The Finance of
British Industry
1918–1976

W. A. THOMAS

The Finance of British Industry 1918–1976

METHUEN & CO LTD
LONDON

First published in 1978
by Methuen & Co Ltd
11 *New Fetter Lane London* EC4P 4EE
© *W. A. Thomas* 1978
Printed in Great Britain by
William Clowes and Sons Limited, Beccles.

ISBN *0 416 67420 8*

Contents

SEP 16 1980

Acknowledgements

I am greatly indebted to the Trustees of the Houblon-Norman Fund for a grant which enabled me to meet several practitioners in the financial world. My thanks are due to many members of the City for patiently answering a host of questions; financial practices change quite quickly and it would be difficult for an academic observer to keep pace with these shifts without the generous co-operation of those who operate in the field. The Bank of England and HM Treasury again left me in their debt by answering queries and providing various tables. I am also grateful to Dr P. L. Cottrell, University of Leicester, for reading and commenting on several chapters.

For all errors I am responsible.

Liverpool 1977   W. A. THOMAS

Introduction

It is probably more important to inform the reader at the outset of what is to follow than to lecture him on the precise conclusions he should draw at the close.

This volume is part of a survey of the financing of British industry from the industrial revolution to the present day and deals with the period since the First World War. Accordingly no attempt has been made to provide background coverage on the structure and trends in company financing prior to 1914. Where it seemed important to make specific reference to pre-war practices so as to clarify developments in the 1920s this has been done.

Coverage centres largely on the manufacturing industry, the main capital using sector, and in the years after 1945 also on public corporations. The figures used and the related text deals for the most part with the activity of incorporated companies. The omission of unincorporated firms is not a damaging lapse since such companies account for a relatively small part of output and probably an even smaller proportion of capital.

The subject matter lends itself to a convenient and sensible division: the inter-war years and the post-war period. There are good reasons for doing it in this way. Firstly, the inter-war years may be taken for this, as for so many other purposes, as a self-contained period bounded by the decisive influence of two world wars. Secondly, a difference of treatment is possible due to the considerably superior statistical series available for the company sector from 1948 onwards. Whereas it is possible to have a series for the sources and uses of funds for the company sector, and for quoted companies, thus permitting an examination of the changes in the structure of financing in a fairly accurate manner, this is not possible for the inter-war years. Clearly it would be admirable if a uniform and continuous series of the sources and uses of funds was available for those years on the lines presented in Chapter 11, but in its absence one cannot in any way use the separate figures for internal and external funds in order to arrive at total sources of funds. It is not that the data is recalcitrant to yield conclusions, it just is not there. The best that can be done is to take a very general look at the underlying forces constituting the demand for funds (Chapter 1) and follow with a far more detailed treatment of the major sources of the supply of funds, that is, internal funds and external funds, dividing the latter into the capital market for long-term and the banking system for short-term funds. The drawbacks attached to each particular source for these purposes is dealt with in some detail in the relevant chapters. The emphasis in the first part is therefore on the finance of industry viewed from the standpoint of the main sources of supply.

The subdivision of financing into internal and external, with the capital market and the banks treated separately, has been copied for the post-war years, but there it has been possible to follow this with a general chapter examining the trends in the sources and uses of funds for the period 1952–76. In some ways this arrangement may be a little tedious but it seems inevitable in view of the large number of detailed influences operating on each source of funds. In other words, the structure of company finance seems to be subject to very rapid and quite violent fluctuations which are due to a succession of business cycles, some moderate and others severe, and by frequent changes in government policy, sometimes on the monetary front but more often, and certainly more influential, in fiscal matters.

The inclusion of two chapters on the contribution of the banking sector to industrial finance, one for each period, may be over-generous but can be defended on the following grounds. Before, and after the last war, when the level of expenditure rose sharply, the deficiency was invariably made good by resorting to short-term external finance, predominantly from the banking system. But the banking system has not been able to provide funds freely in response to demand by companies; internal banking considerations have operated as a constraint, while more significantly various Chancellors of the Exchequer have employed restraint of bank advances as an important monetary weapon. It seemed pertinent to provide fairly full coverage of such changes and the way they affect the ability of the banks to gratify the needs of their industrial customers.

The role of financial intermediation played by the major non-bank financial institutions has also been accorded some prominence. Although the capital market provides a relatively small fraction of the total needs of industry, for many firms this increment is particularly vital. With the change in the pattern of share ownership towards increasing institutional involvement, new industrial issues, on balance, tend to meet with a fairly responsive demand. It has also raised questions about the possibility of more institutional participation in the management of companies, and led to the advocacy of certain continental practices.

The chapter dealing with the 'Macmillan and other gaps' covers the emergence and closing of that famous shortcoming, while other genuine and more illusory ones are also noted. Often, present-day financial commentators are over-zealous in their desire to identify a financial gap, which is frequently the result of their failure to distinguish between cause and effect. There has always been a tendency among outside observers of the financial scene to label any failure or difficulty to obtain funds as further testimony of the existence of the notorious 'imperfections of the capital market'. There are undoubtedly departures from the textbook model but what appears pardonable in other markets attracts instant attention when glimpsed on the financial front.

Chapter 9 deals with several important sources of short-and medium-term finance which do not appear in the aggregate figures of the company sector. This is partly because they are treated as part of the unidentified item, and partly because they do not appear in company balance sheets (leasing), or are an intermediary facility for converting stated assets from one form into another (factoring). Further, inter-company lending, which on occasions has provided a useful supplement to more established channels of finance, does not appear in the aggregate figures for the company sector.

The selection of 1976 as the point to end the narrative is dictated largely by the date at which National Income Blue Books make their appearance. Many items for 1977 are available in a provisional form, but it would be misleading to use them alongside more settled figures for earlier years. Neither is there any discussion of the debate surrounding the proposals put forward by the Sandilands Report (*Inflation Accounting*: *Report of the Inflation Accounting Committee,* Cmnd 6225, 1975) as to the most appropriate accounting procedure to be used in a period of rising prices. There is a long pedigree of somewhat similar debates and it would appear judicious to await an agreed outcome before including such matters as part of a long-term survey.

At the close some international comparisons are noted. Those who make the journey thus far may be struck by the complexity and the ephemeral nature of the influences upon the financing of British industry. To follow the advocacy of some observers who believe that all is perfection on the other side of the national moat, and far beyond, and that what we need is a thoroughgoing transformation with imported practices is, of course, one prescription; but then it might not be the right one.

PART ONE

The inter-war years

1 Some aspects of the demand for funds

the amount of factual information on corporate income . . . policies is far from commensurate with the general interest in their significance.
SERGEI P. DOBROVOLSKY

The study of the finance of British industry involves an examination of part of the mechanism whereby additions to and replacement of the stock of capital are brought about. Frequently belittled, and often ignored, the question of finance raises some interesting and for the early part of this century largely unanswered questions; regrettably, due to the absence of adequate information, only tentative answers can be put forward. Among such questions are those relating to the determinants for long-term funds, changes in the demand for external funds, the division between short- and long-term borrowing, and between debt and equity borrowing, and how effectively industry used the financial resources put at its disposal.[1] Further, the assumption is usually made, on the capital using side, that the only changes that occur, or are important, are those involving the acquisition of real assets. But in the case of business firms, changes in capital formation are almost invariably accompanied by changes in holdings of financial assets. Thus, ideally, the supply of funds (the sources of funds), should be related not only to the level of investment in plant and equipment and stocks, but also to the acquisition of all assets, including financial ones. More often than not it is assumed that additional funds are used solely for the purposes of capital formation and that no part finds its way into financial transactions. It would be desirable to be able to separate the two streams of expenditures, but in practice it is not possible even to identify a rough order of magnitude for the latter for any length of time (see Chapter 4).

In looking at the finance of industry the main distinction made is between internal financing, the user drawing upon his own level of savings, and external, where a claim is made for someone else's savings. In so far as internal funds are concerned the only decision that matters is that of the firm; no external party is involved. But in an indirect way even internal sources are subject to some degree of testing by the market. Buyers must be prepared to pay a price for the firm's product which covers depreciation and yields a net profit, so enabling the firm to finance replacement or expansion from within. External financing, since it draws on the financial resources of other sectors, must pass more stringent tests but one's which are not consistent over time, or common to all borrowers. Also involved in the case of external borrowing is the important distinction between fixed interest (loans of different durations and conditions as to security) and equity capital where there is no fixed date of repayment or rate of return.

The aggregate picture of capital funds brings with it several problems and the need for a great deal of caution in interpreting trends. In such a presentation opposite movements among individual units cancel each other out. The larger the number of units included within the total the greater the likelihood of cancellation. For example, if all companies combined show a negligible net balance for security financing in a given year it does not mean that borrowing was unimportant for every firm; some may borrow heavily from the market while other firms may be redeeming debt. In practice the derivation of net totals tends to understate the share of external borrowing and to exaggerate that of internal funds. Ideally it would be desirable to have available figures of inter-company flows but these do not exist even for more recent periods. The other temptation is to adopt too great a degree of association between sources and uses of funds, and between maturity periods on both sides of the balance sheet. It is all too easy to link depreciation provisions to the financing of gross fixed capital formation alone, but as emphasized below the practice is often different. Industries displaying slow growth use such funds in other ways and this may well be true of all industries in times of depression. In the matter of maturities long-term funds would normally be associated with the financing of long-term investments such as plant and equipment, and buildings, while short-term funds such as bank loans would be used to carry stocks of materials and finished goods, or to acquire financial assets. In practice long-term funds are used for the continuous circulation of short-term assets, while firms with very fast rates of growth may use short-term funds in part to finance long-term assets, and the substitution between maturities is probably greatest in the case of such firms. Normally their long-term liabilities would be given priority in financing long-term assets, and short-term liabilities preference in financing quick assets, but it is essential to be aware that there may well be important exceptions to this general assumption. As a rule, of course, company statements do not show the exact items on which funds obtained from a given source were spent.

Such qualifications and cautionary warnings apply to comparatively recent series on the financing of company activity, such as those for the post-1945 years. Since there are no comparable figures for the inter-war years even greater care and awareness of the problems involved are essential. It was not until the 1948 Companies Act that some long due degree of uniformity was imposed on company reporting; before that it was extremely varied and very haphazard. For the inter-war years there is no composite series on the uses and sources of funds: the information with which to make some inferences regarding the general picture of the demand and supply of funds consists of a series of quite separately derived estimates. The best that can be done, therefore, given the independent nature of the compilation of such items as investment, internal funds, and long-term external borrowing, is to note the extent to which changes in one series coincide roughly with those in another. They can in no way be added together to produce illuminating ratios, that is, one cannot add internal funds to external borrowing to give total sources of funds. While it is possible to make a loose association between uses, corresponding to net changes in assets, and sources, changes in liabilities, it is not possible to compile a table of the sources and uses of funds which come to an identical total.[2] What follows, therefore, is an attempt at some generalizations as to the demand for funds with such severe shortcomings in the material very much in mind.

The pre-1914 financial background

In attempting to provide a general indication of the nature of the financing of industry immediately prior to the First World War, as a background to the more detailed study of inter-war practices, 'we are at once', in Lavington's words, 'met by the great difficulty that the available statistical information is exceedingly meagre.'[3] Such conjectural estimates as are available suggest that the demand for external funds in this period was small, and that even in times of boom when the ratio of external to total financing would be expected to rise, that not more than 10% of real home investment was financed by market borrowing and of this only about a third was raised by new companies.[4] For the period 1911–13 A. K. Cairncross estimated that the value of security issues made by new companies averaged some £8m., but this sum included issues by railways, investment trusts, etc. Earlier, in 1907, the total value of issues for domestic investment purposes, excluding financial and public utility issues and correcting for cash payments to vendors, was no more than £13. 8m. It would seem reasonable to conclude that the volume of new issues by new companies was therefore modest. Such stock market borrowing as was done by such companies appears to have been largely in the provinces with the amount involved being at the most £2m. to £3m. The rest was obtained by private negotiation between business partners or with well-connected wealthy families and 'generally by the investment of their own capital by the directors or owners and their friends'. Extra funds also came from shares privately placed by public companies formed without a prospectus, the shares later being unloaded on the market, and a rough estimate was that such channels produced 'about £12m. in the provinces for the purpose of home investment'.[5]

Companies already in possession of their capital seemed to have raised rather more of their needs from the market. They were responsible, by number, for about half the issues of home industrials on the London market prior to 1914. In the years 1911–13, by value, such issues averaged £22.5m., but this figure includes utilities and financial issues. Making an allowance of some £9m. for the placing of unsold shares and sales in the provinces of the stock of companies not formed under the Companies Acts, a rough estimate of £54m. is obtained which represents the sum subscribed to home industry in 1911–13. Deducting an estimated one-sixth for cash payments to vendors and for purchases of land and existing assets the figure emerges at £45m., which is probably the maximum of the average amount of capital supplied by the stock market for real home investment prior to the war.

It is probable that at least half the additions to the capital of industrial concerns came from undistributed profits. The Colwyn Committee of 1927 (Committee on National Debt and Taxation) in a sample enquiry for 1912 found that out of trading profits amounting to £312m., companies put to reserve £102m., which after tax was £96m., and of this sum £48.4m. was for the manufacturing sector. What was true then of this immediate pre-war period was probably more so of earlier years since a large part of the manufacturing industry was in private hands, the main market borrowers being public utilities and the distributive trades.[6] The general position would appear to have been that 'the vast majority of joint stock companies coming into being each year were either already in possession of their capital or obtained it by way of private negotiation'.[7] Further, that market borrowing by old companies greatly exceeded that by new ones, and that retained profits were a more important source of finance than outside funds. Thus, the amount of external finance going into manufacture as such was not very large and of that amount only a comparatively small proportion was raised by public issue on the market.

The availability of internal finance

From a general standpoint the demand for long-term funds by industry may be taken as dependent on the level of retained income in relation to investment. Savings depend on gross profits less various deductions, while the level of gross profits is mainly dependent on the level of output, the latter also being one of the most important influences on investment activity. As can be seen from figure 1.1 profit behaviour in the inter-war years was closely related to output variations (the correlation coefficient between the two series being 0.71).

After the immediate post-war slump of 1921 the growth of output was quite steady, apart from the 1926 setback and the depression of 1929–32. Profits followed the same general path, tending to fall more abruptly in periods of reduced activity and rising more rapidly than output in periods of recovery; this pattern is consistent with the interpretation that in periods of expansion costs do not rise at the same rate as output and selling prices, while in the recession falling output leads to rising unit costs and reduced profit margins. The overall impression from the index of

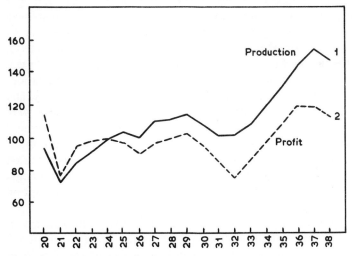

Figure 1.1   Manufacturing production and gross profit, 1920–38 (1924 = 100)

Sources: 1 K. S. Lomax, 'Growth and Productivity in the United Kingdom', in D. H. Aldcroft and P. Fearon, *Economic Growth in 20th-century Britain*, 1969.

2 P. E. Hart, *Studies in Profit, Business Saving and Investment in the United Kingdom 1920–62*, vol. 1, 1965.

industrial production given in figure 1.1 is that the periodic setbacks in output after 1922 were not as sharp as the changes which occurred in other leading economic indicators, particularly unemployment which rose from 10% in 1929 to 22% in 1932. Taking the period 1920-6 the cumulative rate of growth of output was 2.8% per annum, and from 1929–37 it was 3.3% per annum. Among the reasons suggested for this rise was the improvement in the terms of trade, a considerable amount of innovation in the newer industries, cheap money, while rising real incomes sustained consumer demand in the recovery of the 1930s. It had also become less attractive to lend abroad so diverting capital to the home market. Although home investment in money terms in the inter-war period seems rather low (see figure 1.3, p. 11) it should be noted that capital goods were relatively cheap so that domestic investment was in consistent relationship to growth.[8]

While the overall picture of manufacturing output displayed reasonably stable growth, very different performances were recorded by individual industries as measured by comparing the average for 1936–8 with the base year of 1924 = 100. Among those which might be classified as fast growers, whose output rose by more than 75% over the period, were vehicles (215), electrical engineering (213), metal goods (177) and non-ferrous metals (175).[9] This growth in output was associated with increased labour productivity, there being increases in the range of 0.5% to 2.0% per annum in the case of the above industries.[10] Industries which displayed moderate levels of output growth for the period, output increasing by between one-quarter and three-quarters, were food (163), tobacco (153), precision instruments (152), chemicals (143), ferrous metals (132), clothing (130) and mechanical engineering (126). Relative stagnation, however, hit several industrial sectors and they failed to display any significant improvement in output over the period. Among these were textiles (118 – separate figures are not available for cotton which would probably be lower), leather (102), shipbuilding (102 – in 1932 the index fell to 11.3), and mining and quarrying (92). Expansion thus centred on the newer industries and owed its impetus to the fruits of technical change, lower unit costs with economies of scale, and a changing consumption pattern sustained by rising real incomes.

With few exceptions (leather, woollens and paper had little or no trend, and cotton had a clear downward trend) industries in the manufacturing sector experienced a general upward trend in profits in the inter-war years. Fluctuations in the profits of individual industries mirrored in varying degrees the general movements displayed by the index of gross profits for all manufacturing given in figure 1.1. In relation to output changes in individual industries, fluctuations in gross profits moved in sympathy, the latter frequently being greater than the former. For example, in the case of an industry with a record of considerable expansion (vehicles) output increased by 133% between 1924 and 1929, while profits rose by 229%; in the depression output fell by some 20%, profits by 51%, and in the ensuing recovery output rose by 108% causing profits to jump by 234%. In the case of a leading example of a declining industry, cotton, the response of profits to output changes is even more pronounced. Taking the output figures for textiles as an indicator for cotton, output fell continuously from 1924, apart from a brief and minor revival in 1927, being 16% lower in 1931, while profits collapsed to one-tenth of their 1924 level. The recovery of the 1930s brought a 38% improvement in output by 1937, while gross profits rose by 240% on 1931 and by 630% on the 1930 record low figures.

For the purpose of financing investment the available internal funds are those left after certain appropriations have been made against profits. The estimates of gross income for manufacturing given in Chapter 4, table 4.6 are presented in figure 1.2. After deducting dividends, interest and tax (ignoring a small amount for royalties) the remaining stream of gross business saving indicates the amount of internal funds available for financing gross investment. The most notable feature is that savings is a residual and that while dividends fluctuate in sympathy with changes in gross income, the range of fluctuation was less in the case of the latter. Thus abnormally large or small profits in manufacturing were reflected in savings, with dividends maintaining a relatively stable path. This is illustrated quite clearly in figure 1.2, the share of dividends to income remaining relatively stable while that of savings fluctuates greatly, so

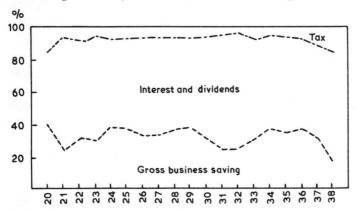

Figure 1.2 Appropriation of company profits in manufacturing industry, 1920–38

Source: P. E. Hart, *Studies in Profit, Business Saving and Investment in the United Kingdom 1920–62*, vol. I, 1965.

taking the brunt of the adjustment of profit swings.[11] Turning to specific instances, in the 1920–1 recession dividends for the manufacturing industry declined by about 12.5%, gross business savings by 63%; in the 1930–2 depression total dividends fell by a mere 21% while savings experienced a sharp fall of 57%, the main adjustment in both periods to the fall in profits being made by savings and not by shareholders income. Equally in the recovery period from 1932–6 total dividends rose by 60%, while gross business saving increased by 176%.

The above pattern is consistent with the belief that savings is a residual and that dividend levels are maintained by companies at reasonably stable levels through periods of boom and recession. This general impression is also supported by the experience of individual industries. For example, in the case of the cotton industry during 1920–38 the ratio of dividends and interest to total income ranged from high figures of 248 and 269 in 1921 and 1932 respectively, to lower figures of 75–80 in the relatively more prosperous recovery periods, while the average ratio for the entire period was 112.6.[12] The high figures for the recession reflected the practice of cotton firms of paying dividends out of reserves. More successful industries, for example, vehicles, experienced the same pattern but the ratio in their case merely changed from 38% in 1930 to 49% in 1932. This low ratio arose not from a 'mean' dividend policy but because of the good profit performance of the industry. It is also significant at the tail end of the period that the imposition of an additional tax burden in the form of the National Defence Contribution was borne not by dividend distributions but rather by the level of savings.

Generating the demand for external funds

The main use of long-term funds by companies is on plant and equipment, and buildings, so that their demand for such finance from external sources depends on the availability of internal funds and the level of investment. Before turning to the question of the sufficiency of the supply of savings a brief indication is needed as to the variations which took place in the inter-war years in the volume of investment. Figure 1.3 gives the fluctuations in gross fixed capital formation for the period at current and constant (1930) prices. The main emphasis will be on gross capital formation rather than with net investment. Part of gross investment is required to replace existing assets, and part to make good wear and tear and obsolescence, that is, the depreciation provision. But, whereas the gross basis may be accepted with considerable confidence, the figures of net capital formation are subject to the difficulties of arriving at reliable

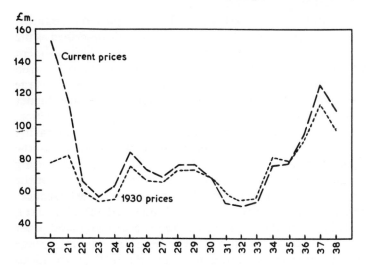

Figure 1.3   Gross fixed capital formation in manufacturing, 1920–38 (current and constant prices)

Source: C. H. Feinstein, *Domestic Capital Formation in the United Kingdom 1920–1938*, 1965.

estimates for depreciation (for inter-war practices in this matter see Chapter 4).[13]

Apart from the early post-war boom the two series given in figure 1.3 move quite closely together. A notable feature of the 1920s is the absence of any growth, the level of real capital formation in 1929 being below the 1925 peak which again was below the 1921 level. Also, the fall in investment between 1920–1 and 1923–4, measured in nominal or real terms, was considerably greater than the 1928–9 to 1931–2 decline; measured in real terms investment fell by 32.5% in the former period compared with 25% in the latter. In the early post-war contraction the trade groups which displayed the largest investment declines were engineering equipment, food, chemicals, motor vehicles, leather, rubber, and building materials; in most of these industries gross investment fell by over 50%. In the second contraction the heaviest falls were in cotton, rayon and silk, and chemicals; the decline in the latter was very severe, gross fixed capital formation at constant prices falling from £14.6m. in 1929 to £4.3m. in 1932.[14]

The investment recovery of the 1930s is particularly strong with gross fixed capital formation in 1937 standing at £112m. (constant prices), more than twice the level of the depression years 1931–2, and greatly above the 1929 peak. It is also significant that, of the total gross fixed capital formation taking place in 1932–7, 73% was in plant and equipment, compared with only 66% in the 1923–9 period. The improved investment performance is to be seen particularly in what are usually described as the newer industries, for example, non-ferrous metals increased its investment in the period 1932–7 by 185%, chemicals by 153%, paper by 130%, rayon and silk by 121% and motor vehicles by 53%. Thus the recovery took the form of increased productive capacity in these industries to meet higher demand associated with rising real income, cheap money, and protection.

Using the data of gross fixed capital formation at 1930 prices and taking the period as a whole, 1920–31, some interesting variations in the performance of individual industries become apparent. Expressing aggregate investment as a percentage of the gross stock of capital at the end of 1920 (at 1930 prices) produces the following range of performance: industries with increases of more than 100% included vehicles (221), rayon and silk (213), tobacco (123), leather and rubber (107), and paper and hardboard (103); those which had increases in the 50–100% range included electrical engineering (90), non-ferrous metals (73), chemicals (61), iron and steel (54); and the slower industries, under 50%, included engineering and shipbuilding (46), and textiles (20). However, the amounts involved in the fast growth industries was relatively small, about 17% of all investment, the medium growers accounting for 52% of all investment, and the sluggish performers taking the remaining 31% of the total.[15]

Reference to the changes in investment given in figure 1.3 and those of output and profits in figure 1.1 indicate that the former follow the latter quite closely. A more formal approach is to use an econometric model to test the relationship between capital expenditure and the rate of change of output. A study of private sector investment in the inter-war period showed that with a lagged relationship between the two variables a coefficient of determination of 0.54 was obtained, while adding profits as a measure of expectations as to future profitability increased the coefficient to 0.69, and the inclusion of share prices as a measure of expectations on future earnings of capital improved the explanatory value of the model giving a coefficient of 0.79.[16] In the case of this model it was found that the rate of interest had little influence on investment behaviour, but that may well have been due to the use of annual data and that for part of the period the rate of interest was 'managed' by the authorities. By contrast a study covering the post-war years 1955–67 indicated that investment activity is significantly related to the level of demand, lagged by one year, and also to the rate of interest, lagged by two years. In the case of the latter it was calculated that the elasticity of investment with respect to the rate of interest was well above unity, but that it was less than the elasticity with respect to output.[17]

While the post-war study cited above lends support to the suggestion that the long-term rate of interest is an important determinant of investment in the manufacturing industry, a study of investment practices in the 1930s gave support to the contrary view. The famous survey described in *Oxford Studies in the Price Mechanism* came to such a conclusion after conducting a pioneering empirical investigation. The Oxford Economists' Research Group analysed 309 completed question-naires out of 1,308 sent out in 1939 but they failed to identify any strong confirmation of the association between interest rates and investment changes. The replies indicated that 'there is almost universal agreement that short term rates of interest do not directly affect investment either in stocks or in fixed capital', while the majority of the respondents 'deny that the long term rate of interest affects investment directly, although some indicate that it is of some importance to them'.[18]

Internal and external funds

A precise analysis of the relationship between available internal funds, the level of investment, and the corresponding need to resort to outside borrowing is not possible for the inter-war years. Figures are not available for these three items which are derived from a common source; all that can be done is to provide a rough impression of the trends using the available independent estimates for the manufacturing sector. At best, therefore, the general trends may be reasonably reliable but little dependence can be placed on short-term movements and comparisons. Figure 1.4 gives the level of gross business savings for manufacturing for 1920-38, along with depreciation, estimates of gross fixed capital formation, and the Midland Bank series of new issues by 'mainly home industries'. On the basis of this information it appears that for most of the period gross business savings was sufficient to support investment activity, the two series coming very close together in the immediate post-war recession, the 1926 reversal, and the 1931–3 depression, which compares with the general relationship found in the post-war period given in Chapter 11. The expected movements are present, that is to say, in periods when investment and output are rising gross business saving also increased – in 1922–4, 1927–9 and 1933–6. This should not be taken to mean that external finance was not drawn upon; resort to outside funds also increased in such periods. The fact that on this aggregate view savings exceeded investment does not imply that this was so for each firm or industry within the manufacturing sector. Unfortunately there are no estimates of savings for each individual industry, which would permit an examination

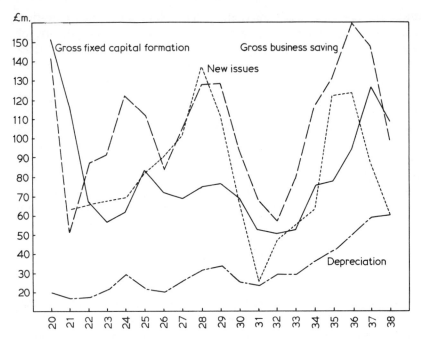

Figure 1.4   Capital formation and finance 1920–38
*1920, £246m.; new issues

Sources: C. H. Feinstein, *Domestic Capital Formation in the United Kingdom 1920–1938*, 1965.
P. E. Hart, *Studies in Profit, Business Saving and Investment in the United Kingdom 1920–62*, vol.
1, 1965. Midland Bank new issue series (see Chapter 2).

of the relationship between finance and investment and how it might have
varied between industries with different rates of growth of assets.

The stream of internal finance consists of two elements, the depreciation
provision computed according to the prevailing accounting practices of
the time, and net business savings. On the basis of the series given in
figure 1.4 it can be seen that depreciation as a proportion of gross fixed
capital formation increased from 36% in 1923–9 to 42% in 1933–7. The
significance of depreciation as a source of internal funds, and its increasing
importance over the period in relation to investment expenditure, may be
construed as implying that a large part of the re-equipment of industry in
the inter-war years was accomplished through the depreciation provision
rather than by net investment.[19] As stressed above, too close an association
between sources and uses of funds should not be made. The significant
feature is that over the period there was a rise in the ratio of depreciation
to capital formation and that this rise in the share of capital consumption

(assuming that depreciation is a rough measure of it) in gross capital formation is not surprising or to be construed as a less desirable method of investment. The growth of depreciation took place because there was a rise in the volume of short-lived equipment, while the proportion of plant and equipment in the investment total increased over the period (see p. 11). Further, if the share of depreciable durable capital in total gross capital formation rises, this will cause a rise in the ratio of capital consumption to total gross capital formation. Given this trend a steady rise in the share of internal finance would then be expected.[20]

If it is assumed, for the moment, that particular sources of funds are related to specific uses then it would be reasonable to expect that the demand for long-term capital from the market, in both equity and debt form, depended largely on the level of investment expenditure in relation to the amount of funds available internally. If the ratio of internal funds to expenditure on plant and equipment and buildings was high then the demand for long terms should be low, and when the ratio was low then correspondingly there should be a stronger demand for external funds. That is, there would be an inverse relationship between the ratio of gross internal financing to investment expenditure and that of new security issues to total financing. Due to the absence of figures for each category drawn from a common source it is not possible to verify such a pattern for the inter-war years. As a consolation it might be worth noting that for the level of aggregation involved in manufacturing, such a clear trend might not assert itself due to the tendency of netting out external borrowing, so overstating the importance of internal funds. The necessary information is also not available at the industry level.

Given the shortcomings the only course is to offer general observations on outside borrowings, as recorded by the new issue statistics, in relation to the movements in the other series given in figure 1.4. Firstly, the changes in internal and external funds are clearly very similar; periods of investment activity are associated with a rise in profit retention and with additional demands for outside funds by means of security issues. This is not so curious as it might first appear. While internal funds appear to be well in excess of gross investment in 1923-4, 1927-9 and 1934-7, all periods of relative expansion, new issues – especially in the last two periods – brought in substantial sums of money. This arose because some companies had low retained incomes, while others with high retained incomes still needed considerable external finance to meet investment expenditure. What is also noticeable in the recovery period of 1933-5 is the lag between security issues and the level of investment and retained earnings. This probably arose from the ability of many firms to finance expansion from current earnings and by drawing on accumulated liquid assets, that is, the phenomenon of parts of industry 'living of its hump' (see Chapter 4). If the gross business savings of individual firms exceeded investment in the pre-depression years this would imply that the surplus was used for the net acquisition of liquid assets.

What can probably be asserted with a little more confidence, but not substantiated for the inter-war years, is that firms with different rates of growth would display different demands for external finance. Where firms increased their assets slowly or at moderate rates then internal funds would generally be sufficient to cover capital expenditure. If firms expanded rapidly, then although profits would also be higher, the rise in savings would be insufficient to meet increased capital expenditure, thus leading to a demand for external finance. This is the experience brought out by the extensive survey on the financial behaviour of firms covering the years 1948–53, and it seems reasonable to assume that it was so in the inter-war years, particularly for the newer industries with large expenditure on capital equipment and little or no opportunity to accumulate a reserve of liquid assets.[21]

Long-term external funds may be procured on the basis of issuing either equity shares or debt, the latter being either short- or long-term. In order to borrow funds by the issue of debt and have a reasonable hope of a full subscription, a company would need to be of a certain size, maturity, and have an acceptable record of past performance, with some assurance that future earnings would be adequate to maintain interest payments. Debt, therefore, is suitable for companies with stable earnings pattern and which also have assets by way of security for such debenture borrowing. Equity issues, on the other hand, are not so demanding in terms of prerequisites. A company can seek equity capital without possessing an equivalent base of assets as security, or a history of past dividend payments; the main asset which is offered is that of future profit earning capacity. It is thus a suitable means of financing activities using small quantities of fixed assets and particularly where profit performance is variable so that dividends can be passed over without threat of bankruptcy proceedings. Given these general features newer industries in the inter-war years tended to use equity finance, for example, in oil, vehicles and aviation, whereas the traditional heavy industries such as iron and steel, and shipbuilding relied more heavily on debt borrowing.

Changes in the broad structure of external borrowing in the inter-war years, as given by the Midland Bank series of new issues of debt and capital is portrayed in figure 1.5. The main influences on the distribution of fund raising as between debt and capital are the presence of boom conditions in 1919–20, recovery and expansion prior to 1929, and recovery from the depression in the mid-1930s. In the 1924–9 period it should be

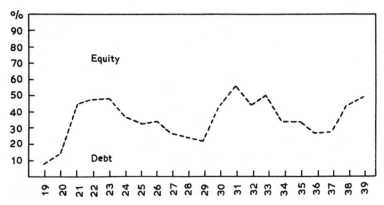

Figure 1.5   Types of company security 1919–39

Source: Midland Bank series (see Chapter 2).

noted that debt borrowing averaged nearly £50m. per annum, so that the shifting pattern is associated with the increase in the demand for equity capital coming from the newer industries where the units tended to be of a smaller size. In the depression years the demand for both debt and equity funds fell off sharply, by some 60% in the case of debt between 1929 and 1932, while equity demand fell in 1932 to about an eighth of the 1929 level. In the recovery of the 1930s the level of fixed interest borrowing remained at around £36m., while the volume of equity finance increased, taking its share of external funds from nearly 50% in 1933 to over 70% in 1936–7. As can be seen from figure 1.5 the structure of external financing in terms of the division between fixed interest and equity, was not markedly different in the mid-1930s to that prevailing in the mid-1920s. On the assumption of a growing economy it might be expected that existing companies would be able to make demands for equity funds beyond that possible for smaller concerns so leading to a long-term fall in the percentage of debt capital. However, the stable structure of external borrowing and fund raising may well have been due to the ability of large companies with fixed capital to draw more heavily for funds on depreciation allowances and internal savings. Established firms, who tended to use debt borrowing, also had insufficient investment expenditure to require large-scale equity issues so that there was no pressure to reduce the proportion of debt in total external finance. Finally, in this period prices were either generally stable or falling which meant that there was no great advantage in increasing the proportion of debt borrowing. All the above were influences making for a stable pattern in the structure of external financing.

Another factor affecting the relative demand for debt or equity funds is the relationship between interest rates on the former and the yield on the latter. In general terms, if the yield on equities is above that on bonds then it would follow that companies should rely less heavily on equity borrowing, while the reverse pattern would be expected to hold if equity yields fell below the rate on bonds. It should be remembered that for most of the newer companies such a choice of borrowing medium was not available. The advance in the share market between 1924 and 1928, and especially 1928–9, produced a sharp fall in yields, the cost of ordinary capital falling appreciably, compared to the modest reduction in debt yields, from around 6.6% in 1924 to 6.1% in 1929, which produced an associated increase in the volume of equity compared to debt financing. The collapse of share prices in 1929, and after, caused yields on equities to rise steeply but it is very doubtful in the circumstances prevailing whether yield considerations had much influence on the choice, or volume, of borrowing medium. The subsequent recovery and fall in yields again made equity borrowing relatively more attractive. It should be emphasized, however, that interest rates relationships do not of themselves explain the proportions of external funds raised through various channels. The most decisive influence was the level of output and the associated demand for it which then induced appropriate profit expectations on the part of firms who tended to raise capital by whatever means was open to them. Large established companies would have had some choice in the selection of their liability, but smaller and newer companies tended to have less choice in the manner with which they could recruit long-term capital.

The return on capital 1920–38

One measure of the efficiency with which manufacturing industry in the inter-war years used the funds accumulated internally and obtained from outside sources is the rate of return on capital. The estimates derived by P. E. Hart are given in figure 1.6 and provide an idea both of the level of return and the long-term trend. However, the available figures are rough estimates and they depend very greatly on the figures of profit and capital used. In the derivation of the figures the denominator was the first cost (without deducting for depreciation) value of fixed assets in manufacturing in current prices, while the numerator was profits without adjusting for depreciation and before deducting tax, dividends or interest payments.[22]

In terms of general movements, following the fall from 7.6% to 6.8% in the post-war recession, the rate of return rose sharply in the recovery reaching 11.6% by 1925 and climbing to 13.2% in 1929. With the

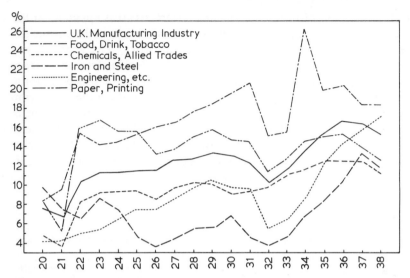

Figure 1.6 Rates of return on capital 1920–38; U.K. manufacturing and five industry groups

Source: P. E. Hart (ed.), *Studies in Profit, Business Saving and Investment in the United Kingdom 1920–62*, vol. 2, 1968, pp. 231, 274.

depression the rate slumped to 10.3% in 1932 (profits in this period fell by nearly 30%). In the recovery it eventually climbed to 16.4%, sliding back somewhat in 1938. The average for the entire period was 12.2%, with a variance of 6.54%. While the fluctuations are quite pronounced (see figure 1.6) the trend for the period is upwards; the average for 1922–8 was 11.5% and for 1932–8 it rose to 14.1%. This applies whether the measures are in constant or current prices.

While fluctuations in the rate of return are associated with the familiar cycles of the period and the significant effect those had on profit figures, the rising trend over the years needs some further explanation. A plausible reason for the increase is that the level of technical progress in the period, particularly in the newer industries, produced a rising trend in the ratio of value added to capital, from an average of 0.448 for the period 1922–8 to 0.521 for 1932–8.[23] That is, the average productivity of capital increased sufficiently during the period to produce a rising trend in the rate of return. Further evidence is to be found in data available for five industrial categories within the manufacturing sector: food, drink and tobacco, chemicals, iron and steel, engineering, and paper and printing. The rates of return for these industries are given in figure 1.6. Only food, drink and tobacco, and paper and printing produced performances in excess of the average rate for manufacturing – 16.7% and 13.6% respectively. However, with the exception of iron and steel an upward trend is apparent in the rates of return produced, and this conforms with the upward trends in the ratios of value added to capital in these industries. The sharpest rise occurred in food, drink and tobacco, the ratios increasing from an average of 0.336 for 1922–4 to 0.433 in 1936–3. Although the value added to capital ratio for the same years improved greatly in the case of engineering, from 0.413 to 0.642, it did not produce a significant increase in the rate of return, possibly because the prices of capital goods did not rise to the same degree as retail prices.[24] In the case of iron and steel the ratio of value added to capital remained virtually unchanged over the period, while its investment record was also pretty static.

Notes

1 Due to the absence of any sort of series for bank lending to industry it is not possible to make an assessment of changes in the relative importance of short- and long-term borrowing.

2 For a masterly treatment of the above problems, and much more, see S. Kuznetz, *Capital in the American Economy: Its Formation and Financing*, New York, 1961.

3 F. Lavington, *The English Capital Market*, London, 1921, p. 200.

4 A. K. Cairncross, *Home and Foreign Investment 1870–1913*, Cambridge, 1953, p. 96.

5 ibid., pp. 96–7. This was Lavington's estimate, which Cairncross was inclined to put lower.

6 ibid., pp. 98–9.

7 Lavington, op. cit., p. 203.

8 K. S. Lomax, 'Growth and Productivity in the United Kingdom', reprinted in D. H. Aldcroft and P. Fearon, *Economic Growth in 20th-century Britain*, London, 1969, pp. 15–16.

9 ibid., pp. 32–3.

10 J. A. Dowie, 'Growth in the Inter-War Period: Some More Arithmetic', reprinted in Aldcroft and Fearon, op. cit., pp. 67–8.

11 P. E. Hart reported that a regression of first differences of gross business savings on total gross income of manufacturing companies for the period 1921–38 gave a coefficient of determination of 0.81, with the value of the marginal propensity to save being 0.69; P. E. Hart (ed.), *Studies in Profit, Business Savings and Investment in*

the United Kingdom 1920–62, vol. 2, London, 1968, pp. 122–3.

12 P. E. Hart, *Studies in Profit, Business Saving and Investment in the United Kingdom 1920–62*, vol. 1, 1965, p. 121. The inclusion of interest in the numerator tends to bias the ratio in the direction of greater stability.

13 C. H. Feinstein estimated that for plant and other equipment over 80% of gross capital formation was needed to make good capital consumption. He notes that the estimates of scrapping (replacement) were not made from actual records of scrapping but 'simply reflect our assumptions as to the useful life of assets'; C. H. Feinstein, *Domestic Capital Formation in the United Kingdom 1920–1938*, Cambridge, 1965, pp. 50–1.

14 ibid., pp. 44–5.

15 ibid., p. 45.

16 P. J. Lund and K. Holden, 'An Econometric Study of Private Sector Gross Fixed Capital Formation in the United Kingdom, 1923–38', *Oxford Economic Papers*, 1969, pp. 62–4. An alternative explanation is that firms attempt by their investment activity to attain some optimum level of capital stock which is consistent with replacement needs, the existing rate of output, and providing for expected future changes in demand. Testing this particular model they found that with allowance for expectations and time lags it provided a satisfactory explanation of private gross fixed capital formation; pp. 65–72.

17 A. G. Hines and G. Catephores, 'Investment in U.K. Manufacturing Industry, 1956–67', in K. Hilton and D. F. Heathfield (eds), *The Econometric Study of the United Kingdom*, London, 1970, pp. 203–22.

18 T. Wilson and P. W. S. Andrews, *Oxford Studies in the Price Mechanism*, Oxford, 1951, pp. 28–9.

19 See note 13.

20 Kuznetz, op. cit., pp. 395–6.

21 See B. Tew and R. F. Henderson, *Studies in Company Finance*, Cambridge, 1959. It is also conceivable that the increased degree of concentration in industry, particularly where amalgamations were involved, led to reduced dependence on external funds. Concentration due to the growth of individual firms may not have had a similar effect if investment was also expanding. For the available evidence on these trends see D. H. Aldcroft, *The Inter-War Economy: Britain 1919–1939*, London, 1970, pp. 140–1.

22 Hart (vol. 2), op. cit., pp. 221–8. Hart also calculated rates of return after adjusting for stock appreciation which produced very sharp falls in the rate for 1921–3; he adds the qualification that the adjustment for this period is not very reliable. Calculation of real rates of return, with adjustment to both numerator and denominator for price changes, produced rates which moved in sympathy with the ratio in current prices but at a somewhat lower level.

23 ibid., p. 231. Making the same calculations for the period 1948–62 Hart found that the trend in the rate of return was downwards from 17.5% in 1948–51 to 14.5% in 1959–62, while the ratio of value added to capital also fell from 0.531 to 0.479 respectively. For a suggested explanation of the trend see Hart, pp. 234–5.

24 ibid., pp. 274–5.

2 The establishment of the domestic new issue market

*That you cannot prevent a fool from his folly is
no reason why you should not give a prudent man
guidance. We believe that our financial
machinery is definitely weak in that it fails to give
clear guidance to the investor when appeals are
made to him on behalf of home industry.*
MACMILLAN COMMITTEE, *Report*

In general economic terms the function of a new issue market is to facilitate the transfer of funds from surplus units to deficit units. More specifically in relation to home industry this can take the form of selling either going concerns or newly constituted companies to the public; the former to provide additional capital or to fund short-term capital, the latter to raise capital for acquiring the physical means of production. The market, however, is concerned not only with transmission but also with the allocation of funds. As Lavington put it, 'capital should be supplied to industrial ventures in accordance with their prospective earning power'.[1] He was careful to point out that this would only occur 'if the proper risks of these ventures, that is, the risks as estimated by well informed opinion, correspond to the estimate of those which are formed in the mind of the capitalist'. Those who demand funds are naturally better placed to identify and assess such risks than the large number of potential investors. Imperfect knowledge on the part of the latter may easily lead to a diminished evaluation of such risks, thus causing capital to flow to companies with low or nil returns, or even to fraudulent promotions. Hence Lavington advocated the need for intimate and expert knowledge to 'examine impartially the prospects of the venture and if suitable, to present it to the public with the implicit guarantee that the enterprise was one with a reasonable claim to the capital for which it asked'.[2] An efficient new issue market therefore requires an elaborate organization to facilitate the movement of funds to those investments with the highest net yield.

The question arises as to the criteria by which the efficiency of the market is to be assessed. Lavington set them out as follows. To facilitate the movement of funds to the points of highest yield two conditions must be satisfied:

> In the first place, the source of earning power must be rightly formulated in order that it may exert its appropriate attractive power upon the available supply of capital; in more practical language, the property must be sold to the public at a price corresponding as nearly as possible to the capitalised value of its prospective net yield; it must be sold at its Investment Value. In the second place, the work of marketing securities must be carried out as economically as possible.[3]

At the outset of the inter-war period there were considerable deviations from these desirable criteria. There was certainly unequal knowledge on the part of buyers and sellers. Buyers found themselves faced with extremely complex circumstances, so much so that 'an accurate estimate can be made only in the light of expert knowledge'. In practice the vast majority of industrial stocks were sold without the assistance of any permanent intermediary group; and in the virtual absence of the great issuing houses, or any institutions equivalent to the German bank intermediaries, issuing work was largely left to makeshift promoters. These were mostly self-interested agents with little concern for the companies they formed apart from the hefty premiums on the overvalued shares they sold. Such persons were apt to maximize the difference between the price at which they bought from the vendors and that which they subsequently sold the company to the public, all making for inflated marketing costs.[4]

Lavington's view as to the deficiencies of the market were not altogether shared at a more official level. The Committee on Financial Facilities, reporting in 1919, believed that 'the machinery . . . is already in existence. It consists of a group of financial houses, comprising investment trust companies, well known issuing houses, merchant banks and others'; it took time, however, for the machinery to change its diet.[5] While Lavington would not concur with such a complacent picture, he was not entirely gloomy. There were certain checks which operated. The public had considerable knowledge of some firms, while others had a reputation for fair dealing. Leading brokers associated with a particular issue frequently satisfied themselves as to the *bona fide* of the issuers, while investors could consult the financial press who often were not slow with general and specific warnings about the worst abuses surrounding issue practices. There were of course legal checks, but numerous devices were used to circumvent these and the spirit of the law was frequently evaded.

The Stock Exchange also had regulations, but these did not extend, and were never so intended, to adjudicate the merits of issues seeking a quotation. Existing companies with a record of past profits allowed a reasonable judgement to be made as to prospective returns, while at a local level knowledge of particular firms and promoters permitted of a fairly objective assessment, but even so there was still plenty of scope for promoters with purely financial interests.

The growth of domestic industrial new issues, 1919–39

The composition of the borrowing undertaken on the new issue market during the inter-war years presents a marked contrast to that which occurred in the immediate pre-war years. On the basis of *The Economist*'s figures for 'mainly home industries', this category represented for the period 1911–13 34% of total borrowing.[6] This low level of home borrowing was only repeated in the inter-war period in three exceptional years, namely 1927, 1932 and 1933. On the basis of the Midland Bank statistics, home industrial issues (including finance) prior to 1927 never fell below 29% of all issues, while after 1927 (with the exclusion of finance), the figure still kept above 28%. What is noticeable is that by the mid-1930s well over 50% of the new issue market's work was concerned with the finance of home industry.

The increasing importance of domestic issues reflected two trends working on the market. Firstly, there was the fact that British lending to Empire and foreign countries was only a fraction of what it had been, while Britain had also ceased to finance foreign railway investment, which had been the largest single component in overseas investment before the war. This decline was associated with several elements. The demand for overseas capital had fallen off, while the United States had entered the market as a large-scale lender. On the negative side London had lost much of its attractiveness to foreign depositors, while its pre-war short-term creditor position had been wiped out by 1918 so that there were few balances seeking international outlets. More important however was the continuous restriction imposed on foreign borrowing in London over the entire inter-war period. An official embargo on foreign issues was imposed during the war and continued afterwards with varying degrees of severity.[7] The system of control was finally formalized by the setting up in 1936 of the Foreign Transactions (Advisory) Committee, later to emerge as the Capital Issues Committee. Its function was to vet foreign applications for capital primarily with a view to protecting the exchanges and giving preference to Empire and sterling borrowers.[8]

The second element making for the increased importance of domestic new issues arose from the need on the part of industry to seek outside capital. *The Economist* put it in these general terms:

> Before the war, the small industrial undertaking obtained a very large proportion of its finance without making a general appeal to the public. From choice or necessity, industrialists now deem it worth their while, in the periods when the market is active, to turn family businesses into public companies with widely diffused shareholdings. The public for its own part is prepared to buy and hold equities in the undertakings about which shareholders know comparatively little and in whose management they cannot hope to have any decisive influence. The result has been to increase the range of enterprise for which the new issue market caters.[9]

In more specific terms the following factors affected the demand and supply elements in the market. In terms of the demand for market capital it seems to be generally accepted that the traditional pre-war sources of local private finance were greatly depleted, while company savings in one industry were not made generally available to new undertakings in that or other industries.[10] Also, the industries seeking capital were moving nearer to the London market. Further, there was an increase in the optimum size of firms due to technical progress. On the supply side it is possible to point to the growing institutionalization of savings associated with investment and unit trusts, insurance companies and pension funds, while investors themselves, drawing on the demonstration effect of the war, increasingly preferred a paper claim which was marketable. The growing burden of death duties also increased the desire to keep capital in a liquid form. The level of post-war taxation may also have led to a redistribution away from rich savers, thus reducing this source of personal sector savings to the market. Against this, however, was the fact that, 'if the large direct investor slowly lost importance, the number of small savers who became more enterprising, if not speculative, increased, hence the preference for a marketable debt instrument'.[11]

Given the nature of the problems involved it was not suprising that the immediate post-war years witnessed some highly unstable financial markets. War delayed the replacement and conversion of existing plant, while peace gave rise to opportunities for new productive investment. High expectations and capital shortage were likely if given full reign to produce a boom market, and the new issue market in 1919–20 proved no exception. From 1916 onwards new issues had been subject to control, but it was not complete, neither was it to everyone's satisfaction. *The Economist* referred to the work of the wartime New Issues Committee as being full of 'freakish anomalies and contradictions that have become a byword'.

New issues certainly appeared but they could not be traded on the London Stock Exchange or any other recognized market, but an unofficial market was made by outside brokers.

Whatever the effectiveness or merits of such controls the end of the war brought strong pressure for their removal and as a result the new issue market was one of the first to be partially restored. In March 1919 home new issues were freed on condition that every prospectus offering to the public for subscription or purchase and any issue made under general licence carried a statement that 'no part of the proceeds of the issue is to be applied for capital purposes outside the United Kingdom, or to replace money which has so applied'. By November even controls on fringe issues had been relaxed.[12]

If industry was ready to use its new freedom to raise funds or to engage in ambitious reorganization schemes, the public was well equipped with resources, if not entirely so with judgement, to take up the resulting supply of investments. Since the middle years of the war the market had been carefully preserved for official issues, and the inexhaustible supply of gilt-edged tap stocks presented the public with little choice by way of asset selection and diversification. The attraction of industrial capital was that it provided an opportunity for participating in future profit growth, which engendered considerable market interest and a tendency for prices to discount future income for many years ahead. War propaganda had popularized securities to a much wider public and the custom of investing, together with accumulated savings, created a ready demand.

The new issue boom was essentially domestic in character. As the statistics given in table 2.1 show home industry was responsible for the bulk of activity, the percentage being higher in 1919 than in 1920. New issue activity in the last quarter of 1918 indicated that a boom was underway since a stream of industrial issues managed to find their way through the Treasury turnstile, leaving little doubt that a long queue waited behind seeking the necessary sanction. The flow continued into 1919, rose by the third quarter, and in the final quarter reached nearly £70.0m. The first quarter of 1920 saw a great rush of prospectuses, the total, on *The Economist*'s figures, involving over £100m. The sum was boosted by large issues of over a million from Lever Bros., Dunlop, British Cellulose, and Crosse and Blackwell. Such pressure was 'too heavy to last' and after Easter, public sobriety began to reassert itself with underwriters being left with large amounts of shares. While the earlier issues 'were well subscribed . . . the later ones are finding it difficult to obtain capital'.[13] By the middle of 1920 the economic indicators were showing a tightening situation; the government deficit had turned to surplus, trade was depressed, bank rate reached 7%, and the banks were rationing credit. By

Table 2.1   Capital issues by home industry, 1919–39; various series

Year	Midland Bank Series[a]		Economists' Old Series[b]		Bank of England Series[c]		
	All issues	Production, trade and transport (home)	Total	Mainly home industries	Total	Industrial and Commercial	Manufacturing component
1919	237.5	151.0†	1,0178*	160.3	—		
1920	384.2	245.8	267.5	241.1	—		
1921	215.8	63.5	389.0	62.9	—		
1922	235.7	66.1	573.7	76.6	—		
1923	203.8	68.6	271.4	69.3	—		
1924	223.5	69.0	209.3	76.3	—		
1925	219.9	82.5	232.2	89.7	—		
1926	253.3	90.0	230.7	80.9	—		
1927	314.7	102.7	355.1	134.1	316.7	140.9	n.a.
1928	362.5	137.8	369.1	141.2	360.6	193.3	93.9
1929	253.7	110.9	285.2	122.0	268.5	163.8	77.6
1930	236.2	65.4	267.8	58.8	244.2	102.4	29.5
1931	88.7	25.3	102.1	35.9	94.5	37.7	13.4
1932	113.0	45.6	188.9	29.9	117.8	78.2	20.2
1933	132.9	54.8	244.8	33.7	136.9	71.4	37.2
1934	150.2	63.0	169.1	54.7	164.6	94.6	58.7
1935	182.8	121.1	236.1	67.7	199.2	155.3	67.2
1936	217.2	123.0	255.7	79.5	244.6	170.8	90.2
1937	170.9	86.8	251.6	72.5	187.2	120.8	69.0
1938	118.0	59.5	180.1	50.0	131.8	77.8	41.7
1939	66.2	29.8	91.7	23.4	73.2	35.5	16.5

* Includes government stock issue to redeem floating debt.
† 1919–26 *mainly* home production, trade and transport.
[a] Midland Bank Series. Records money raised in the U.K. (other than U.K. government) by all issues of marketable securities. Confined as far as possible to subscriptions by U.K. residents. Subscriptions included in full at the time when they are invited.
[b] Economists' Old Series. Issues on the London market by limited companies and other industrial and trading companies, drawn mainly from publicly advertised prospectuses, offers for sale, or press announcements.
[c] Bank of England Series. Relates to cash subscribed by U.K. residents, including their subscriptions to issues made abroad. It excludes subscriptions by overseas residents to issues made in the U.K. Issues were valued at the price paid by the subscriber. For detailed descriptions of the above series see 'Capital Issues in the U.K.', *Bank of England Quarterly Bulletin*, June 1966, pp. 151–6, and R. F. Henderson, *The New Issue Market and the Finance of Industry*, 1951, Appendix A, pp. 155–61.

the third quarter the volume was only a third of the boom level, and although a small recovery occurred in the next three months, the market was somewhat satiated and in spite of offers made on 'alluring terms', underwriters found themselves fulfilling their promises.[14]

Total industrial issues in 1921, for both the Midland Bank and *The Economist* series, fell to a quarter of 1920 level. Investment stocks were still able to find a market but the public would not look at speculative offers. There were some signs of recovery in 1922–3, but the volume remained well below the boom level. At least public subscription to issues that were made was good, and overseas issues were beginning to pick up by this time.[15]

The new issue boom centred on manufacturing, heavy industries and the miscellaneous section. During 1919–20 these industries represented over 60% of issues by 'mainly home industry'. However, the figures given in the new issue series omit a large volume of issuing activity at this hectic time. A very large amount of re-financing went on, some of it needed, but a great deal was sponsored 'by the get rich quick brotherhood'. Ambitious schemes were particularly prevalent in 1919 when easy money market conditions facilitated conversion operations. The bulk of them were made by companies already possessing large capitals and they generally took the form of an issue of fixed interest stock.[16] This sort of activity was to be found not so much in the miscellaneous and manufacturing sectors, but in the motor, cotton and shipping industries.

In the case of the motor industry, a comparatively new arrival, 'capital emissions', amounted to some £23m. during the boom, much of it raised at high rates. Some commentators were fairly complacent that it was needed in every case, but others were not so friendly since the industry was luxury orientated and the shares consequently completely speculative.[17] Activity in the shipping industry was even more doubtful in nature. It had become heavily overcapitalized as a result of the strikingly profitable freights carried in the immediate post-war years, and as H. W. Macrosty relates the episode, with high freight rates 'another orgy of speculation broke out in Cardiff, and in one month alone thirty companies were floated with £4m. capital. The experienced shipowner sold, the ignorant man bought, and the banks financed the deals'.[18] The boom spread to other parts of the country with several shipbuilding yards changing hands at inflated prices.

The most notorious episode of the boom was probably the recapitalization activity in the cotton industry. In the immediate post-war period cotton profits rose rapidly, mainly because of widening margins on a restricted output. Before the war the industry's response to this would have been to expand existing mills and build new ones. However, shortage of resources and time did not permit of such a course in 1919. Instead it took the form of a speculative reconstruction of a large part of the industry. Prices of shares were hopelessly inflated and based on grossly optimistic expected earnings so that the transfer of cotton undertakings took place 'at very full values'. The reconstruction took two forms: firstly, the refloatation of mills on an inflated capitalization – some 217 spinning mills were refloated in this way; secondly, recapitalization which entailed increasing the share capital by issuing new bonus shares which the shareholders later disposed of on the market at a premium enabling 34 mills to be recapitalized.[19]

From the low point of 1923 new issue activity for home industry began to pick up in 1924, with increased use being made of the market, especially by electric light and power companies. It was apparent from the reception accorded to these issues that the public had large resources and in addition 'a willingness to respond with avidity to any offer that possessed reasonable merit or attraction'. Admittedly there were plenty of stags in the market, but the underlying investment demand was also present since issues held their premiums after the stags had taken their profits.[20] Total issues for home industry rose during 1925 and 1926, despite the prevailing pessimism about trade prospects, and a feature of the market was the number of rubber plantation issues in 1925 and of coffee issues in 1926. Indeed in the last quarter of 1925 there was a flood of rubber issues, so that over the whole year they numbered 180 (old and new companies) with the average amount asked for working out at less than £140,500.[21]

By 1927 a new issue boom was well underway (in contrast to the United States the boom was not in established industrial shares) especially in speculative securities, with a large number of greyhound, film, and gramophone shares, and a public 'already on the feed'. With falling yield levels and the public appetite suitably whetted enterprises of all descriptions quickly took advantage of the conditions, and issues of all classes were heavily oversubscribed.[22] The early part of 1928 was notable for issues in the following sectors, as given by *The Economist*, stores and trading, electric light power and telegraphs, rubber, and 'hotels, theatres and entertainments'. The latter persisted into the second quarter of the year, 'all admittedly of a speculative nature', along with a large number of small issues by new companies 'for the exploitation of some patent process'. Following the normal August lull in the market the campaign was quickly resumed with new vigour, the main activity concentrated in such areas as gramophone companies, photographic processes and luxury services of various kinds. By late autumn the market was satiated with speculative offers and issuing houses and underwriters were left with a great deal of stock. In the short space of seven weeks from the beginning of October over 90 issues were made of which only eight were regarded as possessing any investment status, the rest being speculative issues, that is, companies new to the market and largely the creation of active company promoters eager to exploit some new process in the radio, gramophone, or artificial silk industry.[23] By this time, however, the growing instability of the market was becoming apparent. It arose partly from the increasing extent to which securities were carried on loans from the banks, and partly from the vulnerability of low denomination shares, once favourably received, which were sensitive to the slightest reversal since speculators with small means were apt to sell out in a panic.

The boom came to an end in the spring of 1929. The increase in bank rate to 5.5%, disappointment with the speculative issues for not bringing anything by way of the promised returns, and defaulting by a number of flagrantly weak sub-underwriters, were important halting factors. Also, more experienced speculators were increasingly attracted by the prospects of participating in the mounting Wall Street boom. By mid-year prices were falling and underwriters were left with large blocks of stock. The crash on Wall Street and the Hatry Crash at home finally demoralized the market. The volume of issues for the second half of 1929 amounted to only £31m., compared with three times that amount in the first half. As the *Midland Bank Review* put it, 'at the outset properties were appearing with extraordinary frequency and a fair degree of variety; at the end they were almost as rare as a swallow in winter'.

It is particularly interesting that half the issues by number and two-thirds by amount came from existing businesses, and that the subsequent fall in their market value was only of the order of one-third. With regard to new companies several points can usefully be made. In the category of new companies acquiring businesses with past profits stated there were several cases where the capital raised was not used mainly to purchase a business; they were merely technical devices used by the vendors for ends other than a literal sale.[24] Another feature of such issues was that the vendor usually retained a greater part of the ordinary share capital, the public issue consisting of fixed interest preference shares, while those companies that did offer some participation frequently demanded a hefty premium. Successful businesses rarely offered any real participation to the public in their future prospects; those that made the overture were uniformly unsuccessful. Finally, the main groups within the 109 new or virtually new ventures were as follows: gramophone and radio, 21; artificial silk, 10; finance, 10; films, cinemas and theatres, 8; and portrait machines, 7 (all of which had been wound up by 1931 at a loss of £1.1m.). It was in this group, and that of new companies without profits, that depreciation of share values was most severe; it was the new companies that really collapsed.

As to the boom overall, from 1927–9, certain characteristics stand out. There were many issues of a financial nature, in particular, a large volume of investment trust issues; in 1927, £19.5m.; 1928, £33.9m.; and 1929, £29.1m. This, of course, was part of the growing trend towards indirect participation in share ownership, but in these boom markets the trusts did not expand at the expense of direct investment. As to the distribution of investment trust funds between new and existing securities nothing is known. In the miscellaneous and commercial section the amount of capital raised was conspicuously up on previous years, and covered a great multitude of purposes and concerns. Such issues were obviously greatly to the public liking; 'the attractions of whose deferred shares as gambling counters were more regarded by the public than their merits as an investment.'[25] A further feature was the extent of parent and offspring financing that occurred. This type of financing involved a parent company 'having made its own appeal to the investor, sells the foreign rights, as yet unproved, in its particular invention to a brood of its offspring, which in their turn claim the investor's largesse'.[26] Finally, the market continued with its traditional defect of overvaluing issues. The new financial twist in 1928 however was to declare that 'nothing was for goodwill', compared to the previous practice which was 'overvaluation of assets, which were placed at their approximate true worth, and the balance, if any, of the purchase consideration plainly called goodwill'.[27]

In contrast with the preceding two years 1930 was a quiet year for industrial new issues. The start of the decline in activity is clearly shown in table 2.1; in the second half of 1931 only £7.0m. of capital appeared. *The Economist* at the time saw the change thus: 'In a capital boom, like that of 1928, capital is raised by those who think they may need it. In an ordinary cyclical slump it is raised only by those who really need it. In a crisis like that of [1931] ... even necessity looses its compelling power.'[28] Market uncertainty and lack of confidence among investors virtually brought home industrial issues to a standstill. Investors were shaken by the decline in the market quotations of existing securities, which greatly reduced their inclination to take up new offers. Such issues as appeared on the market were, compared to the boom flotations very conservative in nature, but given the public mood even blocks of these were left with underwriters. Companies in such circumstances looked to alternative sources of funds, for example, bank finance, while those of exceptional credit standing resorted to making issues direct to their shareholders.

After Britain's abandonment of the gold standard in September 1931, and a brief spell of high rates, bank rate was reduced to 2%, a move which was quickly followed by the successful conversion of £2,000m. of government debt from a 5% to a 3.5% basis.[29] Once the ban on home issues, imposed to assist the conversion operation, was lifted the stage was set for a revival of home industrial issues, but this was slow in coming, and the market was not really tested for this purpose for some time. Companies had little incentive to approach the market, and such issues as were made after the 'ban' on shares were mainly confined to offers to shareholders and for small amounts.

The path of revival taken by the market and the variations in new issues during the 1930s can be seen from the figures given in table 2.1. At first the pace was exceedingly slow, and low interest rates had little effect on the volume of issues. During 1932–4 average annual issues (*The Economist*'s figures) amounted to £39m., compared with £132m. during 1927–9, but such a comparison does ignore the important effect of falling prices of capital goods. In practice low rates seem to have coincided with the lowest borrowing for a generation, and while expectations remained at a very low ebb cheap money provided little stimulus for industry. Resort to the new issue market, however, is not the only guide to the pace of industrial activity. Industry in 1933 was reported as having very abnormal liquidity and *The Economist* aptly pictured industry as 'living on its hump'.[30] Initial recovery from the depression was thus financed without going to the market so that the secondary phase of financing expansion was likely to be delayed.[31]

Towards the close of 1934 signs appeared that investors were again taking an interest in new industrial ventures, and one indication of this was that preference shares were coming back into favour. By 1935–6 the volume of industrial issues was up greatly on previous years (see table 2.1), a recovery linked with increased industrial activity. Thereafter, however, the volume of issues declined significantly due to adverse risk factors and rising interest rates. By mid-1937 the pace had slackened; many issues were still oversubscribed but some were now being left with underwriters. In 1938 the new issue market was labelled as stagnant with issues being postponed, while those who did brave the market frequently ended up with the underwriters. A tendency had set in to assess business prospects conservatively and the market was left to quality borrowing.

Within the general picture certain features of the new issue market are of interest. In some sectors borrowing was up quite dramatically. For example, on the basis of the Bank of England's industrial classification of issues, coal, iron and steel raised £45m. in 1934–6, a sum used for plant extensions following the granting of tariff protection; land, building, and building materials averaged just over £13.5m. a year for 1933–6, reflecting the housebuilding activity of the time.[32] Property companies also raised considerable sums, with investors displaying a keen interest in the returns available. In 1936–7 there was also an increase in the 'numerical frequency of issues in a narrow range of popular industries', for example, engineering industries remotely connected with re-armament. Favourite issues in 1936 were those in machine tools, aircraft, aircraft accessories, miscellaneous engineering, and any such enterprise which could 'claim a fifth cousinship to the armament industry'.[33] At least many of these had an advantage over their 1929 predecessors in that they had some past earnings but it was common practice merely to use the latest good figures as the basis for the capitalization.[34]

A feature which generated some criticism was the appearance during 1936–7 of relatively small issues involving shares of small denomination. In a survey of prospectuses issued between 1 January and 24 July 1937 by companies involving a total money subscription of less than £150,000, *The Economist* found 45 companies with an average size of only £105,000, while the 62 blocks of securities involved averaged only £76,000.[35] Such small issues were disliked for their restricted marketability, their speculative prospects, and their large non-productive initial expenditure. The subsequent market in the shares depended largely on the reputation and diligence of the issuing houses or promoters. On the whole they did not attract the best issuing houses, but rather the smaller issuing groups eager for a quick profit. The use of shares of small denomination was something of a legacy from the 1928–9 issue boom and over three-quarters of the 62 issues noted above had shares of under £1. Marketability, while it might be assisted by shares of such denomination, did not increase in inverse proportion to size.

An area of activity not indicated by new issue statistics, but which occupied a prominent role in the finance of industry following the introduction of cheap money was that of conversion operations. The resulting fall in the long-term rate of interest made possible an adjustment to the capital charges of industry. The amount of fixed interest stock involved was certainly large; *The Economist* estimated that for quoted companies that there was some £945m. of debenture stock within the conversion zone, while a further £860m. of preference stock would have been eligible if company law before 1929 had not ordained their inconvertibility during the lifetime of the companies concerned – most of these were therefore only convertible by repayment through liquidation.

In the case of debentures a large number were near the conversion zone. It was estimated in 1933 that some £105m. was eligible for conversion within 10 years, but that the bulk of outstanding quoted debentures representing the greater part of post-war finance fell outside this zone.[36] This arose because some stocks had no early redemption date, some companies had marred their credit standing which prevented their debentures from rising above the redemption price, while others, even if their standing was better, had to persist with a heavy interest burden because their issues had been by way of stock 'with a moderate interest rate, offered at a discount'.[37] Indeed it was not easy for companies to take immediate advantage of the cheap money terms since the Treasury embargo laid down that company issues could not use underwriting facilities, without which a large conversion operation was difficult.[38] This did not prevent conversion offers to existing shareholders, underwritten by an insurance company by private arrangement. Industrial conversion operations from 1932–7 are given in table 2.2.[39]

In terms of total stock outstanding only a small portion had been converted during the initial period of cheap money. This, however, was not the only criteria for assessing the importance of the policy for industry. As can be seen from table 2.2 a significant reduction was achieved in the long term rate, but probably more vital still was the timing of the fall. The consequential reduction of some £2m. in the annual interest burden of British industry in the climate of the mid-1930s constituted a welcome addition to disposable profits. In a sample of large-scale conversions made in 1933 E. T. Nevin found that the saving secured was equal to an increase of nearly 6% of those companies' total operating profits in 1932.[40]

Table 2.2   Conversion operations, 1932–7

Year	Total stock converted (£'000)	Yield before conversion %	Yield after conversion
1932	10,536	6.0	4.7
1933	61,334	5.45	4.53
1934	26,592	5.5	4.38
1935	28,236	5.16	3.85
1936	29,012	4.73	4.0
1937	9,303	4.73	4.4

Source: *The Economist*, 12 February 1938, p. 332.

A glance at the main new issue series given in table 2.1 reveals the fluctuations in the volume of funds raised by home industry in the inter-war years. In the boom episodes there is little doubt that the investing public was overly receptive to greatly over-priced issues put out by some unscrupulous company promoters. On the other hand in the downturns investors were still prepared to support issues made to tide companies over a difficult period when funds were not available from elsewhere and when banks were pressing for the repayment of overdrafts. In the midst and between the speculative activity the market helped to provide much-needed capital for expanding productive capacity, and for funding short-term debt, and it did so not only for large companies but over the period for an increasing number of small companies who found that they could not grow without becoming public companies. For the most part the speculative excesses were more numerous than large and as one perceptive observer remarked, 'the instinct of the public was right. The world was certainly going to need more artificial silk, films, cinemas, safety glass, automatic machines and similar things'.[41] The mechanism was deficient, but the new market did accomplish the transition from foreign to domestic service without the aid of the great issuing houses, and before the advent of large-scale institutional investment interest.

Types of capital issued

In general terms if a business can offer assets by way of security, and reasonably stable income to cover the contractual obligation involved, then the tendency is to borrow a high proportion of funds by fixed interest securities. On the other hand, if its main asset consists of profit earning capacity then the tendency is to offer equities to the market. The other main influence on the type of security offered is the state of the economy and attendant market expectations, boom periods being associated with increasing resort to equity financing, while depressions produce the reverse movements. Table 2.3 gives the types of securities issued by companies during 1919–39.

Table 2.3 Midland Bank Series: types of company security*

Year	Debt^a £ m.	%	Capital^b £ m.	%	Total £ m.
1919	21.0	9.6	199.0	90.4	220.0
1920	46.7	15.2	261.0	84.8	307.7
1921	42.2	46.8	47.9	53.2	90.1
1922	48.8	49.5	49.8	50.5	98.6
1923	44.7	49.4	45.8	50.6	90.5
1924	38.1	38.1	62.0	61.9	100.0
1925	45.2	34.2	87.1	65.8	132.3
1926	49.9	35.2	91.0	64.6	140.8
1927	50.0	27.9	129.0	72.1	178.9
1928	65.4	26.0	186.1	74.0	251.5
1929	44.6	22.5	153.9	77.5	198.6
1930	33.9	43.6	43.9	56.4	77.9
1931	23.1	56.0	18.2	44.0	41.3
1932	17.0	43.9	21.7	56.1	38.8
1933	31.2	50.5	30.6	49.5	61.7
1934	35.6	35.4	65.0	64.6	100.6
1935	40.7	35.1	75.4	64.9	116.1
1936	38.5	29.9	90.3	70.1	128.8
1937	33.1	29.7	78.3	70.3	111.5
1938	33.6	45.2	40.7	54.8	74.4
1939	15.2	49.2	15.7	50.8	30.9

* All companies excluding railways, gas and water undertakings.
^a Debentures, notes and similar issues.
^b Shares of all kinds.
Source: *Midland Bank Review*.

The figures include an element for foreign issues, but reference to table 2.1 (p. 27) indicates that home borrowing predominated. Two distinct features of the immediate post-war boom deserve comment. The large figures of capital raised in 1919 and 1920, representing 90% and 85% respectively of all company securities issued, was the highest total for the inter-war period, unequalled even by the excesses of 1929. The figures given in table 2.3 contain preference issues as well as ordinary shares, and on the basis of *The Economist*'s figures the former amounted to some £78.0m. in 1919 and £21.0m. in 1920. At the time many leading industrial companies issued cumulative preference shares, frequently on an 8% basis.

A feature of industrial borrowing in the later stages of the boom, around the end of 1920, was the issue of short-term notes. Although included with debentures in table 2.3 they differed from them in several respects. Usually such notes were a mere promise to pay, while holders were only entitled to rank with ordinary creditors but before shareholders. Seldom was there any definite allocation as to security or provision of a sinking fund, and this lack of collateral was compensated, somewhat, by a higher rate. The only security was the 'past record of the company and the public faith in the names of the directors'.[42] They were used largely because firms wanted fresh capital to tide them over the next few years, and the intention was to fund them when cheap money arrived. They had several attractions to commend them – the expenses of issue were comparatively small, the public liked the high rates offered, and the assets of the company were left free to be mortgaged to banks in case of need. The prevailing type of note was for 6–7 years, generally at 8% (deductible in computing taxable income), and issued at a small discount. Such generous terms indicate the difficulty which industrial companies experienced in raising money in the later stages of the boom. *The Economist* estimated that about £20.0m. was issued in 1920, with only one issue in 1921.[43]

The onset of depression and the market fall quickly brought debt borrowing into prominence, the proportion of funds obtained thereby rising to almost 50% in 1922–3, and it did not fall to 34% till 1925.[44] Depression and low rates induced a tendency among industrialists to increase the percentage of their capital which was subject to fixed interest. They were anxious to borrow long at low rates in order to tide them over a difficult period, and also to replace the use of the short-term note. Market necessity also dictated greater use of fixed interest debentures. In the prevailing conditions the public were seeking safety of principal rather than high yield, and prudent investors sought secured debentures yielding 6.5% to 7.5%. The bulk of the prior charge issues were first mortgage debentures, along with some very well-secured preference shares.[45] Some companies took advantage of lower interest rates to undertake conversion operations, but they could only do so when they had specifically reserved the right to effect redemption at an early date. The effect of this practice was that early redemption stocks lost market favour.[46]

As can be seen from table 2.3 there are two other periods when the percentage of capital raised in fixed interest form rises well above the 40% level. These are the depression years 1930–3, and the period of uncertainty in 1938–9 before the outbreak of war. In the former a similar pattern of events to that experienced in the early 1920s is discernible, with investors insisting on more stringent requirements in the matter of security by means of bond offers. The lowest figure for debt issues during the entire inter-war period was made in 1932, but then there was an artificial handicap on industrial fixed interest borrowing since the authorities were busy grooming the market for their conversion issue. The majority of issues from the manufacturing sector at this time were in the debenture category, which 'geared up' industry, while many of them were conversion operations. During the short period before the outbreak of war borrowers again made relatively greater use of fixed interest issues. The sharp fall in the level of equity issues is clearly shown in table 2.3, and in the prevailing climate of hesitancy the proportion of debt to total issues rose to almost 50%. It was, however, according to contemporary comment, lack of enterprise among investors rather than among those responsible for business flotations that led to the decrease in equity volume.[47]

The remaining interesting feature associated with the types of capital issued occurred during the boom of the late 1920s, and to a lesser extent during the recovery period of 1934–7. In the former boom equity finance rose from 65% of all issues in 1926 to 77% in 1929; in the latter period it rose from 50% in 1933 to 70% in 1937. A practice widely used in the 1928 boom, especially by new speculative issues, was that of dual capitalization. This involved issuing simultaneously high denomination fixed interest preferred or priority shares (which fell to a discount) and low denomination ordinary shares (which rose to a premium). Generally shares of 2s or 1s were offered in conjunction with high value preferred shares. Such combinations were widely used by the patent company promotions of 1928, and P. D. Leake found 50 issues of shilling deferred shares in 1927, and about 16 in 1926, having first appeared in 1924.[48] The public were often required to take up a specified quantity of preferred shares in order to obtain deferred ones, while inside interests were frequently given the latter on special terms and for some consideration other than cash.[49] The priority shares were usually issued in such an amount as to provide 'the whole of the cash capital required for the purchase of the vendors' plant and stock, and for the working capital of the undertaking'. More often than not the deferred shares 'vested the goodwill of the undertaking in their holders by giving them the right to receive by way of dividend the balance of distributable profits earned after payment of a fixed rate to priority shares'.[50] At least since the totals of shilling deferred shares were usually small this placed some limitation on the valuation of goodwill. Since effective voting power frequently resided in the hands of the deferred share holders, and as public participation occurred predominantly through the priority shares, vendors of the business were often left with voting control. It also placed them in a position where they could practice some judicious unloading on the market when the limitation on the supply of such 'gambling counters' produced a premium. 'Knife edge ordinary capitalizations' were understandably popular with market stags.

The use of low denomination shares in the 1930s was associated with the appearance of numerous small issues. In practice, however, marketability did not increase with diminished share denominations. *The Economist* in a sample of 50 companies in 1937 found that 'although no stock in the [Supplementary] list has been in existence for as long as seven months dealings are already quiet, intermittent and irregular'.[51] Although the shilling share had reappeared it was in a 'slightly less objectionable guise' than in 1928, largely because the dual capitalizations were not as highly geared. However, the inside parties continued to do well, the general public being allowed to subscribe, on the average, for 86% of the preference capital but only 55% of the ordinary capital at the time of issue.[52]

Methods of issue

The most commonly used method of introducing securities to the market during this period was a public issue with a prospectus inviting the public to subscribe for a stated amount of shares at a fixed price. In this case the shares were issued directly by the company, the issuing house being paid a fee for its services. The company received a sum equal to the number of shares times the price, the money coming from the public, or if the issue was not a success partly from the public and partly from the underwriters. From the market's point of view the advantages of this system was the attendant publicity, that the allotment of shares was non-discriminatory, and they were widely distributed before dealings began. Its main disadvantage was that the costs of issue were high owing to legal, administrative and advertising expenses, which bore most heavily on small issues. Despite this in the mid-1920s nearly all small issues by companies new to the market were made by public issue.

A somewhat similar procedure, which was becoming increasingly popular, was the offer for sale. By the early 1930s the big issuing houses tended to use it for most of their domestic industrial issues. In the case of an offer for sale an issuing house bought the entire block of shares from the company, thus guaranteeing it the money, and then proceeded to sell the shares by prospectus issue at a fixed price. The proceeds to the company depended on the price paid for the shares by the issuing house, and whether or not any of the costs of issue were divided between the company and the issuing house. The same advantages were present as in the case of a public issue. However, the practice was mildly criticized in the 1920s on two counts. Firstly, that prior to a change in the law in 1927 the purchase by the issuing house of the capital meant that it escaped liability for prospectus statements; after 1927 both company and issuing house were made responsible for the statements made in prospectuses. The other ground for criticism was that in certain cases the margin between the amount received by the business and the sum paid by the public was occasionally regarded as unduly large.[53]

With the fairly constant flow of big domestic issues it was found that the traditional method of underwriting was becoming unsatisfactory. This involved the practice, especially with risky industrial issues, of 'hawking around' the city. When a few failures occurred underwriters quickly became reluctant to commit themselves and closed their books, while the banks would not lend on such securities, thus leaving the underwriters to rely on their own resources for the payment of allotment money and subsequent calls. Such 'hawking around' was in use in the early phase of the 1920 boom, but it was reported as being done 'as much with the determination to secure overriding commission for themselves as to do their friends any particular favour'. In the early 1920s the shortage of professional underwriters induced a wide response in that 'the public are beginning to deal in underwriting to an extent quite unknown even five years ago'; they regarded underwriting commission 'like a gift of free money'.[54] The problem with such small underwriters was that they tended to sell at a discount to secure a small profit from the underwriting commission with the result that the issue would languish below its subscription price till such selling was out of the way.

During the inter-war years the practice quickly developed of the issuing houses becoming the main underwriters, a process reinforced by the tendency among companies to choose those that could guarantee subscriptions. The issuing house entered into the main underwriting agreement and then proceeded to distribute the risk among a large number of sub-underwriters, for which it got an overriding commission. In the 1920s, however, the procedure was not without criticism. Often the main underwriting contract was made by syndicates with only a nominal capital, while the ranks of the sub-underwriters included, according to one observer, numerous 'men of straw'.[55]

The principal sub-underwriters to the big issuing houses were usually large investment institutions, particularly insurance companies and pension funds, along with a small class of professional underwriters. The issuing houses preferred to deal in large blocks and were not disposed to deal in trifling sums. By 1930, however, those that took some interest in home issues were willing to get down to units of £2,500 to £5,000 in order to satisfy a wider clientele. The institutions were the main and most favoured outlets, since they were particularly suited for this sort of work. Many were prepared to take a firm commitment, that is, agree to subscribe for shares whether the issue was a success or not, and on a good issue this meant that they got preferential allotment. More usual was the conditional form whereby underwriters agreed to take up any unallotted shares. In the case of the large issuing houses the arrangements were concluded over the telephone and often the underwriters never saw the prospectus, being prepared to take 10,000 to 20,000 shares 'blind' and rely on the issuing houses 'to make the issue go'.[56] Underwriters knew that the larger houses would support the market if difficulties arose, and they would always be ready to let the underwriters out with a minimum of sacrifice.

Anxiety to get on the underwriting list of an issuing house or leading stockbroker, 'as a means of getting into securities on the ground floor', imposed obligations on underwriters. There was an understanding in the best circles that they would take participations as they came, the rough with the smooth, and they were expected to support an issue by making applications in the normal way. Most important was the understanding that they would not indulge in the cardinal sin of panic selling if an issue proved unsuccessful. Even though powerful underwriters had the underwriting commission available to absorb any sales at a discount on the issue price, and still leave them with a profit, they usually declined to sell until a public demand arose which enabled them to sell stock at something like the issue price.[57] The above obligations might have created a 'pathetic submissiveness' on the part of some subscribers and placed them under the influence of the issuing houses, but increasingly underwriters with greater experience investigated issues more closely and practised discrimination in non gilt-edged issues.

It was not until the Companies Act of 1900 that companies were authorized to pay underwriting commission out of capital, but then only in the case of public issues. The Companies Act of 1907–8 extended this facility to all types of issue, but the payment had to be authorized in the articles. However, prior to the 1929 Act there was no limitation on the amount of commission payable, when a limit of 10% (on the nominal value of the shares underwritten) was set.[58] Before 1929 the best companies tended to set a limit of 25%, but commissions of 50% were paid out, with the resulting tendency of issuing shares at a very heavy discount, an undesirable market practice and hence the imposition of the 10% limit. In most cases the actual rates paid were well below the permitted minimum. In the late 1920s it was generally 4% on ordinary shares, with 1% overriding commission.[59] By 1937 it had fallen to 3%, with overriding commission of 1%. Preference shares, on the other hand, were generally underwritten at 2%, with 0.5% overriding commission. For established companies and public bodies the charge was even lower.[60]

It was seldom the case that the cream of issues by way of underwriting or sub-underwriting was accessible to the outsider, but an alternative was to hand, by way of stagging first class issues, a popular practice in the early post-war boom. It was reported to be so acute that the 'lists of many of the more attractive issues had to be closed within a few hours'; lists were open for a few days. By the late 1920s the practice developed that lists were opened at 9.00 a.m. and closed at 5.00 p.m., while by the war they were closed at 1.00 p.m. The main danger in these occasional great campaigns of stagging was that of stock 'being heavily oversubscribed by people who have neither the money for, nor the intention of keeping it, and who clamour to get out immediately a market is made. The consequence is that for a few days the market is swamped with small selling orders, which are not offset by such buying as is pretty certain to be attracted as soon as the stocks become better known; genuine buyers tended to hold off till the stags had cleared out.'[61]

While the practice of a private placing followed by a Stock Exchange introduction, that is, seeking permission to deal, was anything but new, its popularity increased greatly after the war. Its early use was linked with doubtful and speculative borrowing, reflected in *The Economist*'s observation that 'under cover of this introduction habit, dozens of concerns have received Stock Exchange sanction to utilize all the machinery of the House for facilitating transactions in the shares'.[62] Before the war a mild suspicion was attached to shares that came to the market in this manner. However, it was later resorted to by companies of standing and made considerably more respectable. The progressive tightening of Stock Exchange requirements as to the disclosure of material facts helped in this. Also, by about 1930 some borrowers of high standing – 'known names' – were reported as being increasingly impatient with the 'heavy stagging of recent public offers', and within a few years it was used for large issues. It was popular in investment circles since it put shares their way on the ground floor, and Stock Exchange members liked it because it brought a wider spread of commissions compared to public issues. In the prevailing moribund market just before the war it was widely used.

No precise figures are available of its use over the entire inter-war years.

The following figures (table 2.4) of the number of issues by prospectus and information statements compiled by *The Economist* for the years 1926–33 give some indication of its use. Although it increased in popularity in 1928–9 most of the cash raised came from public issues. In another series of calculations *The Economist* found that the nominal capital arising with introductions was as follows: 1931, £8.8m.; 1932, £15.0m.; 1933, £34.8m.; and 1934, £28.2.m.[63] During the mid-1930s the volume increased, which was reflected in a new series of figures prepared by *The Economist*. The figures in the new series of capital issues included indirect placings which had reached the public through the Stock Exchange after the granting of permission to deal. For the category 'other British' the

Table 2.4　Issues publicly advertised

	By prospectus	By information statements
1926	194	118
1927	321	85
1928	390	261
1929	200	173
1930	145	49
1931	59	17
1932	98	33
1933*	100	80

* To October.

Source: *The Economist*, 14 October 1933, p. 723.

figures ranged from £215m. in 1936 to £40m. in 1939. For 1936 the Midland Bank calculated that there were 240 publicly advertised private placings, compared with 186 the year before.[64]

The usual procedure was for the shares to be allotted in the first place to a broker, issuing house or syndicate, and then made available to the public who made purchases through their stockbrokers. Occasionally, even in advance of permission to deal being granted, the stockbroking firm drew up a list of names of people who came to them requesting that they, 'the prospective purchasers shall be put down on the waiting list for the purchase of the shares when a market in them starts. As the list grows, so, it occasionally happens, does the price rise, and even before permission to deal is given some people have bought and sold.'[65] A certain amount of information was required to be made available to the public, and from

1919 onwards the Stock Exchange stipulated that an advertisement should be placed in two leading London newspapers. Even this had its defects since on occasions full details were dispensed with and merely a brief statement inserted. Variations of this form were also used in that such advertisements might invite the public to subscribe for shares without supplying any of the details obligatory in a prospectus issue.[66] Market dealings began at prices above the original price, and the placing price was no doubt fixed so as to allow a reasonable profit for risk-taking. In an analysis of a sample of introductions made during 1933–5 (involving mainly ordinary shares) *The Economist* found that the premium paid averaged 57% of the nominal value involved.[67] Apart from the exorbitant margins seen in 1929 it was not often that the public appetite for placed shares was sufficient to establish very large speculative premiums on the placed price.

In many respects this method was an attractive one for bringing shares to the market. Legal and administrative costs were considerably lower than with prospectus issues, with no underwriting expenses. Of course, the agents, who did the placing, allowed for a margin of profit for themselves and for their clients when dealing began. The suggestion was also made that there was little prospect of deception with the general run of experienced city investors, and indeed, the growing use of this method rested on the increasing investment interest of the main financial institutions in the industrial security market. It was undoubtedly well suited for small issues, and also for public companies who wanted to market shares previously in private hands.

Against these advantages there were several drawbacks. The particulars published were much less complete and less 'circumscribed by regulations' than with prospectus issues, and issues of doubtful merit had possibly greater opportunity of evading scrutiny. From a Stock Exchange viewpoint there was the criticism that no precise knowledge existed of the number of shares available for the market, and this was further exacerbated by their lack of diffusion which made it easier for prices to be manipulated. Suspicion that the placing method had been used for private reasons, where a normal prospectus method would have been more appropriate, led to representations being made to the Stock Exchange and in 1936 it was decided that 'all issues, particularly those of ordinary capital, should be made by prospectus or offer for sale unless from the public stand point the necessity or advantage of a private placing is indicated by the circumstances'.[68] Thereafter the Stock Exchange required to know full details of the volume of shares placed, with whom, and so forth, thus enabling them to form a picture of probable supply conditions to the market.

The price of capital, 1920–37

The most accessible information on the average rates paid on new capital is the series compiled by *The Economist* which gives the average yields calculated on the issue prices of prospectus offers for new money. Table 2.5 sets out the figures of the average yields of gilt-edged, industrial debentures and preference stocks and shares. It is noticeable that debenture rates provide a better guide as to the general trend of rates, exhibiting a much more stable differential with the gilt-edged rate, while preference rates show much greater fluctuation reflecting the variation in the type of instrument issued and the varying risks attached to them. It is, of course not possible to measure in the same way the cost of borrowing by ordinary shares, since they carry no rate of interest in the accepted sense of that term.

Table 2.5   Average yields on new issues: prospectus offers for new money (%)

Year	Gilt-edged	Debentures	Preference	Year	Gilt-edged	Debentures	Preference
1920	7.0	8.0	8.1	1929	5.0	6.1	6.6
1921	5.7	8.1	8.4	1930	4.7	6.0	6.0
1922	6.0	6.7	7.2	1931	no issue	6.3	6.5
1923	5.3	6.4	6.6	1932	3.5	5.4	6.3
1924	4.7	6.6	6.3	1933	3.0	4.6	5.3
1925	4.7	6.4	6.1	1934	3.1	4.5	5.0
1926	5.0	6.5	6.7	1935	2.2	3.8	5.0
1927	4.7	6.2	6.7	1936	2.9	4.2	5.0
1928	4.8	6.1	7.4	1937	2.6	4.1	4.9

Source: *The Economist*, 8 February 1936, p. 292, and later issues. Figures are not available for 1938–9.

A distinctive feature of table 2.5 is the downward trend of rates from a high point of around 8% for industrial fixed interest borrowing in the immediate post-war years, to a 4–5% basis in the mid-1930s. Within the trend there are some distinctive and interesting interruptions. The collapse of the post-war boom brought a relatively rapid decline in rates over the next two years, a fall checked in 1923–4. An interesting feature of 1924–5 is the appearance of what might be called a reverse yield gap between debentures and preference stocks. The lowering of the preference yield, when their volume was increasing quite sharply, was probably due to the appearance of several large, good quality issues with very adequate cover of the preference dividend. From 1926 until 1931 the debenture rate declines gradually, in contrast to the greater fluctuation in the level of gilt-edged yields. Compared with the quiescent debenture rate the preference rate behaved erratically. It rose from just over 6% in 1925 to nearly 7.5% in 1928. This level was partly a reflection of the increased volume of preference issues, but probably more decisive was the dubious investment value of numerous prospectuses. The rise in the rate could be regarded 'as the price paid for the specious popularity of the Shilling deferred share, linked with high yielding preference shares of doubtful security'.[69]

The onset of the depression brought a fall in the rates, but this was temporarily interrupted by a technical upward move associated with the events of the 1931 financial crisis. With the adoption of cheap money policy rates fell sharply, but during 1934–6 preference rates levelled off, a check associated with re-armament finance and the re-emergence of some of the dubious practices of the 1928 boom. A further influence in arresting the fall was the increase in the number of small share issues which commanded an additional risk premium in the market.[70] Debenture issues were mainly used by established companies of sound credit standing, and the fall in debenture rates followed the downward path of gilt-edged. The fall in debenture rates was also influenced by the reduction which took place in the average life of new debentures being offered to the market during 1931–7, their average life falling from 39 to 28 years.[71] The fall in rates was maintained despite a significant rise in the volume of debt issued. From 1936 onwards the general tendency was for rates to rise, and the market became increasingly sensitive to the volume of defence borrowing, with the rise in gilt-edged rates reflected in the industrial sector.

Costs of issue

These were mainly incurred in the acquisition of two services, those of publicity and expertise. They involved payments to brokers, solicitors, accountants, bankers, advertising and prospectus costs, and underwriting commission; stamp duties were an additional item. However modest the profit taken by promoters and intermediaries it was difficult to reduce them below a certain point. For example, in the case of advertising a prospectus it was quite easy to spend around £5,000. Modesty was not the hallmark of every intermediary since 'some firms of brokers consider themselves but poorly remunerated by a fee of 1000 guineas for merely giving the promoters the right to print their name on a prospectus'.[72] Most of the costs involved were of a fixed nature, very few of them varied with the size of issue. In the case of large issues such charges represented a relatively small percentage, but on small issues of around £100,000 they were proportionately burdensome.

For the 1920s there are difficulties in arriving at reasonably accurate costs for issuing. R. F. Henderson examined several prospectus issued in 1926 and found that many did not provide sufficient information for the accurate calculation of issue costs, especially in the case of the smaller issues where he suspected that issue costs were high. Accordingly, any figures arrived at were likely to underestimate the costs involved. Similar problems were encountered by a group of Cambridge economists who undertook a survey of issues made in 1927–33. In their results, 'ambiguous' expenditures absorbed a large percentage of issue proceeds, while identified issuing costs (termed 'preliminary expenses') were rather low, ranging from 0.5% to 3.4%.[73]

The most reliable figures available for the 1920s are those compiled by R. F. Henderson for 1926. For all methods of issue (predominantly public issues, even for small sums), 14 issues by new companies, with an average size of £214,000, produced average issue costs of 12.7%, which was probably an underestimate.[74]

Calculations are more numerous, and more reliable, for the mid-1930s. A detailed investigation undertaken by J. B. Selwyn of issues made in 1937 produced some interesting figures. Particularly noticeable was the range of expenses, from 1% to over 30%. For the purpose of his survey expenses were defined as the difference between the amount the company received and the sum the public paid for the shares. For all public offers analysed the cost of issue was 8.5%, but such issues of less than £150,000 produced issue costs of 15%, and those above, 7%. Also, offers for sale proved more expensive than public issues for all size groups, being 10.5% and 6.7% respectively, possibly because the former method was used for smaller issues. Even with their advantage for new companies, introductions produced costs of 14.2%, but old companies using this method got away with 5.9%.[75] Similar figures were arrived at by R. F. Henderson for 1937. In the case of his new money only issues, 9 preference share issues (average size of £183,000) had costs of issue of 7.5%, while 19 issues of ordinary and preference (average size of £164,000) produced a figure of 12.0%. Compared with costs in the 1920s there would seem to have been a reduction, while in addition the size of issues had fallen along with that of the net asset size of the issuing companies, suggesting that more smaller firms were making use of the new issue market.

While in general costs were falling most commentators argued that for small issues they continued to be too high; as *The Economist* put it, 'the midwife's fee appears economically high'. Given the incidence of fixed cost items in the issue process differences were bound to occur in the percentage costs of big, medium and small issues, but even so, the market was seen to be requiring an additional premium for handling small issues. In the matter of underwriting higher rates were charged for small issues, due to the greater risks involved and the possibility of 'institutional lock-in' of the shares for some time, but it was not altogether clear why a much higher percentage was taken. J. B. Selwyn's investigation revealed that more than one-third of the issue costs went to finance houses, which might have represented in the case of the smaller houses a participation by the vendors taking their profits indirectly. For small issues the entry of the established issuing houses into the domestic new issue market did not provide a solution by way of cheapening the cost of supplying funds. 'It is difficult to escape the conclusion', A. T. K. Grant wrote in 1936, 'that either some of the smaller issues should not be made at all, or else, that they should have been made more cheaply.'[76]

The above generalizations applied to London issues, but it is worth noting that issue costs were lower in the provinces, so much so as to make 'possible issues of considerably smaller size, down to £50,000 at reasonable costs of issue'.[77] The factors responsible for this were firstly, that a company was better known locally so that sales resistance was less; secondly, local brokers were content with smaller profits in the interests of keeping local custom; thirdly, certain fixed issue costs were lower; fourthly, there was less stagging in the provinces; and finally, there were better markets in the issued shares.[78]

In practice high costs did not deter issues. It could be that they were paid since this was the price of getting marketability for the capital sunk in an industrial activity. Further many were prepared to pay simply to get the prestige of a quotation, in the hope that subsequent issues could be made on a lower cost basis; a Stock Exchange quotation conferred financial status, at a price. It is also possible that some minimized the apparent cost by regarding it as an annual charge.

The institutions of the new issue market

The need for the 'interposition of some expert responsible body which could examine impartially the prospects of the venture' was certainly recognized in the immediate post-war years.[79] Generally companies had to present their case to the public without the aid of any well-known intermediary. In the opinion of the Macmillan Committee the position had not changed much by 1931, since with the exception of a few issuing houses and leading stockbrokers 'the public is usually not guided by any institution whose name and reputation it knows'.[80] In the case of many leading issues a clearing banker's name was prominently displayed in the prospectus, but they merely received subscriptions and took little responsibility for the issue, apart from a very superficial view of its respectability, while they in no way looked after the market subsequently.[81]

The most experienced and respectable institutions in the new issue market, the established issuing houses such as Baring, Rothschilds, Lazards, Schroeders, Hambros and Erlangers, had traditionally concentrated on high-quality overseas issues, along with a few large domestic issues. Their sponsorship gave a special standing to the issues they handled, and they invariably watched carefully over issues after they had been made. However, the reduction in the volume of foreign issues made in London after the war, and especially after 1931, brought a gradual switch to home issues. The transition was a somewhat reluctant one on the part of the issuing houses and they were still reproached for being better informed on conditions in South America than in Lancashire or Scotland. From their standpoint they were entering a field where the record was unimpressive, and a business which in the 'best circles' was classed as 'second rate'. The industries best suited to use their expertise, the heavy industries, were at the time in no state to make frequent market appearances. In the period 1926–8 only four of the leading houses handled domestic industrial issues, and of the fifteen made by them, half were done by one house, while on the foreign side they did about a dozen each.[82]

More specifically their reluctance to take up domestic industrial issues arose from the size of most issues, and from questions of liquidity. Compared to overseas issues the domestic ones presented to them were for the most part small and involved proportionately greater dealing problems. They felt, in addition, that their investigation machinery was not adequate for small industrial issues. The liquidity aspect was expressed as follows by Sir Robert Kindersley to the Macmillan Committee: 'An Acceptance house must keep its funds liquid, and it has to confine itself to the issue of what it believes to be first class bonds or debts. It cannot assume liabilities which are going to mean a great locking up of money or it cannot father a particular industry. It cannot father a company, in my opinion it should not.'[83] The Acceptance Houses also claimed that firms did not approach them because they did not give out 'cash advances' prior to an issue.

The above, however, possibly overstates the degree of their domestic inactivity. Though they were not active in sponsoring public issues on the open market they had been involved with a certain amount of placing activity. Sir Robert Kindersley told the Macmillan Committee that his house had 'purchased from English industrialists and have placed with our own clients and through agencies'; during 1918–30 Lazards had placed some £24m. industrial securities.[84] The issuing houses were also involved in numerous industrial reconstructions, aided by the finance companies with which they had connections. This usually involved rearranging a company's financial structure with a fairly drastic writing down of a big part of the capital and cutting out fixed interest 'dead wood'.

As a rule issuing houses seldom made issues for an entirely new business, they confined their activity to large and well-established companies. This preference for size and quality to some extent explains their relative inactivity in the middle 1930s when most industrial issues tended to be on the small side. Usually the issuing house procedure was to buy the amount to be offered outright and sell it on the market on an offer for sale basis, arranging the necessary underwriting with the leading investment trusts with which the older houses had very strong links.[85]

Another group of intermediaries, the finance houses, had traditionally played a significant part in the financing of home industry, and those operating in the years after the war received modest praises from Lavington, 'they are permanently engaged in financial operations, and that having a reputation to loose, they give the public some measure of assurance of the worth of their issues'.[86] Among the most active in the inter-war years were British Shareholders Trust (registered 1921), British Trusts Association (1917), Charterhouse Investment Trust (1925), H. Wagg & Co. (1919), Investment Registry (1903), London and Yorkshire Trust (1919), Standard Industrial Trust (1920), and Scottish Finance Co. Ltd (1926). Their financial resources were not limited to their own capital since they had developed important connections with leading financial institutions who were taking a growing interest in industrial shares from the late 1920s onwards.

The third group of agencies in the market were the various syndicates formed by company promoters to launch particular issues, with the probability that vendors were also involved. Such mushroom houses flourished in the 1919 and 1928 booms and were again in evidence in the mid-1930s. They were, at their height, to be found in every trade centre, 'syndicates of not too scrupulous individuals bent on garnering a rich harvest'. Following the experiences of 1928–9 *The Economist* portrayed the activities of these obscure and often irresponsible company promoters as follows:

The speculative promoter or issuing house as a rule, regards issue business largely from the angle of *salesmanship*. He is concerned to discover new enterprises which will 'go well' when offered to the public, and, after making an issue, is anxious to 'get out' as quickly as possible. He lacks inclination, knowledge or resources to enable him to place a potential operation against the background of the general welfare of the country, or to 'nurse' a new concern and exercise a wise control over its future fortunes. He gives the public what it wants rather than what is good for it, so that any industry which has shown more than average profits is flooded with new companies, to the ultimate disadvantage both of the latter and the industry itself.[87]

The gullibility of the public and the low quality of many of the syndicates does not mean that the method is essentially a bad one.

Finally there were the large stockbroking firms with established connections who could handle issues by themselves. Their activity varied with the state of the new issue market, the number of issues handled by London brokers increasing from 281 in 1926 to 1,004 in 1929, falling to 82 in 1931 and recovering to 285 by 1933.[88] In all some 260 brokers were involved, but the bulk of them only handled a few small issues, the majority of issues being undertaken by about eight brokers.

Notes

1 F. Lavington, *The English Capital Market*, London, 1921, p. 103.
2 ibid., p. 109.
3 ibid., p. 190.
4 ibid., pp. 190–1.
5 Report of the Committee on Financial Facilities, 1919, para. 41; reproduced in A. W. Kirkaldy (ed.), *British Finance, 1914–1921*, London, 1921, Appendix IX.
6 F. W. Paish estimated that of the £150m. per annum net home investment before 1914 only about £30m. was financed through the capital market; 'The London New Issue Market', *Economica*, 1951, p. 2. On the same point see also T. Balogh, *Financial Organisation*, Cambridge, 1947, p. 253.
7 For a detailed account of its operation see Balogh, op. cit., pp. 268–71. See also J. Aitken, 'Official Regulation of Overseas Investment 1914–1931', *Economic History Review*, 1970, pp. 324–35. Although Treasury regulations were removed in 1919 an unofficial embargo operated in the 1920s against foreign government and company issues, the aim being to protect the pound when under pressure and to reserve the market for home government borrowing.
8 The effect of these restrictions was very marked in the 1930s. During 1931–8 the annual average of Empire issues amounted to £25m., compared with £62m. in 1928–1930; foreign issues averaged only £3m.,

compared with £34m.; *The Economist*, 6 January 1940, p. 27.
9 *The Economist*, 11 September 1937, p. 508.
10 T. Balogh asserted that the extent of 'the decline of the local finance is shown in the most striking way in the increase of the relative importance of issues for home purposes relative to total savings'; Balogh, op. cit., p. 281.
11 For a full treatment of these trends see A. T. K. Grant, *A Study of the Capital Market in Britain from 1919–1936*, London, 1937, pp. 179–82.
12 *The Economist*, 5 March 1919, p. 514; 3 January 1920, pp. 9–10.
13 *Statist*, 27 March 1920, p. 594.
14 *The Economist*, 10 April 1920, p. 770; 8 January 1921, pp. 5–6.
15 *The Economist*, 30 December 1922, p. 1210; 7 April 1923, p. 725.
16 *The Economist*, 3 January 1920, p. 9; *Statist*, 8 January 1921, pp. 50–1.
17 *The Economist*, 6 December 1919, pp. 1029–1030.
18 *Statist*, 8 January 1921, pp. 50–1; H. W. Macrosty, 'Inflation and Deflation in the U.S. and the U.K., 1919–1923', *Journal of the Royal Statistical Society*, 1927, p. 72.
19 W. A. Thomas, *The Provincial Stock Exchanges*, London, 1973, pp. 156–8.
20 *The Economist*, 5 July 1924, pp. 4–5; 3 January 1925, p. 8.
21 *The Economist*, 2 January 1926, pp. 4–6. In

all they involved £13.2m. ordinary, £55,000 preference, and £560,000 debentures securities.

22 Grant, op. cit., p. 143.

23 *The Economist*, 24 November 1928, p. 953.

24 S. A. Harris, 'A Re-analysis of the 1928 New Issue Boom', *Economic Journal*, 1933, p. 455.

25 *The Economist*, 10 November 1928, p. 854.

26 *The Economist*, 24 November 1928, p. 950. *The Economist* calculated that about three quarters of the inventions cited in recent prospectuses had not been granted a patent.

27 *Statist*, 10 December 1927, p. 1078.

28 *The Economist*, 13 February 1932, p. 344.

29 For details of the conversion operation see E. Nevin, *The Mechanism of Cheap Money*, Cardiff, 1955, pp. 92–8.

30 *The Economist* analysed a large sample of company accounts covering 1930–2. It found that over the period working capital had increased by 6.5% and that the increase was very marked in the case of large companies. Certain industries showed increases of around 50% in net liquid assets (excluding stock in trade) – in tea, breweries, motors, textiles and miscellaneous groups: 3 June 1933, pp. 1196–7.

31 Company boards at this period were reported as being conscious of the high level of tax on distributed earnings, which inclined them to put funds to reserve for future bonus issues rather than pay out higher dividends and then proceed to ask shareholders for new capital: *The Economist*, 26 December 1936, pp. 625–6.

32 Bank of England figures of industrial issues, 1928–36, are given in Grant, op. cit., p. 149.

33 *The Economist*, 25 July 1936, p. 173; 10 October 1936, p. 71.

34 *The Economist*, 10 October 1936, p. 71: 'Rearament Boom Finance'.

35 *The Economist*, 31 July 1937, pp. 253–4. Most of the armaments companies were in the small to medium size category. On this subject see also Nevin, op. cit., pp. 224–5, who found that during 1935–6 a larger share of issues was made by small firms (net assets under £1m.) than during the other years of the decade.

36 *The Economist*, 23 December 1933, p. 1236.

37 *The Economist*, 30 July 1932, pp. 230–1.

38 The Regulation read: 'there are to be no issues involving either underwriting or an undertaking to subscribe to new cash for the optional replacement of existing issues.'

39 These are broadly similar to the Bank of England figures given by Nevin, apart from 1934 and 1935; the Bank of England figures being £44.3m. and £44.6m. respectively; Nevin, op. cit., p. 227.

40 Nevin, op. cit., p. 228. *The Economist* reported that 'the recent reports of some of the largest British concerns have suggested that internal adjustments – in costs, interest charges – have been sufficiently extensive to make production at least moderately profitable, even under the depressed conditions of the time', 3 June 1933, p. 1196.

41 Grant, op. cit., p. 146.

42 *The Economist*, 20 November 1920, pp. 900–1.

43 *The Economist*, 28 January 1922, pp. 118–119. During the 1920s most companies which had issued short-term notes funded them: see *The Economist*, 30 July 1932, pp. 230–1.

44 Some industries during 1921–8 displayed a very high percentage of debt issues; tramways and omnibuses, 56%; electric light and power, 53%; iron and steel, 49%; *Midland Bank Review*, 1929.

45 *Statist*, 8 January 1921, pp. 50–1; 28 May 1921, pp. 993–4.

46 *Statist*, 30 December 1922, p. 1124.

47 *Midland Bank Review*, 1939.

48 P. D. Leake, 'Shilling Deferred Shares', *The Accountant*, 4 February 1928, pp. 168–9. *The Statist* claimed that this particular artifice had been imported from abroad, but the British capital market in earlier years was never short of 'watering' or 'gearing' exponents; they would seem certainly to have links with the well-known founders shares.

49 *The Economist*, 24 November 1928, p. 950.

50 Leake, op. cit., p. 168.

51 *The Economist*, 31 July 1937, p. 253.

52 *The Economist*, 10 October 1936, pp. 71–2.

53 Grant, op. cit., p. 161.

54 *The Economist*, 27 November 1920, p. 939; 23 February 1924, p. 419; 5 July 1924, p. 13.

55 D. Finnie, *Capital Underwriting*, London, 1934, pp. 205–6. There was no need at this time to disclose the capital of either the main or sub-underwriters. On the diffi-

culties arising from weak underwriting in 1928 see Finnie, ibid., p. 69. In its evidence to the Departmental Committee on Company Law Amendment of 1945, the London Clearing Banks asserted that they had come across very little bogus underwriting. One bank had handled 307 industrial issues involving £196m. over a period of 25 years and in only two cases had the underwriters not stood up to their commitments. Lloyds Bank experience was that they had 'never known underwriting break down in any shape or form'; Q. 4758.

56 *The Economist*, 1 November 1928, p. 850. Lord Kindersley stated to the Macmillan Committee: 'you are supposed to look after the market'; Q. 1309.

57 *The Economist*, 23 February 1924, p. 419.

58 Finnie, op. cit., p. 56–7.

59 In *The Economist*'s survey of 10 November 1928 (p. 850) of issues advertised in April–June 1928, total capital offered for subscription was £28.8m. and the total underwriting commission was £821,938, that is, 3%.

60 Balogh, op. cit., p. 291.

61 *The Economist*, 21 July 1923, pp. 97–8.

62 *The Economist*, 23 May 1925, p. 1018.

63 *The Economist*, 21 December 1935, p. 1266.

64 Grant, op. cit., p. 163.

65 *The Economist*, 15 January 1927, p. 105.

66 *The Economist*, 30 April 1927, p. 903.

67 *The Economist*, 21 December 1935, pp. 1266–7.

68 Grant, op. cit., p. 163.

69 *The Economist*, 8 February 1936, p. 292.

70 Nevin, op. cit., p. 213.

71 ibid., p. 216.

72 Lavington, op. cit., pp. 218–19.

73 G. D. H. Cole (ed.), *Studies in Capital and Investment*, London, 1935, p. 125.

74 R. F. Henderson, *The New Issue Market and the Finance of Industry*, Cambridge, 1951, p. 141.

75 Balogh, op. cit., pp. 294–5.

76 Grant, op. cit., p. 169.

77 Henderson, op. cit., p. 83.

78 ibid., pp. 83–4; see also Thomas, op. cit., p. 255.

79 Lavington, op. cit., p. 109.

80 Committee on Finance and Industry, *Report*, para. 388 (Macmillan Committee, 1931).

81 Macmillan Committee, *Minutes of Evidence*, Q. 1298; see also Qs 1485, 1101, 2397. The Westminster Bank read through prospectuses but did not look into the estimates given, these were 'usually vouched for by the people we know'; Q. 2387.

82 *The Issuing House Year Book and Financial ABC*, 1929.

83 Macmillan Committee, *Minutes of Evidence*, Q. 1308. See also Henry Clay, 'The Financing of Industrial Enterprise', *Manchester Statistical Society*, 1932, p. 217; H. F. Foxwell, 'The Financing of Industry and Trade', *Economic Journal*, 1917, pp. 519–20.

84 Macmillan Committee, *Minutes of Evidence*, Q. 14818.

85 Balogh, op. cit., pp. 258–9.

86 Lavington, op. cit., p. 184.

87 *The Economist*, 15 February 1930, p. 364.

88 *The Issuing House Year Book and Financial ABC*, 1934. For provincial activity see Thomas, op. cit., pp. 249–50.

3 The clearing banks and industry

It is not the most approved business of a bank to furnish the fixed capital of an enterprise.

C. A. PHILLIPS

From a strictly banking viewpoint it is not a major function of the banking system to provide funds, either short-term or long-term, for industry. The banker's function may, however, be said to consist of meeting the contract between himself and his creditor, that is, the depositor, so that deposits placed on demand may be so realized, while those placed for seven days or longer can be realized on agreed terms.[1] In general his assets should match these commitments. The assets held will generate income which will be used for the payment of interest on the liabilities, meet the operating expenses of the bank, allow what is deemed desirable to be placed to reserve, and what remains is profit. It so happens that one of the most profitable outlets for bank funds is through making short-term advances to industry and the personal sector. If, however, other more lucrative outlets offer themselves, and they are consistent with the nature of a bank's liabilities, then from a banking viewpoint the acquisition of such assets is perfectly reasonable. In other words there is no duty upon the banking system to provide finance for industry; in the inter-war period there were many voices proclaiming such an obligation.

Banks provided short-term credit by means of advances, either by way of loan or overdraft; 'in the South of England financial assistance is usually given by a banker in the form of a fixed loan, whereas in the North the floating overdraft on current account is the more generally recognised'. Usually they were for short periods of between six and twelve months and in the case of industrial users were usually made to finance stocks of raw materials, work in progress or finished goods, and quite often they were renewed for new transactions.[2] A cardinal point of English banking practice was that there should be no 'lock-up' of funds, a view which was endorsed by the Committee on Financial Facilities of 1919.[3] In making advances banks had to be reasonably confident that the transaction would be self-liquidating in the short term, or that the amount advanced could be obtained with 'reasonable promptitude' if the bank demanded repayment. In so far as banks confined the bulk of their lending to seasonal working capital purposes their loans were not only self-liquidating but also fairly secure since a company's fixed capital could easily provide a loan with a safe margin of cover. The reluctance of banks to 'go long', in this and other periods, was tied up with the increased risks involved, and this risk factor in the opinion of one authoritative writer 'is a wholly sufficient reason for confining bank advances, in a system of the British kind, mainly to the provision of circulating capital and for avoiding any extensive locking up of banking funds in fixed capital or long-term securities'.[4]

The structure of banking after the First World War

The pre-war years had already seen a large number of bank amalgamations but what was distinctive about the surge of mergers in 1918–19 was that they took the form of 'unions of two joint stock banks, both already possessing large funds and branches spread over a wide area'. During a comparatively short space of time 19 amalgamations took place, involving 38 large banks. Indeed the public became somewhat alarmed at the pace of the movement and in March 1918 the Treasury set up the Committee on Bank Amalgamations, chaired by Lord Colwyn and which reported in May of that year. The Committee recommended that all subsequent amalgamations should be subject to the approval of the Treasury and the Board of Trade. Among the reasons it gave for such a recommendation was that the newly formed units were 'large enough to meet the requirements of the immediate future, at any rate if supplemented, so far as may be necessary by combinations for special purposes.'[5] The most important mergers occurred in 1918, while those of the following year were in the main consolidations. As a result the banking system was clearly dominated by the newly emerged 'Big Five', namely, the National Provincial and Union Bank of England, London County Westminster and Parr's Bank, London Joint City and Midland Bank, Barclays Bank, and Lloyds Bank.

One immediate consequence of the mergers was that the ratio of paid up capital to total deposits for all banks fell from the pre-war level of 10% in

1910 (*The Economist*'s estimate) to 6% in 1918. Even this low figure was an overstatement since only about half of this was actual capital, while the rest was undivided profits liable to be 'trenched upon'. This decline in the capital position followed from the fact that amalgamation schemes usually meant a reduction in the total paid-up capital and uncalled liability of the two pre-amalgamation banks.[6] In order to strengthen the position several appeals were made in 1919–20 to the capital market.[7] It is interesting to notice in the case of the independent Lancashire banks that they were affiliated rather than merged; for example, in 1919 Barclays Bank obtained control of the Union Bank of Manchester, a policy designed to avoid a clash with local feeling which had been roused when mergers had been threatened before the war.

One of the important reasons advanced by the banks in support of their amalgamation moves was that it was necessary to keep pace with the growth in large business firms generally. They claimed that wartime experience had provided them with a foretaste of the growing financial needs of firms. The chairman of Barclays Bank stated in 1915 that their amalgamation was motiviated by the need 'to meet the demands for extra accommodation made by manufacturers and contractors who were obtaining government contracts for raw materials which were beyond their ordinary capacity to carry'. A somewhat similar reason was put forward by Walter Leaf to justify a merger by the Westminster Bank in that the anticipated requirements in the near future when general trading was resumed would be 'beyond the resources of a comparatively small local bank, but which are well within the compass of a bank such as our own with its exceptional liquidity and large deposits'.[8] Large sums were needed not just for the growth of industrial units but also for the reconstruction needs of industry, both at home and abroad, and this reason was also noted in justification of the merger activity.

Among the other benefits likely to accrue to industry from an increase in the unit size of banks were the following. Firstly, it was thought that a large bank would be able to lend proportionately more than a group of small banks of equal aggregate resources since the former worked to a smaller reserve. Secondly, it was felt that the acquisition of the accounts of firms engaged in diverse industries gave added strength to the banking system since 'the policy of a large bank may be more stable than that of a small', and because 'the specialised experience of bankers operating in areas concentrating on similar types of industry was focussed under one, instead of many roofs'.[9]

However, various qualifications were also voiced as to the degree of assistance banks could render to industry. The Colwyn Committee commented that 'if both the amalgating units have, before amalgamation, lent up to their full resources, home trade *as a whole* cannot gain any increase in accommodation as a result of the amalgamation'.[10] Further, *The Economist* pointed out that very large firms were accustomed to going to more than one bank. However, a 'firm which was entitled to credit to the extent of £100,000 each from the two banks is not likely to get £200,000 from the combination. It is difficult to understand why this should be so, but we are assured that it is.'[11] Also, combination did nothing for the supply of longer term capital from the banks, and in this respect their capital ratios were well below continental levels. To meet these needs the banks would require large-scale resort to the capital market, while the longer commitments involved would require 'more careful investigation and judgement than the kind of business that has hitherto been done by our great banks'.[12] It would also require a radical shift towards long-term liabilities. Finally, there were some more pointed regional reservations. Industrial producers in the North of England were somewhat suspicious of the benefits of amalgamations, while they strongly disliked the tendency of banks to move towards increased safety by restricting 'heavy loaning done without security'.

Procedures for advances, bills and acceptances

Bank advances to customers were made either as loans or overdrafts. Loans would be of a fixed sum usually for a given period, the sum being placed to the credit of the borrower and interest charged for the full sum even if only a part was used. Generally such loans were secured by adequate collateral. During the inter-war years this was the general form of accommodation in use in London.[13] Overdrafts on the other hand involved a bank granting permission to draw on an account up to a maximum limit, and the customer was only charged interest as he used the credit. Collateral security might be required where the limits granted seemed large in relation to a client's resources. Generally small overdrafts were given on balance sheet and personal considerations, although in the late 1930s there was a growing tendency to obtain collateral from borrowers. The overdraft form was widely used in the provinces, about half of them being unsecured, while in Scotland practically all trading advances were on fluctuating balances, with none being made as fixed loans. Indeed, contemporary observers were of the view that overdrafts were rapidly replacing loans for fixed periods; Frederick Hyde, managing director of the Midland Bank, stated to the Macmillan Committee in 1930, that 'the overdraft system with our trading customers is very largely supplanting the old system of making loans of fixed amounts for fixed periods'.[14] The amount of the unused overdraft in a sense constituted a liability on the bank, although if necessary this could be cancelled. At the time of the Macmillan Committee the banks refused to disclose the sum involved for fear that it would 'shake confidence'. In any case such a figure might well be misleading since there was little danger that it would all be used at the same time.

Loans were mostly granted for periods of up to a year, although in a meritorious case a bank might go up to three years. However, all advances came up for reconsideration every year on the grounds that the banks preferred where possible to secure an annual reduction, but a good deal of latitude was allowed where this was not easily possible. In theory overdrafts were for seasonal purposes, to finance transactions which would soon liquidate themselves. However, the banks were not averse to considering loans for capital expenditure purposes if they could see how they could get their money back, for example, by means of a subsequent share issue. Also, sympathetic consideration was given to applications from customers in difficulty where the bank felt that loss of business was due to external causes, but such loans were made on fairly stringent conditions.

The procedures by which the main clearers considered applications for advances was a mixture of centralization and de-centralization. Three of the clearers, Midland, National Provincial and Westminster, operated on a centralized basis, Lloyds had a sort of compromise, while Barclays had a policy of de-centralization. In the case of the centralized system the discretionary limit allowed at branch level was small so that most applications went to the head office where in the first instance they were considered by regional controllers or supervisors, and if they were above a certain limit they went to higher management levels. No application was turned down except at the highest level. Lloyds had local committees which gave opinions on loan applications, and which were useful in establishing contacts and providing information. By contrast Barclays Bank had local boards which enjoyed considerable powers, and reference was only made to head office in exceptional cases. On the whole the commercial banks felt that no contact had been lost with local trade and industry as a result of the amalgamation programme. Centralization, however, did cause some concern outside the banks. In the view of *The Economist* in the early 1920s 'far too much goes to London', adding that 'one section is centralising its work to a degree that savours of the government office and rations its credit on a mathematical basis, that takes little heed of trade imponderabilia'.[15] Other criticisms revolved around the reluctance of the banks to 'apply general rules under expert guidance to their particular problems'.[16] Certainly, when compared to the vetting procedures used in the United States, the British practice seemed particularly undeveloped. While there was concern for the security of the collateral there was little in the way of 'searching credit analysis' when granting loans.[17]

Head office had not only to look at the merits of each application but it also had to look to the overall advances position of the bank, the ratio of advances to total deposits and the distribution of advances. The general aim was to secure the maximum of diversification so that if a particular trade or location seemed to be on the decline, or likely to face difficult times, then the bank could attempt gradually to shorten its commitments in such areas. In practice it proved more difficult to achieve this objective than the banks would have liked.

The rates charged on advances were tied to bank rate. In the 1920s they were usually 1% above bank rate, with a minimum of 5%. Large borrowers with good collateral could secure loans at 0.5% above bank rate, with a minimum of 4.5%. Only in exceptional cases would industrial loans be made at more than 1.5% above bank rate, while in Scotland the banks granted secured loans at 0.5% cheaper than those without collateral. With the advent of cheap money in the 1930s the banks found that the well publicized minimum was constantly being 'shaded' downwards, and influential customers were able to extract even more favourable conditions by threatening to move their accounts or avail themselves of different sources of finance.[18] By 1938 *The Economist* reported that the banks' slogan of 'one above bank rate, minimum five' had gone by the board; loans at 4.5 to 4% and even less were readily obtained by large customers.[19]

Bank auditors annually examined all loans and advances, and satisfied themselves that adequate provision had been made wherever necessary. The provision took the form of deductions from the profit and loss account, such sums being placed to inner reserves. This sum naturally tended to increase in the years of depression, although the transfers required were reduced by the realization of security held against such debts. Indeed, even after the declaration of profits further appropriation might often be made in the form of an allocation to contingencies. The inner reserves were also boosted by profits made on investments realized at prices over and above book values; it was the practice never to write up investment values in line with current appreciation. Further, the inner reserves were increased by making transfers from the published reserves. This arose when sums were drawn from the published reserves to provide for the depreciation of investments, but any profits which subsequently accrued were appropriated to the inner reserves.[20]

Banks could also offer financial assistance to industry by discounting bills of exchange and by granting acceptances. A bank could either discount a bill directly for a customer, which thereby provided accommodation closely similar to granting an advance, or the banks could buy bills on the market which had initially been drawn to finance an industrial transaction and which had been accepted by a leading bank or an acceptance house. The former type of bill certainly lacked the security of the latter. Unfortunately, for the period under review, there is no indication of the proportion of each in the portfolios of the banks.

Although they carried a lower rate of return than advances, the banks were nevertheless favourably disposed to bills. They regarded them as a clean and compact form of finance, while fine bank bills were a desirable liquid asset. In a speech to the Institute of Bankers in 1928 a prominent commercial banker claimed that 'if a banker has to choose between a more or less secured advance and a bill of exchange representing and secured on a definite transaction, he will choose a bill every time. If British traders would revert to the use of the bill of exchange they might find that bankers would . . . give them greater facilities than they can at present.'[21]

Industry, however, showed an increasing tendency to use less of bill finance. Industrialists found that advances gave them greater freedom of action and they preferred this to having their 'obligations definitely dated by their acceptances'. Many preferred to pay cash in order to get a trade discount and would not therefore accept bills.[22] A further reason, according to The Economist, was that 'first class British firms do not like to have bills bearing their name brought into circulation, and prefer to pay the higher interest charged on bank loans, as in doing so even the comparatively limited publicity of their credit transactions involved in operations in the bill market can be avoided'.[23] In the face of these tendencies the volume of commercial bills declined. By the late 1920s six-months bills had become virtually obsolete, and even bills of shorter issuance were relatively scarce. The Macmillan Committee reported that commercial bills had 'largely disappeared as part of the mechanism of home business', but even so went on to praise the instrument: 'To those who find it necessary for good reason to give extended credit, finance would be rendered more easy if their 'accounts receivable' were in the form of commercial trade bills rather than in the form of mere debts.'[24] By the 1930s revival was thought to be hindered by the fact that the average provincial trader or manufacturer had never been taught how to draw or accept a bill, while 'many branch bank managers can neither give their customer the necessary advice, nor have any experience of arranging credits themselves'.[25]

Finally, banks could aid the financial activities of their customers by accepting a bill, which for a small commission transformed its status.[26] The clearing banks in particular were well placed to undertake such business since in relation to their capital and deposits the volume of acceptances was very small. Generally the acceptances of the big banks were on behalf of 'banks and firms of undoubted repute', but these seldom came onto the market in the ordinary course of business. The other items more often than not included with acceptances were engagements on account of customers, and endorsements.[27]

Advances during the inter-war years

The immediate post-war boom produced a quick surge in the level of bank advances, as the figures of the London clearing banks given in table 3.1 indicate; changes are examined using total bank advances since for most of these years no consistent industrial breakdown is available. The high point of bank advances was reached in the spring of 1920, the peak figure being £861m. in March and April, which gave the clearing banks an advances ratio of just under 51%. Thus between January 1919 and April 1920 bank advances rose by £385m., an increase of 81%. The banks accomplished this by reduced lending to the government, but chiefly by expanding their deposits by some £250m.[28] The reasons underlying this sharp rise in bank lending over so short a period of time were set out by *The Economist* in the following terms:

> bankers have been subjected to continual pressure from their customers who wish to take advantage of apparently profitable opportunities to expand enterprise, and in order to do so made persistent demands for further credit from the bankers. Thus the banks were between the devil and the deep sea. Increased output was demanded on every side. The cry for more goods as the most wholesome way of reducing prices was everywhere heard, and manufacturers and merchants thus had a very strong case when they went to their banks and asked for increased facilities in order to carry out the necessary expansion and so produce a greater volume of goods. Prices of commodities were still rising, and were involving a much greater outlay and a much greater lock-up in order to finance a given quantity of goods. Morever, owing to shortened hours and reduced output, industry was working slowly, making the time during which credit was required to cover the process of production much longer than it had been; and when the goods had actually been produced, the congestion of transport facilities was again prolonging the time that they took between the close of the production period and their actual delivery to the customers. There was another very important fact, that a great many potential buyers of the goods produced were unable to pay for them with anything like the former promptitude, owing to the impoverishment of many countries which

had once been our regular customers, and owing to the general dislocation produced in markets abroad and the economic system of the world as a whole from the results of the war.[29]

Table 3.1 London clearing banks: Advances, commercial bills discounted and acceptances 1919–22 (£m.)

Date	Advances	Commercial bills discounted	Acceptances outstanding
1919 March	506.9	93.1	47.3
June	527.6	89.5	52.5
September	652.0	107.6	68.9
December	731.0	133.6	108.4
Monthly average (12 months)	579.6	106.8	61.4
1920 March	861.7	138.2	99.0
June	844.4	121.3	64.2
September	831.2	133.1	54.2
December	815.1	142.8	69.3
Monthly average (12 months)	831.6	144.2	75.8
1921 March	844.5	125.2	42.5
June	795.7	132.1	36.6
September	767.7	126.2	29.4
December	735.5	130.8	39.9
Monthly average (12 months)	790.2	134.1	39.4
1922 March	725.8	101.3	36.2
June	701.7	113.5	33.3
September	695.8	105.3	29.6
December	717.3	116.4	47.5
Monthly average (12 months)	711.8	113.3	36.5

Source: Committee on Finance & Industry, Report, 1931, App. 1, Table 1, pp. 284–5.

There can be little doubt that the credit policy pursued by the banks in the boom was far from conservative and it was spurred on by a competitive spirit. The annual reports of the banks emphasized their willingness to accommodate business needs arising from increased activity, the high prices of labour and raw materials, and in specific cases, where firms changed over from war to peacetime production and so lost government financial backing. Barclays Bank assisted many provincial mills and factories with loans 'to extend their productive capacity'. They found that the demand for funds exceeded the amount they felt justified in lending; they lent 'to the fullest extent prudence would allow'.[30] The Westminster Bank similarly experienced a large demand for advances 'for all stages of manufacture'. By the close of 1920 the District Bank found its advances ratio standing at 55%, but 'a considerable portion of this percentage is due to overdrafts fluctuating according to seasonal requirements and is therefore sufficiently liquid'.[31] Reginald McKenna admitted in the Midland Bank annual report for 1920 that it had been the policy of the bank to sell investments 'even at a loss in order that we might be prepared to meet any legitimate demand for credit which might occur. An alternative would be to impinge upon our liquidity but we preferred to face the loss on investments.'[32]

With the collapse of the boom and the fall in prices the total of advances of the London clearing banks fell off gradually during the next two years (see table 3.1), reaching a low point of just under £700m. in September 1922, with the advances ratio declining to 42%. From the 1920 peak advances fell by 19% by September 1922, but the fall in prices over the same period was of the order of just under 50% which suggests that the proportion of loans frozen may have been quite large. With the collapse of the boom the banks found that they could not realize some of their loans, particularly where manufacturers had built up stocks of finished goods and now relied upon bank finance to carry them.[33] In the case of the cotton industry it was estimated at the end of 1920 that stocks were from £50–£60m. in excess of the usual volume because of reduced foreign demand.[34] It may have been the policy of some banks to have a certain proportion of banking advances renewable, but the 'trade slump made it impossible, or at any rate inexpedient to call them in'. In many instances, however, they only had themselves to blame since they had not been sufficiently discriminating with their loans. For example, the textile industry reconstruction was heavily financed by bank loans, while loans were used for speculative excesses in re-financing private companies and for carrying commodity stocks at inflated prices. The banks, of course, admitted that bad debts had been incurred but hastened to add that they had fully provided against such contingencies, and also for 'all probable bad debts'. The continued decline in advances over 1921–2 reflected the running down of stocks carried with bank finance, while no fresh accommodation was required.[35]

The trend of discounts and acceptances followed that already described for advances. While commercial bills declined in relative importance (cf. bank deposits) the volume in circulation certainly increased with the trade boom and the commercial banks quickly expanded their portfolio to accommodate customers' needs (see table 3.1). Between January 1919 and April 1920 the volume of commercial bills held by the commercial banks increased from £91.7m. to £148.5m., a rise of 62%. These were mostly approved trade bills and fine bank bills with less than three months to maturity, and at least in the case of the Midland Bank in 1920 'all of them good'. The volume of bills held continued to rise, reaching a high level at the end of 1920 and early 1921, with manufacturers carrying stocks on bill finance. With the onset of the slump and the running off of stocks in the ensuing months the volume of bills in the banks' portfolio fell back at the close of 1922 to about the mid-1919 level. This, plus the lessened trade demand, and reduced prices, kept the level low. The banks were not altogether too happy with this position since it left them with little alternative 'but to invest our surplus money in Treasury Bills'.[36]

At the end of the war the volume of acceptances was low due to transport difficulties and delays in the presentation of bills drawn. However, the volume doubled with the boom (see table 3.1) which was associated with the growth of commercial bills and in particular the large increase in cotton stocks.[37] Subsequently, the volume declined with the fall in prices and of trading in cotton. At this time the bulk of the acceptances of the major clearers represented the movement of commodities to this and other countries, and all were well secured.

In the recovery period from 1923 to 1929 the level of advances of the London clearing banks rose from £729.5m. to £964.0m. It was a more-or-less continuous increase (see table 3.2) but, of course, the aggregate figure for advances contains such a diversity of uses that it should not be taken

Table 3.2   London clearing banks: Advances, commercial bills discounted and acceptances 1923–9 (£m.)

Date	Advances	Commercial bills discounted	Acceptances outstanding
1923 March	733.0	108.4	46.6
June	733.8	119.3	38.4
September	722.6	115.9	38.3
December	742.9	129.8	60.2
Monthly average (12 months)	729.5	119.8	44.9
1924 March	771.6	113.1	56.9
June	778.2	126.8	47.1
September	778.0	121.3	44.1
December	794.8	132.1	70.9
Monthly average (12 months)	774.2	125.5	54.5
1925 March	827.9	120.6	67.1
June	835.6	110.9	47.3
September	814.8	129.3	50.9
December	834.5	126.7	68.7
Monthly average (12 months)	821.7	127.6	60.5

Table 3.2—cont.

Date	Advances	Commercial bills discounted	Acceptances outstanding
1926 March	855.9	114.2	58.4
June	861.6	105.0	44.9
September	861.5	90.7	43.4
December	887.3	95.0	51.8
Monthly average (12 months)	858.0	107.8	52.1
1927 March	897.6	88.1	51.6
June	909.4	96.2	47.0
September	909.1	94.6	44.6
December	907.6	101.0	53.1
Monthly average (12 months)	899.2	98.4	49.5
1928 March	922.7	101.3	60.3
June	927.6	122.8	62.5
September	919.2	117.8	66.9
December	943.4	125.0	83.3
Monthly average (12 months)	923.6	118.2	65.3
1929 March	968.9	124.2	81.2
June	978.9	118.3	74.5
September	960.2	117.7	64.7
December	962.3	116.9	66.6
Monthly average (12 months)	964.0	122.9	73.6

Source: Committee on Finance & Industry, Report, 1931, App. 1, Table 1, pp. 286–9.

as an accurate measure of the provision of bank finance for industry. It is, however, the best approximation available. The increase in advances in 1923 and 1924 was largely due to increased trade demands.[38] Not only did the banks sell investments to accommodate the demand for advances, but they were at the time only 'too desirous to make loans and give additional credits' since their ratio of advances to deposits was unprofitably low, standing at 45%.[39] Industry, instead of being squeezed, was given the opportunity of borrowing more than it needed. The expansion of advances continued into 1925, but the pace slowed up in the second half of the year; the sheltered industries were doing all right but demand for finance from the export industries showed little signs of improvement.

The rise in imports and the continued expansion of production in 1926 was reflected in the level of advances. The figure was also increased since the banks made advances to customers who were in difficulties due to the coal stoppage.[40] Despite the absence of active trade conditions in 1927 the level of advances remained relatively high. This was because many of the loans extended during the stoppage remained outstanding for an unusually long period.[41] Barclays Bank in its Annual Report for 1927 commented on the very slow liquidation of old loans, and held out the hope that a revival of trade would speed up that process. Meanwhile there was some increased demand from new and old customers. The suggestion was made at the time that the reason for the high level of advances in the prevailing trade conditions was that banks were lending abroad at the expense of home industry because of the attractions of higher interest rates. However, only about 1% of all advances were made abroad; 'not only are many of these advances made simply against remittances in transit (the foreign borrowers being creditors of British firms) but foreign balances maintained with London banks in all probability exceed the total of foreign advances–overseas connections thus increasing rather than diminishing the banks' power to finance domestic trade.'[42]

New loans made by the banks during 1927 and 1928 were mostly to business in and around London, and the larger provincial towns. The Lancashire banks, catering for the staple industries, found their advances contracting as a result of the continued depression in the area.[43] In such a climate most banks claimed that 'no reasonable application is turned down', and they staunchly rejected criticisms as to their record. They maintained that they met all legitimate needs and one bank chairman's pointed reply to the critics was that 'an assignment of a series of book debts, or the issue of a debenture upon buildings, machinery, or other fixed assets is from a bank's standpoint not always adequate collateral'.[44]

Advances continued their rise throughout the closing months of 1928 and well into 1929, reaching their high point of £978.9m. in June, with the average advances ratio for the year being 55.5%. The banks were undoubtedly eager to lend, but part of the high level was due to the 'gradual accumulation of frozen loans'.[45] In the midst of the Stock Exchange and new issue booms the banks endeavoured to keep loans for financial purposes as low as possible, thus retaining the bulk of the facilities for industrial and commercial use.[46]

Although commercial bills were less profitable than advances the banks' holdings of bills remained fairly stable during this period. If anything, the gradual return of business confidence and trade in 1923 and 1924 was accompanied by an increase in the volume of commercial bills coming onto the market, and one of the leading London discount houses was able to report in 1925 that 'for the first time for several years commercial bills formed the greater part of our portfolio, and attained their pre-war figure in money value'. The commercial banks' holdings at this time were almost entirely of fine trade bills. Acceptances, usually on behalf of banks and firms of undoubted repute, also increased gradually. The revived use of

London for this purpose was due to it being a relatively cheap centre for short-term credit, but on the domestic front the volume of acceptances was affected by the depressed state of the staple industries, notably cotton, and the rise in rates at the end of 1929.[47] Another banking facility which industry made use of was that of forward exchange cover. In the period 1923 to 1925 traders made extensive purchases and sales of forward exchange, but it was very noticeable that once the exchange rate was stabilized in 1925 'engagements' declined. However, their popularity seemed to have been established and traders continued to use them as a means of insuring against even comparatively small exchange fluctuations.[48]

The extent of the decline in economic activity in the depression may be illustrated by the following few statistics. Between 1929 and 1932 the Gross National Product at factor cost fell by over 13%; production in the manufacturing sector fell by 10.3%; production in mining and quarrying fell by 18.6%; and the national unemployment rate rose from 10.4% to 22.1%. Against this background the volume of advances declined from £988m. in the first quarter of 1930 to £784m. during the last quarter of 1932, a fall of nearly 21% (see table 3.3).[49] The most important reason for this trend was the state of industrial activity, while the accompanying fall in prices, especially commodity price levels (wholesale prices fell by 27% between 1930 and 1932) also brought a reduction in the demand for advances for stock carrying purposes.[50]

Over the initial stages of the depression the fall in advances was fairly slow. This was because it proved difficult to reduce outstanding, and largely frozen, industrial loans; *The Economist* was of the view that 'there is still much dead wood to be cut away'. The banks themselves were certainly conscious of their inability to force the pace of liquidation, and they made increasingly large allocations to contingency funds to provide against losses which rationalization might bring.[51] Banks in areas of heavy industry felt the pressures quite quickly, judging by their dividend policy. Williams Deacons and the Manchester and City Bank dropped their dividends in mid-1930, and in 1931 Lloyds Bank followed suit on its A shares, which served to change the prevailing view that bank dividend levels were immutable. The rate of fall of advances accelerated in 1932, reflecting the state of trade and the lack of confidence which deterred businessmen and traders from seeking bank accommodation on the usual scale, while the liquidation of stocks meant that outstanding advances were being paid off.[52]

The fall in advances was 'sometimes interpreted as betraying pressure by the banks for repayment and reluctance in granting fresh advances'.[53] From the evidence available there is little support for the view that the

banks created strong pressure for repayment. For example, the Westminster Bank in 1930 found money flowing back and there was 'no calling
in of loans from productive industry'.[54] Reginald McKenna was also of
the view that the decline in business activity was not traceable to undue
pressure on the small borrower, but simply to the shrinkage in demand.[55]
There was on the other hand an understandable reluctance by the banks
to extend new loans. They exercised care and discrimination in respect of
every individual application for accommodation, and made stringent
provision for bad and doubtful debts.

Criticism was levelled at the banks for not bringing down the rate on
advances to the full extent of the fall which had taken place in the level of
bank rate. This feeling was possibly accentuated in the public mind by the
erroneous belief that the banks were still enforcing the alleged minimum
of 5%, but in practice the average charged was nearer 4.5%. The
minimum had been abandoned not only for large borrowers but for small
ones as well. It was hardly likely in the prevailing climate that a further
adjustment of 0.5% would have had much effect, even for those companies
on low profit margins. If the banks had not put down rates substantially
they had at least in some instances been forced to renew loans in the face
of the continued depression, which blurred the distinction between short-
term liquid loans and the continental and United States banking practice
of medium- and long-term finance. In the light of the latter's experience
in the depression, the adherence by the British banks to the principle of
self-liquidation with adequate security had stood them in good stead.

The general picture with regard to discounts and acceptances was very
much the same as that for advances. The collapse of trade brought a
reduced volume of commercial bills, which was reflected in the amount of
bills held by the banks. In 1930 the London clearing banks held £127.2m.
(average of monthly figures); R. J. Truptil estimated that by 1932 the
volume of their bill holdings had fallen to £58m., and to £44m. by 1933.[56]
Although rates on bills compared quite favourably with those charged for
overdrafts, traders were apparently reluctant to resort to them; they 'had
a prejudice against giving their acceptances instead of paying cash, fearing
that it might reflect on their credit, and preferring to get the cash discount
which is frequently allowed for prompt payment'.[57]

The depressed state of trade also brought a drop in acceptances, and
reduced commissions to the banks. Acceptances were down due to the
contraction in the volume of trade and fall in prices, and perhaps also due
to a certain hesitancy to draw on London after the suspension of the gold
standard. During the year from March 1930 the amount of acceptances
held by the clearing banks fell from £64.4m. to £47.4m. The overall
figures for acceptances, endorsements, etc. for the clearing banks declined

from £161m. at the beginning of 1930 to £96m. in the first quarter of 1932. However, this cannot be taken as representing the fall in acceptances since one of the most striking features of balance sheets after the abandonment of the gold standard was the increase in the amount of contracts for forward exchange. This was indicative of the growing use of facilities for covering the risks involved in trade conducted in foreign currencies under conditions of widely fluctuating exchange rates.[58]

Probably the outstanding feature of bank advances during the early phase of recovery from the depression was that they contracted. As Reginald McKenna remarked in 1934, 'factors have operated to permit a large recovery of trade not only without additional advances, but with an actual contraction'.[59] Advances by the clearing banks fell from £784m. at the end of 1932 to £740m. at the close of 1933. The first consequence of the trade revival for the banks was that firms were able to pay off outstanding advances as they used up stocks and as their general financial position improved. Indeed, in some cases frozen loans were repaid by borrowers whose advances had been written off as total debts.[60] The banks later saw this process as vindicating the decision to nurse some customers through the worst years of the depression. From an internal standpoint it meant that the banks could reduce the sums they had felt it necessary to add to reserves to meet possible losses, and in many cases they were able to bring previous allocations back to the profit and loss account.[61]

At the same time fresh borrowing, of a thoroughly healthy character, was taking place up and down the country; with better economic conditions the quality of advances was greatly improved.[62] In 1933 the Midland Bank reported that the demands for larger accommodation to finance improving trade had been up, but that this had been slightly more than counter-balanced by the volume of payments. For their part the banks had ample resources with which they could grant advances. In February 1934, for example, they could have expanded advances by some £200m. if suitable borrowers had been available.[63] Indeed, judging by the remarks of some of the bank chairmen, they approached applications less critically than previously, without reference to 'purely theoretical principles'. In particular, small firms who had fewer openings to other sources of funds, were reported to be making 'more extensive use of overdraft facilities'.[64] The District Bank in its Annual Report for 1934 stated that whereas their advances were still low, the number of borrowers on their books had 'materially increased'.

The decline of total bank advances is not a totally reliable indicator of industrial borrowing during the early phase of the recovery. The composition of the advances figure is an obvious qualification. For example, most banks in the mid-1930s included 'transit items' with advances, while as late as 1937 only Lloyds and Martins Banks had adopted the recommendations of the Cunliffe Committee and later the Macmillan Committee, on bank balance sheet presentation. More significantly, however, there were several developments, particularly in the period 1934–6, which reduced the dependence of firms on the banking system. These were alternative sources of funds, the effects of integration, new issues, the use of company internal funds, and sales of investments.

Table 3.3   London clearing banks: Advances
1930–9 (Quarterly: £m.)

Year		Amount	Year		Amount
1930	I	988.2	1935	I	758.4
	2	976.5		2	733.5
	3	953.1		3	767.3
	4	934.3		4	775.4
1931	I	928.3	1936*	I	828.4
	2	932.6		2	867.8
	3	910.8		3	876.4
	4	903.2		4	887.6
1932	I	903.1	1937	I	906.0
	2	868.2		2	954.3
	3	818.4		3	971.1
	4	784.5		4	983.0
1933	I	765.4	1938	I	980.0
	2	771.2		2	985.0
	3	756.8		3	973.0
	4	740.1		4	966.0
1934	I	743.2	1939	I	978.0
	2	757.0		2	989.0
	3	756.2		3	992.0
	4	754.8		4†	1,003.0

*Figures inclusive of District Bank.
†To September 1939 average of weekly balances,
thereafter average of balances on the last working
day of the month.

Source: 1930–7, *Statistical Abstract for the U.K.*,
1938;
1938–9, *Annual Abstract of Statistics*, 1947.

The 'abnormal' competition came from certain non-bank financial institutions with liquid funds on their hands, and from a hitherto unsuspected direction. The most striking example was the extension of insurance activities into essentially banking transactions. In many cases insurance companies 'stepped in with offers of short- and medium-term credit for industrial reconstruction and extensions of plant', secured to some extent on fixed assets and for a length of time well beyond the orthodox banking usage.[65] Insurance companies found themselves with a large volume of liquid funds, and with low yields on gilt-edged investments they were eager to find suitable outlets.[66] At such a time a well-secured mortgage at a good rate of interest was a very desirable asset since it was not subject to capital depreciation and the rate of interest was above that yielded on the better class of Stock Exchange security. Such commitments were probably better suited to insurance companies than banks, but for the latter it represented a loss of business and income.[67]

Another point of competition came from hire purchase companies who borrowed short term from the banks in order to lend on medium term to their clients. Companies in this field were reported as being prepared 'to finance the sale and purchase of almost anything (preferably productive assets) on terms of repayment by instalments over periods up to 5 years or even more.[68] Further finance for industry was reported as coming from the plethora of money in London, with *The Economist* claiming that 'large city houses and even leading Stock Exchange firms are offering money to industrial borrowers at low rates', and the chairman of Lloyds Bank in 1933 referred to competition from financial houses, usually involved in investment or merchant banking business, as taking the form of 'loans of a purely joint stock banking character'.

A more ephemeral and certainly surprising source of funds were the American banks. This arose because the discount on forward dollars yielded a profit of about 3.5% per annum on American funds employed in England, and accordingly some New York banks were offering loans to English borrowers at absolutely nominal rates. The use of such funds was most noticeable in Liverpool for the finance of the cotton trade. These facilities, however, were dependent on the presence of the forward dollar discount which rendered the finance particularly susceptible to rapid withdrawal.[69]

Bank accommodation was further reduced by the progressive integration of industry: 'Big business means ... small overdrafts.' As Reginald McKenna put it to the Midland Bank shareholders in 1934: 'It has been no infrequent occurrence for a company with large credit balances to come under joint control with another who is in debt to the bank, and then to finance the whole combination out of its own resources.' One consequence then of the rapid extension of rationalization and cartelization was that a given volume of trade could be conducted on a smaller sum of direct bank credit than previously.[70] It was also probable that the increased size of firms led them to enjoy 'economies in investment and dis-investment of short term funds', which made for a further decline in the use of overdrafts.[71] In the United States in this period the increasing average size of business enterprise was an adverse factor in the use of bank credit, since the relative dependence on such credit was, in general, least among concerns of largest size. Large corporations indulged in the acquisition of fixed assets and in investments in other companies to a marked degree which served to place increased emphasis on long-term financing.[72]

The recovery and freeing of the new issue market meant that companies could resort to funding their advances and obtain their working capital from the open market on advantageous terms.[73] This facility, however, was only available to firms of good standing and reasonable size, that is, well above the Macmillan limit. The Chairman of the Midland Bank was of the view that 'money raised by new issues of capital had been used to pay off many millions of bank advances'.

Companies also reduced their dependence on bank finance by drawing increasingly upon internal funds. Indeed Reginald McKenna was of the view that the 'principal explanation' of the fall in advances was that business undertakings 'in the mass have been in a position to use their own resources to a much larger extent than before'. The tendency applied particularly to the more solvent firms who found with trade recovery that cash was readily thrown back on their hands. But more important that this accumulation of cash was the fact that they had liquid assets which, with the high level of security prices, induced them to sell for capital gains and use the proceeds for expansion, or the repayment of bank debts. In other words, with falling interest rates holders of gilt-edged sold instead of using them as collateral to obtain bank advances, which they might well have done if interest rates were rising. *The Economist* was of the opinion that it was largely through this means that 'the credit created by the authorities has percolated through to the business world'. The investments of the banks at this time rose rapidly, for while there was no major increase in the supply of new stock, the sales of the business sector were probably absorbed by bank purchases amounting to £335m. between 1932 and 1935.

Some observers were critical of the banks' record in this connection. The complaint was not that the banks were not buying sufficient gilt-edged, – 'a bank cannot be expected to buy securities beyond a reasonable limit' – but rather that their policy as to charges on advances was not sufficiently flexible, and that this forced firms to sell investments rather than seek out advances. The minimum rate of 5% had certainly gone by the board, and those with ample security behind them could obtain advances at rates of between 4 and 5%, while any reduction beyond this was most improbable. One bank spokesman argued that a 1% all round reduction in the advances rate would have involved a complete suspension of dividend payments. Given the banks' heavy overheads the margin between average rates received and paid out was 2.2% in February 1934. The estimated average interest received was 2.8%, the estimate average paid out was 0.6%.[74] The average earned on advances was put at 4.375%, while the net profit of the Big Five was equivalent to a rate of 1.25% upon advances. With this position there was little scope for a sharp fall in the advances rate, and anyway the demand elasticity of advances with respect to interest rates was probably quite low.

Despite encouraging progress in industrial and manufacturing activity advances were only making a slow recovery by 1936. The Midland Bank reported that 'little more than $\frac{1}{3}$ of the rise over the year' could be accounted for through the increased needs of more trade. At least some of the factors making for reduced resort to the banks had by late 1936 spent their force, and advances were regarded as definitely, if only slightly, on the upgrade.[75] The figure of clearing bank advances for 1936 was, however, complicated not only by the inclusion of the District Bank figures, but also by the appearance in advances of sums lent for the French credit of £40m. In the following year advances rose at a faster rate with the banks accommodating the rise by running down their investments.[76] At the close of 1937 the advances ratio for the clearing banks was still only 41%, and to restore it to the 1929 level would have required an expansion in advances of some £300m. There was, of course, no compelling reason for such a restoration; prices were higher in 1929, industry was less integrated, and had smaller internal liquid resources.

The spurt of advances in 1937 (see table 3.3.) was followed, after the usual lag, by a contraction in the second half of 1938 arising from the recession in business activity which began some months earlier. The extent to which industry was receiving assistance at this time was hidden by the repayment of the French credit so that changes in aggregate advances understated the changes in advances to industry. This figure was kept up by the growing needs of the armament industries, and by the less propitious state of the new issue market. During the months prior to the outbreak of the war several cross-currents were at work influencing the level of advances. The increasing demands of the armament industries due to their accelerated production and costs required temporary financing, and added to this was the rise in commodity prices. On the other hand, the banks were consciously discouraging advances for non-essential purposes; the Midland Bank felt bound 'to examine applications for advances with first regard to national needs'. A further factor was the increasing direct intrusion of the government in trade and production which to some extent caused repayments of advances. Stocks of certain staple commodities were acquired by the government which therefore relieved customers of the banks from needing temporary finance to carry

them. Also under war conditions traders worked on low inventory stocks
(see Chapter 7).[77]

With regard to discounts and acceptances the aggregate figures for the
London clearing banks are of little assistance in revealing the extent of
their involvement with commercial bills, or in granting acceptance credits.
Even in the case of individual banks only Lloyds Bank, of the Big Five,
gave separate bill figures for the whole of the 1930s; the Midland Bank did
so as from 1934. Both banks gave figures for 'Acceptances and Confirmed
Credits'; of the smaller banks Williams Deacons and Martins Bank gave
such particulars. The figures available for discounts and acceptances are
given in table 3.4. The activity of the banks in the commercial bill business
were mainly directed towards attempting to encourage its greater use.
Bankers put out the claim that it would help the mobilization of accounts
receivable, and enable traders to obtain cheaper and more ample finance.
Whatever return to popularity there was, the commercial banks did not
overindulge by way of rate cutting. The *Statist* commented in 1934 that
the 'scarcity of commercial paper and the maintenance by the banks of
minimum buying rates at a level rather higher than that which obtains in
the open market are sufficient to prevent these bills from reaching the
banks'.[78]

Table 3.4   Discounts, acceptances and endorsements, 1933–9; Lloyds, Midlands,
Williams Deacons & Martins Banks (£m.)

Year	Other bills discounted		Acceptances	Endorsements, exchange contracts, guarantees, etc.
	Lloyds	Midland		
1933 Dec. 31	3.2	n.a.	16.4	49.2
1934	7.5	18.5	16.2	52.7
1935	6.7	29.6	18.1	39.1
1936	4.0	21.8	18.5	42.3
1937	3.8	30.6	19.4	41.2
1938	6.7	21.5	15.0	53.0
1939	6.9	19.7	12.2	44.9

Source: *Statist*, 1 June 1940.

One feature of competition for the banks was the return to 'popularity
of the domestic acceptance'. Admittedly it made little progress compared
to the total of bank loans, but in certain spheres it established itself at a
significant pace:

This is true, for example, of the Lancashire textile trade, where the
financing of cotton in warehouses as well as the import of raw material

is now being increasingly affected by acceptance credits granted by the big London merchant houses. This may be a reversal to early practice, but nevertheless it involves the disturbance of arrangements which have now persisted for close on two decades. During the war the habit had grown up of financing the cotton trade within Lancashire through bank loans. The relative difference between the cost of financing by way of acceptance and of overdraft facilities respectively was not sufficient to cause a borrower undue concern; for one thing, he was then working on such a generous profit margin that a mere one per cent. difference did not count. Moreover, the overdraft and bank loan facilities provided certain advantages in the shape of elasticity of maturity dates, and so on, which the bill of exchange does not possess. And this habit having struck root persisted until the recent fall of discount rates and the relative rigidity of bank loan rates provided an opportunity for the acceptance houses to regain the business which was lost during and after the war to the clearing banks.[79]

It should be added that this form of finance was not amenable to most of the commodity or manufacturing processes in use in the 1930s; 'the essential desideratum of the self-liquidity of the bill and of the termination of the transaction coincidentally with the maturity of the bill is not easily found.' As to the item engagements, the banks were offering much better facilities. The presence of persistent currency instability led to a considerable increase in forward exchange business in the early 1930s and this again came to the fore in 1938.

Several accusations were made against the behaviour of the commercial banks in the 1930s. Their conservatism was frequently cited, the claim being made that they denied finance for purposes which constituted 'eligible banking accommodation'. Individual instances of such refusal may well have taken place but the impression from the above survey of the available evidence is that the banks did not generally behave with such reserve. There is no evidence that the banks exerted undue pressure for repayment of advances in the depression years, indeed they appear to have nursed many customers through their worst difficulties – self-interest may of course have dictated that course. At the close of the period the banks may well have felt that they had given more credit to depressed industries than was good both for their own balance sheets and for encouraging the necessary changes within firms and industries.[80] That they were inflexible in their lending methods is not borne out by the available data; they shifted from fixed loans to overdrafts, a facility which industry preferred whereas loans have several advantages from a banking viewpoint; short-term accommodation often revolved to become medium-term advances; they were keen to promote the discount facility but the demand from industry was in the main sluggish; and they offered foreign exchange cover when flexible rates replaced the certainties of the gold standard. Finally, it was claimed that the banks preferred to lend abroad and for financial purposes rather than to home industry. Very little foreign lending was made by the banks in this period, while they often stated that in general they kept financial loans low so that they could accommodate industrial needs; overindulgence in the financial category does not accord with the aim of keeping a reasonably balanced distribution of assets. It might well be that the slow growth of advances, especially in the 1930s, was taken as reluctance on the part of the banks to meet genuine industrial needs but more often than not it was the absence of demand for funds which was the main problem. The banks do not appear to have turned away much 'eligible banking accommodation'.

The industrial classification of advances

The Cunliffe Report of August 1918 called attention to the fact that 'a committee of Bankers' had recommended that banks should publish a monthly statement of a standard form showing the average of their weekly balance sheets during each month. It was to be several years before the banks followed their own advice; Lloyds Bank did so in 1927, with the others following rather spasmodically. In 1931 the Macmillan Committee recommended that the London clearing banks should publish a regular analysis of their advances in accordance with the classification drawn up by the Committee, and on the basis of which they presented figures for 1929–30, the only aggregate classification available for the 1920s. It was not for another five years or so that a regular analysis became available.

In its memorandum to the Macmillan Committee the Federation of British Industries had urged that the banks should keep and publish an industrial classification of advances, with a view to seeing when aggregate credit granted 'begins to be in excess of industrial requirements'.[81] Some of the bankers had been doing this for a few years, on the basis of their own classification, but they were by no means all agreed as to its desirability. For example John Rae of the Westminster Bank was firmly of the opinion that such an industrial analysis of advances was detrimental and anyway was largely accidental due to amalgamations, and the industrial regions so covered.[82] Some notion of the distribution of advances between industries and other uses prior to 1929 can be obtained from the information provided in annual reports of a few of the clearing banks. Table 3.5 gives part of the Lloyds Bank classification 'towards the end of 1926', that of Martins Bank at the end of 1927, and that of Midland

Table 3.5 Classification of advances: Selected clearing banks

Lloyds Bank: circa end 1926	£m.	Martins Bank: end 1927[b]	%	Midland Bank: 26 June, 1928[c]	%
Retail	13.2	Shipbuilding	2.4	Textiles	12.25
Cotton	3.8	Cotton	9.6	Building &	
Iron & Steel	3.2	Iron & Steel	3.8	land	11.25
Coal	3.9	Coal	1.5	Wholesale &	
Chemical &		Wool	4.8	retail traders	11.25
fertilizers	0.9	Timber	1.9	Heavy industry	7.75
Oils & fats	1.7	Paper	0.7	Food, drink &	
Paper, printing		Leather	0.6	tobacco	6.0
& publishing	1.8	Builders	1.5	Leather, rubber	
		General Produce	11.0	& Chemicals	4.0
Trade and industry	28.5	Retail	4.7	Shipping	3.5
				Coal	3.5
		Trade & industry	42.7	Miscellaneous	
Personal &				trades	4.0
professional	43.5				
Agriculture	18.5	Agriculture	3.5	Trade and industry	62.5
Local authorities	7.1	Local authorities	14.2		
		Personal	18.4		
Total[a]	97.6	Miscellaneous	21.1	Agriculture	6.5
				Finance	8.0
				Stocks & Shares	8.75
				Entertainments	2.5
				Local authorities	3.5
				Personal &	
				professional	6.5

[a] This figure in no way corresponds to that in the published balance sheet which is for 31 December, 1926, the total there being £194.8m. The figures were taken out at different dates; several important categories are not given above, e.g., engineering, shipping, shipbuilding, brewing, foodstuffs, etc., also the balance sheet figure 'included overdrafts in India, and various accounts, such as outstandings between head office and the branches, which strictly, do not come under the heading of overdrafts'; see *The Economist*, 5 February 1937, p. 288.

[b] The advances total for Martins Bank at the end of 1927 was £36.7m. which was divided between 22,472 lenders, 26% of which were in the trade and industry grouping.

[c] Further details on individual items: textiles, include advances to brokers, merchants, spinners and manufacturers; building land, this includes temporary advances for investment in land and houses, but the larger part was lent direct to builders, contractors, etc; of the retailers it was estimated that ⅔ had a single place of business, while part of the accommodation granted to wholesalers may have been used to give credit to customers; heavy industry included iron and steel, metals, and shipbuilders. There were 180,000 borrowers at this particular date.

Source: Annual Reports

Bank for 26 June 1928. The Lloyds Bank classification was based on the industrial grouping adopted by the Federation of British Industries.[83]

Table 3.5 indicates that the three banks concerned were not excessively committed with advances to heavy industry, indeed their holdings seem to have been spread fairly well over the entire range of industrial activity. In the case of the Midland Bank some 63% of its advances was in the broad category of industry and trade, and of this about 23% concerned the staple industries. The percentage which Martins Bank had in industry and trade was considerably lower, being some 43%. It is not possible to indicate the extent of Lloyds Bank's commitment, since the available figures do not give all the categories in which advances were made. In terms of individual industries it is possible to make some general comparisons. In 1928 Midland Bank had 7.5% of its advances in iron and steel, engineering and shipbuilding; in 1929 the percentage of all clearing bank advances in this category was 6.4%. The Martins Bank figure for this category in 1927 was 6.2%. The total of advances for the cotton industry made by Lloyds Bank in 1926, a sum of £3.8m., is of interest, since in the following year the figure had jumped to £7.0m., which arose from increased advances to cotton brokers following on the rise in the price of cotton. In the same year, 1927, Barclays Bank commented that the banks had already advanced large sums to the cotton industry and that there was little room for further advances with safety.

The position for the clearing banks at the end of 1929 and early 1930 is of course given by the Macmillan Committee analysis of advances (see table 3.6). As can be seen some 49% of advances went to trade and industry but judging by the experience of the Midland Bank, and that of Martins Bank, mentioned above, it is not safe to assume that such a figure represents the position for each bank. Variation from this aggregate picture could have been quite considerable. Information as to the position between 1930 and 1936, the first year of regular statistics on advances classification, is particularly scanty. The Midland Bank reported in 1932 that almost all groups except building and related trades showed declines, while in 1934 the only group to show any significant increase was miscellaneous manufacturers which included many new and small enterprises. The District Bank noted the same tendency for the building trade in 1933, while advances to the staple trades were just maintained.

The changes which took place between 1929 and 1936, and then during the ensuing years, can be gleaned from table 3.6. Admittedly, the interval of time involved is rather long so that such a comparison can only be of limited value, but the relative changes are certainly of some interest. Between 1929 and 1936 total advances fell by 12% (13% if the District Bank element is added to the 1929 figure), but the decline in some categories was much greater than this. Advances to trade and industry were down by some £126.0m., a fall of 26%. However, within this total there are some very significant changes, particularly among the staple industries. Advances to mining and quarrying fell by 40%; those to heavy

Table 3.6   London clearing banks: Classification of advances (£m.)

Industry	Ten banks[1]		Eleven banks[2]					
	1929[a]	%	*1936*[b]	%	*1937*[c]	%	*1938*[d]	%
Textiles (cotton, wool, silk, linen, jute)	81.6	8.3	39.9	4.6	43.8	4.6	38.1	4.0
Heavy industry (iron, steel, engineering, shipbuilding)	63.0	6.4	40.7	4.7	49.9	5.2	45.9	4.8
Mining & quarrying (including coal)	30.0	3.0	18.1	2.1	15.1	1.6	15.2	1.6
Food, drink & tobacco	63.2	6.4	29.4	3.4	32.5	3.4	36.1	3.8
Leather, rubber & chemicals	22.0	2.2	12.6	1.5	15.3	1.6	14.0	1.5
Building trades	47.8	4.8	61.5	7.1	68.2	7.1	68.1	7.1
Miscellaneous trades	146.5	14.9	67.4	7.7	74.7	7.8	69.1	7.2
Retail			60.1	7.0	64.0	6.6	66.4	7.0
Shipping & transport (including railways)	25.2	2.6	23.2	2.6	20.1	2.1	26.5	2.8
Trade and industry	479.3	48.6	352.9	40.7	386.6	40.0	379.4	39.8
Agriculture & fishing	68.6	6.9	57.7	6.6	60.1	6.2	62.5	6.5
Local authorities & public utilities	52.4	5.3	50.4	5.8	54.2	5.6	59.2	6.2
Amusements, clubs, etc.	26.5	2.7	40.5	4.6	44.5	4.7	46.6	4.9
Financial	142.5	14.4	109.6	12.6	118.2	12.2	109.0	11.4
Other advances	218.4	22.1	258.5	29.7	300.4	31.3	298.0	31.2
Total	987.7	100	869.5	100	961.0	100	954.3	100

[a] Various dates from 22 October, 1929 to 19 March, 1930.
[b] Nearest available date to 31 October, 1936.
[c] Various dates between 4 August and 26 October, 1937.
[d] Various dates between 3 August and 31 October, 1938.

Sources: 1 Macmillan Committee Report.   2 *Bank of England Statistical Summary.*

industry (iron and steel, engineering and shipbuilding) by 35%, and textiles saw a large fall of 51%. Among the groups to display large gains were the building trades, 29%; amusements, 53%; while other advances (including personal and professional) went up by 18%.[84] The largest declines generally occurred in the depressed industries which arose partly from the fact that some of their heavy debt accumulations were paid off during the recovery from the depression. One prosperous industry, food, drink and tobacco, managed to exhibit a large fall of 53%, but this probably reflected increased reliance on self-finance with rising profits.

The figures for 1936–8 provide some broad outlines of the changes which were associated with the rise to the 1937 trade peak, and the subsequent recession. Total advances to trade and industry rose, and this was reflected in the increased need for bank credit from textiles, heavy industries, building, and miscellaneous trades. Only in the case of shipping and mining and quarrying (which includes coal) were there falls in the volume of advances granted. The shrinkage of business activity and the fall in commodity prices in 1938 brought a reduced demand for credit which is reflected in the figures for textiles, heavy industry, and the miscellaneous trades (see table 3.6).

Notes

1 The banks at this time accepted large sums for periods running into several months and they paid competitive rates, 'appreciably above market rates' for such funds; see *The Economist*, 19 July 1930, pp. 109–10.

2 Another example of self-liquidating loans were those made to companies about to make a new share issue;'in cases where shares are offered for sale, we frequently lend money against the shares pending the issue being made'. However, advances were never made for the expenses of such issues; *Departmental Committee on Company Law Amendment, 1943–44*, Q.4763–4, evidence of the Committee of the London Clearing Bankers.

3 F. E. Goodenough, chairman of Barclays Bank, was a member of this Committee.

4 Manning Dacey, *The British Banking Mechanism*, London, 1958, p. 91.

5 *Treasury Committee on Bank Amalgamations, Report*, para. 6 (Colwyn Committee 1918); reprinted in J. Sykes, *The Amalgamation Movement in English Banking*, London, 1926, pp. 218–27. See also R. S. Sayers, *The Bank of England 1891–1944*, Cambridge, 1977, vol. 1, pp. 235–55.

6 Sykes, op. cit., pp. 101–2.

7 Finance issues amounted to £26.8m. and £19.6m. for 1919 and 1920 respectively; Midland Bank series. The total paid up capital of all banks rose from £68.9m. in 1919 to £94.0m. at the end of 1922; Sykes, op. cit., p. 102.

8 Sykes, op. cit., p. 87.

9 ibid., p. 92.

10 Colwyn Committee, *Report*, para. 6.

11 *The Economist*, 14 September 1918, p. 328.

12 *The Economist*, 31 August 1918, pp. 263–4.

13 T. Balogh, *Studies in Financial Organisation*, Cambridge, 1950, p. 74. For practices before the First World War see C. A. E. Goodhart, *The Business of Banking 1891–1914*, London, 1972, pp. 153–4.

14 *Committee on Finance and Industry, Minutes of Evidence*, Q. 1067 (Macmillan Committee, 1931).

15 *The Economist*, 21 May 1921, p. 1037.

16 Balogh, op. cit., p. 84.

17 See evidence of O.M.W. Sprague to the Macmillan Committee, *Minutes of Evidence*, 49th Day.

18 Balogh, op. cit., p. 75; Macmillan Committee, *Minutes of Evidence*, Q. 2439; *The Economist*, 8 October 1932 (Banking Supplement).

19 *The Economist*, 1 January 1938, p. 27.

20 *The Economist*, 14 May 1932 (B.S.)

21 Reported in the *The Economist*, 17 November 1928, p. 885.

22 *Memorandum* by G. J. Scott and Sir Alexander K. Wright, Royal Bank of Scotland, to the Macmillan Committee, vol. I, p. 157, para. 5. The banks regretted this resistance to bills since, 'The customer was able to obtain credit from the bank on the bill discounted, which gave the bank a document bearing two or more names for the obligation.' See S. Nishimura, *The Decline of Inland Bills of Exchange in the London Money Market 1855–1913*, Cambridge, 1971, for an account of the reasons for the decline in the use of bills before 1914.

23 *The Economist*, 27 December 1930, pp. 1215–16; 13 May 1933 (B.S.). In the early 1930s the cost of this sort of accommodation, including accepting commission, bill stamp and discount, was about 2.25% for the larger firms and no more than 2.75% for the smaller ones; *The Economist*, 24 March 1934, p. 635.

24 Macmillan Committee, *Report*, para. 391.

25 *The Economist*, 24 March 1934, p. 635. On the discounting of commercial bills by the Bank of England see 'Commercial Bills', *B.E.Q.B.*, December 1961.

26 Acceptance credits were granted either against the collateral security of goods, or could be done without such security; reimbursement credits were not given directly to customers but to foreign banks which guaranteed their clients to the London bankers; see Balogh, op. cit., p. 154.

27 *The Economist*, 19 October 1918, p. 488; 23 October 1920, p. 642.

28 E. V. Morgan, *Studies in British Financial Policy 1914–1925*, London, 1952, p. 298.

29 *The Economist*, 23 October 1920, p. 642. Loan demand also rose at this time because strikes forced companies to carry large stocks, while the disorganization on the railways made distribution slow and thereby delayed payment for finished goods.

30 Barclays Bank, Annual Report, 1920.

31 District Bank, Annual Report, 1920.

32 The District Bank in 1920 also sold War Loan at an 'unsatisfactory price' in order to meet industrial demands.

33 Lloyds Bank, Annual Report, 1920.

34 Barclays Bank, Annual Report, 1920.

35 Barclays Bank, Annual Report, 1922. The Midland Bank's advances total, however, was up to 1922 in contrast to all the others; the Annual Report cited this as 'evidence of exceptional assistance to industry'.

36 Midland Bank, Annual Report, 1921.

37 Martins Bank, Annual Report, 1919. The increase in acceptances was particularly noticeable in the case of the Lancashire banks.

38 Barclays Bank, Annual Report, 1923; Midland Bank, Annual Report, 1923.

39 The banks made substantial profits on the sales which were put to inner reserves rather than to the current profit and loss account.

40 Barclays Bank, Annual Report, 1926. The 1926 Annual Report of the National Provincial Bank spoke of the abnormal requirements of their industrial accounts in the provinces, mostly taking the form of bridging finance for the strike. Coal imports were financed by bank advances.

41 *The Economist*, 12 November 1927, p. 828.

42 ibid., p. 829.

43 Martins Bank, Annual Report, 1928.

44 *The Economist*, 17 November 1928, p. 885.

45 *The Economist*, 10 May 1930 (B.S.).

46 *The Economist*, 25 July 1929, p. 108–9; Midland Bank, Annual Report, 1929; National Provincial, Annual Report, 1929.

47 District Bank, Annual Report, 1926. The acceptances of this bank were almost entirely in respect of imports of raw cotton.

48 Midland Bank, Annual Report, 1926.

49 It should be noted that some industrial groups showed increases in advances during this period, especially the newer trades such as entertainments and chemicals; see Lloyds Bank, Annual Report, 1930.

50 *The Economist* survey (3 June 1933, pp. 1196–7) of the experience of 110 companies over the period 1931–2 concluded that their stock in trade declined by some 16%.

51 Bank balance sheet figures were obtained after writing off all bad debts and deducting full provision for claims regarded as doubtful. The Hatry Crash merely added to their caution.

52 District Bank, Annual Report, 1932.

53 Midland Bank, Annual Report, 1932. It is conceivable that the fall in advances in 1931 and 1932 may have been overstated given the very stringent provision for bad and doubtful debts.

54 Westminster Bank, Annual Report, 1932.

55 Midland Bank, Annual Report, 1932.

56 R. J. Truptil, *British Banks and the London Money Market*, London, 1936, p. 98. This decline is reflected in the bill holdings of Lloyds Bank, the only major clearer to give details of its bill portfolio. Commercial bills fell from £12.4m. in December 1929 to £5.7m. in December 1932. In its 1930 Annual Report the National Provincial Bank reported reduced customer demand for bill accommodation, and in 1931 that their commercial bill holding was down by £5.5m.

57 Lloyds Bank, Annual Report, 1932.

58 Midland Bank, Annual Report, 1932. In its Annual Report for 1930 the District Bank noted that acceptances, mainly for raw cotton, continued to be small, but that forward exchange cover was well up.

59 Midland Bank, Annual Report, 1934.

60 *The Economist*, 15 May 1937 (B.S.).

61 *The Economist*, 12 October 1935 (B.S.).

62 A. M. Allen, 'Bank Advances', *The Banker*, April 1936.

63 The banks at this time were refraining from adding to their bill and security holdings because they would get unremunerative assets as a result. They feared that capital losses might arise from forced realization of securities.

64 *The Economist*, 14 October 1933 (B.S.); 21 July 1934, pp. 118–19.

65 Insurance company accounts were drawn up in such a way that it was not possible to distinguish between loans on mortgages to industrial and commercial firms and those made to private householders. This may have accounted for A. M. Allen stating in *The Banker* in 1936 that the public accounts of insurance companies did not reveal any such change of policy.

66 Insurance companies in the United States in the 1930s also increased their segment of the business credit market; see W. H. Jacoby and R. J. Saulnier, *Business Finance and Banking*, New York, 1947, p. 13.

67 In the Annual Report of the District Bank for 1935, it was noted that the experience of companies set up during the early 1930s to deal with advances of a nature not regarded as coming within the description of eligible banking accommodation had reinforced the caution of the banks after 'practical acquaintance with the applicants'.

68 *The Economist*, 13 May 1933 (B.S.).

69 *The Economist*, 14 October 1933 (B.S.); 15 May 1937 (B.S.).

70 On trends in the size structure of industry see J. H. Dunning and L. J. Thomas, *British Industry: An Economic Analysis*, London, 1961, pp. 43–61. It was not until 1935 that there were any official statistics on the size of firms so that changes before that are impressionistic. Certainly the depressed industries moved towards a more concentrated output, and some of the newer trades quickly evolved ologopolistic tendencies, e.g. dyestuffs, soap, and air transport.

71 R. S. Sayers, *Modern Banking*, Oxford, 2nd ed., 1947, p. 240. Keynes in his *Treatise on Money*, vol. I, London, 1930, p. 42, suggested that large firms made greater use of overdrafts, which given the prevailing picture of bank advances leaves a lot to explain.

72 Jacoby and Saulnier, op. cit., pp. 4–5, 78.

73 A sample survey of company issues during 1933–4 indicated that the rise in debenture issues was closely associated with the paying off of bank debts, and this purpose was also a feature of the 1936 debt issues; see E. T. Nevin, *The Mechanism of Cheap Money*, Cardiff, 1955, pp. 249–50.

74 For 1934 the average rate paid on London deposits was put at 0.5%; but the rate on country deposits was estimated at 1.625%. The banks also paid higher rates than those on some long-term deposits.

75 Barclays Bank, Annual Report, 1936; District Bank, Annual Report, 1936.

76 The Midland Bank did this since 'the demand for short term industry and trade advances has shown an appreciable revival during the year'. The banks were only prepared to sell gilt-edged to the extent that they could secure loans which conformed to their prevailing standards. The problem for the authorities was to ameliorate the rise in rates arising from sales of bank investments.

77 Lloyds Bank, Annual Report, 1939; Martins Bank, Annual Report, 1939.

78 *Statist*, 19 May 1934, p. 787.

79 ibid., p. 786; see also *The Economist*, 1 August 1936, p. 119. In the cotton trade this recovery was assisted by the fact that special forward exchange facilities were made available and used in conjunction with the acceptance credits. London merchant banks provided this combined service.

80 For an authoritative account of the involvement of banking system in the rationalization and reorganization of heavy industry in the period see Sayers, op. cit., vol. 1, ch. 14 and vol. 2, ch. 20.

81 Macmillan Committee, *Minutes of Evidence*, vol. 2., pp. 240–1.

82 Macmillan Committee, *Minutes of Evidence*, Qs 234–51. This reticence was reflected in the annual reports for the 1920s since in contrast to other banks nothing was said of the industrial division of the advances.

83 Lloyds Bank full advances classification contained about 30 groups. This was not the first such analysis for them to make, one had been drawn up in 1925 in order to show that the bulk of the additional loans granted had been for 'the purpose of financing extended trade', and that very little had been needed to tide firms over bad times and to cover their trading losses; see Lloyds Bank, Annual Report, 1925.

84 In its annual report for 1936 Barclays Bank gave a detailed breakdown of its professional and personal loans; see also *The Economist*, 23 January 1937, p. 180.

4 Internal funds

But in this age of statistics no official agency has made itself responsible for assembling the facts about the finances and resources of industry.

The Economist *had been making bricks, with a certain amount of straw, for forty years, and had succeeded in building a respectable structure of information on this question.*

THE ECONOMIST

Internal funds are obtained by retaining part of the revenue which a company receives from its trading and other operations. It consists of two main parts, namely, depreciation which essentially represents funds retained for the purpose of replacing fixed assets, and undistributed profits which can be used to finance additions to fixed assets. In the case of manufacturing activity internal funds may be expected to represent an important part of total financing. Firstly, because it is a growing sector of the economy using a considerable amount of capital it retains and reinvests some fraction of earnings in order to take advantage of market opportunities, and secondly, with its generally high ratio of capital to output, depreciation provisions constitute an important contribution to total finance. However, for the reasons given below the following discussion will centre around *net* savings.

In general terms the amount of *net* savings would be arrived at in the following way. After deducting from gross profits a provision for depreciation, and the sums necessary for the payment of fixed interest on debt and for taxation, the remainder is available for distribution to the ordinary shareholders of the company. What is then not allocated to the payment of dividends can be put back into the business. But in practice certain difficulties present themselves, and they are even more acute when attempting to assess the volume and significance of company savings during the inter-war years. These relate to depreciation practices and to taxation.

In assessing the costs to be placed against revenue an allowance needs to be made for wear and tear (depreciation), which should approximate to the actual deterioration of the plant and machinery employed. Fixed assets can thus be written down by periodic sums over an expected life (a few years for machines, longer for other fixed assets) until zero. The resulting accumulated funds can either be kept for replacement purposes or used as working capital. The usual method used for such calculations in the inter-war period was the reducing balance approach, partly because it presented fewer book keeping difficulties, and partly because the Inland Revenue made allowances on this basis.[1] Most firms treated depreciation as a definite charge on the profit and loss account, but firms with relatively small ratios of fixed assets to total assets were not always so financially prudent. The amount of such allowances was a matter of judgement. With bad trading results the depreciation provision was sometimes put aside altogether so that the true fall in profits was not shown, or somewhat less drastically the depreciation provision was reduced, thus maintaining working capital by the conversion of fixed capital. *The Economist* observed in 1932: 'Unfortunately, there is no uniformity between companies in the principles of charging depreciation. Most of the figures of net profit as returned seem to be struck after making some provision for depreciation, but not an entirely full provision.'[2] Also in profitable years a higher charge was made to depreciation in order to understate the extent of the improvement in profits. As a rule, however, firms did not write off more for depreciation than they were allowed for tax purposes, and this consideration was an important element in depreciation practices. A company's accountant would seek to obtain a liberal allowance for tax purposes since depreciation was an allowable expense, but the Inland Revenue, conscious of the need to protect the public interest and secure the revenue, took a less liberal view.

Compared to recent practices statutory allowances in 1918 were still in their infancy. When Income Tax was introduced in 1842 no relief was allowed for the wear and tear of any asset, and it was not until 1878 (Customs and Inland Revenue Act, s. 12) that a statutory allowance was introduced 'as representing the diminished value by reason of wear and tear during the year' of plant and machinery used for the purposes of trade. However, although the law did not admit of such allowances before 1878:

> there is evidence that the practice had been otherwise and that certain bodies of local Commissioners were making general allowances for wear and tear of machinery. From the first, too, a liberal construction had been placed upon the rule allowing repairs or alterations of

implements and this enabled taxpayers to claim amounts expended on renewals or replacements.[3]

The legislation of 1878 thus gave formal sanction to allowances which had existed for several years, and which had varied from area to area, and industry to industry; the Inland Revenue accepted 'in the great manufacturing districts the scale allowed by the manufacturers themselves sitting as Commissioners'.[4]

It was the rapid growth in the volume of medium-term assets during this period which focused the attention of the Revenue and accountants on the problem of depreciation allowances. But wear and tear allowances did not cover obsolescence, that is, loss in value due to the need to install new or improved machinery for that which had become out of date before it had worn out. Thus in 1897 an administrative concession (legalized in 1918) admitted the principle of an allowance for obsolescence, 'the deduction being so much of the cost of replacement as was equivalent to the written down value of the old plant or machinery less any sum realized by its sale.'[5] In 1918, mills, factories and other similar premises, were brought within the scope of depreciation allowances in recognition of the wear and tear to which they were subject, the measure of the allowance being one-sixth of the gross annual value under Schedule A.

Appeal could be made to the General Commissioners of the Inland Revenue as to the amount of the wear and tear allowances, and gradually a complex body of practice governing the rates of allowance in various trades was built up based on the decisions of different bodies of Commissioners. Up to 1932 the general principle followed was that the wear and tear allowance should correspond to the depreciation of the year as measured in commercial accounting. Since industry needed help in 1932 the first step was taken towards a modern view of capital allowances as a positive investment incentive, and an increase of one-tenth was made in all the rates of wear and tear then in force, while the Finance Act of 1938 brought the addition to one-fifth.[6]

The state of reporting of the tax paid by companies was as casual as that of depreciation. Profit figures were frequently published after deducting taxation, without the amount of taxation being made public. The estimate of profit made by the Inland Revenue was not always that declared by the directors to the shareholders, and the different practices of companies makes for considerable difficulty in attempting to generalize as to whether reserves included any tax provisions or not. With the customary delay in the payment of tax companies enjoyed an internal source of funds over and above net savings, especially companies with steadily rising profits.

Inter-war taxes levied on company profits may be summarized as follows. Throughout, profits were subject to income tax, the standard rate falling from 6s. in 1919 to 4s. in 1925–6, and for most of the 1930s it was between 4s. 6d. and 5s. Companies with few shareholders were also subject to super-tax (surtax after 1927); up to 1927 the number was 50 persons, thereafter it was five. The 1922 Finance Act said that the whole income of a closely controlled company would be subject to tax if a reasonable portion was not distributed, thus bringing it within the surtax net.[7] For a short time after the war companies were subject to the wartime Excess Profits Duty, an exceedingly complex tax, and their liability for this ended at various dates between August 1920 and August 1921. In order to get some boom profits into the Exchequer a short-lived Corporation Profits Tax was introduced in 1920, being repealed in 1924. It was levied at 5% during 1920–3, and 2.5% until June 1924. The definition of profits used in its assessment was similar to that used for income tax purposes. In April 1937 a National Defence Contribution was imposed and levied at 5% on companies, with 4% on unincorporated firms.

Internal funds may also be supplemented by past accumulations of savings held as liquid assets of various kinds, e.g., bank deposits, shares, government securities. Generally such holdings could be realized quickly and used to cover working or permanent capital needs, or for extending a loan or credit to other firms. Although such items were given in company balance sheets, there are no uniform series available for the inter-war years, partly because of the complete absence of uniformity in the presentation of balance sheet items, and partly because there was no collecting agency. What is available from the endeavours of *The Economist* is given at the close of the chapter.

Profit and savings series for the inter-war years

Before providing an account of the main fluctuations in industrial profits for these years a brief description of the two series used is useful. They are the profits series of *The Economist* and that compiled by P. E. Hart.[8] *The Economist* series was based on an analysis of published company accounts from 1909 onwards. For the most part they were companies quoted on the London Stock Exchange. For 1909 (which can be taken to relate to profits earned in 1908) the reports of 775 companies were analysed, showing net profits of just under £47m. By 1937 the series covered 2,279 companies, with some £280m. net profits, equivalent to just under a quarter of total profits assessed for income tax purposes under Schedule D. Since the series was based on quoted companies it tended to under-represent groups such as retailing, food, and certain parts of the textile industry, that is, activities largely conducted by unquoted or unincorporated businesses, while it may have over-represented such industries as steel, engineering, and other capital goods industries whose profits in this period were liable to cyclical swings. In so far as it dealt with the quoted sector it was biased towards the more successful companies.

It was not exclusively related to home industry, or to commercial activity. Profits derived from overseas activities in tea, rubber, oil and nitrate were included, but as table 4:1 shows, the profits of domestic industry predominated. While it did include investment trusts, it excluded banks, home and foreign railways, and gold or base metal mining operations.

Net profits appear after deduction of debenture interest, and after making allowances for depreciation and taxation on company savings. Preference interest and ordinary dividends were not deducted. The emphasis on net profits after deduction of debenture interest was designed to highlight fluctuations in the dividend paying capacity of industries. Broader changes may be illustrated after adding back the debenture interest. Its exclusion made the series less stable since it represented a relatively constant sum.

Since company law at the time did not set out in detail the composition of profit and loss accounts, there was little uniformity as between companies, and diversity within companies over time. Neither was there any uniformity in accounting years. In compiling the series *The Economist*, as far as possible, attempted to analyse profit and loss accounts on a uniform basis, but with the growing importance of taxation and the diverse methods of dealing with it in accounts, a rigid treatment was difficult. The picture was further complicated by changes in tax rates which reduces the usefulness of the series for long period comparisons.[9]

Table 4:1   Net profits; broad classification (£m.)

Category	1913*	%	1924	%	1930	%	1935	%
Mainly domestic industry	44.9	63.4	98.4	65.5	132.4	70.6	158.7	70.8
Mainly overseas	8.6	12.1	22.3	14.9	18.9	10.1	18.1	8.1
Commercial and transport	10.1	14.3	18.0	12.1	17.3	9.3	26.2	11.7
Finance†	7.2	10.2	11.3	7.5	18.9	10.0	21.0	9.4
Total	70.8	100.0	150.0	100.0	187.5	100.0	224.0	100.0

* Not wholly comparable with other years due to changes in classification.
† Includes investment trusts, land and financial companies.

Source: The Economist, 17 December 1938, p. 597.

Consistency was made infinitely more difficult by the reporting practices of companies; there was no prescribed period within which declarations had to be made. The delays in publishing profit and loss accounts after the end of the trading period varied greatly between companies, while the time lag was greatly increased in the case of holding companies. Further, even one company's accounts might be published in different quarters of successive years so that it became difficult to make accurate comparisons for more than a year at a time.[10]

From the standpoint of getting a uniform series the chief drawback was that the sample of companies for one year with its successor was quite distinct from the sample that compared that successor with the following year. For example, in the calendar year 1937 2,279 companies had net profits of £282.4m., compared with profits of £240.3m. in 1936. The enumeration for the calendar year 1936 was for 2,186 companies which had net profits of £239.1m. The totals of net profit were somewhat similar, but the sample of companies was different. However, each pair of years provided a percentage relationship, and taken as a whole, they provided a chain of comparable percentage links. Thus, it was possible to construct an index which expressed in a common term the whole series, which showed the relation not only between two adjacent years but also between any separate years in the series. A chain index, based on 1936, of net profits for 1919–38 is given in table 4.2.

The figures upon which the series was based were not identical with those rendered by the companies to the tax authorities. In the first place, as noted above, income tax allowances for wear and tear were somewhat arbitrary, while the amounts deducted by companies in their published accounts were likely over time to be nearer the true requirements for depreciation and obsolescence. Secondly, profits disclosed to shareholders were usually subject, before publication, to adjustments by way of allocations from and to unspecified internal reserves, which had the effect of smoothing out fluctuations in published profits. The practices pursued to minimize results in good years and maximize them in bad years did not altogether survive taxation scrutiny so that assessments should not, other things being equal, fluctuate more widely than published profits. Finally, *The Economist*'s totals did not necessarily reflect the true aggregate earnings of holding companies, where the latter's subsidiaries made their own reserve appropriations and the parent company brought in as profits only the net balances which the subsidiaries had declared as dividends.[11]

Despite these qualifications the series was particularly useful. Prior to post-war work it was the only long-term one available. At the time the figures, on a quarterly basis, were available well ahead of those provided by the Inland Revenue, while the breakdown of the figures to various

Table 4.2   Net profit series of The Economist, 1919–38

Year in which profit earned^a	Number of companies	Net profit (after deb. interest) Year given	Net profit (after deb. interest) Preceding	Index 1936=100	Profits earned for ordinary^b	Put to reserve or carried forward^c	Col. 6 as % of Col. 2
	1	2	3	4	5	6	7
		£m.	£m.		£m.	£m.	
1919	1,406	119.2	98.5	92.8	104.0	41.9	35.2
1920	1,353	138.5	126.9	101.4	117.7	39.9	28.8
1921	1,386	80.2	139.8	58.2	58.1	–6.3	–7.9
1922	1,358	115.6	99.5	67.6	90.3	17.6	15.2
1923	1,406	135.0	120.8	75.6	108.6	27.3	20.2
1924	1,443	150.0	136.6	83.0	120.7	33.5	22.3
1925	1,475	164.9	153.6	89.2	134.5	34.8	21.1
1926	1,699	179.1	182.9	87.4	145.6	32.1	17.9
1927	1,700	173.4	163.9	92.5	140.5	35.9	20.7
1928	1,742	197.3	193.9	94.2	158.9	39.6	20.1
1929	1,771	198.5	191.3	97.8	156.9	37.0	18.6
1930	2,053	187.6	219.8	83.6	144.3	29.5	15.7
1931	2,017	139.4	189.7	61.6	98.0	7.6	5.5
1932	1,949	137.1	146.9	57.1	97.7	12.2	8.9
1933	1,960	159.6	142.4	64.1	118.3	27.4	17.2
1934	2,072	193.0	161.5	76.7	148.8	40.4	20.9
1935	2,132	224.0	199.0	86.4	177.1	55.2	24.6
1936	2,271	266.5	230.5	100	216.7	73.2	27.5
1937	2,337	298.8	263.2	113.5	250.9	91.6	30.7
1938	2,387	285.6	307.0	105.3	234.0	84.1	29.4

^a Based on reports published during 12 months to 30 June of ensuing year, in each case. H. Parkinson's calculations gave 5 December as the mean date to which 82% of the profits declared during the 12 months to 30 June 1937, were made up. Thus, taking the reports issued in the 12 months to 30 June gave a 'reasonably accurate basis' for indices of profits earned in the preceding calendar year: The Economist, 17 December 1938, p. 599.
^b After deduction of preference dividend from column 2.
^c After deduction of preference and ordinary dividend from column 2.
Source: The Economist, 17 December 1938, p. 600.

appropriations provided a useful indicator of the practices of companies in relation to internal financing.

The most useful index of gross trading profits (before deduction of tax, debenture interest, royalties and long lease rents) available for the inter-war years is that compiled by P. E. Hart. It is partly based on Inland Revenue sources, the definitions employed are similar for those used in official post-war series, and the industrial grouping is that of the Standard Industrial Classification. As far as possible the index follows official definitions and methods. The basis of the time series were the figures of absolute gross trading profits calculated by the Oxford Institute of Statistics for the years 1927, 1932, and 1936–8, which were based on official estimates.[12] The figures for 1928–31 and for 1933–5 were estimated by interpolation. These processes were based on index numbers of profits constructed from a variety of sources. For the period up to 1930 the records of the London Stock Exchange were used, and a set of Moody cards for the rest of the period, supplemented by additional sources.[13] The formidable problems of sampling from a highly skewed distribution of companies – the estimates were partly based on samples of the accounts of relatively large companies quoted on the London Stock Exchange – were dealt with by using a log normal sampling scheme.[14] The index numbers of profits obtained were then reconciled with the benchmark of absolute profits in each industrial group as estimated by the Oxford Study.

The gross profits of the major industrial sectors of the U.K. for the period 1920–38 are given in table 4.3. It is noticeable that manufacturing and distribution are the two largest sectors and what errors of estimation, coverage, sampling, etc., that occurred in these governed the presence of errors in the aggregate figures. Fortunately, the least accurate were those for construction, which had relatively little weight in total profits; as did public utilities but they were the most accurate. Even allowing for the fact that the benchmarks were accurate to within plus or minus 3%, 'on the whole it seems prudent to place the accuracy of the figures of total profits in category B, that is, between 3 and 10% error'.[15]

Within manufacturing it was possible to estimate the gross profits of thirteen industrial groups, and a summary of the series is given in table 4.4. In general they exhibited fluctuations in profits similar to those for manufacturing as a whole. Each one experienced an upward trend over the period, except woollens, leather and paper, whose profits had little or no trend and cotton with a decidedly downward trend. Seven industries (metals, engineering, vehicles, metals not elsewhere specified, cotton, woollens and other manufacturing) had fluctuations greater than those for manufacturing as a whole, while the profits of the four metal-using trades were very volatile. The drink industry had the most stable profits.[16]

Table 4.3 Summary of the time-series of gross profit by industrial sector, United Kingdom, 1920–38 (£m.)

Year	Extractive industries	Manufacturing	Construction	Public utilities	Transport	Distribution	Total
	1	2	3	4	5	6	7
1920	233.6	326.9	11.0	14.4	47.6	291.7	925.2
1921	123.1	179.2	8.0	12.3	30.8	262.4	615.8
1922	132.8	242.3	6.0	17.3	79.8	295.7	773.9
1923	146.1	261.8	5.0	17.4	76.8	296.8	803.9
1924	124.6	269.9	6.0	16.6	77.5	320.2	814.8
1925	101.6	258.5	11.0	17.0	74.8	320.8	783.7
1926	96.0	229.1	15.0	15.9	59.6	313.7	729.3
1927	68.0	267.2	17.0	20.7	82.9	334.7	790.5
1928	73.9	277.2	6.0	22.0	84.6	345.4	809.1
1929	91.7	274.8	13.0	22.4	87.8	339.3	829.0
1930	99.9	252.1	9.0	25.6	82.0	312.8	781.4
1931	83.5	220.2	8.0	21.3	70.2	295.1	698.3
1932	82.7	185.2	9.0	23.2	54.5	265.1	619.7
1933	104.0	218.7	13.0	23.1	66.4	279.9	705.1
1934	121.8	255.3	15.0	23.4	74.9	300.7	791.1
1935	117.2	304.4	15.0	25.0	82.7	322.2	866.5
1936	135.5	351.1	19.0	26.6	88.9	342.2	963.3
1937	118.6	392.5	19.0	28.3	111.0	351.1	1020.5
1938	116.9	379.0	20.0	28.4	96.1	333.9	974.3

Source: P. E. Hart, Studies in Profit, Business Saving and Investment in the U.K. 1920–62, 1965, p. 21.

Table 4.4   Gross profit in manufacturing industries: yearly average (£m.)

	Food	Drink	Tobacco	Chemicals etc.	Metals	Engineering	Vehicles
1920–24	17.1	29.4	9.0	20.3	38.6	19.9	4.5
1925–29	21.9	32.5	11.9	24.5	17.3	28.4	9.4
1930–34	24.1	28.5	11.7	25.1	17.5	22.4	8.9
1935–38	29.3	32.7	14.8	35.0	43.0	54.7	18.3

	Metal goods N.E.S	Cotton	Woollens etc.	Leather etc.	Paper & printing	Other	Total manufacturing
1920–24	7.0	11.9	32.7	18.0	27.1	20.5	256.0
1925–29	7.5	8.2	23.2	21.5	30.0	25.0	261.4
1930–34	6.1	3.8	13.0	15.1	26.8	23.4	226.3
1935–38	13.6	7.3	20.1	17.9	34.1	35.9	356.8

Source: P. E. Hart, *Studies in Profit, Business Saving and Investment in the U.K., 1920–62*, 1965, p. 70.

This series can claim several advantages over others. Firstly, previous series were calculated before the authoritative benchmarks of the Oxford Study were compiled. Secondly, since the Oxford figures provided a detailed industrial breakdown it was possible to make the series consistent with the Standard Industrial Classification. Thirdly, in the compilation of the series an attempt was made to overcome the problem of estimating the profits of an industry from a knowledge of only the largest firms' profits by the use of a log normal sampling scheme. Fourthly, in some of the other series the figures used were those of profits after taking out certain items. *The Economist* index is based on profits after depreciation, debenture interest, and taxation on company saving have been deducted, which raises the possibility that it may be influenced by changes in tax rates, debenture interest, and by somewhat arbitrary provisions for depreciation, and none of these may reflect changes in profit.[17]

A comparison of Hart's index with that of *The Economist* (both reworked to 1936 = 100) indicates that for general movements over the period they moved very much in sympathy (see figure 4.1). Movements in *The Economist* index are somewhat more erratic, reflecting its composition.

Estimates of company savings

Business saving is very much a residual item. Following the various appropriations of company profits, such as depreciation, debenture and other fixed interest payments, and taxation, the remaining sum – 'earned for ordinary' – can be allocated to a dividend and the remainder carried forward as a balance or put to stated reserve funds. Such undistributed profits can be held as idle balances, temporarily invested in securities,

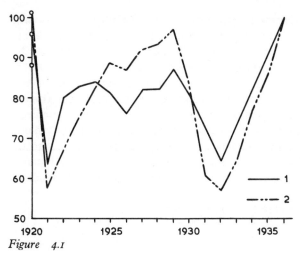

Figure 4.1
1. Hart – total gross profit
2. *The Economist* Index.

Source: P. E. Hart, *Studies in Profit, Business Saving and Investment in the U.K. 1920–62,* 1965, p. 32.

used for short-term loans, or for making additions to fixed or working capital. The savings flow thus depends on the size of total profit and the appropriations from it. However, in the inter-war period procedures were not so straightforward, since the practice was common of making allocation to internal or other secret reserves which were not shown in the profit and loss statement. Their existence only became known when directors thought fit to capitalize or distribute them in some form to the shareholders.[18] Since savings is a residual it follows that savings fluctuated more with earnings levels than did the dividend level. With a protracted slump there would be a tendency to lower dividends so that the full impact of earnings fluctuations would not fall on savings, but in the occasional bad year the inclination was for directors to draw heavily on reserves and balances in hand to maintain dividend payments. In the short term a firm making a loss could pay as good a dividend as one making a profit.

The aggregate figures of savings for the sample of companies analysed by *The Economist* is given in table 4.5. As noted above the figures are for companies reporting during the twelve months to June of each year, which relate in the main to profits earned during the previous calendar year to which they have been credited in both tables. The savings flow is based on deduction from net profit (after debenture interest) of the preference and ordinary dividend. The reserve column includes the amounts added to the balance carried forward, as well as specific allocations to various reserve funds. The cyclical fluctuations in savings will be discussed below, but one figure deserves some explanation, that is, the debit item of £6.3m. for 1921. This arises because the debit item for the industrial groups exceeded the surpluses for that year. It should not be assumed for *The Economist*'s sample of companies that a sum of that amount was taken out of reserves to pay dividends and interest payments. It did not follow that if a company made no profits, or indeed made losses that it cut into its capital reserves in order to meet its dividend payments. The figure arose because an industrial group's aggregate profits minus the dividends disbursed by the profitable companies left a debit balance. Undertakings which carried a loss forward as a rule paid no dividends.

Table 4.5   Estimates of net business savings 1919–38

	The Economist[1]		Hart[2]	
	£m.	% of profit	£m.	% of profit
	1	2	3	4
1919	41.9	35.2	—	—
1920	39.9	28.8	121.7	45.3
1921	−6.3	−7.9	35.5	21.4
1922	17.6	15.2	69.8	30.2
1923	27.3	20.2	70.1	27.8
1924	33.5	22.3	91.9	37.7
1925	34.8	21.1	83.9	34.1
1926	32.1	17.9	64.3	30.8
1927	35.9	20.7	77.6	30.8
1928	39.6	20.1	96.3	35.3
1929	37.0	18.6	94.2	36.7
1930	29.5	15.7	68.3	27.8
1931	7.6	5.5	44.0	20.6
1932	12.2	8.9	29.1	17.4
1933	27.4	17.2	50.5	27.3
1934	40.4	20.9	70.5	29.4
1935	55.2	24.6	89.4	30.6
1936	73.2	27.5	109.4	32.9
1937	91.6	30.7	88.8	25.3
1938	84.1	29.4	37.4	10.1

Sources: 1. *The Economist* series, see table 4.2 (p. 89).   2. P. E. Hart, *Studies in profit, Business Saving and Investment in the U.K. 1920–62*, 1965, pp. 118, 128; col. 4 is a percentage of total income less royalties and tax – see table 4.6 (p. 96).

Hart's estimates of business savings, given in col. 3 of table 4.5, only cover the manufacturing sector; they do not purport to be estimates for industry in general.[19] The Oxford Survey, which was an important ingredient in the compilation of the profit estimates, did not examine the appropriation of company profits. To obtain such a series, therefore, a benchmark was obtained for 1936 from Inland Revenue reports and then estimates were made of appropriations for 1920–35 from the changes in profit appropriations in the sample of company accounts used to estimate profits of the manufacturing sector. The 1938 estimates are reliable to within 3%, but the results for 1920–35 are less reliable 'and should probably be placed in category B, with less than 10% error'.[20]

The derivation of net business savings from the estimates of income is given in table 4.6. Most of the items are self-explanatory, but some need a little comment. 'Other income' consists of that part of profit which the Inland Revenue imputed into the ownership of property and taxed under Schedule A, plus interest on government securities and other assets, whether directly assessed for taxation or taxed at source. Clearly this is an important contribution to company income throughout the period (overall it accounts for about one-third), and its availability probably influenced company decisions on dividend policy. The deduction of interest and dividends covers payments by companies to their debenture, preference and ordinary shareholders. The tax paid on this item by the company is subsequently recovered from the shareholders. On the average, for the period, the taxation of company savings was some 10% of the total.[21] The residual represents estimated net business savings for the manufacturing sector.

Fluctuations in profits and savings 1919–39

The series described above for profits and business savings are on an annual basis, and while they provide a reasonably good guide to the movements and the main turning points during the period they provide little by way of detailed coverage of each cycle. The only available guide on a quarterly basis are the figures compiled by *The Economist*. These have many shortcomings, which have already been noted, but with regard to their use as a kind of quarterly guide it should be heavily stressed that the returns for each quarter relate to the reports analysed in that quarter, which on average would be for annual accounts with years ending at anything up to six months before that quarter. They *do not relate in any way* to profits earned within a particular three months. Deficient though this series is, it is the only one available and will serve as a rough guide.

The general picture for the immediate post-war year is shown by figure 4.1 (p. 93). In the case of *The Economist*'s index it stood at 76.5 in 1918, climbed during the boom to 101.4 in 1920, fell back sharply with the 1921 slump to the low point of 58.2, and with recovery gradually rose to 83.0 in

Table 4.6   U.K. manufacturing industry: Appropriation of company profits, 1919–38 (£m.)

	1920	1921	1922	1923	1924	1925	1926	1927	1928	1929	1930	1931	1932	1933	1934	1935	1936	1937	1938
Gross true income	254.7	151.4	204.8	221.2	228.1	218.4	187.9	225.8	249.3	240.3	221.0	192.6	161.1	193.0	227.9	275.3	320.3	363.8	354.2
less depreciation	19.5	16.2	17.5	20.8	29.1	21.5	20.1	26.0	30.9	33.9	25.3	23.7	28.6	28.1	35.6	41.0	50.1	57.2	59.7
plus other income minus losses	92.6	53.2	73.7	78.7	78.2	77.3	66.0	78.5	85.7	81.0	76.7	66.1	51.5	64.3	74.8	91.0	105.0	101.3	149.8
TOTAL INCOME	327.8	188.4	261.0	279.1	277.2	274.2	233.8	278.3	304.1	287.4	272.4	235.0	184.0	229.2	267.1	325.3	375.2	407.9	444.3
less dividends and interest	146.9	130.7	161.0	181.7	151.6	162.3	146.4	174.3	176.7	162.7	177.3	169.4	138.2	152.6	169.1	203.0	222.9	261.9	333.5
less royalties	7.0	7.0	7.0	7.0	7.0	7.0	7.0	7.0	7.0	7.0	7.0	7.0	7.0	7.0	7.0	7.0	7.0	7.0	7.0
Gross business savings	173.9	50.7	93.0	90.4	118.6	104.9	80.4	97.0	120.4	117.7	88.1	58.6	38.8	69.6	91.0	115.3	145.3	139.0	103.8
less tax on business saving	52.2	15.2	23.2	20.3	26.7	21.0	16.1	19.4	24.1	23.5	19.8	14.6	9.7	19.2	20.5	25.9	35.9	50.2	66.4
NET BUSINESS SAVING	121.7	35.5	69.8	70.1	91.9	83.9	64.3	77.6	96.3	94.2	68.3	44.0	39.1	50.5	70.5	89.4	109.4	88.8	37.4

Source: P. E. Hart, Studies in Profit, Business Saving and Investment in the U.K., 1920–63, 1965, p. 118.

1924. The Hart index, starting in 1920, shows a similar pattern, except that it does not fall so far and recovery from the slump is rather faster. Gross profits of all industries as given by the Hart series fell from £925.2m. in 1920 to £615.8m in 1921, a drop of a third, and the fall was not fully recovered until 1936. As can be seen from table 4.3 the decline was concentrated in the manufacturing sector, with a fall of 45.2%, and in the extractive industries with 47.3%. The latter industry never restored its 1920 profit levels during the inter-war years.

The peak profit level of 1920 was reached after a period of increasing profits during the war. In 1914 *The Economist* index stood at 51.7, compared with 76.5 at the end of the war. However, the annual changes during the war were by no means gradual. After the first year *The Economist*'s surveys indicated a drop of 3% in profits, followed by a substantial rise of 29% in the following year. The increase in 1917 was only 10% due to the incidence of taxation, while rises in working costs in the last year of the war brought the increase down to a low of 1.6%. From the standpoint of company financing a notable feature of the war period, as indicated by *The Economist*'s sample, was that dividend distributions fell from 56% in 1914 to 51% in 1918, as a percentage of net profits, while reserve allocations rose from 27% to 33.8%. This re-appropriation of profit did not become evident at the outset of the war; indeed, *The Economist*'s figures of reserve percentages do not rise until 1916.[22] However, the fall in shown dividend distributions was frequently made up by bonus distributions of capitalized reserves.

The precise level and changes in profits during the war and immediate post-war years is difficult to establish owing to the incidence of Excess Profits Duty.[23] It was introduced in September 1915 at a rate of 50%, which increased to 60% in April 1916, and became 80% in April 1917. In 1919 it was reduced to 40%, but was soon back at 60%, and finally removed in 1921. Dropping the rate to 40% in 1919 proved to be something of an embarrassment for the Treasury since it led to a drastic fall in revenue. Even more significant was that the reduction generated expectations of the removal of the tax and this led to a fall in declared profits. Some of these were postponed by 'one dodge or another', in the expectation that if brought into 1920 they would be tax free; that proved a mistake since the rate went up to 60%. During its operation it brought in over £93m. (excluding arrears due), or nearly 25% of total revenue exclusive of borrowing.[24]

The most general fear at the end of the war was of a large fall in prices, and that with large stockholdings, coupled with Excess Profits Duty, industry had been prevented from making prudent allocations to reserves.[25] Thus, there was little room to manoeuvre if stock values fell quickly, merely to write down profits drastically. However, the unease about reserves could hardly be blamed on Excess Profits Duty since during the war many companies had paid out higher dividends. Fortunately, the fall in prices did not come immediately. The returns of *The Economist* for the middle quarter of 1919 (relating mainly to activity in 1918) indicated a falling off in profits, and, indeed, of reserve allocations (see table 4.7); the reduction of Excess Profits Duty and the Armistice probably lessened the degree of caution among many directors. However, the reports for the ensuing five quarters all showed increases in net profits, while the proportion put to reserve was restored to a more traditional level. Shareholders did not suffer unduly in this since the practice had become increasingly popular of making distributions of bonus shares, which as a rule were not made from profits in that particular year but from accumulated profits in the form of reserves, both known and secret.[26]

The upswing in profits in the boom, which lasted from Spring 1919 to Summer 1920, was helped by the reduction in Excess Profits Duty. As to savings during this period, textiles and shipping headed *The Economist*'s list of reserve appropriations; in the case of shipping it was the practice to place large amounts to depreciation and reserve funds before striking profits.[27]

Table 4.7   Quarterly changes in net profits (A) and percentages put to reserve (B) 1919–1924

Quarter	1919		1920		1921		1922		1923		1924	
	A*	B†	A	B	A	B	A	B	A	B	A	B
1st	+10.4	35.8	+26.9	35.6	+3.5	29.3	−43.4	−19.1	+41.4	22.0	+8.7	22.3
2nd	−5.1	29.3	+37.8	35.6	−8.4	21.4	−33.7	−4.1	+22.1	15.8	+3.0	16.9
3rd	−3.4	29.7	+41.9	31.3	−42.4	3.1	−23.5	−10.1	+65.2	26.7	+2.3	22.4
4th	+10.5	38.0	+27.1	36.6	−52.9	−4.0	+3.9	N 15.7	+11.4	19.3	+13.3	24.7

* Col. A: The comparison is with the same companies in the previous year's quarter.
† Col. B: The percentage of net profits for returns in that quarter.

Source: The Economist.

The Economist's figures for the first quarter of 1921 (see table 4.7) do not show up the trade depression which started in the summer of 1920, but a falling off is certainly evident. In the second quarter the effect of the depression becomes evident, but the fortunes of individual industries differed somewhat. Some sections felt the depression before others. Motors, textiles and rubber showed big falls in profit, but there were also some conspicuous rises, especially nitrate which made a remarkable recovery from the early post-war setback it had suffered. Reserve appropriations also showed signs of falling and several companies drew on their balances in hand to pay dividends. The third and fourth quarter returns reveal the sharp drop in profits since the accounts cover the year ending around June 1921, the period of depression. It should be noted, however, that a great deal of the fall in profits was the result of price reductions which involved writing down stock in trade to such an extent as largely to neutralize any margin of profit there may have been on trading conditions. All industries, except tea and nitrate, showed profit falls compared with their previous year's performance. Some industries suffered particularly large decreases in profits, for example, rubber companies reporting in the third quarter of 1921 showed profits down by 84.2% on the previous year, textiles down by 141.5%, iron and steel by 52%, miscellaneous industries by 43.6%, rubber by 115%, and motor cycles by 175%.[28]

As shown by the reports for the first two quarters of 1922 (see table 4.7), the rate of fall of profits abated somewhat, but this was due not so much to an improvement in profits as to the fact that the levels with which they were compared had actually passed the top point. In the first quarter of 1922 only four industrial groups showed increases, with three in the second quarter. In the first quarter heavy falls were reported by iron and steel (-41%), textiles (-50.7%), miscellaneous (-53.3%); in the second quarter by rubber (-89.8%), textiles (-74.6%), and miscellaneous (-51.9%). The third quarter returns contained companies which benefited from early recovery so that seven out of the 13 industrial groups in *The Economist*'s analysis showed increases in profits on the previous year's figures, with striking recoveries in tea and textiles. By the fourth quarter the corner had been turned, but profit levels were well below what they were in 1918.

In this profit fall it was the reserves which suffered, as can be seen from the figures for the quarters from 1921 (4th) to 1922 (3rd). The buoyancy of dividend levels is shown by the rise from 45% in 1920 to 69% in 1921 of the ratio of dividend and interest to total income for all manufacturing industries (see table 4.6).[29] On the basis of Hart's figures net business savings for manufacturing fell from £121.7m. to £35.5m. during 1920–1. Many companies drew on balances in hand to pay dividends, while others withdrew large sums from accumulated reserves. Thus dividends, albeit at a reduced level, were paid out basically at the expense of savings. Companies which displayed trading losses, as distinct from a fall in profits, did not pay out dividends to their ordinary shareholders.

Recovery from the depression began early in 1922, and continued until 1924. In the case of manufacturing industries it involved a rise in profits from £179m. in 1921 to £270m. in 1924, an increase of 107%, while for all industries profits increased over the same period from £616m. to £814m., a gain of 32% (see table 4.3). Recovery from the low position of 1921 was rapid, but during 1922–4 it was at a slower pace. The general pattern is indicated by the quarterly figures given in table 4.7. One reason for the rapid rise from 1921 (as shown by the 65.2% gain in the third quarter returns for 1923) was that greater stability of commodity prices and reduced stock holding removed the necessity of any further sharp writing down of stock values.[30] Within the general gains there were some very notable rises in net profits, particularly in rubber and textiles. However, coal, iron and steel did not share in the improvement because of the heavy falls in profits for many of the larger concerns.[31] Despite the general recovery, however, profits were still below the pre-depression level.

While the proportion of net profits put to reserve were gradually improving they were still well below the traditional 30% level (see table 4.7). These allocations to specific reserve funds, or in the form of additions to balances carried forward, differed appreciably between industrial groups. Textile companies reporting in the third quarter of 1923 put aside 45%, while in the first quarter motor cycles made the best showing, but it did have a great deal of leeway to catch up. The low figure of reserve appropriation in the second quarter of 1924 was due to the payment by some companies of preference dividends in arrears from the depression.

The recovery in profits after the 1921 slump was arrested in 1925 when Britain went back to the gold standard. The General Strike brought a sharp fall in the following year, particularly in the manufacturing and extractive industries. The path of profit movements can be clearly seen in figure 4.1 (p. 93); movements in *The Economist*'s index were less pronounced due to the inclusion of several activities which were largely overseas in nature. Thereafter profits improved and the recovery lasted until 1929, when profits were not far below their 1920 peak level.

Despite the slackening of activity in 1925, profits, as measured by *The Economist,* continued to improve (see table 4.8). However, the improvement was by no means general. Iron and steel suffered heavy falls in profits during these years, while some of the larger companies were consistently showing *net* losses; in the four quarters of 1925 this group's profits as shown by *The Economist*'s analysis had decreases ranging from 23% in the first quarter to 72% in the fourth. Textiles and shipping had similar, if less pronounced, trends. By the third quarter of 1926, if the overseas component in *The Economist*'s compilations is taken out, company profits reported in that quarter were down by 5.4% on the previous year's level, and the same adjustment to the fourth quarter's figures produced a decline of 3.7%.[32] These decreases arise from the bad results in the domestic heavy and staple industries, particularly with such firms as United Steel and Dorman Long. The first two quarters of 1927 (see table 4.8) show up the effects of the General Strike on industrial profits, but even so some industries continued to do well, for example, food, tobacco, and the motor industry. Those which suffered appreciable falls were metals, cotton, and woollens (see table 4.4, p. 92).

Table 4.8   Quarterly changes in net profits (A) and percentages put to reserve (B) 1925–30

Quarter	1925		1926		1927		1928		1929		1930	
	A*	B†	A	B	A	B	A	B	A	B	A	B
1st	+9.1	23.9	+7.6	23.1	−4.0	18.8	+15.2	23.0	+1.5	21.1	+1.9	18.4
2nd	+11.1	19.8	+8.3	18.1	−5.7	13.9	+1.3	19.5	−0.7	16.5	+8.6	18.6
3rd	+4.8	17.6	+2.8	17.4	+2.4	14.7	+9.7	26.3	−3.0	20.6	−6.4	18.3
4th	+6.4	25.5	+3.8	23.7	−0.3	22.0	+3.1	23.2	+1.4	18.0	−18.1	15.1

* Col. A: The comparison is with the same companies in the previous year's quarter.
† Col. B: The percentage of net profits for returns in that quarter.

Source: *The Economist.*

Although the quarterly series given in table 4.8 shows net gains in the latter part of 1927, it was not until early 1928 that gains on an appreciable scale appear, indicating that at last a satisfactory recovery from 1926 was taking place. Even the reports of iron and steel companies in the first quarter of 1928 showed a large improvement, but these gains should be reviewed against the previous depressed state of the industry. Much better profits were also recorded in the cotton industry.

Despite the fact that in general domestic industry continued to record satisfactory advances in profits, signs were present early in 1929 that some setbacks were taking place. This was so in iron and steel, shipping, and textiles; profits in heavy industry were suffering from price cuts and keen competition. The gradual slowdown in industrial activity from the spring of 1928 is reflected in the figures for the second and third quarters of 1929 (see table 4.8). Decreases in profits at this stage were confined to a few industries, but many showed declining rates of increase. In contrast to the declining profits of heavy industry, 1929 proved a peak year for consumer goods industries, engineering and the motor industry (see table 4.4, p. 92).

Changes in business savings during this period reflect the behaviour of profits. Column 3 of table 4.5 indicates the fall in savings in 1926 in manufacturing, and the build up to 1929; from 30% of profits to 36.7% respectively. While the general picture is one of savings on the increase (see table 4.8), the experience of individual industries differed greatly. The decline in profits in the iron and steel industry (see table 4.4 – Metals) led to a sharp fall in their reserve ratio, and frequently funds in hand and in reserve were used to keep up dividend payouts.[33] The largest drafts on earnings by companies in the heavy industries occurred shortly after the restoration of the gold standard and the coal stoppage. An industry which managed to indulge in heavy ploughback over this period was the motor industry, which not infrequently put to reserve some 50% of its net profits. *The Economist* calculated that a group of 17 motor cycle companies put 42% to reserve in 1925 and 31% in 1928, but that taking the companies making profits the relevant percentage was 57% and 46% respectively. Hope calculated a savings ratio (net undistributed profits to total net earnings for ordinary capital) for the period 1924–9 of 66% for non-commercial vehicles, and 65% for commercial ones. He also identified seven other manufacturing industries with savings ratios in excess of 30%; motor accessories, engineering, clothing, electrical engineering, paper, brewing and food.[34] This is not to infer that all heavy industry firms indulged in the division of profits 'up to the hilt'; where they could iron and steel companies tended to pursue conservative financial practices with relatively stable dividends, putting what they could to reserve.

The landslide in profits which occurred with the onset of the depression is shown by the following figures for the manufacturing sector. As measured by the Hart series gross profits fell from £275m. in 1929 to £185m. in 1932, a decrease of 33%.[35] Certain other sectors fell even more abruptly (see table 4.3, p. 91), but these were less important than manufacturing. The only other large sector, distribution, the biggest at the time, suffered a relatively modest fall of 22%. For both the Hart and *The Economist*'s series the low point comes in 1932 (see figure 4.1, p. 87), although the latter index falls more sharply than the former due to the inclusion of overseas activities.

The onset of the decline and the extent of the fall was by no means similar among the numerous industrial groups. As early as 1927–8 there were signs that the capital goods industries were suffering a mild setback, the consumer goods industries reached a peak in 1929, while the food industry did so in 1931 (see table 4.4, p. 92). As to the fall in profits, experiences differed greatly. In the manufacturing sector, using the Hart series and taking the high point and the low point within 1928 and 1932 for each industry, cotton and woollens had falls of 91% and 76% respectively, engineering and vehicles 51%, metals 50%, leather and metal goods 43%, paper 34%, drink 32%, food 20%, tobacco 24%, and chemicals 14%. The severity of the decline diminished through the ranks of the staple export industries, heavy industry, domestic consumer goods industries, to the newer industries. Taking the results for all industries as a norm consumer goods had results above the norm, so that profits on the average were either increasing or falling less rapidly than in the case of all industries taken together. On the other hand, profits in the capital goods industries were on the average falling faster than they were in industry as a whole.[36]

The results declared by companies in the first quarter of 1930 (see table 4.9) showed that the upward trend was beginning to flatten out. This was confirmed in the second quarter results, since if oil companies are excluded, the gain is merely 2.4%. The third quarter's reports (mainly covering the year ending June 1930) indicates the start of a general downward movement, which gains speed in the following quarters. The results in the last quarter of 1931 show significant falls, the last quarter of the year providing the largest drop ever elicited by *The Economist*'s analysis. The progressive fall in profits due to the depression was accelerated by the unusually large proportion of gross profits which had to be allocated to provide for the depreciation of stocks.[37] As the depression worsened trading losses became more numerous among the groups in *The Economist*'s analysis. The tendency towards lower profits was uniform – 150 companies in the miscellaneous groups in the fourth quarter of 1931 had falls in profits of 56.8% – but it should be noted that group fortunes could be distorted by the adverse fortunes of one or two large concerns.

The declining percentages continued into 1932, but at lower levels than for the end of 1931.[38] The small fall recorded by companies reporting in the fourth quarter of 1932 – 2.9% – conceals the fact that if allowance is made for a 16% gain by 165 companies in the miscellaneous category, a fall of 19.0% is registered. The miscellaneous group included a high proportion of new industries whose products were mainly distributed on the home market. The figure for the first quarter of 1933 shows that the decline was being arrested in the case of companies reporting in that quarter, there being merely small diminutions over a wide range of companies rather than any outstandingly large losses. By this time company earnings figures seemed to indicate that the worst was over, and the arrest of the fall was probably contributed to by the use of tarriffs, the depreciation of sterling, and to internal company economies in expenditure which strengthened their financial position.[39]

The effect of the depression on company savings could not be anything but severe. Net business savings of the manufacturing sector fell from £94m. in 1929 to £29m. in 1932 (see table 4.5). With the decline in earnings company reports quickly reflected a tendency to put less back into the business.[40] This followed from the need to maintain dividends; by the fourth quarter of 1930 *The Economist* reported that amounts put to reserve were sharply down and this continued into 1931. Company reports for the third quarter of 1931 revealed that about £1.5m. of reserves had

Table 4.9 Quarterly changes in net profits (A) and percentages put to reserve (B) 1930–3

Quarter	1930		1931		1932		1933	
	A*	B†	A	B	A	B	A	B
1st	+1.9	18.4	−10.6	16.2	−14.3	9.6	−8.9	12.2
2nd	+8.6	18.6	−19.4	14.8	−24.2	11.1	+3.3	12.6
3rd	−6.4	18.3	−35.5	−8.9	−28.6	3.2	−5.5	4.0
4th	−18.1	15.1	−53.9	−20.0	−2.9	−7.8	+30.3	12.3

* Col. A: The comparison is with the same companies in the previous year's quarter.
† Col. B: The percentage of net profits for returns in that quarter.

Source: *The Economist*.

been used up, which had not happened since 1921. It should not, however, be assumed that loss-making concerns paid out dividends from capital resources; it was simply that in the compilations the group aggregate profits minus dividends paid out by profit making concerns left a debit balance. For the most part, therefore, the dividends paid represented legitimate distributions. The negative items for the last quarter of 1931 and the final quarter of 1932 in table 4.9 reflect the losses carried forward in the profit and loss statements. However, in terms of *The Economist*'s figures superficially this can be taken to mean that several groups were 'trenching' on their reserves to a rather disquieting extent. With the recovery that began in late 1932 companies resumed more normal allocations to reserves which aided the financing of the capital expenditure programmes needed to increase the momentum of the recovery in manufacturing production.

The general pattern of recovery from the depression during 1933 to 1937 is conveyed in figure 4.1, p. 93, while the 1938 recession is also clearly evident. All the main industrial sectors, as identified in the Hart figures (see table 4.3, p. 91) shared in the revival although at somewhat unequal rates; manufacturing profits increased by 81%, transport by 67%, construction by 46%, while in the lesser orders distribution and public utilities had gains of 25% and 22% respectively, followed by 14% in the extraction industries.[41] Within the manufacturing sector the profit revival presented a rather diversified picture (see table 4.4, p. 92). The most rapid gains were certainly in metals and engineering with impressive increases of over 270%, followed by vehicles 182% and metal goods 127%. Tobacco and cotton managed slightly over 60%; food, chemicals and paper and printing attained 45% increases; drink a third, while leather and wool trailed badly with 16% and 8% respectively. This wide range of recovery experience among industries was in marked contrast to the depression phase when industrial groups showed a greater degree of uniformity in the trend of their profit changes.

The recovery in profits, which for most industrial groups was fairly continuous, was aided by the protection afforded to certain key industries, the recovery of the home market, which was especially important for the domestic consumer goods industries, and the depreciation of the currency which assisted the export industries, particularly after 1934, in regaining some of their lost markets. In the latter phase of the recovery the metal industries were greatly helped by mounting armaments expenditures. Companies also pursued cost savings policies and so increased their profit margins. On the basis of *The Economist*'s figures of profits and business activity, profits increased at a faster rate than activity during this period, which was the converse of the picture during the depression phase. With declining turnover the proportionate burden of overhead charges increased; in the recovery the opposite occurred. Profits were also helped by price rises which brought inventory gains; the depression had lead to large stock losses.

The onset of the 1938 depression brought a decisive fall in profits, which can be seen in all the main profit series. Manufacturing profits as presented by the Hart series fell by £21m. and *The Economist*'s series also produced a fall of £21m., but their coverage is, of course, different. The quarterly series of *The Economist* given in table 4.10 shows up clearly the falling trend of profits for the reports examined in the third quarter of 1938, which for the most part dealt with companies with years ending on 31 March. Subsequent quarter figures confirmed the fall, especially those for the first quarter of 1939 which dealt with companies with years ending on 31 December 1938. In the manufacturing sector (Hart series) the only industry groups to escape this setback were drink, tobacco, and engineering, while the staple industries of cotton and wool suffered the worst falls; Courtaulds had a very bad year.[42] It was noticeable that the impact of the recession on profits in the heavy industries was softened by controlled prices and by the growing stimulus of rearmament expenditures.

What is perhaps more surprising for this period is not so much the increase in profits, but the distinct change in policy towards savings. In absolute terms, as computed by the main series given in table 4.5 (p. 94), the trend is decidedly upwards during 1933–7. Of greater interest is the increased percentage put to reserve, which is also indicated by all the main series. The Hart series relating to manufacturing shows a return to the pre-depression level of the savings ratio, while *The Economist* series show the same development with peak savings ratios in 1936–7. The quarterly

Table 4.10   Quarterly changes in net profits (A) and percentage put to reserve (B) 1933–9

Quarter	1933 A*	B†	1934 A	B	1935 A	B	1936 A	B	1937 A	B	1938 A	B	1939 A	B
1st	−8.9	12.2	+5.3	18.5	+14.6	19.4	+13.3	22.2	+11.9	23.6	+10.5	29.7	−9.9	27.7
2nd	+3.3	12.6	+18.2	20.6	+17.8	22.9	+10.6	26.6	+19.9	29.9	+12.9	31.1	−8.2	26.8
3rd	−5.5	4.0	+27.7	18.5	+12.2	23.7	+14.3	29.7	+19.2	28.5	−1.4	29.5	−7.4	32.2
4th	+30.3	12.3	+32.9	20.5	+16.9	25.8	+15.2	29.0	+20.2	32.7	−4.4	37.3	−7.1	37.9

* Col. A.: The comparison is with the same companies in the previous year's quarter.
† Col. B: The percentage of net profits for returns in that quarter.

Source: The Economist.

series given in table 4.10 shows that from 1934 to 1938, almost without exception, the savings ratio (reserves/net profit ratio) gradually rises reflecting increasingly conservative financial attitudes on the part of company directors. After the slump many firms took to a lower level of 'conventional' dividend with a flattening out of the savings curve which indicated a greater willingness on the part of directors to allow dividend payments to fluctuate more with earnings.

There was thus a discernible increase in the savings ratio of industry due not only to increased prosperity, but also to a distinct swing towards directoral conservatism. Taking the amount paid in ordinary dividends as a percentage of net profits in 1929 and 1930 the figures are 60% and 61% respectively (*The Economist*'s series). This compares with a much lower figure for the recovery years – between 1934 and 1938 the payout ratio of net profits rose from 51% to 54%.[43] The reasons for this trend are fairly straightforward. During the depression heavy drafts were made upon reserves so that directors were eager to rebuild their positions. The period of recovery involved replacement and extension of plant with a corresponding need to obtain finance; a period of revival offered opportunities for the profitable investment of increased liquid capital. *The Economist* reported in 1938 that much the greater part of such funds had gone not into gilt-edged but rather into active and immediate employment at higher rates of return.[44] When the ratio of internal funds to plant and equipment outlays is high the demand for long-term external funds declines, which at this time had important implications for bank finance and the capital market.

The increasing amount put to savings was also aided by the steady decline in the effective rate of interest on debentures during the 1930s, which thereby released a somewhat larger proportion of earnings for the preference and ordinary shareholders, and for reserve purposes. In the preference area the level of rates paid, although fluctuating, had not changed by anything like the same extent as total earnings so that residual profits available for ordinary shareholders had varied more than profits as a whole. This, coupled with increased conservatism in the board rooms added to the flow of earnings going to savings.[45]

In general terms the picture which emerges for the mid-1930s is that a savings ratio of one-quarter to one-third had been achieved. Taking the results for the year ending June 1936, as reported by *The Economist*'s sample of companies, the average savings ratio (net profit put to reserve) for all industries was 25%. Some industries, however, were notably in excess of this level and relied heavily on self-finance to sustain their expansion. The better than average industries included building materials, 32%; iron, coal and steel, 41%; electric lighting and power, 45%;

electrical equipment, 46%; motor cycles and aviation, 47%; and shipping, 64%.[46] Among these industries were some of the best performances in terms of profit increases, and they were inclined to be more conservative in their distribution policies than some of the less successful industrial groups.

With savings being the main means whereby companies finance investment, the actions of company boardrooms as to dividends levels attracted a good deal of attention. Not infrequently the naive view was held then (and by some now) that lack of investment, or its variability, could be ascribed to changes in the level of company saving. In the inter-war cycles company savings varied greatly due to changes in company profits and to the policy of keeping stable dividends, which with falling income was only possible at the expense of savings. The impression that the declining industries (heavy industries) distributed up to the hilt arose because directors pursued conservative or stable dividend policies which on falling profits left little by way of surplus. Successful new companies pursued equally conservative policies as to dividends but with rising income they could display high savings levels. With a fairly widespread policy of stable dividends the degree of risk attached to equity capital was somewhat reduced – the main brunt of the adjustment to fluctuations in the level of production was taken not by dividends but by company savings. The post-Second World War government policy of discouraging company distributions was in many ways merely a continuation of the traditional policy of dividend conservatism pursued in the boardrooms of the 1930s.

Liquid assets

It can be seen from the profits and savings series given above that periods of recovery, for example, 1921–4, 1926–9, and 1932–7, were characterized by higher savings ratios so that industry was able to meet part of its working and fixed capital needs from the annual flow of income. But the flow of annual savings was not the only way in which companies could avail themselves of internal funds. By making adjustments to the liquid items in their balance sheets, on both the liabilities and assets side, companies could add to their supply of funds for spending purposes.

In balance sheet terms the components which are of interest in this context are those which constitute the supply of working capital, or, the surplus liquid assets of a company. On the liabilities side these are mainly sums owed to creditors, amounts required for dividends, sums by way of loans and bank overdrafts, sums due for tax and accrued interest and dividends; on the asset side the main items are stock in trade, investments, sums owed by debtors, and cash. A company may use undistributed profits to add to some items, such as investments and cash, while it may supplement its own resources by borrowing within the company sector in the form of larger and longer trade credits, sums from other companies (especially in the case of subsidiaries in holding companies), or use sums set aside for dividend or tax payment purposes. It can thus manage its state of liquidity, to add to or reduce sums available for expenditure.

If all companies had reported on a uniform basis and at the same calendar dates it would be possible to compile a very illuminating series for the company sector of changes in surplus liquid assets during the various cycles of the inter-war years. The diversity of accounting dates has already been mentioned; the diversity of accounting practices at this period is even more bewildering. Some examples will suffice to make the point. In many balance sheets bank loans were not separated from amounts owing to other creditors (i.e., trade credit); the item sundry creditors often contained an element of 'secret reserves'; cash would often be added to bills receivable, while investments would frequently include both securities and long-term trade investments in other companies. These pitfalls preclude an accurate assessment of the volume and changes in surplus liquid assets for the period.

However, thanks to *The Economist*, some limited findings are available which serve to show how the management of balance sheet liquid claims were used to finance activity. The surveys available cover two relatively short periods, one the sharp fall in profits associated with the depression years 1929–32, the other the recovery from 1932 to 1935. The general impression might be that during a phase of depression, with a protracted decline in profits, that industry would be tending towards being denuded of its liquid resources, while in the recovery stage it would have little to fall back on internally, and would seek outside capital, especially bank funds, to finance increased production. The experience of several companies as portrayed in the sample surveys of *The Economist* for the decline and the recovery in the cycle do not bear out this particular expectation.[47]

The Economist examined the records (balance sheets and profit and loss accounts), of 110 companies in eleven of the main industrial groups for the years 1930, 1931, and 1932. A summary of the findings is given in table 4.11. For these companies gross trading profits fell by 10%, with the heaviest fall taking place in rubber, shipping, tea, and iron and steel; among the more stable industries were textiles and the miscellaneous groups.[48] However, the fall in profits was not accompanied by a loss of working capital. Indeed, rather than pile up liabilities and part with assets, the reverse happened. As can be seen from table 4.11 liquid assets increased during 1930–2 by 6%, a rise common to seven out of the eleven groups in the analysis. And the rise was not due to a build-up of stocks since this item fell by 16% over these years, a fall due not only to price declines but to a volume reduction as well. Leaving aside stock-in-trade, net liquid assets increased by 20% in 1930–1, and by 16% during 1931–2.[49] With this enhancement in liquidity the signs were that recovery could be aided by such a reserve of spending power.

Table 4.11   Trading profits and liquid assets (110 companies: £000)

Profits & Assets	Mainly 1930	Mainly 1931	Mainly 1932
Gross trading profits	75,063	67,719	66,612
Surplus liquid assets	111,490	115,148	118,562
Stock-in-trade	66,509	61,161	56,117
Net liquid assets	44,981	53,987	62,445

Source: *The Economist*, 3 June 1933, pp. 1196–7.

The Economist's survey for the recovery period includes a smaller sample of companies, twenty in all, and compares their position in 1932 with that in 1935–6, depending on the latest balance sheet date available – ten for December 1935, with most of the remainder around mid-1936. Although there are fewer companies, more detail is given of the components included in the compilation of surplus liquid assets. A summary of the

Table 4.12   Profits, liquid assets and liabilities (20 companies) £000

	1932	Reports for Dec. 1935–Sept. 1936
Profits	32,685	41,920
Surplus liquid assets	103,365	110,327
Stock-in-trade[a]	43,041	54,107
Investments	54,885	64,868
Debtors	19,731	25,960
Creditors	38,734	47,584
Cash	34,749	29,989

[a] Figure for 13 companies.

Source: *The Economist*, 9 January 1937, pp. 71–2. The companies were: I.C.I., Unilever, Vickers, P & O, Associated Newspapers, Imperial Tobacco, Distillers, Watney Combe, J. Lyons, Marks & Spencer, F. W. Woolworth, J. P. Coats, Courtaulds, Morris Motors, Dunlop, General Electric, Associated Portland Cement, Stewart & Lloyds, United Steel, and Turner & Newall.

analysis is given in table 4.12. During this period, 1932–5, production in the manufacturing sector rose by 28%, and aggregate profits rose by the same amount.

Surplus liquid assets increased by 7%, but after deducting stock in trade, net liquid assets fell by 9%.[50] This decrease, however, is well below the level of the increase in activity, or profits. Liquid investments were not reduced, and registered an increase of £10m., 18% up on 1932 holdings; part of this may have been due to rise in values, but a volume increase is more probable here, given the tendency to value investments conservatively. The items debtors and creditors both showed substantial increases, debtors up by 31%, and creditors 23%; clearly inter-company credit was a concomitant feature of the revival, and this group of companies increased their net trade credit use by some 15%. There was a drop of 13% in their cash holdings over the period which provided a further financing item.[51] Clearly, then, the manipulation of working capital items provided an important source of finance during the recovery period and further work is needed on this unexplored corner of industrial finance.

Notes

1 For details of depreciation practices in the inter-war years see P. Taggart, *Profits and Balance Sheet Adjustments,* London, 1934, ch. IV; and P. D. Leake, *Depreciation and Wasting Assets,* 5th ed., London, 1948.

2 *The Economist,* 30 April 1932, p. 955; P. E. Hart, *Studies in Profit, Business Saving and Investment in the United Kingdom 1920–1962,* London, 1965, p. 42.

3 Royal Commission on the Taxation of Profits and Income, *Final Report,* Cmd 9474, 1955, para. 309.

4 ibid., para. 313.

5 ibid., para. 311.

6 *Report of the Commissioners of H.M. Inland Revenue,* Cmnd 4838, 1971, pp. 9–14.

7 *Report of the Commissioners of H.M. Inland Revenue,* Cmnd 5804, 1974, pp. 14–16; P. W. S. Andrews and E. Brunner, *The Life of Lord Nuffield,* London, 1955, pp. 162–4.

8 Hart, op. cit., pp. 11–34. Other profit series for the inter-war years are those by Sir J. C. Stamp, 'Industrial Profits in the Past Twenty Years – A New Index Number', *Journal of the Royal Statistical Society,* 1932, pp. 658–78; A. S. Carruthers, 'The Trend of Net Profits of Commercial and Industrial Enterprises, 1928–37', *Journal of the Royal Statistical Society,* 1939, pp. 63–80;

and R. Hope, 'Profits in British Industry from 1925–35', *Oxford Economic Papers,* 1949, pp. 159–81.

9 Hart, op. cit., p. 90.

10 *The Economist,* 23 April 1932, p. 901; see also L. Luboff, 'Some Aspects of Post-War Company Finance', *Accountancy Research,* 1956, pp. 154–200.

11 *The Economist,* 17 December 1938, p. 597 ('British Industrial Profits, A Survey of Three Decades', Hargreaves Parkinson).

12 G. D. N. Worswick and D. G. Tipping, *Profits in the British Economy 1909–1938,* Oxford, 1967.

13 For the drawbacks of the various sources used see Hart, op. cit., pp. 41–3.

14 See Hart, op. cit., ch. 2 and ch. 5 for full details.

15 ibid., p. 25.

16 ibid., pp. 69–84.

17 *The Economist* itself noted some of these drawbacks in its commentaries, see 23 April 1932, pp. 901–2. Further details on comparisons are given in Hart, op. cit., pp. 86–92.

18 While the practice was known before 1914, it was certainly a growing fashion in the early 1920s; *The Economist,* 11 October 1919, p. 571.

19 These are confined to manufacturing because this sector is more important than distribution, and since the traditional concept of the theory of the firm 'is formulated with manufacturing in mind'; Hart, op. cit., p. 117.

20 ibid., pp. 119–20.

21 ibid.

22 *The Economist*, 26 July 1919, p. 125, 'Six Years of Industrial Profits'.

23 A munitions levy was also imposed; see note 7.

24 U. K. Hicks, 'The Taxation of Excess Profits in War Time', *Transactions of the Manchester Statistical Society*, March 1940, *pp. 3–4*. See also E. V. Morgan, *Studies in British Financial Policy 1914–25*, London, 1952, p. 91.

25 *The Economist*, 25 January 1919, p. 97; see also a report by the Ministry of Reconstruction in 1919 (Cmd 9224).

26 *The Economist*, 17 January 1920, p. 94. This practice quickly went out of fashion with the onset of the depression in the summer of 1920. With falling profits it produced a reduction in the return on capital.

27 *The Economist*, 12 October 1918, pp. 444–445.

28 Companies which had a large volume of preference outstanding simply passed the dividend. During the subsequent recovery preference dividends were made up at the expense of reserve allocations.

29 The ratio of dividends and interest to total income for some industries in 1921 reflects their plight, e.g., chemicals, 99.1%; metal goods, 145.2%; and cotton, 248.6%; see Hart, op. cit., p. 121.

30 *The Economist*, 21 April 1923, pp. 830–1.

31 Profits in the coal industry recovered from a net loss of £18m. in 1921 to £20m. in 1922, and to £40m. by 1923, but then fell back to £24m. in 1924; see Hart, op. cit., p. 60: Hart's index of gross profits (1936 = 100) for iron and steel fell from 65 to 44 in 1922, recovered to 54 in 1923, but then fell to 46; see Hart, op. cit., p. 81.

32 *The Economist*, 16 October 1926, pp. 613–614; 15 January 1927, pp. 93–4.

33 *The Economist*, 17 July 1926, pp. 90–100; it was reported that Ebb Vale, Armstrong Whitworth, and Bolckow Vaughan had drawn down reserves by £300,000, £900,000 and £249,000 respectively.

34 Hope, op. cit., p. 177.

35 Gross fixed capital formation in manufacturing, measured in 1930 prices, fell from the 1929 peak of £73m. to £54m. in 1932, with the largest declines occurring in cotton, rayon and silk, and chemicals where it was particularly sharp; C. H. Feinstein, *Domestic Capital Formation in the United Kingdom 1920–1938*, Cambridge, 1965, pp. 44, 102–4.

36 Hope, op. cit., p. 166.

37 At this time there was a tendency to lower general depreciation charges which were based on high original costs from a more prosperous era. On old plant such depreciation charges appeared high compared with those incurred by competitors putting up new plant constructed at lower depression prices.

38 The percentage falls in profits for the first quarter reporting companies was usually lower than for other quarters. This was deemed to be because an unusually large proportion of them consisted of somewhat 'sheltered' undertakings accustomed to ploughing back a safe percentage of their earnings; *The Economist*, 16 April 1932, pp. 841–2.

39 *The Economist*, 15 April 1933, pp. 798–99.

40 At the onset of the depression industry requested the Chancellor of the Exchequer to consider the abatement of income tax on company reserves used for re-equipment, but it was refused; *The Economist*, 19 July 1930, pp. 112–13.

41 During 1933–7 gross fixed capital formation (at 1930 prices) rose from £55m. to £112m., the largest increases taking place in the metal and metal-using trades, chemicals, paper and printing, and building materials; Feinstein, op. cit., pp. 102–104.

42 D. C. Coleman, *Courtaulds: An Economic and Social History*, Oxford, 1969, vol. 2, pp. 320–2. Its trading profits plus investment income slumped from £4.2m. in 1937 to £1.0m. in 1938.

43 This trend is also reflected in the ploughback expressed as a ratio of ordinary capital. *The Economist*'s calculations put it at 1.4 for 1932 increasing to 3.5 by 1935; *The Economist*, 18 April 1936, p. 118. In the United States companies during the 1920s had followed a policy of high savings and self-financing. In the mid-1930s they found that taxation policy sought deliberately to curb this trend. During 1936–7

a graduated undistributed profits tax was in effect. In the case of large manufacturing companies the percentage of reported net income retained dropped to 22%, compared with over 40% for selected years in the 1920s. The evidence indicated that the tax had its greatest effect on the income retention policies of highly profitable companies, and that it had little consistent effect on less profitable concerns; see Sergei P. Dobrovolsky, *Corporate Income Retention 1915–43*, New York, 1951, pp. 61–3.

44 By the first quarter of 1936 *The Economist* calculated that the ratio of net profit to capital had recovered to 10%, compared to the low point of 3.2% in the fourth quarter of 1931. The 1929 figure of 11% was not attained, but this time the capital base had been enlarged by bonus and other issues for cash at less than current market prices; *The Economist*, 17 July 1937, pp. 117–18.

45 *The Economist*, 5 January 1938, pp. 103–4.

46 The experience of some of the motor car firms has been examined in detail by G. E. Maxcy and A. Silbertson in *The Motor Industry*, London, 1959. During 1934–8 six large firms ploughed back about 32% of earned for ordinary; they were Austin, Ford, Morris, Rootes, Standard and Vauxhall. Also their retained earnings were slightly more important as a source of funds than the capital market, and if depreciation provisions are added then internal funds were distinctly more important: £19.3m. cf. £7.5m. (pp. 161–2).

47 *The Economist*'s sample was based on big quoted companies which tended to have easier access to outside funds than small business. For these companies the problem of getting outside help could have meant a sharp run down of liquid assets with the depression.

48 The textile industry's problems pre-dated the depression; the miscellaneous group had successfully 'rationalized' before the onset, especially some of the larger companies.

49 Only iron and steel and the retail trade had debit net liquid assets, i.e., an excess of liabilities over assets. Unfortunately *The Economist* did not give detailed figures for the composition of net liquid assets. The United States experience of the depression period as recorded by F. A. Lutz in *Corporate Cash Balances 1914–43*, New York, 1945, indicated that large corporations, with little bank debt, accumulated surplus cash through liquidation of inventories and receivables. (In 1921, they had large bank debts so that no free cash made its appearance.) Smaller companies had less of an increase in free cash because of their large dependence on bank funds.

50 Most of the increase in stocks recorded by the sample was due to one company, Imperial Tobacco. *The Economist* was of the view that financial problems had been reduced by the success of companies in keeping down to moderate levels their stock holdings.

51 Cash holdings fell in the case of 13 of the 20 companies.

5 The Macmillan and other gaps

great difficulty is experienced by the smaller and medium-sized businesses in raising the capital which they may from time to time require, even when the security offered is perfectly sound.

MACMILLAN COMMITTEE, *Report*

Over the past fifty years the contribution of the small firm sector within manufacturing to economic activity has been declining in importance, small firms being those who employ about 200 or less workers and are either incorporated or unincorporated. The available measures indicate the trend quite clearly. While the total number of people employed in manufacturing increased by a half between the early 1920s and the early 1960s, the proportion of the manufacturing workforce employed in small establishments fell from 44% in 1924 to 29% in 1968. Measured in terms of enterprises (a unit controlling one or more establishments) small firm representation declined from 38% in 1935 to 20% in 1963. The contribution of the small firm sector to net output (on an establishment basis) fell from an estimated 42% in 1924 to 25% in 1968, with a particularly sharp fall since the last war; on an enterprise basis the trend is similar, from 35% to 16% respectively. Even more dramatic are the changes in the number of firms. Small establishments in 1924 stood in the region of 160, 000 with an increase in the late 1920s recovery to 164,000, but thereafter the decline has been continuous reaching 82,000 in 1963; on an enterprise basis there was a fall from 136,000 in 1935 to 60,000 in 1963.[1]

The reasons for the decline in the importance of the small firm sector are to be found more in the falling birth rate among companies than in an increasing death rate. Small firms have had to make their appearance in increasingly difficult surroundings, and even the mitigating factors of a commitment to full employment and growth in real income after the war did little to encourage them. The unfavourable factors have been many and will only be briefly mentioned here. Firstly, technological developments and associated increases in plant size works against small units; it is probable that while these elements tipped the balance against the small firm in the inter-war years, they have not been as critical in post-war years. Secondly, many processes require large expenditures on research and development, but this probably has not been a decisive influence since many significant advances have indeed originated from small concerns. Thirdly, transport developments have rendered local markets into national ones exposing small companies to powerful and often overwhelming outside competition. Fourthly, and possibly the most significant factor is that small firms cannot avail themselves of the considerable economies of scale obtainable in marketing. Fifthly, growing state intervention has produced a preference for large units in purchasing and tendering, while over the years there have been periodic preoccupations with policies aimed at encouraging concentration, from the rationalization programmes of the 1930s to the short-lived official bodies of recent years. The growth of public sector activity effectively closed out small companies from several areas of activity, less so in manufacturing than in other industries. Even in the private sector the growing importance of the large firm produced equally trying conditions in that they also prefer to deal in large quantities, and they can attempt to erect barriers to entry, so shutting out small firm competition.[2]

More generally the growing burden of taxation was probably one of the most important factors inhibiting the formation of new firms and the growth of existing ones. High taxation is seen as one of the main obstacles to the accumulation of savings from profits and particularly so as it applies to close companies, that is, a company controlled by five or fewer persons or by its directors. Of the 320,000 active companies within the charge of corporation tax in 1971 some 220,000 or 70%, were close companies. Where the distributions of such companies falls short of the required standard they are liable to an assessment of income tax at the standard on the shortfall, and the shortfall may be apportioned to the participants in the company on which tax would be levied at rising rates. For a trading company the maximum required standard is 60% of the trading income, plus 100% of its investment income. In 1969–70 the amount of income tax and surtax assessed under the shortfall provision was about £4.5m. This maximum requirement can be reduced by so much of the company's income as it 'shows could be distributed without prejudice to the requirements of the company's business' and in arriving at the required standard 'regard shall be had not only to the current requirements of the company's business but also to such other requirements as may be necessary or advisable for the maintenance and development of that business' (Section 290, Income and Corporation Taxes Act, 1970). Devised in the 1920s (see Chapter 3) as a means of preventing private companies from being used as personal tax shelters, the system has probably left private firms short of capital. For very small companies special relief is available if the trading income after corporation tax is less than £5,000 (recently raised to £25,000), such income being ignored in calculating the required standard.[3]

No detailed surveys are available of the financial structure of small firms in the inter-war years, but it was probably along the lines discernible in the post-war period. From a major survey conducted by the Bolton Committee for the year 1968 it appears that small firms obtained a smaller proportion of finance from external sources by borrowing than did the average large firm. Long-term loans and bank overdrafts provided finance for 14% of total assets, compared with 19% for quoted companies. An earlier survey for 1956 provided the same picture, with 8.7% and 12.8% respectively.[4] The general impression is that they have always tended to rely more heavily on internal funds than their larger quoted counterparts. Fast-growing small firms, however, tended to rely more on external borrowing, which is true of all fast-growing concerns, and for small firms bank finance constituted an extremely important channel of funds. Such a dual dependence on internal funds and bank finance prompted the question in the past, and indeed in recent years, whether the long-term capital market was discriminating systematically against small firms. The most celebrated short-coming was identified by the Macmillan Committee in its *Report* in 1931, while other types of 'gaps' have been suggested in recent years.

The Macmillan Gap

It would appear that up until the First World War there was no significant gap in the provision of medium- to long-term funds for small firms. Industry had little difficulty in obtaining outside finance, and did so without making use of the public issue of negotiable securities. In the words of the Macmillan Committee:

> Industry in those days was, so far as each unit was concerned, on a comparatively small scale; its basis was in the main a family basis; ... its capital was provided privately and it was built up and extended out of profits, insofar as it required banking facilities, it found them from the independent banks, ... which in general had their headquarters in

the provinces, and particularly in the Midlands and the North, where the new industries flourished. Moreover, there had existed for many years in this country a large class of investors with means to invest, who exercised an independent judgement as to what to invest in ... Industry therefore ... maintained its independence of any financial control.[5]

In the post-war world, however, several forces were at work, on both the demand and supply side, which rendered this degree of self-support less general. On the demand side technical progress was persistently increasing the optimum size of units, thus creating a pressure for additional funds. On the competitive front small units found that size conferred benefits by way of reduced costs through bulk buying of raw materials.[6] There was, thus, a need for permanent capital to finance technical efficiency and competitive advantage. Also the incidence of direct taxation must have made it more difficult for the smaller firms, and especially new firms, to accumulate capital for purposes of expansion. It was, of course, possible to economize on the use of long-term capital by resorting to short- to medium-term credit on a revolving basis, but increasing centralization in the provision of bank finance placed a penalty on small units, while in the area of mortgage funds from institutions such as insurance companies, firms needed adequate collateral, and the facilities of hire purchase for the financing of productive equipment was only just beginning.[7] Given such limitations on the availability of short- to medium-term funds, long-term finance for small firms grew in importance.

The pressures on the supply side were perhaps even more decisive in making for the formation of the celebrated Macmillan Gap. The incidence of direct taxation probably reduced the flow of funds to industry from private capitalists — the declining ranks of rich savers — while those with surpluses to invest increasingly sought to obtain realizable capital gains in addition to a source of interest income.[8] Others — the growing ranks of small savers — placed their savings with financial institutions. These funds were not entirely lost to the capital market but such institutions preferred at this time marketable assets, and usually fixed interest securities rather than equity holdings. On all these counts there was a discernible preference for quoted as against unquoted securities.

This change in public taste for quoted investments had a considerable influence in creating the Macmillan Gap. In this new environment, small issues, say £50,000 to £150,000, failed to meet the conditions of a free market which investors demanded. From the lenders viewpoint small amounts meant not only higher risks but also higher costs. On the stock market small issues tended to generate little turnover, and the lack of ready negotiability, once the initial flush of premium hunting was over, further reduced investors' interest. Such lack of marketability had to be compensated for by the offer of a substantially higher yield. On top of this was the fact that from the companies standpoint the costs of issue could be fairly prohibitive. It has been estimated that the cost of a small issue by new companies in 1926 was around 13%.[9] These calculations were based on London issues, indeed the whole discussion of the 'Gap' was carried on with only London in mind, and it has been suggested that small issues would be made at lower cost and more readily on provincial markets.[10] In addition to the above general factors the experience of the wartime issue of securities, and particularly the post-war boom, had encouraged a vogue for quoted securities.

Given these trends and that the new issue market had at no time been greatly concerned with small issues, indeed hardly at all with home issues, the difficulties of the small firm in its search for long-term capital were easily detectable.[11] The Macmillan Committee identified the 'Gap' in the following terms, indeed para. 404 has attracted more lasting attention than anything else in the *Report*:

It has been reported to us that great difficulty is experienced by the smaller and medium-sized businesses in raising the capital which they may from time to time require, even when the security offered is perfectly sound. To provide adequate machinery for raising long-dated capital in amounts not sufficiently large for a public issue, i.e. amounts ranging from small sums up to say £200,000 or more, always presents difficulties. The expense of a public issue is too great in proportion to the capital raised, and therefore it is difficult to interest the ordinary investor by the usual method: the Investment Trust Companies do not look with any great favour on small issues which could have no free market and would require close watching; nor can any issuing house tie up its funds in long-dated capital issues of which it cannot dispose. In general, therefore, these smaller capital issues are made through brokers or through some private channel among investors in the locality where the business is situated. This may often be the most satisfactory method. As we do not think that they could be handled as a general rule by a large concern of the character we have outlined above, the only other alternative would be to form a company to devote itself particularly to these smaller industrial and commercial issues. In addition to its ordinary capital, such a company might issue preference share capital or debentures secured on the underlying debentures or shares of the companies which it financed. The risks would in this manner be spread, and the debentures of the financing company should, moreover, have a free market. We see no reason why with proper management, and provided British industry in general is profitable, such a concern should not succeed.[12]

While the Committee had clearly demonstrated the existence of the 'Gap' it did not indicate whether the initiative 'to form a company' should come from the private or public sector. The formation of a powerful agency with official approval was delayed until 1945, but some State assistance did flow through other channels. Meanwhile, the response came largely from numerous city interests and institutions in the form of several investment companies specializing in the provision of finance for small businesses. The three most important institutions were formed in 1934–5; Charterhouse Industrial Development Co. Ltd, and Credit for Industry, both formed in 1934, and in 1935, Leadenhall Securities Incorporation. There were also several other small institutions — loan or nursing agencies — which aimed at providing financial facilities for small firms, e.g., the New Trading Company, Industrial Finance and Investment Corporation, Lonsdale Investment Trust, Northern Territories Trust, Private Enterprises Investment, and the Glasgow Industrial Finance Company.[13] In addition to these specialist institutions some stockbrokers and several merchant bankers went some way to finding methods of selling small issues to institutions and creating markets for them with the general public. These were issues of about £50,000 and they were mostly flotations of the whole or part of the capital of existing companies.[14]

Credit for Industry was set up in June 1934 by United Dominions Trust, which itself had been formed in 1925 with the assistance of the Bank of England. The new company was to meet the capital requirements of small concerns which could not be satisfied by means of instalment financing which was provided by the Trust itself.[15] The Company offered long-term credit — up to 20 years — between the range of £100–£50,000, secured by bonds or mortagages and repaid in equal instalments. The rate of interest 'is said to have been somewhat lower than the yield on preference shares of firms of standing similar to that of the borrower, varying between 4.5 and 7%'.[16] Companies requesting loans had to show a profit record for at least three years and six if possible. It was a lending institution based on security and achievement; it was not one which offered participation on the basis of future prospects. It was flooded with applications, but its stringent criteria did not permit of great expansion, and by July 1939 its loans, less repayments, amounted to £384,909.[17]

The Charterhouse Industrial Development Co. Ltd, a pioneer 'nursing' institution, was also established in June 1934.[18] It was set up by the Charterhouse Investment Trust in conjunction with the Prudential

Insurance Company and two of the main clearing banks. It had an initial capital of £250,000, later increased to £500,000, and its general object was to provide finance for small undertakings in amounts ranging from £10,000 to £100,000. Unlike Credit for Industry it was prepared not only to grant loans, but also to take participations in companies. Its requirements, however, were fairly stringent since it set out to provide finance for the expansion of existing undertakings. It was not its intention to provide finance for speculative or untried ventures.[19] The client company had to show a three-year profit record, good growth prospects, and those running the business had to have money in the business themselves; the emphasis was on a good 'track record' and growth. It preferred participation in the form of preference shares, while occasionally participating in the equity of a company, and its investments were relatively long-term, averaging about seven years. Frequently the shares were 'nursed' along until they were floated off by a specialist subsidiary.[20]

Broadly speaking the present operations of Charterhouse Industrial Development continue the lines laid down at the outset, but there have been several changes of detail. It now seeks investments of not less than £50,000, but the issued amount is generally in the £100,000 to £200,000 range, and occasionally much more. Also it looks for concerns capable of earning pre-tax profits of not less than £50,000 per annum. In order to participate in the future profitability of a client company it normally requires a holding of ordinary shares, usually some 20–30% of the equity. If the subscription to the ordinary shares does not provide all the new money required it will provide the remainder by a medium-term loan or subscribe to redeemable preference shares. The period of the investment is now about three to four years. The intention is still to build up a company with a view to a market flotation, but more often than not most holdings are sold off to a trade buyer.[21]

The third most important institution of the pre-war years was that set up in 1935 by the merchant bank J. Schroeder & Co, namely, Leadenhall Securities Corporation Ltd. It had a capital of £250,000 and was to 'engage in the finance of medium and small home industrial business for which the machinery of the London market is inappropriate'. In terms of operation it had more in common with C.I.D. Co., than with Credit for Industry. It preferred companies with a good business record and with prospects of future expansion. It tended to make its investments in the form of redeemable preference shares along with part of the ordinary shares for periods of from four to five years, after which time the shares were repurchased by the proprietor of the firm.[22]

Even if their example was considerable their combined capital resources was below a million, and the value of business correspondingly small; part of the 'Gap' therefore remained despite these efforts on the part of the private sector.[23] Much of the potential demand for capital from small businesses remained unsatisfied. They were not, of course, without their critics. It was claimed that the emphasis on lending rather than participation restricted the number of suitable clients, but caution in the recovery from the depression was hardly surprising. Further, that they helped existing concerns rather than new undertakings, that is, smoothed the road from a successful start to large-scale success. On the other hand if they had spread their resources too widely a single failure would probably have brought down the entire project. Finally, those companies that did grant participations were 'nursing' agencies so that clients could 'ripen' to a size appropriate for a public issue — they were mere forcing houses for potential market material. In other words, they did not in the main tackle the problem of finding a home for unquoted issues. Certainly, for this purpose their capital was inadequate.

The Industrial and Commercial Finance Corporation Ltd

It was not until July 1945 that 'a company to devote itself particularly to ... smaller industrial and commercial issues' made its appearance following a recommendation to the government in a report of the Steering Committee on Post War Employment in January 1944, and the initial moves were made through the then Governor of the Bank of England, Lord Catto. The precise form of the Corporation was drawn up by a drafting committee composed of the chief general managers of the main clearing banks. The resulting project, however, 'was embraced with some reluctance by the English and Scottish banks', who along with the Bank of England constituted the shareholders.[24] The clearers subscribed in proportion to their resources as gauged by deposits, while the Bank of England held a token subscription. By virtue of their shareholding the banks had full control, but they were careful from the outset not to interfere with the day-to-day management of the Corporation.

Its capital consisted of a share subscription of £15m. from the banks, with powers to borrow up to £30m. from them, and while the reasons for this division are not clear at least it gave the capital structure some gearing and flexibility.[25] It also 'provided a way for the banks to obtain some return from the outset, since the first £30m. of resources was to be called up in slices of £1.5m. on the shares, plus £1.5m. on loan, in that order.' However, this procedure was soon modified so as to increase the return to the banks, and in 1949 payment on the shares stopped at £7.5m. By 31 March 1958 the sum of £7.5m. had been paid up on the shares, while

£25m. had been drawn for loan capital, leaving £12.5m. of uncalled resources.

Experience with this form of capital structure generated criticism on both sides, and also drew comment from the Radcliffe Committee. The banks, following their reluctant fathering, found the undertaking to provide funds burdensome, and the various credit restrictions in the 1950s forced them to curtail their line of credit to the Corporation. From the latter's viewpoint, not only did the 'narrow bed' laid down at the outset prove restrictive, but the practice regarding the cost of funds also proved harmful. Some of the banks viewed part of the loan capital to the Corporation as an advance callable at any time, and in line with their practice after 1952 for other bank advances they charged a variable rate of interest which meant that when bank rate went to high levels the Corporation, whose lending rates were not altogether of their own choosing, found themselves with squeezed margins.[26] Indeed for a time after the introduction of flexible bank rate the Corporation revised some customers' contracts and probably lost a lot of well-earned goodwill as a result.[27]

The Radcliffe Committee commented on the reluctance of the banks and noted that the feeling had grown with the total of Corporation borrowing. At this point, therefore, it was agreed that the banks would pay up the remaining equity and allow the Corporation to seek funds from the open market. Part of the resorces would be used to repay bank loans and the rest to provide new funds. This policy was, of course, in line with the original notion of the Macmillan Committee.

Admittedly such market funds would probably be more expensive, but at least the rate paid would be known, as would their maturity. The first public issue of debentures was made in 1959, £10m. at 5.5%, secured on a floating charge and maturing in 1980–2. Most of this issue was taken up by the institutions. The Corporation has since made several issues of debenture stock in blocks of £10m. to £15m. at varying market rates, with redemptions at the twenty-year range. However, recent high levels of long-term interest rates prompted a series of shorter term borrowings since it was found undesirable to raise money for a term in excess of the average lending period. By 1972 four issues of medium-term unsecured loan stocks had been made, which were quickly oversubscribed, and some of which were continued on a tap basis; by March 1975 the volume of unsecured loan stock was £36m. The opening of a gap between medium- and short-term rates brought another change of policy since the Corporation found it expensive to borrow medium-term in advance of customers requirements. They therefore sought short-term money and intend to fund it later through issues of loan stock. At 31 March 1975 its

short-term borrowing represented 22% of all borrowing, being just over
£35.5m. To cover these short-term borrowings it arranged a standby
facility in the form of a $25m., five-year, Eurodollar credit.[28] Thus at 31
March 1975, the Corporation had £229.2m. of capital in the form of
secured and unsecured loan stocks and other borrowing. Its share capital
stood at £55.0m.[29] In 1973 it became part of the Finance of Industry
Group.

The principal object of the Corporation, as outlined in its Memorandum
of Association, was to 'provide credit by means of loans or the subscription
of loan or share capital or otherwise for industrial and commercial business
or enterprises in Great Britain, particularly in cases where the existing
facilities provided by banking institutions and the Stock Exchanges are
not readily or easily available.'[30] The sums lent were to be over £5,000,
and up to £200,000 — the ceiling being an echo of the Macmillan
Committee recommendation. In the opinion of the drafting committee
small sums could be got from banks, while sums over £200,000 could be
raised from the market. This ceiling was certainly found to be 'hampering'
and in the late 1950s the banks agreed that in exceptional cases assistance
could be extended to £250,000, while the Radcliffe Committee urged that
the ceiling should correspond 'to the lowest practicable amount for a
market issue', which would allow for the decline in the value of money
and institutional trends in the new issue market.[31]

It is the policy of the Corporation to publicize and make available its
facilities as widely as possible and to this end it now has eighteen branch
offices, compared with only five in 1958. Indeed the policy over recent
years has been to decentralize operations and area managers are assisted
by legal and industrial advisers.[32] Loan applications, which usually come
through bankers, accountants, etc. are carefully assessed by experienced
technical staff and funds are made available whenever there are acceptable
standards of competence and the purposes are reasonable. By and large the
Corporation seeks companies with a good profit record and a reassuring
balance sheet, selecting those which can be expected to earn enough
profits to service an investment throughout its life. Generally finance is
required for capital investment in the form of new fixed assets, as working
capital for expansion, and occasionally to fund 'hard core' bank overdrafts,
for capital transfer tax purposes, or financial re-organization.[33]

The Corporation does not insist that funds should be seen to be not
available elsewhere, but according to one commentator 'it frequently
works on that principle'.[34] Inevitably there has been much business that
the Corporation found itself unable to accept due to the nature of the risk
and the security offered. Where possible, however, there is always an
attempt to provide the most suitable form of finance, and often applications

are sliced down. Where needs exceed the funds currently available, and the project is thought suitable, the Corporation lay off a marginal amount of business in a form which will interest an insurance company or other financial institution.[35] In this instance the institutions prefer redeemable securities of a term something under twenty years. When the business is accepted, the Corporation make a charge of about 1% which covers everything except the borrowers legal expenses. Originally, they made no charge at all.[36]

The general growth of business over the post-war years is reflected in the following figures. In 1950 the total of advances outstanding stood at £15.7m., by 1960 it was £38.4m., and in 1975 it amounted to £224.7m., involving 2,331 active customers. In the early 1950s the annual rate of *net* new investment stood at about £3.5m. but towards the second half of the decade the rate declined, due to pressure on the resources of the Corporation. Certainly for most of the 1960s it only ran at something around £4.0m. a year. Over recent years, however, the volume of business has picked up appreciably, running at well over £10.0m. a year, and reaching £21.1m. in 1971. Possibly this was associated with restrictions on the availability of short-term credit following on a persistent credit squeeze and the accompanying need to resort to funding. Since then annual net new investment has declined somewhat partly due to the willingness of the clearing banks to make longer loans than previously.

The methods by which the lending was done is given for various years in table 5.1. Several features merit comment. The emphasis upon secured lending against debentures and other security has increased during the 1960s, but it should be noted that some of the fixed interest loans carry conversion options. The loans are redeemable, generally by annual instalments, which maintains a flow of funds; repayments and realizations averaged some £13.0m. over 1969–71, and £25m. during 1972–5. By contrast unsecured lending has declined in relative importance. A similar trend is evident with redeemable preference shares which are redeemable only on maturity and carry dates varying from 15 to 30 years. The introduction of corporation tax made them expensive for borrowers and after 1965 they became less popular. The fluctuations in the volume of non-redeemable preference shares arises because it is well adapted for capital reorganization of private companies. The other important feature is the growth in the volume of equity shares held, rising from 10% in 1960 to 24% of the Corporation's portfolio in 1975. However, on occasions in the late 1960s the volume did not rise as fast as was hoped because of the preference of customers for options rather than direct subscription for ordinary shares.[37] Indeed, critics have long advocated an increase in the Corporation's equity holding claiming that it would, amongst other

Table 5.1 Financial facilities analysed by method; amounts outstanding 31 March (£m.)*

Financial Facility	1953	%	1960	%	1965	%	1972	%	1975	%
Debentures & secured loans	10.8	41.1	16.0	41.7	33.2	50.0	84.5	49.6	106.5	47.3
Unsecured loans	5.7	21.7	6.9	17.9	5.7	8.6	10.3	6.0	12.8	6.0
Redeemable preference shares	4.9	18.6	7.7	20.0	10.0	15.1	9.3	5.5	8.8	3.9
Non-redeemable preference shares	2.9	11.0	3.7	9.6	5.0	7.6	3.1	1.8	2.4	1.0
Preferred ordinary shares	—	—	—	—	—	—	8.5	5.0	12.4	5.5
Ordinary shares	2.0	7.6	4.1	10.7	11.5	17.4	37.7	22.2	54.1	24.0
Property, plant & equipment	—	—	—	—	0.9	1.3	16.9	9.9	27.7	12.3
Total	26.3	100.0	38.4	100.0	66.3	100.0	170.3	100.0	224.7	100.0

*Figures exclude shipping finance facilities and leasing.

Source: I.C.F.C., Annual Reports. Separate figures are not available for I.C.F.C. after 1975.

things, bring larger capital gains enabling it to widen its lending activities. Of the total investment holding at March 1975, £26.2m. (at cost) were quoted securities, but presumably some of these, although quoted on London and regional exchanges, would seldom have a real market. The net book value of the unquoted investments amounted to £140.6m. of which £25.6m. was unquoted equity securities.[38].

Table 5.2 Financial facilities outstanding analysed by amounts, 31 March: Percentages*

Amount	Customers				Aggregate amounts			
	1953	1964	1972	1977	1953	1964	1972	1977
Up to 20,000	39.0	33.2	40.8	35.2	8.4	6.1	5.8	3.5
20,001–50,000	26.6	29.9	26.0	26.4	16.9	16.3	12.0	9.5
50,001–100,000	15.6	17.4	15.9	16.2	22.0	20.6	15.9	12.1
100,000 & over	18.8	19.5	17.3	22.2	52.7	57.0	66.3	74.9
Total no. of customers	64	952	2.294	2201	£4.1m.	£57.5m.	£170.4m.	£211.9m.

*Small sums include the remaining balances of some large loans.

Source: I.C.F.C. Annual Reports.

Also of interest are the trends in lending analysed by amounts. Table 5.2 gives such an analysis for various years. It appears that despite the fact that small loans of around £5,000 do not pay, the Corporation has continued to do as much as it can which is a useful contribution to the 'venture' capital gap. In 1977 over 35% of customers had loans outstanding of less than £20,000, compared with 41% in 1972, an expected trend given the level of price increase over the period.

While it may not do enough in this area, which is regarded by many to be a critical stage in the growth of firms, the amount lent is at least encouraging. By contrast most institutions believe that profitable business cannot be done at this level, where total net assets are below £100,000 or turnover is less than £150,000.[39] It is apparent from table 5.2 that nearly two-thirds of customers had loans of less than £50,000, while loans in excess of £200,000 went to relatively few customers. Indeed the average size of first advances has remained constant over recent years at about £44,000, which implies a fall in real terms.[40] The typical customer would seem to have net assets below the £250,000 range, only about 10% of the Corporations customers have net assets in excess of £500,000. Loans over the old Macmillan limit of £200,000 numbered 228 in 1977 which, although small, as a percentage of customers absorbed 57.3% of the aggregate amount outstanding.

The rates charged by the Corporation are not those which the 'market will bear', but even so many firms who previously relied on bank overdrafts find the rate levels something of a shock. The general policy has been not to charge high rates, and they are very much regulated by the rates charged by other institutions especially insurance companies; 'they are really the pacemakers in all these rates on loans, particularly on property and things like that. We stick rather close to them.'[41] A fixed rate is usually charged for the entire period of the loan on the sum outstanding. A further feature is that the interest rates charged have been concentrated within a relatively narrow range, and the smaller loans may well cost the Corporation more than the interest received on them. Such small loans tend to incur higher costs per unit of funds because of the costs of investigation, policing and collecting of both principal and interest.

At various times the Corporation has laboured under certain difficulties which served to hinder the growth of business. Until it was given powers to raise capital on the open market it found itself operating with restricted means, and its operations further complicated by periodic embarrassments arising from credit squeezes which limited bank accommodation. For example, in 1955 for some months it could do no lending, and in 1957 it was particularly short of funds when small and medium-sized companies were also suffering from an acute shortage. It has also had to cope with two other difficult problems. Whether due to lack of publicity or other factors there is an alleged reluctance on the part of businessmen to go to I.C.F.C. — it was said to the Radcliffe Committee that a businessman would only go there if the 'bank manager took him by the hand and led him there'. Secondly, those with knowledge of the institution amongst the ranks of small and medium-sized firms are very reluctant to raise additional share capital since this would dilute control. Given such reluctance it has proved difficult to increase the flow of risk capital through this particular channel. In 1959 Lord Piercy reported that there was 'the greatest possible repugnance' by such concerns towards parting with any of their equity, 'even though there are some propositions which the Corporation would finance on a partnership basis, but which are not suitable for loans'.[42] Indeed, some companies were prepared to pay high rates on preference capital since they were not inclined to part with any equity or give options on equity. However, a recent survey has reported that this traditional resistance is declining. With the prevailing level of inflation and taxation a firm wanting to obtain finance for expansion is left with little alternative but to giving an equity stake. Increased equity holdings by the Corporation could provide opportunities for a greater flow of funds through realizations, which might permit it to become a little more venturesome in its policies.[43]

This particular policy has in fact been pursued over recent years since with high interest rates the Corporation found that the margin between borrowing and lending rates narrowed to an uncomfortable extent, which led it to look increasingly for increased profits to a modest participation in the customers equity directly or by way of option.[44] It should be noted, however, that the scope for obtaining a regular and large flow of funds from realizations is hindered by the size of the investment in individual companies, by undertakings given in certain cases as to the disposal of shares, and by market conditions.

The main criticism laid against the results achieved by the Corporation is that it could have done more. It has been argued that there has not been a sufficient tendency to concentrate assistance in the lower range, which is claimed to be the critical point in a firm's growth. Although I.C.F.C. and other financial institutions have lent to some firms there are still many more whose growth has been impeded due to lack of access to long-term capital and that this has led them to rely heavily on internal funds, and occasionally on less desirable and more costly short-term sources.[45] The charge that only a few hundred or so loans a year are made when there are some 50,000 small firms (10–500 employees) is an appealing statistic, but as to what proportion of these actively seek long-term funds it is not possible to say. They all cannot need outside long-term funds, and the percentage of those who do must fluctuate with several factors, e.g., profits, interest rates, alternative sources of funds, etc. No doubt many firms remain unsatisfied, so that the gap cannot be entirely filled.

The criticism has also been made that only the best risks obtain funds, which is in conformity with the Macmillan Committee assessment that there was difficulty 'even when the security offered is perfectly sound'. It has been suggested that the 'Gap' is wider than such a narrow interpretation would indicate and the problem is that many firms cannot offer normal security or a satisfactory balance sheet and profit record.[46]

Some other 'Gaps'

In terms of the long-term gap as defined by the Macmillan Committee two problem areas remain. Firstly, the matter of unquoted securities. There are a large number of companies whose securities though perfectly sound are not suitable for the general investor, and which are not eagerly sought after by the investing institutions. It has been suggested that an improved market for these secondary securities would aid the raising of capital by companies in the Macmillan size category, and at a lower cost than hitherto. The other problem is the small sum of money wanted for a business with prospects but with no record and little security — the so-called 'venture capital' problem. Both these areas of need have over recent years been accorded some official and unofficial attention.

Unquoted securities

An alternative to seeking a quotation for a relatively small issue, say under £250,000, is to obtain through private negotiation a placing of shares with private persons or financial institutions. To this end certain professional services such as solicitors and accountants put clients in contact with good, small firms, while 'there is an important though small scale activity by certain issuing houses and stockbrokers who will make private placings of unquoted shares'.[47] The volume of long-term finance provided in this manner is, however, quite small. There are few individuals able to invest substantial sums, and it has to be of some size to be worthwhile from the company's viewpoint, while those who have such means often find it difficult to find a promising small company. In the case of financial institutions the proportion of their total investment passing into the equity of small companies is very low.

Most financial institutions impose minimum size requirements, which are often related to the size of pre-tax profits, and they must be confident as to good growth prospects. Since there is no ready market in unquoted securities there is the distinct possibility that capital may be tied up for some considerable time. As a result such investments could not be compensated for by a fixed charge only, and most firms would probably find it difficult to pay an additional premium. Institutional investors therefore require an equity interest so that the finance is normally provided by a mixture of equity and convertible loan stock. While this avenue does offer a company an addition to its long-term capital it may involve parting with some equity, and reluctance to do this may render it a last resort method. There are indications, however, that the hostility of firms towards outside equity participation is on the wane.

Faced with continuously rising costs institutions are placing increasing emphasis on short-term holdings so that added importance attaches to the prospects of going public within a reasonable period, say, 3–5 years. The current cost of capital has made it difficult to lend for long-term at around 12% so that to make the operation profitable regular realization of equity for capital gain is desirable, that is, rapid turnover of the portfolio. The alternative is to seek higher returns of 18–20%, which even firms with outstanding growth prospects might be hesitant to commit themselves to. Increasingly the emphasis is on eventual marketability which means that the difficulty of placing unquoted stocks for long periods with institutions remains for all but the very fastest growers in the small company range. The small personal saver cannot offer much to fill the gap. He prefers a minimum of risk and illiquidity, and although he might indulge in a speculative flutter he would prefer to do so for the prospect of very large gains.[48]

Such difficulties arise for the financial institutions, and indeed for private investors, from the very nature of the small firm sector. Selection is difficult, while there are no regular and reliable market reports of the kind associated with quoted companies, and the shares acquired cannot be thrown onto the market if any doubts arise. In the case of investment trusts it appears that they are not greatly interested in unquoted shares, partly because of the management problems that arise, but also because they do not need to diversify their portfolio in that direction. While insurance companies do give assistance to small firms, few offices feel suitably equipped to deal satisfactorily with the provision of finance; 'the absence of a market for shares and debentures of the companies is less an obstacle for a life office than the difficulty of vetting propositions and maintaining a close watch on future performance.'[49]

Equity capital is also sought for reasons other than to provide working or permanent capital. One such purpose is to provide for the payment of death duties (capital transfer tax since 1974), and to obtain such funds without resorting to a public issue or the breaking up of a firm. The best-known institution which takes on equity to provide cash is the Estate Duty Investment Trust (EDITH), set up by I.C.F.C. in 1952 because it found itself doing such business. Indeed it continues to provide some facilities of this kind for companies below the EDITH preferred size. The problem for a small company arises from the difficulty in selling some of its shares, or at least selling them at a fair price, into safe hands; it is virtually impossible to do this where there is some urgency. Also some shareholders will be anxious that control should not pass from them. Prior to the availability of such institutional channels as EDITH, companies sometimes attempted to raise money by making bonus issues of securities of a fixed interest type, which was not entirely satisfactory since it used up borrowing power and created charges which might later prove onerous.

The business of EDITH consists of 'holding minority interests in private companies, affording a safe home for securities of this sort, and a reasonably profitable investment'.[50] The bulk of its share capital is held by investment trusts and insurance companies. The practice is either to buy equity outright from some or all of the shareholders in a company, or purchase some or all of a bonus issue of preference or preferred/ordinary shares made to the ordinary shareholders.[51] These securities may be held by EDITH for long periods, or occasionally they may be placed, particularly so the fixed interest type, among its shareholders and other institutions. However, EDITH is not normally prepared to invest less than £20,000 in any company, and will not hold more than a minority interest, which rules out access to it by very small companies with say pre-tax profits of less than £15,000 per annum.[52] In 1958 its portfolio plus outstanding commitments amounted to £2.4m.; at the end of March 1976 its investments totalled £13.7m., of which £12.9m. were unquoted securities. These were mainly in the form of closed issues of convertible preferred ordinary shares with preferential rights both as to capital and dividend.

Other institutional investors have also entered this sort of business. Many merchant banks and investment trusts have some estate duty investments, while insurance companies sometimes provide funds by accepting a long-term mortgage on land and buildings. More specifically, in 1953 an issuing house set up Safeguard Industrial Investments Ltd, a quoted company with a capital of £1.0m., and which holds both quoted and unquoted investments. Also established in 1953 by merchant banking interests was Private Enterprises Investment Company. It is reported that they rarely participate in sums of less than £20,000 and confine themselves to businesses which are expected to become viable within a relatively short space of time.[53]

It has been suggested that some of the difficulties which small firms experience with unquoted shares might be eased if there was a secondary market in them. This is likely to prove a difficult exercise since the market for many of the smaller quoted issues is very narrow, while that for unquoted securities is narrower still. However, if such an organized market could be developed it would then be both easier and cheaper for small firms to raise long-term capital.

The existing channel is very much a rudimentary placing market between issuers and institutions and a few rich individuals. There is a small trade between institutions in unquoted shares but their scale of operations in these shares seems unlikely to grow to provide a good supporting base for a viable secondary market. From the standpoint of the institutions these shares have high risks, information is not always easy to obtain, there is the problem of the size of their holding relative to the total of stock outstanding, and finally there are the cost and expertise aspects of managing a portfolio of small holdings.[54] Further problems arise with syndicated investments, while the creation of a market might well infringe the partnership notion which is an important aspect of the relationship between small companies and the financial institutions with investments in them.

The firms that handle issues of such shares recognize an obligation to make a market in their own particular issues. Thus, an intending seller can go back to the issuer who will either find another buyer or take in the security himself and then rely on his contacts to dispose of it. In the absence of such a facility sellers can wait for a buyer to come along, but the delay could well be long and the price fluctuation forbidding, and there remains the problem of valuation on an illiquid market. It had been suggested that the present informal contacts could be systematized through the circulation of lists, which might bring marginal relief. Previous experience with such lists would indicate that they would quickly degenerate into carrying the 'dregs'. The position could perhaps be eased by dealer participation but this would involve costs which probably would not be covered by turnover. Apart from handling costs (which vary little with the size of bargains) there would be the costs of shopping around, of carrying illiquid securities, and in addition, the overheads of expertise. Unfortunately, such costs bear more heavily on small firms' securities than on large, and there would soon come a point, with the existing levels of commissions and mark up, where it would not pay to make a market.[55] The American Over-the Counter market has been cited as an example to emulate, but the companies dealt on it are much larger and numerous than those contemplated here, the commission levels are relatively higher, and marketability for many issues is very low.[56] Dealers anticipating taking a position would need high mark-ups and they would understandably mark prices up or down sharply if they were long or short of stock. If the small company share market already had sufficient turnover dealers might be persuaded to run a book; if dealers attempt to run a book as it stands it is doubtful if turnover would be greatly encouraged.

The most reasonable hope is that an increase in general demand for large company securities will benefit smaller ones, since as yields fall investors might be tempted to widen their interest into the secondary range of investments and down the size scale. Given this more realistic possibility dealers might be inclined to carry lines in small company securities along with their more profitable activities in popular equities.

Venture capital

When the Radcliffe Committee looked at the financing of small businesses it was of the opinion that 'with certain modifications ... the existing institutions can look after the ordinary requirements of small businesses for capital'.[57] However, it did feel that the finance of innovations for small companies presented a special problem. The development of a new technique or a new line of business means an increase in the scale of operations, or in the risk of loss, that may make it necessary to obtain outside capital. It is, therefore, important that small firms, particularly those engaged in exploiting new technical knowledge, should have access to such funds. In terms of the provision of such venture capital the Radcliffe Committee identified two problems; firstly, that the needs of such companies may be large in relation to their existing capital structure and earning prospects, larger in fact than most institutions would accept, and secondly, the increased risks attached to the commercial exploitation of technical innovation. To assist in closing this venture capital gap the Committee recommended the setting up of a corporation to guarantee any loans made by an existing financial institution to borrowers wanting finance for 'novel processes or the manufacture of new types of product', but such guarantees should be limited to a proportion of the loan to ensure that institutions behaved cautiously.[58]

The other stimulus to the U.K. venture capital movement, which got under way in the early 1960s, came from the experience of the United States, where there are several experienced companies in this sort of activity. However it is certainly a field for experts. One United States company which has twenty years experience in venture capital backed an equal number of winners and losers, but since the gains proved very large and because they got out of losing situations, the gains outweighed the losses. Even for the experts it is not possible to combine high returns with safe investments.[59]

The number of institutions in the venture capital field in this country is small, though many of the major financial institutions are associated with such finance in some way or other.[60] There are only two institutions of major relevance, the National Research Development Corporation, and Technical Development Capital Ltd, and these account for a large part of institutional venture capital finance. The remaining sources are subsidiaries of various financial institutions, frequently taking the form of joint undertakings.

The National Research Development Corporation (N.R.D.C.) was founded in 1948 and is a government-backed organization which largely concentrates on financing the research and development efforts of small companies. Technical Development Capital (T.D.C.) was set up in 1962 in response to the 'Radcliffe Gap' and was primarily aimed as a complement to the facilities provided by N.R.D.C. in that preference would be given to products which had passed the prototype or development stage and required finance for production and marketing. When established it had an issued capital of £2.0m. subscribed by I.C.F.C. and numerous insurance companies and other financial institutions. However, in its first years of operation it received a large number of applications from almost every branch of technology and in the interests of economy and of providing stronger backing it was fully integrated with I.C.F.C.[61]

Private venture capital companies, several of which have appeared since the early 1960s, provide finance mainly for production and marketing. They are mostly subsidiaries, some jointly owned, set up by merchant banks, investment trusts, holding companies and insurance companies. There is also one clearing bank subsidiary in the business. Merchant banks had always done some lending in this field, but hiving off the business to specialist subsidiaries was felt to create conditions conducive to faster development. Further avenues are provided by some merchant banks who are prepared to arrange facilities from institutional and private investors 'where finance is needed to exploit an outstanding new technological development'.[62]

The most suitable method of providing finance is an equity subscription to a company combined with a long-term loan, with the proportion of one to the other depending on the assessment of the risks involved. From the standpoint of the venture capitalist it is important, since few investments turn out to be winners, that a reasonable share of the equity is acquired to provide an element of appreciation. Borrowing companies obviously want to minimize their release of equity, but they also want funds and a minimum fixed interest burden.[63] Both N.R.D.C and T.D.C. have equity elements in their investments, but usually a minority interest. In the case of the latter institution it is usually less than 30% of a company's equity.

Such an equity stake may take several forms, such as a subscription to new ordinary shares, a purchase of existing ordinary shares, or the acquisition of some form of convertible preference share. Where a fixed loan is used this is repayable, in the case of T.D.C. over a given period according to the projected budget, and the loan is made at I.C.F.C. rates of interest. They are usually secured by a fixed or a floating charge. In the case of N.R.D.C. the funds may be recovered by a levy on sales, a not altogether satisfactory method since it can reduce the cash flow at a tender stage in the company's growth.

Both the institutions provide finance for periods of over seven years thus permitting the development and manufacture of new products. By contrast the venture capital companies are seldom interested in new products. Rather they seek companies with fast growth prospects and their time scale of five to six years to the realization of their usual equity stake rules out such nursery activity. Venture companies also tend to go for investments in the £40,000–£130,000 range, although they occasionally go below £20,000. On the other hand, over half the investments of T.D.C. involve sums of less than £30,000, and the bulk of the remainder are under £50,000. The aggregate amount of funds lent is however comparatively modest and dominated by the N.R.D.C. and T.D.C. In the year ending March 1972 T.D.C. had investments of just over £2.0m., while at December 1969 N.R.D.C. had investments of £3.6m. It was estimated in 1971 that the private venture institutions made available less than £1.0m. a year.[64]

The general outlook for the provision of venture capital is that it will continue to be available in comparatively small amounts and the standards set will continue to be high. At least in the experience of T.D.C. the casualty rate had fallen well below expectation. Even so on the supply side the high costs and risks attached to such investments, which seem inescapable for small firms, will continue to make institutions apply high standards of credit worthiness.[65] On the demand side it is likely that small firms will not part easily with equity, or readily pay high, fixed interest charges. The latter reluctance in particular is partly due to the legacy of having access to cheap and easy overdraft facilities, which rather than being used as working capital has frequently been used for medium- to long-term financing. There is therefore an understandable reluctance to pay a realistic rate for long-term funds from the market. The prospects were well summarized by the Bolton Committee: 'We cannot anticipate any significant improvement in the provision of equity capital for small business; it will remain available only to the most promising and successful.'[66]

Other sources of long-term capital

Mortgages

Long-term finance may be provided in this instance by a mortgage loan where the lender has a fixed charge on specific assets, land or buildings, of the borrower. It involves regular interest payments, and the loan may be repaid over a specified period by direct repayments or by an endowment policy maturing at the end of the period. The lender will attempt to ensure that the resale value of the assets will always be at least equal to the balance owing to him. As a result loans tend to vary between 50–70% of valuations, while the proportion also varies with the age of the property and the specialization of its use. The lender will also be interested in the evidence as to the future earning capacity of a firm, whether it will be sufficient to justify a loan and adequate to service it. It is not necessary for the borrower to have good prospects of going public.

The periods for which loans are made tends to vary, but often they are as long as 20–25 years. As to their size most companies have a normal lower limit in the range of £25,000–£50,000 although some may go below this for policy holders. In fixing the rate of interest the main influence is the prevailing rate on first class debentures, and the present rate on mortgages is between 10.5–11.5%. Generally the rate is fixed for the period of the loan, although some companies have experimented with variable rates.[67]

The volume of funds provided for small firms through this particular channel is, however, relatively small. In 1971 it was estimated that only some 1% of mortgages held by insurance companies involved small firms, 'and the total flow from this source must be well under £5.0m. a year'. As for pension funds it has been estimated that they contributed around £2.0m. per annum.[68] The size of the flow of funds from this source is unlikely to change greatly in the future for the following reasons. On the demand side few companies have sufficient assets of the kind suitable as security against which to borrow, and anyway many such assets would be highly specialized and probably unsuitable as a result. Further, there are legal, accounting and survey charges payable by the borrower and while these items obviously vary with the size of the loan, they do not do so proportionately so that they bear heaviest on the smaller transactions.[69] On the supply side insurance companies set fairly high standards as to security and quality of trading results, and few firms are able to meet them. Perhaps of greater point is the fact that investigation costs for the lender are high, which induces them to set a high minimum level on transactions. Also, the recurrent costs of lending tends to be large if the progress of borrowers is to be continually surveyed, and many institutions are reluctant to incur such costs. In any case they often feel that they lack the necessary expertise for this type of work. Indeed it is often stated that insurance companies do not seek to publicize the facilities they can offer small firms; only those with specialist departments seek out mortgages.[70]

As noted above the flow of funds is small and a high proportion of applicants are refused, but this should not be taken to mean that the facilities are entirely inadequate. It may merely be a reflection of the fact that with the attendant risks and costs, small loans at normal rates may not be justified. Two avenues may, however, be available so as to widen the availability of the facility. In 1970 one insurance company set up a mortgage scheme for loans as small as £5,000 for short periods (5–15 years), and if necessary repayable by monthly instalments, while a lower class of property was accepted as security.[71] It is also possible that with the rate of increase in property and land values that the customary valuations are unduly conservative and a relaxation in this area might help to widen the range of eligible borrowers.

Leaseback

In many ways this method is similar to the above since it involves raising capital on the security of property. A company sells its factory or similar industrial property to an insurance or property company and it is then leased back at an annual rental. In exchange the seller has a capital sum available for investment. This facility, however, is only provided by institutions who normally include property among their investments. The length of leases varies greatly, ranging from the usual 21 years to those of 42 or even 99 years. There tends to be a lower limit in the region of £25,000–£50,000 for sums negotiated. Generally the method is regarded as a form of equity investment and therefore in fixing rents companies look at future growth prospects, yields on alternative investments, etc. Consequently rates expressed as a current running yield are subject to bigger fluctuations than interest rates on mortgages. In 1970/1 interest charges (expressed as a ratio of rental to purchase price) of 10–11% were recorded, but the true cost is difficult to ascertain because of the practice of inserting clauses allowing rental reviews as a protection against inflation.[72]

For a small firm with suitable assets this is a ready method of obtaining long-term capital. But such firms are only a very small minority in the small firm sector since it is essential for the property to be attractive in itself as a long-term investment for the lending instituition. Therefore, the facility is of limited availability and is probably more suitable in the distributive trade than any other. For the lender the primary test is whether the property is of the kind which would be held if the seller could not continue with the lease.

The facilities described above have to a considerable extent filled the various gaps in the provision of long-term funds for small firms so that they can proceed with their growth. Some disquiet remains, however, but this stems from the imposition of periodic credit squeezes which impinge more severely on small than large firms, and from the nature of the borrower rather than from any conspicuous gap in the supply of finance.[73] For example, small firms tend to pay higher interest rates than large borrowers because of greater risks and administrative costs; some institutional facilities are available to large firms which are not so readily available to small ones — indeed they may be ignorant of their existence or prefer not to use them. Such disabilities may well constrict the supply of funds available, but since they do not stem from imperfections in the market for financial facilities it is doubtful if any further special provision should be adopted by way of institutional arrangements or by some form of subsidy on interest rates to lower the cost of funds; the former might well distort the flow of funds between institutions, the latter distort the flow among alternative industrial uses.

Notes

1 Committee of Inquiry on Small Firms, *Report*, Cmnd 4811, pp. 55–60 (Bolton Committee, 1971).

2 ibid., pp. 75–81.

3 ibid., pp. 203–4.

4 J. Bates, *The Financing of Small Business*, London, 1971, 2nd ed., p. 18.

5 Committee on Finance and Industry, *Report*, Cmd 3897, para. 377 (Macmillan Committee, 1931).

6 T. Balogh, *Financial Organisation*, Cambridge, 1950, p. 275.

7 It was estimated that some £10m. was outstanding in 1939 for finance of productive equipment; R. F. Henderson, *The New Issue Market and the Finance of Industry*, Cambridge, 1951, p. 63.

8 The incidence of estate duty tended to encourage the formation of trusts, with the accompanying legal and cautious behaviour of trustees; R. Frost, 'The Macmillan Gap, 1931–1953', *Oxford Economic Papers*, June 1954, p. 196.

9 This is the average cost of 14 preference issues, with an average size of issue of £214,000; on this basis an issue of less than

£100,000 would probably cost over 20%; Henderson, op. cit., p. 141. For further details of issue costs see Chapter 2.

10 See Henderson, op. cit., pp. 83–5; W. A. Thomas, *Provincial Stock Exchanges*, London, 1973, pp. 261–2.

11 The position of the City was clearly put by Lord Kindersley in reply to a question from J. M. Keynes during the Macmillan enquiry; *J. M. Keynes*; 'take an English industrial concern of good credit but of small size which wants to raise, say, £50,000 on debentures, any larger sum being out of proportion to its scale. Is there any regular machinery through which its requirements can be satisfied?'

Lord Kindersley; 'Well, I am bound to say I do not know of any myself. I think it is a great weakness in the City of London that there is not such machinery. It is very difficult to place small issues. If people come to us with small issues and they are perfectly good we cannot do anything with them largely because the average investor today does not like to have anything without a market, and you cannot possibly have a market with £50,000 of stock or £100,000 for that matter; there is bound to be no market in stock and it is very difficult of negotiation in consequence'; Macmillan Committee, *Minutes of Evidence*, Q. 1526.

12 Macmillan Committee, *Report*, para. 404. The Committee also urged the setting up of a strong institution to engage in industrial financing to perform very much the range of services now offered by the large merchant banks. In addition it looked at the provision of short- and medium-term, and intermediate, credit, but concluded that adequate provision was available; para. 392–3.

13 For further details on these companies see A.T.K. Grant, *The Capital Market in Britain from 1919–1936*, 2nd ed, London, 1967, pp. 217–19; N. A. D. Macrae, *The London Capital Market*, London 1957, pp. 121–2.

14 Lord Piercy, 'The Macmillan Gap and the Shortage of Risk Capital', *Journal of The Royal Statistical Society*, 1955, p. 2. Lord Piercy stated in evidence to the Radcliffe Committee that in the 1930s 'one or two people thought they had discovered a new line in floating small issues, and a lot of it was done'. These small issues were attractive mainly to the private investor, 'they had to be very attractive for an institution to take an interest'; Committee on the Working of the Monetary System, *Minutes of Evidence*, Q. 12646 (Radcliffe Committee, 1960).

15 Grant, op. cit., p 215.

16 Balogh, op. cit., p. 301.

17 ibid., p. 302.

18 Sir Nutcombe Hume stated in his evidence to the Radcliffe Committee that the practical experience of turning away small applications for capital, and the recommendations of the Macmillan Report 'stimulated me and my colleagues into forming a company, a greenhouse in which the more tender plants were allowed to grow under our supervision until they were big and sturdy enough to face a public issue'; Radcliffe Committee, *Minutes of Evidence*, Q. 12753.

19 In a memorandum to the Radcliffe Committee Sir Nutcombe Hume noted that thousands of proposals were rejected as uncreditworthy; Radcliffe Committee, *Memoranda of Evidence*, vol. 3, p. 129.

20 Balogh, op. cit., p. 302; Grant, op. cit., p. 216; Macrae, op. cit., p. 121.

21 In 1959 it was reported that C.I.D. had some 90 investments, but this figure probably included some quoted stocks; at present it holds about 40 investments.

22 Grant, op. cit., pp. 216–17; see also *The Economist*, July 1935, p. 80. It had a London and a Birmingham office.

23 Some assistance was also rendered to small firms through various forms of state aid, e.g., financial facilities by the Trade Facilities Acts which guaranteed the interest and/or principal of loans raised by industry, but this scheme was not considered a success. Further assistance flowed from the Special Areas (Development and Improvement) Act of 1935, which later led to the setting up of a Special Areas Fund; Balogh, op. cit., pp. 303, 305–6.

24 Radcliffe Committee, *Memoranda of Evidence*, vol. 3, memorandum submitted by Lord Piercy, p. 195.

25 The Corporation was not permitted at the time to borrow elsewhere, or accept deposits.

26 I.C.F.C., Annual Report 1953.

27 Brian Rew, 'I.C.F.C. Revisited', *Economica*, 1955, pp. 232–3.

28 See I.C.F.C., Annual Reports, 1971, 1972, 1975.

29 In 1965/6 the banks agreed to convert the outstanding loans to share capital so that the Corporation could go to the market unencumbered by outstanding bank borrowing. With other adjustments the share capital was rounded up to £40.0m.; Annual Report, 1965–6.

30 Lord Piercy, Memorandum, op. cit., p. 199.

31 Radcliffe Committee, *Report*, para. 946 (1959). Lord Piercy stated in evidence to the Committee that it was very seldom that I.C.F.C. wanted to go above £300,000.

32 In the 1950s regional experience varied greatly. In Birmingham 'we take peoples fancy — we find it very difficult in Manchester'; Lord Piercy's evidence to Radcliffe Committee, op, cit., Q.12666. More recent experience is as follows:

The number of financings and the amount of funds provided were the biggest at the London Branch, followed by Leeds, Glasgow was third in number of financings but Leicester was third in amount of funds. There is a considerable variation also among the branches with respect to the comparative significance of their first financings and their further financings; some branches appear to have a concentration of one and some the other. (R. C. Osborn, *Financing Small and Medium Sized Businesses*, I. C. F. C., London, 1972, p. 5).

33 C. Allen, *Small Firm Survey 1970*, London, 1970, I.C.F.C., p. 7.

34 J. Bates, 'The Macmillan Gap in Britain and Canada', *Bankers' Magazine*, 1962, p. 204.

35 Lord Piercy's evidence to the Radcliffe Committee, op. cit., Qs.12682, 12692. The process of laying off larger propositions is not looked upon too favourably by some of the shareholders.

36 ibid., Q.12716. Unless a loan is offered no charge is made and expenses incurred must be recouped out of general revenue.

37 I.C.F.C., Annual Report, 1967.

38 I.C.F.C., Annual Report, 1975.

39 See Bolton Committee, *Report*, para. 12. 59. The policy of the small business investment companies in the United States is to place fewer and larger loans with the larger 'small' enterprises.

40 ibid., para. 12.36. For small businesses receiving their first assistance from I.C.F.C. the contribution was particularly important since it added, on the average, two-thirds or more of the total capital they employed. This is a very high level of assistance compared to United States practices; see R. C. Osborn, op. cit., p. 34.

41 Lord Piercy's evidence to the Radcliffe Committee, op. cit., Q.12701.

42 Lord Piercy, Memorandum, op. cit., p. 196. I.C.F.C. has never tried to obtain voting control of companies, although it may well appoint a director to the board.

43 The vogue for take over bids has helped this particular flow and in 1966–7 a subsidiary was set up to promote mergers. It found that potential buyers far outnumbered potential sellers by some 4:1.

44 I.C.F.C., Annual Report, 1971.

45 See. J. Bates, 'The Macmillan Gap in Britain and Canada', op. cit., p. 207.

46 ibid., p. 208.

47 Bolton Committee, *Report*, para. 12.52.

48 For the difficulties of attracting small savings see Bolton Committee, Research Report No. 4, *Financial Facilities for Small Firms*, pp. 63–4.

49 Memorandum of British Insurance Association to the Radcliffe Committee, Memorandum, vol. 2. p. 39.

50 Lord Piercy, Memorandum, op. cit., p. 197.

51 Brian Tew, 'Edith', *The Three Banks Review*, June 1955.

52 Bolton Committee, *Report*, para. 12. 62.

53 See Brian Tew, 'Edith', op. cit., pp. 27–8; J. Bates, *The Financing of Small Business*, p. 107.; Macrae, op. cit., pp. 126–7.

54 For a detailed discussion of these problems see *Financial Facilities for Small Firms*, p. 62.

55 ibid., pp. 62–3.

56 Bolton Committee, *Report*, para. 12.72.

57 Radcliffe Committee, *Report*, para. 940. Here the term venture capital is taken to mean finance for the development of new products, or for the commercial exploitation of a new process — in professional parlance, 'a start-up situation'.

58 ibid., para. 949–50.

59 Bolton Committee, *Report*, para. 12.65.

60 In the early 1960s the City turned its attention to the unquoted sector, especially to highly technological firms with few managerial overheads and high growth rates.

61 I.C.F.C., Annual Report, 1967.

62 P. R. M. Holborn and E. C. N. Edwards, 'The U.K. Venture Capital Market', *Banker*, May 1971, pp. 488–90.

63 Neither N.R.D.C. nor T.D.C. seek board representation to influence policy; private venture capital companies sometimes have managerial representation.

64 N.R.D.C. helped 20% of applicants; T.D.C. 6%; the private companies helped only 1–2% due to the fact that they look for very fast growth; *Financial Facilities for Small Firms*, p. 52.

65 In its evidence to the Bolton Committee enquiry N.R.D.C. indicated that investigation costs as a proportion of a loan fall very sharply as the size of the latter increases. These costs were recovered from part of the proceeds of a levy on sales. N.R.D.C. felt that small firms were unlikely to cover the full cost of their share of overheads and the costs of failure; *Financial Facilities for Small Firms*, p. 52.

66 Bolton Committee, *Report*, para. 12. 67.

67 *Financial Facilities for Small Firms*, p. 33.

68 ibid., p. 31. For insurance companies as a

group *net* investment in 1970 in other mortgages and loans for long-term purposes amounted to £77.7m.; British Insurance Association, *Facts and Figures*, 1970. Before 1960 Building Societies could provide funds through mortgages of small business properties. The Building Societies Act 1960 restricted the amounts which societies could lend to companies and also the amount they could lend in sums above £5,000; *Financial Facilities for Small Firms*, p. 31.

69 ibid., p. 34.
70 G. Clayton and W. T. Osborn, *Insurance Company Investment*, London, 1965, p. 119.
71 *Financial Facilities for Small Firms*, p. 121.
72 ibid., pp. 33–4, 111; Bolton Committee, *Report*, para. 12.48.
73 On the differential effect of bank ceilings on advances to small firms see Chapter 7.

PART TWO

The post-war period

6 The capital market

A mechanism for the distribution of industrial
investment must . . . be in operation that will
enable British industry to make . . . [the] . . .
necessary adjustments with the minimum of
friction, waste, or delay. That is one reason for
the importance of the capital market.

R. F. HENDERSON

The basic function of the new issue market is to enable the flow of funds
generated within the economy to be made available to those who need
them on terms acceptable to the lender; in other words to assist in the
efficient transmission of funds from surplus to deficit sectors. An effective
new issue market cannot of course operate without an active trading
market in securities since the latter provides future marketability of long-
term obligations and an indication of the terms on which new capital can
be raised. At the company level capital requirements may be met either
from internal or external sources and in the latter instance with a choice
between short- and long-term borrowing. In the British tradition the
volume of long-term capital raised, although variable with the level of
industrial activity, had been relatively modest, probably financing about
a fifth of the addition to fixed assets, but the role of new issue market in the
provision of funds should not be assessed solely in proportion to that
figure. For fast-growing firms it has provided a significant portion of
funds, for all borrowers an opportunity to choose various proportions of
debt or equity depending as to the nature of the business and the desired
relation between borrowing and shareholders capital, and it provides as it
were a last resort channel where risk capital can be obtained, at a price,
from existing shareholders or from new ones if all other sources fail.

In supplying funds over the post-war years the capital market has
operated in the presence of various kinds of official action which have to
a lesser or greater degree affected its normal workings. The Capital Issues

Committee in the immediate post-war period exercised control over the nature of market issues with the intention of directing capital to uses deemed to be in the 'national interest'. In practice the control proved 'negligible to the point of irrelevance'.[1] Over the same years the enormous government programme of gilt-edge issues associated with nationalization, together with restraint on dividends and other limitations (see p. 237) all served to affect the flow of funds to the private sector. Institutional participation by investment and unit trusts was deliberately restrained prior to 1953 in the mistaken belief that their issues diverted funds away from productive needs; the quantitative effect of the control was probably small but the action displayed a marked lack of appreciation of the workings of the capital market. Throughout the post-war period there have been periodic admonitions on the volume of funds going to non-productive uses, but where it occurred the market merely reflected deeper influences and was not making arbitrary decisions on the allocation of funds. If the rate of return from productive investment is below that offered by other uses then the cure for such a differential is not to be found in the compulsory redirection of investment. Also, throughout these years there has been changing emphasis in the matter of company taxation which produced significant swings in the type of securities demanded by the market, ranging from periods when distribution of profits was discouraged to others when a neutral view was adopted by the government of the day. In the stock market industrial equities have suffered discriminatory treatment compared with gilt-edged, since dealings in the latter have been free of stamp duty and of capital gains tax if held for more than a year. In the presence of such varying influences and fiscal treatment it is not surprising that the market had been less than perfect in the eyes of some observers; indeed markets less subject to official actions are no more perfect but they have not attracted such a lasting label as 'imperfections of the capital market'.

One of the most significant influences on the new issue market in post-war years has been the growing importance of institutional investment and the decline of direct investment by private savers. For the past twenty years or so the personal sector has been a persistent net seller of shares, for example, in the decade to 1976 average sales per annum amounted to £1,100m. Since personal savings were increasing at this time, reaching record levels in the mid-1970s, such sales could hardly be for expenditure purposes, rather they reflect changes in the composition of personal wealth affected by many factors, not least, the desire to obtain assets offering tax advantages, such as house purchase, insurance policies and pension plans. As a result the ownership of quoted equity by the personal sector fell from 55% in 1963 to 42% in 1973 of the total shares outstanding.[2] The increased flow of savings from persons to the financial institutions, done largely on a contractual basis (for most of the past ten years the contractual element was about 60% of personal savings) provided sufficient resources for them to absorb both the sales of the personal sector and the new issues offered by industry. Thus the main institutional holders, insurance companies, pension funds, investment trusts and unit trusts, increased their holdings of fixed interest industrial securities from 42% of the total outstanding in 1953 to 63% in 1974 and in the case of equities from 13% to 52% respectively. The dominance of the institutions in the market over recent years is confirmed by the figures of market turnover, their share of fixed interest activity rising from 60% in 1965 to 78% in 1974, and in the case of equities from 28% to 39% respectively.

The weight of institutional holdings and the annual addition to their funds constitutes an important element in the absorbtive capacity of the new issue market; such a demand for large blocks of securities makes the market less prone to fits of 'indigestion'. However, with portfolios containing several hundred companies they prefer issues with ready marketability and they accordingly seek out large issues of high quality. They are understandably reluctant to hold more than a limited portion of any issue (they have no special desire to get involved in industrial management), and combined with this is the need for substantial units since small sums are administratively difficult. This would suggest that the bar of size for new issues is constantly rising but this does not rule out occasional institutional interest in smaller issues with good growth prospects.

The flow of issues

Since the Second World War the new issue market has been more or less entirely orientated towards meeting the requirements of domestic borrowers. Almost without exception the percentage of home funds raised, as recorded by the Midland Bank new issue series, amounted to over 90% of total annual issues. The transition from an international market to a predominantly domestic one was nearly complete. The absence of overseas borrowing was of course linked with the ban on capital exports arising from the persistently weak balance of payments position and the low level of reserves, which prevailed for most of the post-war period. During the war capital issues were rigorously controlled and public offers of securities were prohibited except where Treasury approval was obtained through the agency of the Capital Issues Committee. In practice there was very little need for financial control since the rapid introduction of comprehensive physical controls served to ensure that resources only went to essential activities. During the period 1940–5 total new issues for 'production' amounted to only £30.7m. with a further £5.7m. for trade, transport and finance. The flow of savings in the capital market was directed largely towards taking up War Loan issues.

The end of the war brought a relaxation of controls and new guidelines for the C.I.C. Issues larger than £50,000 required the consent of the C.I.C., while those over £100,000 had to follow instructions from the Bank of England as to timing. Control over the method of issue was restored to the Stock Exchange. As to purposes, new issues were allowed for 'approved purposes' which included such activities as exporting, public utilities, transport, production of capital goods and essential consumer goods. Issues were not normally allowed for the retail and distribution trades, or for hire purchase finance. Also controlled were bonus issues and issues involving the acquisition of existing firms. The machinery of the new issue market was therefore quite speedily restored to the public, which was 'a triumph for commonsense over doctrinaire policy imposed with little apparent solicitide for, or even, knowledge of, the detailed functioning of an intricate machinery'.[3]

The first major security issue soon appeared and was an offer of new preference capital by John Summers towards the close of 1945, while in 1946 the market made up somewhat for the lost opportunities (see table 6.1). More money was raised in one year than in all the war years together, and during the next few years some £80 to £90m. was raised annually for the production category of the Midland Bank series.[4] Funds at the time were plentiful, not least from institutional investors eager to lower their gilt-edged commitment. However, the fuel crisis and the convertibility exploit with sterling occasioned temporary difficulties and the postponement of some issues. It was noticeable that funds were going predominantly to the capital intensive heavy industries where re-equipment expenditure exceeded the supply of internal finance. An interesting feature of the 1945–7 market was that there were a large number of issues by small firms. R. F. Henderson found that there were 91 'no new money' issues involving £18.3m. and 68 'new money' issues raising £14.3m., which provided £6.9m. of actual funds to companies.[5] During 1948 the volume of new issues declined marginally, which may have been due to revised instructions to the C.I.C., and to the introduction of the new and short-lived bonus tax. Also, investors after their first flush of freedom were becoming more discriminating so that some issues were heavily under-subscribed. Over the next two years the volume of funds raised remained roughly the same and issues were only absorbed with increasing difficulty and slowness. The attractions of equity issues were of course diminished by continued dividend limitation and by the relapse of the share market during 1949–50. The re-introduction of monetary policy and higher bank rate in 1952 added new uncertainties, while the fall in raw material prices and the decline in demand experienced by some industries clearly affected calculations as to permanent capital needs, so that requirements which seemed pressing nine months previously were quickly revised.[6]

Given the extent of capital depreciation and the replacement that was needed after the war, on the surface it is a little surprising that the volume of new money issues was comparatively modest (see table 6.1). In nominal terms the figures are on the same sort of level as those recorded in the mid- and late 1930s; in real terms, however, they only represent about half the pre-war level. It was not that the C.I.C. restricted their volume, but that for most of the transition period industry was able to finance itself extensively from internal and other sources. Many undertakings emerged from the war with large reserves, some held in gilt-edged, while others had tax recoveries due to them. Additional help was given in the form of larger depreciation allowances provided for in the Finance Acts, and war damage compensation in many instances further supplemented available funds.[7] With the cheap money policy the banks were ready to provide temporary assistance, although loans not paid off were later funded through the new issue market. On the supply of funds side, voluntary dividend limitation and heavy discriminating taxation of distributed profits reduced the reception accorded to new issues, but on the whole there is no evidence that there was a serious shortage of investable funds in the market.

That is not to say that the market was unimportant to industry as a source of finance. During the period 1949–53 nearly one quoted company in three resorted to the market, and the total sum raised represented nearly 30% of their *net* investment. The market facility was of even greater significance to fast growing companies (net assets increasing by over 100%). For these companies net proceeds of all issues represented over 40% of the growth of net assets and three out of four fast growing companies made capital issues. Companies in fast growing industries, e.g., the electrical and chemical industries made considerable use of the new issue market, while large companies (net assets over £4m.) resorted to the market more often and to a greater extent than the average company.[8]

The main new issues series available are designed to indicate the volume of funds raised for companies through the market. They, therefore, omit issues which do not raise new funds for firms, i.e., non-cash issues, which in this period had many purposes. During the early post-war years they often took the form of offers for sale for the purpose of dispersing capital holdings and widening the market in a company's shares. Placings of shares particularly with institutions, were also used for this end.[9] With the

Table 6.1　Capital issues by companies 1940–69 (£m.)

Year	Midland Bank series [a]				Bank of England series
	Production Manufacturing	Trade and transport	Finance	Total	
1940–44	17.6	1.4	0.4	19.4	—
					(Old series)[b]
1945	13.1	3.1	0.8	17.0	16.4
1946	73.5	26.9	11.3	111.7	80.1
1947	82.3	25.5	4.8	112.6	106.6
1948	75.6	33.2	5.0	113.8	114.0
1949	80.2	7.5	7.8	95.5	94.3
1950	94.4	8.9	4.6	107.9	143.6
1951	108.1	12.8	7.0	127.9	130.6
1952	94.4	15.2	7.6	117.2	108.2
1953	56.0	26.8	9.0	91.8	107.1
					(New Series)[c]
1954	138.4	10.5	36.6	185.5	137.4
1955	165.5	25.1	28.8	219.4	174.5
1956	158.4	18.1	34.2	210.7	157.8
1957	250.3*	15.7	27.8	293.8	261.7
1958	143.0	11.6	24.9	179.5	174.8
1959	180.1	68.1	136.8	385.0	144.7
1960	146.5	96.1	114.5	157.1	212.1
1961	295.3	97.2	131.8	524.3	209.8
1962	162.6	102.1	121.3	386.0	181.5
1963	199.0	132.1	100.1	431.2	177.7
1964	224.0	98.5	62.2	384.7	234.3
1965	378.7	81.4	39.9	500.0	264.3
1966	430.5	73.5	126.9	630.9	430.4
1967	273.7	52.7	89.0	415.4	312.9
1968	390.4	113.8	146.2	650.4	313.1
1969	338.2	109.5	123.3	570.9	276.5

*Includes an issue of £41.0m. by B.P.

[a] Midland Bank Series: the figures record the amount of 'new money' raised from investors in the U.K. by the issue of marketable securities; they exclude sales of existing securities which do not add to the resources of the issuer; the figures are based on prices of issue.

[b] Bank of England — old series: relates only to cash subscribed by U.K. residents; within the limits of the information available, it includes subscriptions to issues made abroad, but excludes subscriptions by overseas residents to issues made in the U.K.

[c] New series: relates to cash raised by issues made in the U.K., including subscriptions from residents of other countries; estimates relate to new money raised by issues of ordinary, preference and loan capital; figures based on prices at which securities are offered to the market; subscriptions are recorded under the periods in which they are due to be paid.

Sources: Midland Bank Review, February issues; *Bank of England Statistical Abstract*, No. 1, 1970, pp. 87, 93.

prevailing low levels of interest rates a number of conversion operations were undertaken. Shares were also issued for take-over purposes and finally, scrip or bonus issues, though subject to regulation were occasionally made. In the case of the 2,549 companies examined in the Tew and Henderson survey covering 1949–53, the amount of non-cash issues amounted to only £69m. compared with £590m. for cash.[10]

Mr Butler's investment boom of 1954–5 and its aftermath brought about some interesting fluctuations in the volume of new issues. The boom itself had several contributory causes — the relaxation in 1953 of direct controls, the growth of consumer demand especially instalment buying, falling interest rates, and increased bank lending coupled with the ending of C.I.C. examination of the repayment provisions in applications for bank accommodation.[11] In addition there were certain fiscal stimuli. In 1954 the Chancellor substituted a system of investment allowances for the initial allowances which had been re-introduced in the previous year. The new allowances, introduced at 20% for plant and machinery, were very generous, in that they permitted more than 100% of the cost of an asset to be written off over its life. They constituted an outright subsidy by increasing cash flow whereas initial allowances merely re-arranged the time stream of tax payments.[12]

The 1954 boom produced the usual danger signals — rising wages and prices, worsening trade position and a fall in the exchange rate. Restrictive measures on the monetary front then followed mainly in the form of a higher bank rate and periodic requests to the banks to curtail advances. While the monetary restraint may have contributed to the slowing down of capital investment in the manufacturing sector, there is little doubt that the accompanying uncertainty affected the new issue market. In volume terms the market produced large totals for the years 1955–7 (see table 6.1). Companies who had made issuing plans went ahead, and those that shelved them were replaced by other borrowers in the queue — the market counterpart to the long queue for capital goods.[13] But while the flow continued other problems arose for the market; there was temporary congestion in the market and growing uncertainties saw large blocks of shares left with the underwriters who responded by widening their commissions. For the private sector the price of entry to the market went up sharply, helped by competing public sector needs, with dividend yields rising from 5.75% to 7% between 1954–7 and debenture yields going up from 4.5% to 6.5%.

The credit squeeze ended in July 1958 with the removal of the restrictions on bank advances and hire purchase, and the C.I.C. limit was raised from £10,000 to £50,000. Also freed from control were bonus issues made to capitalize reserves except those involving the issue of redeemable securities. Tax changes and the re-introduction of the 1954 investment allowances a year later took the expansionary policy a stage further. However, activity in the new issue market did not match up to this general relaxation. Compared with 1957 there was a marked shrinkage of activity. There were several reasons for this. Although bank rate came down from 7% to 4% during 1958, long-term interest rates remained at high levels due to vigorous official funding operations in gilt-edged; relaxation of credit policy brought access to other sources of funds; and there was hesitancy in some branches of industry to raise long-term capital until uncertainties in the business outlook had been entirely removed. Perhaps the most noticeable feature of market activity in 1959 was the flood of issues associated with amalgamations, take-overs and other forms of integration. Such share operations have no place in the main new issue series.[14]

The familiar post-war cyclical programme re-asserted itself during the next few years. Concern for the balance of payments in 1960 produced high interest rates and calls for Special Deposits, while the run on sterling a year later brought forth a July Budget, credit restrictions and a call for a pause in the growth of wages, salaries and dividends. The large new issue totals for these years reflected in part official measures restraining other forms of borrowing. Banks were increasingly reluctant to provide finance other than for priority needs and day-to-day, short-term business requirements. In many instances companies would have preferred to defer issues, but the banks were not very accommodating.[15]

As a result of the 1961 measures industrial production remained more or less at the same level for the next two years and manfacturing investment declined. Gross fixed capital formation for the manufacturing sector fell by 15% between 1961 and 1963, and in real terms the fall was over 19%. This reduced demand for market capital was very apparent in the case of chemicals, engineering and metal manufacture. Where companies did seek funds they often did so by rights issues to shareholders.

The expansionary fiscal and monetary measures introduced in 1962 soon generated a balance of payments crisis, and by autumn 1964 bank rate was back at 7%, restrictions were re-introduced and further reinforced in the spring of 1965. Despite these policy measures the new issue market remained quite buoyant, and indeed 1965 proved to be quite a remarkable year for new issues. The production category of the Midland Bank series reached £379m., which included some large issues, while over 90% of company issues consisted of debt instruments.[16] Among the important influences making for this new issue boom were the following: companies needed money to fund bank loans, particularly those not in the priority lending categories; the buoyancy of the gilt-edged market spread to the fixed interest industrial market, thus encouraging the raising of exceptionally large sums; and throughout, investment persisted at a high level — gross fixed capital formation in manufacturing rose by nearly 25% between 1963 and 1965.

The record figures of 1965 were quickly surpassed in the following year. In the first half of 1966 manufacturing raised £270m. (Bank of England series). It should be noted, however, that there were two very large issues during the year. In February B.P. made a rights issue of £60m., and in September I.C.I. made an issue of £60m. unsecured loan stock. Half the former was subscribed by the government, and I.C.I. had no difficulty with its issue; the nominal amount of applications amounted to over £2,000m. On a more modest plane a substantial number of companies raised relatively small amounts by way of placings of fixed interest stocks, while in equities the market was reported to be doing two years' business in one. The need to resort to outside funds arose from the intensification of the credit squeeze especially on the banking front, and from the fact that profits became more difficult to earn, thus reducing internal funds. Also company liquidity was put under strain by the introduction of S.E.T., the continuation of the import surcharge, and by changes in arrangements for tax payments under Schedule F.

Compared with the record performance of 1966 the ensuing year was relatively quiet. The reduced demand for funds was largely due to the fall, the first since 1963, in real capital expenditure in the manufacturing sector which was down by 3.3%. While there was no queue of large borrowers some interesting features emerged. On a rapidly rising equity market a crop of small companies appeared, mostly going public to avoid death duties, actual or prospective.[17] On the whole then 1967 represented a pause for the market, which perhaps was not surprising since companies had probably extended their borrowing base during the previous few years.

The sharp recovery in issues in 1968 was due to a number of factors: although company profits rose in 1968 tax liabilities increased substantially; an intensification of credit restraint led to the usual promptings from banks for the funding of overdrafts; industrial stocks had fallen to low levels in 1967 and restocking needs required resort to external finance; finally, fixed capital investment was up on the previous year, aided by a change in fiscal incentives. The level of new issue activity continued into the first half of 1969 despite falling share prices. However, some large issues ran into difficulties later in the year, and hopes of future falls in interest rates reduced the flow of issues, and 1970 produced the lowest figures since the early 1960s (see table 6.1, p. 148). At the time interest rates on loan stocks were higher than those on bank advances so that companies had little incentive to fund short-term borrowing even when they came under pressure from the banks to do so. Also, liquidity pressures were eased by reductions in the rate of corporation tax, the reduction in the import surcharge, and for a time access to the Eurocurrency market.

While industrial issues nearly reached £400m. in 1971 (see table 6.2), fixed investment was on a very depressed level with a fall of 7% on the previous year (at 1963 prices).[18] Also, bank credit became readily available but there was little by way of urgent demand from industry. The high level of activity in the market, in contrast to the domestic economy, was induced more by the supply of funds than by any pressing demand for them. The low issues figure for 1972 (in particular in 'other group', table 6.2) reflected the availability of alternative funds, and the sluggish rate of capital investment. This trend continued into 1973 and some of the issues made were not fully subscribed, while others were quoted at a discount on the basic price when trading started. Company issues slumped further in 1974 (see table 6.2) and of the £162m. raised for all companies nearly 40% was for an insurance company. In the manufacturing sector the Bank of England series recorded an unprecedented net repayment of funds. The dramatic collapse of the equity market made large issues impossible, while the sharp rise in fixed interest yields also discouraged such borrowing; companies financed themselves by resorting to various short-term expedients.

Table 6.2   Capital issues by companies 1970–6 (£m.)

Year	Midland Bank series [a]					Bank of England series
	Capital goods	Consumer goods	Other group	Other companies [b]	Total	Manufacturing
1970	105.3	73.9	68.0	106.3	353.4	121.7
1971	68.9	160.8	158.1	275.8	663.6	149.5
1972	78.2	179.0	18.1	681.1	956.4	223.0
1973	18.7	66.9	25.7	99.2	210.5	67.9
1974	8.3	9.9	0.6	143.3	162.1	−8.0
1975	245.0	505.6	220.8	607.0	1578.4	686.3
1976	185.2	176.7	433.9	365.1	1160.9	532.0

[a] The Midland Bank altered the classification of business by borrower from 1974 onwards so as to accord with revised Stock Exchange practice; figures for 1970 to 1972 were reworked as far as possible on the new basis. See table 6.1 for definition of series.
[b] Includes waterworks, commodity and financial.

Sources: *Midland Bank Review*; *Bank of England Quarterly Bulletin*.

A remarkable recovery took place in 1975, the total for all companies reaching £1,578m. of which some 60% was for industry and the bulk of it obtained through rights issues of ordinary shares. Even after adjusting for price changes this figure had only been surpassed once in the previous ten years. This, to some extent, answered the current criticism that the private capital market could not provide finance on a large scale for home industry. The recovery was associated with a marked rise in share prices which prompted companies to reduce their short-term indebtedness and improve their liquidity, thereby restoring more normal levels between equity and short-term borrowing. On the supply side financial institutions benefiting from record levels of personal sector saving had large amounts of investable funds.[19] Such a pace could not last for long and the volume of issues dwindled as 1976 wore on. Once the flow of funding issues was over and with no prospect of a quick recovery in the economy the expenditure demand for funds fell off. The low level of company borrowing in the second half of the year accompanied by large gilt-edged issues prompted the cry that industry was being 'crowded out' of the capital market but there is little evidence to support this view.

Types of securities issued

Loan capital

The volume of debentures issued by industry in the post-war period (see table 6.3, p. 155) has fluctuated largely in response to three factors: the level of interest rates; the ease or difficulty of raising finance, especially in large sums, on the equity market; and finally, and by far the most important, the incidence of taxation.

Taking the period as a whole the influence of the level of interest rates has not been particularly prevalent. There were occasions, however, when interest rate considerations were reported as having an influence on the composition of capital raising by companies. For example, with the introduction of a flexible monetary policy in the early 1950s higher interest rates were a deterrent to contractual finance despite tax considerations.[20] Again during 1954 when the redemption yield on debentures fell from 4.7% to 4.4% the volume of fixed interest borrowing displayed a marked increase (amounting to 64% of all borrowing) since some companies found it cheaper to raise long-term money on a fixed interest basis. The bulk of the borrowing was done by the issue of unsecured loan stock, a form of security used widely in recent years by companies involved in North Sea oil exploration. By the end of the following year yields had risen sharply to 5.4% and this caused 'hesitancy to incur new debt obligations,

not withstanding the tax advantage obtainable thereby'.[21] The existence
of the reverse yield gap after 1958 also had its influence. For example, in
1967 when debenture yields had risen to 8.0%, and earnings yields on
equities was only around 6.0%, many companies found an issue of
ordinary shares less costly to finance than one of fixed interest. The
influence of historically high rates continued into 1968 and the size of the
gap (reverse yield gap) widened still further and companies were reluctant
to borrow for long periods at such levels.[22] The sharp drop in fixed
interest borrowing in 1973 and 1974, the lowest sums since 1948, arose
because of the high and rising interest rates which made companies
hesitant to burden themselves with long-term debt, a reluctance which
produced record low levels of debt borrowing in 1976 (see table 6.3).

The ease or difficulty of raising equity capital on occasions proved a
decisive influence on the level of borrowing. In the immediate post-war
years, especially 1950, there was a big rise in the proportion of debt issues
partly for this reason. This factor, along with others, also operated to
induce companies to bring out unsecured short-term notes. At the time,
of course, the equity market's absorptive capacity may have been adversely
affected by the imposition of dividend restraint. More recently in 1975–6
when conditions in the equity market favoured large-scale rights issues
the fixed interest sector was virtually ignored.

However, the most important influence on the volume of fixed interest
borrowing has been the incidence of taxation. The essence of the system
which operated from 1937 to 1965 was that companies were subject to
income tax on all profits, and this was credited in the case of distributed
profits to individual shareholders. In addition, profits tax was levied on
the whole of their profits but defined so as to exclude interest on borrowed
money. It was this exemption which brought about the large increase in
debt issues in the early 1950s (see table 6.3) since dividends in ordinary
and preference capital attracted distributed profits tax at the rate of 30%.
Being subject only to ordinary income tax, financing by loan stock was a
fairly orthodox move. With the removal of the discriminatory rate of tax
in 1958 and the introduction of a uniform rate of profits tax of 10% the
incentive to use debt borrowing from tax considerations was reduced.
Thereafter, although still present, the incidence of profits tax was less
influential in determining capital structures and gearing ratios.

The change to corporation tax in 1965 greatly increased the incentive
for companies to borrow by way of debt rather than equities. Debt interest
payments continued to be chargeable against profits as a cost for tax
purposes, but profits available for distribution as dividends was now taxed
more heavily than before. Debt capital thus became cheaper to service
when compared with ordinary shares. Thus, the net of tax cost of

Table 6.3   Types of company security (£m.)

	Debt		Preference	Ordinary	Total
	Convertible	Other			
1946	—	20.1	30.5	77.8	128.4
1947	—	32.3	40.5	61.1	133.8
1948	—	15.6	24.9	100.8	141.3
1949	—	34.0	30.3	50.0	114.3
1950	—	71.5	10.9	46.2	128.6
1951	—	49.1	19.7	61.1	129.9
1952	—	36.7	4.1	87.8	128.6
1953	—	53.1	7.9	44.3	105.4
1954	—	101.0	28.3	73.0	202.3
1955	—	65.1	18.9	154.9	238.9
1956	—	76.0	3.1	145.7	224.7
1957	(100.0)*	183.3	1.7	155.2	340.2
1958	(19.0)*	95.2	1.0	92.6	188.8
1959	(17.9)*	119.5	10.7	274.0	404.2
1960	(6.4)*	121.8	10.4	345.5	477.7
1961	28.1	120.0	2.8	408.9	559.8
1962	41.0	132.8	5.3	233.9	413.0
1963	35.3	236.2	14.7	163.9	450.1
1964	60.2	173.8	10.7	168.9	413.6
1965	28.1	426.5	3.2	45.5	503.4
1966	38.4	441.0	16.4	142.5	638.4
1967	29.7	313.8	5.7	72.6	421.9
1968	128.3	181.3	3.1	363.7	676.4
1969	213.7	165.7	—	195.0	592.4
1970	101.3	211.6	17.2	51.9	382.0
1971	96.7	273.4	12.8	310.4	693.3
1972	96.4	213.6	10.9	649.9	970.8
1973	21.6	21.3	14.0	153.6	210.5
1974	25.6	17.2	—	119.3	162.1
1975	117.0	95.8	44.9	1320.7	1578.4
1976	14.8	77.7	44.5	1023.9	1160.9

*Estimates of convertible stock included in 'other' column.

Source: *Midland Bank Review*, *(February issues)*.

debenture borrowing was substantially reduced; the old system reduced the cost of fixed interest finance by up to 15%, the new system by the prevailing rate of corporation tax. Debt capital was subject to income tax, while dividends were subject to corporation tax and income tax, which in 1965 meant a total payment of 64.75% on the stream of dividends.

The effects on the composition of company borrowing are readily discernible in table 6.3. In the period 1965–7 fixed interest debt ranged from 63% to 75% of all securities issued.[23] By the late 1960s, however, the volume fell off because the demand, especially for unsecured issues, declined and companies thought themselves sufficiently well geared. Obviously there was a point where further equity would be needed to provide cover for the loan capital.

During 1948–51 companies resorted to raising funds by issuing short-term, unsecured notes. (These were only included in the Midland Bank series where permission to deal had been obtained from the Stock Exchange.) Following the success of a private placing of £10m. of such notes in 1948, several other large companies resorted to the same device. During 1950 the Midland Bank estimated that roughly £70m. was raised in this way, with a further £14m. in 1951.[24] Generally the issues were of notes or loan stock, usually unsecured, running for terms of 5 to 20 years, and they were issued to shareholders or privately placed with a fairly narrow circle of institutional investors.[25] Not only were such arrangements employed by large companies, but modest sums were also raised by smaller companies. The reasons for these issues were largely temporary: the incidence of profits tax; the stamp duty on issues 'with an element of bonus'; and the difficulties of marketing large blocks of ordinary shares.

One of the most important developments in company finance over the post-war years has been the adoption of convertible loan stocks. Although such securities have been commonly used in the United States, for rail, steel, and public utilities, and on the continent, they had not featured in the mainstream of British company finance. In the early 1950s convertibles were confined to such speculative activities as South African mining, but in 1957 attention was seriously focused on them following their use by I.C.I.

Basically a convertible loan stock is a borrowing agreement under which the lender has the option within a specified future period to convert all or part of the loan into equity share capital on predetermined terms. If the lender does not exercise the option the stock runs through to maturity and repayment occurs in the usual way. The stocks are of some 25-year maturity (this being most acceptable to institutional investors), with the option to convert during a specified period of the loan, usually from the third to the seventh year of the stock's life. Some convertibles are made by way of offers for sale, but mostly they are made, in accordance with Stock Exchange requirements, by way of rights offers to existing shareholders.[26]

The duration of the average conversion period may be thought of as roughly the time it takes for the project being financed to reach a full profit-earning level – a sort of bridging requirement; and it also reflects the extent of the effective planning horizon for most companies. In practice, during the past ten years, both the period over which conversion can take place and the actual period elapsing before conversion, have tended to increase. In the early 1960s they tended to be around two years, but by 1967–8 the average period had lengthened to about five years, with some companies going on to seven and eight years.[27] During the 1960s conversion prices (the conversion premium – 'the excess of the price at which the first conversion can be made into the equity, over the price of the equity on the day of the issue of the convertible expressed as a percentage of the latter') tended to rise, since the prices of shares rose, and also to provide an incentive to convert the stock at the earliest opportunity, thus reducing the amount of borrowing and giving the capital structure greater certainty.[28] The coupon rate for the stock was arrived at by deducting 'the value of the equity sweetener' from the current cost of debt, but the prevailing practice is to add 'an element' to the grossed up dividend yield of the ordinary shares to which the conversion is offered.[29] With expectations of rising equity prices it was sometimes possible to get a lower coupon rate by having a short period before conversion. A growing tendency has been to use a constant conversion premium at a higher level than previously (with the price tending to start some 10–15% above the market price at issue), and lengthening out the period of conversion; this arose since the tax advantage of fixed interest borrowing tended to delay conversion. Also from the company's standpoint the constant conversion price tends to encourage holders to defer conversion so long as the yield on the stock exceeds the yield on the equity.[30]

The traditional view of convertible loan stocks was to regard them as a form of bridging finance for essentially short-term purposes. For example, a company entering on a risky venture but with the possibility of high rewards, might finance the initial development with an issue of convertible stock. If the project succeeded the stock was converted; if not the lender had the right to full repayment of the loan. Again, a privately owned company in need of finance but not ready to come to the market could offer a convertible stock. Also, they could be used for financing the recovery of an established company so that the decision between lender and ownership status could be deferred to the future.

Two major factors, however, transformed this temporary bridging instrument into a 'deferred' equity. The first was the introduction in 1965 of corporation tax which rendered fixed interest borrowing, after tax, cheaper than share capital. With the tax advantage, which applied so long as the stock was unconverted, there was an incentive to delay conversion. It was no longer desirable to convert as soon as the short-term bridging problem was over, but the stock could be regarded as a deferred equity. The second was the attraction of convertibles during the merger boom of the late 1960s. In a take-over the consideration can take several forms –

cash, but this became increasingly scarce in successive credit squeezes; ordinary shares, which were not only expensive to service but also involved the dilution of the existing shareholder's interests; and debt which had inflationary drawbacks. In these circumstances convertible loan stocks had distinct advantages:

> For the shareholder whose shares are being bid for, there is a guaranteed income at an attractively high rate; there is an option to convert into equity as a hedge against inflation; there is deferment of capital gains tax liability (which applied to cash payments); and there is the longstop of a fixed date for repayment at par if things go wrong. For the company making the bid, there is a lower interest cost than would be with a straightforward loan stock; there is tax relief on the servicing cost; there is a breathing space before conversion in which to achieve and consolidate the benefits of the merger, ... and there is the enormous advantage of making the bid in a form attractive to recipients.[31]

Apart from the general advantages of convertibles already outlined they had other attractive features from a borrower's standpoint. In the period when C.I.C. control operated, the issue of a convertible for a fixed sum had the attraction that once the new capital had fructified the conversion could be exercised, and the ordinary capital then increased without application to the C.I.C. They also have an appeal for companies if the amounts to be raised are small in relation to company capital, and where future capital needs are unlikely during the period over which the option remains alive and if earnings grow sufficiently to ensure that no dilution of the existing equity occurs. However, many companies are prepared to pay more for a conventional issue rather than place themselves in an equivocal position with a conversion issue. The option to convert lies solely with the lender and if he decides not to exercise it the company may be left with a weight of loan service for some considerable time. Capital structure is thus at the mercy of the market rather than company directors and their freedom to manoeuvre is restricted when raising further capital.

For the lender a convertible provides a prior claim on profits and assets, if prospects do not materialize; and if matters go right a claim on earnings. Their widespread use has, of course, been influenced by lenders' requirements, especially the institutions, who value the prospect of an ultimate stake in the equity along with high current income. The expectation of continuing inflation was, and is, an important element in generating institutional demand. But there are risks to the existing equity holders who may be required to accept a dilution of the ordinary capital when the conversion rights are exercised, and the cost of the equity holder in this instance would depend on the extent of the dilution.

The volume of convertibles raised over the post-war years is given in table 6.3 (p. 155). It was not until 1957 that there was a high proportion of such issues, issued mainly to meet lenders' needs. Subsequent fluctuations in the volume of convertibles for cash have reflected the varying conditions in the equity and loan markets. In 1964 there was a sharp rise in the convertible issues due to the uncertain conditions in the market. The largest volume to date occurred in 1968 and 1969, and two possible explanations can be put forward for this wave of convertibles. Firstly, that companies had become fully geared as a result of expanding debt to take advantage of the 1965 tax changes and therefore when they needed further capital they could only get it by offering equity or near equity (deferred equity) which carried a tax advantage. Secondly, companies were able to raise funds at 'a substantially lower coupon rate than would otherwise have been possible without the conversion option'.[32] Indeed, in the first half of 1969 it was reported that the stream of convertibles was only being held up by the 'indigestion of the market'.[33] Later, with the increased buoyancy of the loan and equity markets, issuers were more inclined to offer straightforward stock of either type, and the convertible hedge declined in volume falling to low levels in 1973–4, but experiencing a sharp rise in 1975 in its role as deferred equity for institutional investors.

Preference capital

Since the early 1950s the preference share has lapsed into virtual disuse, except in the case of a few industries. Even so, the volume of preference outstanding is still appreciable; at 31 March 1976 the nominal amount quoted on the London Stock Exchange was £1,088m., with a market value of £544.5m. Leaving aside the influence of corporation tax, their unpopularity (see table 6.3) is in some way surprising given that they possess certain advantages. For example, payments on some kinds of preference shares do not have to be made if no profits are available; there is no obligation to provide security in the case of default of dividend payments, or the return of capital; and they constitute part of the borrowing of a company. The above features involve extra risk for which investors want an additional premium, but in the past many companies willingly paid higher rates rather than use the more demanding debenture form.

The volume of preference shares in the immediate post-war years rivalled that of debentures. The subsequent decline owed something to the courts, interest rates and taxation. In 1949 a court decision on the rights of preference shareholders to the surplus assets in a winding up reduced their appeal to investors, although they did stage a small recovery after this.[34] The rise in interest rates from 1951 onwards certainly restrained the use of contracted finance, while on the demand side the growing preference for equities by investors gave companies little scope for choice. Again, taxation was a particularly important influence, in that profits tax was levied on preference as well as ordinary dividends, while the increase in tax on distributed profits in 1956 led to further replacement of preference issues by other forms of fixed interest capital.[35] Despite the fact that by the end of the 1950s profits tax was levied at a flat rate, even yield considerations proved inadequate to attract company directors to use more preference finance.

During the 1960s the amount of new preference shares issued, especially after the introduction in 1965 of corporation tax, would have been almost non-existent had it not been for several large issues by water companies who were given transitional tax reliefs under the Finance Act of 1965.[36] Under corporation tax arrangements the dividends on preference shares were not treated as a cost against profit so that with the net of tax cost of debentures thereby appreciably lowered, the disuse of preference shares was inevitable. Indeed, there was an incentive for companies to convert outstanding preference shares into debentures. However, several obstacles prevented widespread conversion. Firstly, there were legal difficulties surrounding such exchange schemes. Secondly, financial institutions (holding about half the outstanding volume) obtained franked income from their holdings (i.e., income already subject to corporation tax) and they were reluctant to loose this for unfranked debenture income. Thirdly, companies with uncertain profit records preferred to retain their preference shares rather than be committed to debenture interest payments. Fourthly, the level of gearing in some companies was already high, and although this had little relevance to the dividend level received by shareholders, there might well have been a 'greater risk of insolvency where debentures have replaced preference shares'. Finally, many large U.K. companies had to take into consideration the reactions of international investors and differing tax treatment, which greatly limited their freedom of action.[37]

Ordinary share capital

Early post-war company issues consisted for the most part of shares brought out on a rising market. As can be seen from table 6.3 (p. 155) equities dominated the new issue market until 1949–50, when the reversal of the post-war price rise caused a sharp increase in dividend yields. Despite the existence of dividend limitation, it seems to have exercised far less influence on the type of issue than might have been expected. With the rapidly rising share market of the 1950s equities dominated the new issue figures, reaching a peak of £408m. in 1961. This was associated with the weakening, and ending, of formal dividend limitation, the rising cost of fixed interest finance, and the growing attractions of equity ownership with inflation, especially for the important institutional investors.

The introduction of corporation tax in 1965, with its advantages for debt borrowing, reduced the level of ordinary shares issued to the low figure of £45.5m., a mere 9% of all issues. The gradual revival of equity issues in the late 1960s can be explained by the size of the reverse yield gap, thus offsetting the advantage of raising new capital by debt issues, the reluctance of companies to incur heavy long-term fixed interest costs, and the fact that companies wished to reduce their gearing ratios. On the demand side, the rising equity prices of 1970–1 created a strong pressure on a market short of stock, following the effect of take-overs and capital gains tax, while the desire of institutions to add to their portfolios after the lean years of the mid-1960s supported the revival.[38]

The adoption of the imputation tax system for companies in 1973 whereby all profits, whether distributed or not, are subject to the same corporation tax rate, will doubtless encourage them to distribute rather than retain profits, and then go to the market when they want funds. This will probably shift the balance towards raising new money by equities rather than by fixed-interest stock, and this tendency may be strongly reinforced by the continuation of high interest rates. In the market conditions of 1973–4 little equity borrowing took place, and where it did rights issues were used. However, the volume of equity issues in 1975 and 1976, predominantly rights issues (see pp. 170–1), amounted to a massive £1,321m. and £1,023.9m. respectively. The main cause of this was a desire to restore a more normal relationship between equity and short-term borrowing on a receptive market and when interest rates were high. In the latter year share issues accounted for no less than 88% of total issues by companies.

Methods of issue

Companies seek a stock exchange quotation for several reasons. A quotation may be desirable in order to obtain marketability for shares so that existing shareholders may adjust their portfolios more easily; shares in unquoted companies usually can only be sold after considerable delays and search costs. A market price may be sought simply to get a valuation on shares for death duty purposes, or in addition, for sale to pay off such duties (provincial issues were viewed – mistakenly – as being exclusively for this purpose). A more compelling reason is that associated with the tax position of small unquoted companies. A 'close company' controlled by five or fewer persons or by its directors are expected to distribute a certain proportion (a 'required standard') of profits so that the company is not used as a tax shelter by the shareholders. However, a company is not 'close' if shares carrying at least 35% of the voting power are held by the public and are quoted and dealt with on a recognized stock exchange. More positive motives for obtaining a quotation are associated with the need to obtain funds for growth purposes. Following an initial quotation to improve the status of a company a cheaper second issue for cash may be made. Funds from institutional sources are generally more forthcoming in reponse to offers from large quoted companies, while banks are known to lend more readily if they have an assurance that such debts can be funded by a market issue of shares. Also, growth by acquisition may be made easier since a quoted company can make payment in the form of quoted shares which are preferable to unquoted shares and to cash which will attract capital gains tax.

Public issues and offers for sale

The basic mechanics of these two methods have already been outlined in Chapter 2. Briefly, they involve for a public issue the direct sale of shares or stock by the company to the public through the agency of an issuing house or stockbroker, who is paid a fee for such services. With an offer for sale the issuing house normally buys the shares from the company and then sells them to the market. Such issues are made at a fixed price determined by the issuing house, the broker to the issue, and the company. The general practice is to pitch the price so that 'the shares promise a dividend yield slightly higher than the dividend yield obtainable on quoted shares which are as closely comparable as possible to those in the issue'.[39] This is done to get a market advantage since the essential problem 'is to sell as many shares in a particular company to the public in a single day as they would buy in a year or more'.[40] In addition, a conservative price may be set to allow for changes in market conditions in the interval between the setting of the price and the public offer of the shares (see p. 176). The contents of the prospectus are prescribed in detail by the Companies Act and by the appropriate Stock Exchange regulations. It serves as a means of advertising the issue as well as giving the relevant information.

During the immediate post-war years all issues of new capital by prospectus required the consent of the Capital Issues Committee. Apart from dislike of supervision city interests complained of slowness by the C.I.C. in dealing with applications and they were reported as being reluctant to make offers for sale, resorting instead to placings because of the uncertainty about the treatment they would get from the official supervisor.[41] From the viewpoint of marketing and cost there was little doubt that for large issues offers for sale was by far the most suitable method, and the exercise of supervision possibly delayed the development of specialization according to size for the various methods of issue. Oddly enough, several small public issues continued to be made in the 1950s, usually involving small firms going public and handled by stockbrokers, but the introduction in the mid-1960s of a Stock Exchange rule that 35% of the equity had to be put on the market rendered this form of small issue difficult; up to 1966 the minimum figure was 25%.[42] For the most part, however, the public issue and offer for sale methods are used for large issues, as the figures in table 6.4 indicate. By number it is the least frequently used, but the amounts are certainly larger per issue than for the other methods given in the table.

Table 6.4   Domestic company capital issues: Method of issue, 1949–58

Year	Public issues and offers for sale		Placings and introductions		Issues to shareholders		Capitalization		Others	
	£m.	no.	£m.	no.	£m.	no.	£m.	no.	£m.	no.
1949	n.a.	75	n.a.	231	n.a.	165	n.a.	n.a.	n.a.	21
1950	n.a.	45	44	164	56	193	98	338	n.a.	60
1951	45	44	52	186	79	226	24	263	30	92
1952	34	20	37	150	80	192	104	327	45	108
1953	80	21	63	129	40	156	171	272	41	90
1954	134	49	47	201	128	174	218	457	23	105
1955	93	31	83	309	126	243	568	734	47	126
1956	69	21	61	156	146	321	239	494	76	139
1957	65	10	64	106	172	189	215	283	52	174
1958	85	14	59	129	233	159	186	338	107	266

Source: The Times Issuing House Year Books.

Although the terms of an issue are set with a view to obtaining a full subscription, the possibility of undersubscription is invariably covered by the use of underwriting. In the uncertain markets of the early post-war years some issuing houses took the additional precaution of having a portion of an issue underwritten firm, i.e., the underwriter purchased shares outright on underwriting terms.[43] In the bullish markets of the 1950s underwriters generally profited from their commitments and gladly took all that was offered to them. The commission provided profit, and as they were usually investors, underwriting, at worst, meant taking stock into their portfolios for a while at less than the public paid for it. Indeed, a survey by Merrett, Howe and Newbould for the period 1959–63 (one of fairly buoyant markets) of 168 public issues, tenders and offers for sale, found that losses averaged only 14% of the underwriters' receipts.[44] Quite apart from any capital gains obtained on shares taken up, they appear, in this period at least, to have enjoyed a fair renumeration for the risks actually undertaken.

With the resumption of public issues and offers for sale after the war the familiar problem of oversubscription quickly became apparent, particularly in the case of the smaller issues. As a result applications were scaled down, a considerable administrative burden, but the allegation was made that the public benefited very little from this since shares went largely to favoured applicants.[45] To reduce this criticism the issuing houses adopted what is probably the fairest method of coping with a flood of applications, allotment by ballot, with the device if necessary of scaling them down.

In many instances oversubscription contains a large element of stagging. The aim of the stag is to get a share at the issue price and sell at a premium later. If they have no ready cash to meet the initial deposit they then hope to sell and use the proceeds to meet their own cheque for the initial allotment. They certainly aspire to sell before meeting later calls. Although the risks of being a stag are normally very small the potential profits are also limited by the fact that selling out will keep the premium down. The contribution which the stag makes to the marketing process is, of course, subject to some debate; at worst it is held that he denies genuine investors opportunity to get stock and that he destabilizes the market; at best that he supports the market at the point of issue, while later selling enables the public to absorb the issue over a longer period of time.

The various devices which have been used by stags have been fairly successfully countered over the years. In 1946 the Stock Exchange required that initial instalments for new issues had to be at least 25% of the initial price.[46] Later, in 1948, the Companies Act made applications firm for three days, thus ending the previous practice of stags who withdrew their applications before allotment if they thought an issue was going badly. A practice which was widespread after the war was that of using fictitious names, but in 1947 the Stock Exchange threatened to discipline members involved in the practice, and with the use of proper names it was more difficult to indulge in mass applications. Nowadays even where stags submit multiple applications it is less of a problem since issuing houses and stockbrokers have their own methods of detecting them. Another deterent is to clear all cheques before proceeding to allotment, but that takes up some time. Perhaps the only effective means is to remove the incentive of the premium, if, of course it is assumed that is a desirable end.

Table 6.5   Capital issues; U.K. public companies; method of issue, 1959–76 (Gross issues: £m.)

Year	Public issues and offers for sale	Tenders	Placings	Issues to shareholders		Total
				Ordinary shares	Preference and loan capital	
1959	32.0	3.2	71.9	302.3		409.4
1960	35.6	5.2	72.7	359.9		473.4
1961	29.2	5.0	98.1	436.1	32.6	601.0
1962	69.3	7.1	113.3	206.3	58.6	454.6
1963	54.0	17.6	202.3	144.1	60.5	478.5
1964	29.0	8.2	253.9	181.5	76.0	548.6
1965	55.0	2.9	329.7	61.2	42.0	490.8
1966	164.2	1.9	373.8	116.9	75.9	732.7
1967	74.5	2.1	321.7	64.0	74.6	536.9
1968	30.6	10.2	199.3	352.4	107.6	700.1
1969	112.4	10.0	139.2	175.5	196.9	634.0
1970	28.6	37.2	140.2	62.7	92.6	361.3
1971	102.3	34.3	253.4	169.9	66.1	626.0
1972	293.7	24.4	323.3	359.1	116.7	1117.2
1973	93.3	8.0	89.6	71.0	26.5	288.5
1974	23.3	15.1	30.8	114.6	0.8	184.5
1975	102.6	36.2	70.6	1225.5	103.9	1538.8
1976	102.8	31.2	100.5	1024.7	31.6	1290.9

Sources: *Bank of England, Statistical Abstract, No. 2, 1975, p. 112; Bank of England Quarterly Bulletin.*

Placings and introductions

A Stock Exchange placing is a method whereby the shares of a company are acquired by an issuing house or stockbroker who then places them with private or institutional clients, and also with Stock Exchange jobbers.[47] Usually this is done at a price above that paid by the issuing house which leaves a 'turn' for the latter, although placings are occasionally done for a fee. The Stock Exchange rules require that the placing amounts to at least 35% of the issued equity capital, and 30% for fixed interest stock. Also, that not less than 25% of the amount of equity placed (20% for other securities) must be offered to the public through the medium of the market. The placing letter and other documents constitute prospectus information. The present Stock Exchange rules, however, only accede to a placing as a concession in cases where the issue would not be appropriate for a prospectus issue. Generally this would apply to companies having a market capitalization of under £1.5m. As can be seen from tables 6.4 and 6.5 it is a popular method of issue, and the figures in table 6.4 suggest that the average size is much smaller than for other methods.[48] One interesting feature of placings which emerged from a survey of those done between 1961–5, was the dominance of provincial activity. London recorded 139 for the period, with 153 for the provinces; in 1963–4 the provincial figure was 85 against London's 33. The average size of provincial placings was well below the London figure, £106,000 compared with £183,000; also numerous placings of less than £100,000 occurred in London (31) and in the provinces (52).[49] However, the introduction of minimum quotation figures in 1966, that a company needed an expected minimum market value of £250,000, while any one security for which quotation is sought needed normally an expected market value of at least £100,000, put paid to such avenues to the market. Recently these figures have been raised to £500,000, and £200,000 respectively, although in exceptional cases lower capitalization may be accepted where the Stock Exchange is satisfied as to marketability.

The traditional problem with the method was that the scope for public participation was limited, especially for smaller placings, so that the benefit of appreciation over the issue price became reserved for a few. The popularity of placings after the war merely served to highlight some of the main difficulties. Among them were the erratic price movements, the margin between what the public paid and the borrower received, and the fact that frequently long-term investors had to pay a handsome profit to 'insiders' if they wanted to get any shares. All, of course, reflected the root cause, that available stock was insufficient to meet a substantial proportion of the effective demand near the introduction price. However, it is this very premium that is the attraction which makes placees easy to find among the institutions. The intervention of the Treasury in placing arrangements in 1945 did not help either. The temporary regulations they introduced banned the resale of placed securities until permission to deal had been granted, which was not given for six months after the placing. Indeed, brokers were required to give assurances on this point, and to encourage this they were urged to distribute shares to 'strong investors such as institutional investors, trustees, and other long term holders'.[50] This boycott of personal placees merely worsened criticism of the selectivity of the method.

Widespread dissatisfaction with the placing method produced in 1946 a Memorandum of Guidance from the Stock Exchange which removed the worst abuses. The case for a placing had to be made to the Council (who tended to be more lenient on very small placings) and if approved, orderly marketing was to be assured by making a 'substantial number' of the shares to be placed available through the market at 'one price', and that the market should only take a modest 'turn'. The Council also introduced a rule to reduce irresponsible stagging of placings. This put an obligation on the purchaser to make a firm application and to accept an allocation of shares which, subject to permission to deal being granted, could not be revoked.[51]

Further requirements were brought in by the Stock Exchange Council in 1959 which specified that not less than 25% of the equity capital (20% for fixed interest) should be placed, and of this not less than 25% (20%) be made available to the market.[52] This left the sponsoring broker with up to three-quarters of the placed equity for his clients, and he was debarred from participating in the disposal of the securities reserved for the market. Further, only after the broker had done his placing were the jobbers to proceed with theirs, and they were urged only to retain a reasonable proportion for their opening dealings so that public demand would be more fully met. Although the Stock Exchange rules state that the opening price 'need not be closely related to the placing price' it does urge the participants to ensure that it 'should be realistic'.

Stock Exchange introductions do not, by themselves raise new money for companies, but the importance of the method arises as a means of acquiring a quotation so that future capital raising can be made more easily and cheaply. It also has the attraction that the conventional costs of issue are significantly lower than those of any other issue method. An introduction is only considered where there is no commitment to sell the security, where it is widely held, and there are no other circumstances that require special marketing arrangements. Generally, the Stock Exchange look for fifty to one hundred shareholders, and no undue concentration of holders. Although no shares have to be made available to the market the sponsors of the issue generally know where they can get some should the need arise. Sometimes an introduction may be linked with a rights issue so that a quotation helps in getting all the rights taken up, and thereby new money can be raised.

Offers for sale by tender

Prior to the First World War tendering was commonly used by companies and public bodies as a method of issue. However, they were replaced by fixed price issues, partly because the widespread adoption of underwriting ensured a full subscription at a fixed price, while administrative costs were lower for a fixed price issue, an important point in the case of large issues. More recent reluctance to use the tender method was based on the allegation that there would be no market after the issue and the suspicion that the price would weaken, that the public was not very taken with the idea, and that a smaller volume of subscription money would come forward, especially since stags might hold back because of the absence of a fixed price. Some might also have been reluctant to put in tenders for fear of making fools of themselves, and the small investor might well have felt at a disadvantage compared with the large institutions. On the company side some positively welcomed a large oversubscription and a hefty premium on their shares since it brought good publicity, but little by way of long-term benefit. Finally, many issuing houses and brokers felt that the tender system meant an abrogation of their responsibility to fix a price. There is also a feeling that an issue should not 'screw the market for its last penny' and then within a short space of time come back with a rights issue.

The tender method has been in continuous use by water companies. This arises because they are required by Act of Parliament to provide water as cheaply as possible, and so to raise capital on the cheapest terms. Under the Act they are subject to restrictions on the level of charges and the amount by which their total revenue over the year may exceed their operating expenses. There are also restrictions on the dividend level, but most have paid the maximum allowed for many years and they have in effect become preference shares in the eyes of investors.[53] Applicants for a new issue apply for a stated amount of stock at a price above the minimum offer level. The shares are alloted to the highest bidder, and it is usually necessary to make a proportionate allotment to one group of applicants to exhaust the balance of the stock.

Following heavy oversubscription and large premiums on fixed price issues in the late 1950s, and after some doubts had been expressed in some quarters about the legality of the usual method of making allotments when an issue is oversubscribed, namely by ballot, the suggestion was made to the Council of the Stock Exchange in 1960 that it should permit tender issues for industrial companies. A year later it decided to grant a trial run for a property company issue. In this case the issuing house stated the minimum price at which the shares had been underwritten, while allotment at a uniform price was designed to cover the issue and give a fair spread of shareholdings. In the words of the prospectus; 'In deciding the basis of allocation due consideration will be given to the desirability of spreading shares over a reasonable number of applicants in relation to the number of shares offered, the size of the company, the obtaining of a quotation and the establishment of a market.'

In the case of subsequent tender issues the usual practice was for the issuing house to buy the block of shares from the company at the (unknown) allotment price, or at this price minus a few pence per share for its turn. Allotment to applicants was invariably made at a single price, the striking or clearance price (where two prices were allowed, as an experiment, they were very near each other). The striking price was invariably below the highest prices tendered, and fixed so as to ensure a wide spread of holdings, since the Stock Exchange liked to have about a hundred holders or more, but of course there was no guarantee that concentration of holdings would not occur. Certainly preferential allotment to those tendering at the highest prices was discouraged.

The closing months of 1963 witnessed some 15 issues of industrial ordinary shares by tender. The success of the early experiments, and the rising share market, more than anything else accounted for the crop; it is doubtful that they occurred because there were special pricing problems attached to the issues.[54] With subsequent fluctuating markets there was a lull in tender issues, and on such weaker markets there was less likelihood of fixed price issues being badly underpriced. A resurgence of tender issues took place in 1967, and continued into 1968, allegedly because the heavy premiums on fixed price issues prompted many company directors to opt for the tender method. In 1968 there were 35 tenders, but many were 'no new money' issues (20 tenders raised some £10m.). On the ensuing weaker markets only four tenders were made in 1969 and apart from water companies, none have since been made.

The tender method appears to have been more successful than alternative methods of issue in reducing the size of the market discount. In an analysis of 15 tender issues made in 1963 Merrett, Howe and Newbould found that the average market discount was significantly less than that on offers for sale and placings made in the same year, and indeed over the longer period of 1959–63.[55] This, it was felt, established a strong *prima facie* case for the superiority of the tender method, since from the standpoint of existing shareholders new ones did not come into a company at preferential terms, and where shareholders were selling their shares on the market they obtained a better price than they would get by other methods of disposal. The tender method, however, was not without its oversubscription and stagging problems. Overpriced subscriptions from stags in 1969 led to unduly high striking prices, and subsequent falls in the market price resulted in a total loss of forward momentum with the shares standing at a discount to the issue price.

Issues to shareholders (rights issues)

As can be seen from tables 6.4 and 6.5 rights issues has been a popular method of raising capital by companies, both by value and number, culminating in a figure of £1,329m. in 1975, and of £1,028m. in 1976. It is, of course, for quoted companies a Stock Exchange rule that in 'the absence of exceptional circumstances the issue for cash of equity capital, or capital having an element of equity, must be offered in the first place to the equity shareholders unless these holders have agreed in general meeting to other specific proposals', and that such an offer 'must normally be made by way of right as opposed to an open offer to shareholders'. The procedure thus enables the shareholder to maintain his proportion of the security in issue.

It is important that the sum involved must be reasonable in relation to the amount outstanding, and that the current market price is well above the nominal value. It is expected that the company will be able to maintain its rate of dividend. If the rights issue was large in relation to the existing capital shareholders would probably doubt the company's ability to maintain the prevailing return on capital, and the rights would then go at very low values.

The use of rights issues has usually been associated with some of the following circumstances. The supply of securities to the market tends to increase if there is a continuous squeeze on bank accommodation which necessitates funding operations; when there has been a build up of fixed interest borrowing which has unbalanced the equity base and used up all the mortgageable assets – as happened in the period following the introduction of corporation tax; and when high interest rates prevail with falling equity dividend yields the attractiveness of rights issues in cost terms are increased.

A rights issue involves an offer of shares to the existing shareholders in proportion to their holding, and normally at a price below that of the existing shares. Sometimes an issue is made without limiting the number of shares for which a shareholder may apply but this would then be made at a price closer to the prevailing market level than that of a conventional rights offer.[56] If a shareholder cannot afford to take up an offer he can sell part of the rights and use the proceeds to purchase a limited number of shares; if he decides not to take up the offer he can sell the rights for cash, which in effect compensates him for the fall in the value of the shares he already holds. The reaction of investors would seem to depend on the value of the rights, the prevailing degree of monetary restraint, and the state of expectations as to future share prices. A sample survey of rights issues made in 1957–8 indicates that existing shareholders usually take up over 80% of issues.[57]

The rights are of course valuable in that the price of the new shares will normally be below the market price of the enlarged share capital.[58] The actual price at which the issue is made is, however, largely immaterial. The new supply of shares will cause the price to fall, but it follows that the shareholders' portfolios will have the same value afterwards as the value of the shares before the rights issue plus the actual cash that is subscribed; or put another way the total market value of the company's shares after the issue will be equal to the total value before the issue plus the sum of money received from the issue. The price after the issue determines the value of the right to subscribe at the special issue price. The price of the rights themselves will not be constant but will vary over the period for which the rights are excercisable and with the expectations of the existing shareholders.

As to the margin between the issue price and the existing market price, this tends to be variable. For a sample of 110 rights issues made in 1963 Merrett, Howe and Newbould found that the average percentage difference was 35.6%, with the majority of issues in the range of 10–50%.[59] The more receptive the market the smaller the margin between the two price levels. Many rights issues are underwritten, but opinion is divided as to the need for this protection. If the price is fixed at the correct level so that the rights have a significant value, then it is likely that the issue will be taken up since every shareholder will be better off than if he allows the rights to lapse. In their survey of rights issues for 1963 Merrett, Howe and Newbould found average underwriting costs to be 1.4% (as a percentage of the issue price) and concluded that they were 'substantial in relation to the likely risks involved'.[60] If prices are fixed so that the right to subscribe is in danger of becoming valueless then underwriting may be necessary. But underwriters are only likely to take losses if the value of the shares and rights is less than the price, that is, the rights have a negative value and they decide to sell immediately.

Capitalization issues

Although this is a means of issuing additional shares free of charge to shareholders it is an important part of the new issue market's activity in a broader sense. Such issues usually involve changing accumulated reserves into issued capital and doing so by allotting additional shares to existing shareholders in porportion to their holdings. The latter's portfolio will have the same total value, while the market price of the increased number of shares will approximate to whatever fraction of the old price the old number of shares is of the new number. Companies also resort to annual capitalizations of reserves, and do so by small bonus issues representing re-invested profits. Nominal capital is thus kept in step with actual capital, and the practice is to keep a constant rate of dividend on an increasing number of shares.[61]

Apart from the desirable feature of keeping actual and nominal capitals in step certain other important advantages spring from capitalization issues. A company with a successful profit record and high ploughback will find that its shares earn a high dividend and will be quoted above nominal values. A bonus issue can reduce the nominal rate of dividend to more normal levels and prevent the share from becoming too 'heavy'. Some investors have a prejudice against shares which stand well above their nominal values, while it is generally accepted that shares with lower values enjoy a wider market.

During the immediate post-war years bonus issues were subject to various degrees of official control. During the war they had been expressly forbidden, but when the war ended restrictions were relaxed somewhat. This enabled companies to proceed with new issues containing an element of bonus, and many of these were essential to the conversion of industry at a much higher general level of prices. The C.I.C. approved of some but not others, while *The Economist* pointedly noted that restrictions merely 'served the political purpose of exposing high rates of dividend on irrelevant legal capital'.[62] An additional restraint was imposed in 1947 by Section 60 of the Finance Act which levied a 10% duty on the value of the bonus shares, or the bonus element involved in a proposed issue. During the next two years the nominal value of bonus issues amounted to about £12m. However, due to its inhibiting effect on companies which needed to raise new money, it was abolished in 1949.[63] The abolition spared large issues from having to assume big risks when they had to strike a balance between a fair and attractive price, and keeping the duty as low as possible. However, on the political front they were suspect as a means of evading dividend limitation, and the C.I.C. in 1949 suspended all applications for this reason.

Despite continued surveyance from the C.I.C. the volume of capitalization issues in the mid-1950s was rapidly catching up on previous restrictions. Companies were also overcoming some of their earlier reluctance to capitalize, and investors were quickly getting accustomed to frequent scrip issues from companies whose boards were market conscious. These for the most part took the form of capitalizations of reserves by means of free scrip issues, but some also took the form of restoring the nominal value of shares which had previously been written down during a period of difficulty, and was done mainly for prestige reasons.[64]

New issue costs

Apart from the interest rate which prevails in the market at the time of issue, and which is a continuous charge against the revenue of the company in the form of a fixed payment or a variable dividend, other costs are incurred when an issue of securities is made through market channels. They may be subdivided into conventional costs, which include the administrative, legal and underwriting costs, all of which have over time received much attention, and the other discernible cost, which has until recently received no extensive examination – though it is pertinent to note that commentators were aware of its existence – that is, what is termed the 'market discount'. This is taken as the excess of the market valuation of the issue over the fixed price received by the issuing house. Lavington put the matter somewhat differently, but the object was the same. In an efficient market 'the source of earning power must be rightly formulated in order that it may exert its appropriate power upon the available supply of capital.'[65]

To turn to the conventional costs of issue. The most extensive recent work on this aspect of issue costs is that done by Merrett, Howe and Newbould, covering 391 prospectus between 1959–63 which involved issues of ordinary shares by new quoted companies. They obtained the results given in table 6.6.

Table 6.6 Conventional costs as a percentage of size of issue (1959–63 averages, weighted by the size of issue)

Issue	Number of issues	Average size	Costs %
Public issues	34	£1.3m.	3.5
Offers	149	£482,000	9.6
Placings	193	£186,000	8.6
Tenders (1963 Only)	15	£921,000	6.4

Source: A. J. Merrett, M. Howe and G. D. Newbould, *Equity Issues and the London Capital Market*, London, 1967, p. 113.

As can be seen costs vary with the method of issue. Despite the smaller average size of placings it appears to be a cheaper method than an offer for sale, a cost advantage explained by economies on allotment, printing and advertising.[66] The cost advantage of placings over offers was highly significant for all placings except for the very smallest issues of under £100,000 net size, and 40% of the placings analysed were in this category.[67] Whatever the method of issue at this size the costs of issue averaged about 25% of net proceeds. Even for issues in the size class £100,000–£200,000 the average costs were 17.8% of net proceeds for offers and 13.6% for placings. By present-day standards these are very small issues indeed.

Unfortunately it is not possible to make a detailed comparison of the above costs with those identified by R. F. Henderson for the period 1945–7, since the latter not only worked on a gross basis but his analysis also included old and new companies making both ordinary and preference issues. In the case of the more recent survey companies having a quotation rarely used the above methods of issue, while preference issues were indeed a rarity. However, some points might usefully be made. Henderson found that for public issues and offers by new companies the average costs of issue for 24 items was 11% (no new money raised); while for 12 issues of between £100,000–£250,000, it was 13%. For small placings by new companies (new money and no new money) it was 23–4%.[68] Since the basis for the calculation of Henderson's placings costs was different from that used by Merrett, Howe and Newbould little can be inferred as to the cheapening of issuing expenses. On small issues the costs were then high and this has been the case for the recent studies. This is not surprising since there are large overhead elements such as administrative and marketing expenses. Such costs are undoubtedly a heavy burden for a small company, but subsequent issues tend to be cheaper whether done by rights or through the market. What companies are buying is marketability and part of this cost can be offset by the reduction in future issue costs through being an old company. One means of lessening costs for small firms is to seek a provincial quotation where costs have been identified as being lower. In a survey covering 1951–60 J. K. S. Ghandi found that the 'provincial exchanges were able to make placings of small size for new firms more economically than could be done at London'. However, in the case of offers for sale, 'there does not appear any basis to discriminate between them'.[69] Although some time has elapsed since this survey, and the stock exchanges have been united with London it is still likely that provincial overheads retain an advantage over London levels.

In the case of the sub-division (underwriting, administrative costs, and renumeration to advisers) some interesting features came to light from the Merrett, Howe and Newbould investigation. With underwriting the usual practice is to pay a fee, but sometimes part of the issuing house's fee, or the 'turn', may be in lieu of the underwriting commission, while in several of the prospectuses they examined no underwriting commission was disclosed. It might be that in the buoyant share market of the 1950s some issues dispensed with underwriting. Their main finding was the relatively low average cost of underwriting in any year, or for any method of issue. Expressed as a percentage of the issue price of each share the highest was for offers, 2.4% in 1959, while the lowest was for tenders, 1.3% for 1963 issues. Compared with Henderson's figures for 1936–7 the post-war period witnessed a fall in underwriting commissions. The average commission for 49 offers in 1936–7 was 3.6%, with 4.0% paid on some issues. The reasons for this decline are probably that the equity market has been generally rising, thus presenting lower risks; rising share prices brought forth a greater supply of underwriters; and financial institutions competed actively to get on to the regular underwriting lists of brokers so as to get stock on good terms. Both Henderson, and Merrett, Howe and Newbould noted the uniformity of commission levels, whereas they might be expected to vary with the risks attached to each issue. Presumably the uniformity is due to the practice of underwriters of spreading risks over several issues, so there is no need to match each fee to the risk.[70]

Administrative costs represent a somewhat heterogenous collection, comprising Stock Exchange quotation fees, capital dues, printing and advertising, administration of the allotment, bankers and legal fees, and reporting accountants' fees. Some items vary with the size of issue, others with type of issue. Administrative costs for offers for sale done in 1959–63 ranged from 5.1% to 9.5% of the size of issue, while for placings the figures were 4.2% to 6.3%. The figure for public issues made in 1963 was 1.6%. Tenders done in the same year worked out at 4.1%.[71] Placings involved lower administrative costs than offers in view of savings on several items, for example, printing, advertising, and allotment expenses, while the large sizes of public issues give low percentage figures. Henderson's counterpart, specific costs, for 1936–7 were similar for offers by new companies of ordinary shares of less than £250,000 – these were mostly in the range 8–11%, and for larger issues in the range 4–7%.[72] With regard to the net remuneration of advisers Merrett, Howe and Newbould found that for public issues made in 1962–3 it was 0.3% of the size of issue, while for offers made during 1959–63 it ranged from 1.1% to 2.0%, and with placings from 2.9% to 4.2%. The remuneration for the latter was consistently higher since the risks were greater, and the sums involved were smaller, so giving high percentage figures. There seems to have been some reduction in both the level and range of remuneration from pre-war days since Henderson's figures for offers of under £500,000 ranged from 0.3% to 14%, and for large issues from 2–10%.[73]

The main objective in fixing the issue price is to pitch it at or as near as possible to the equilibrium market price of the shares. If there is then a large identifiable market discount it is maintained that this is due to inaccurate pricing. The general practice with fixed price issues is to adopt a price which gives a slightly higher yield than that available on comparable investments, thus making the newly marketed shares somewhat more attractive. A market discount is then identified if the price fixed proves to be less than some subsequent market price (corrected for general share price movements). This is taken as an avoidable discount and deemed to represent a loss to existing shareholders and a cost alongside the more conventional costs of issue. Not only do existing shareholders loose in terms of price level, but new shareholders are admitted to share in company profits on favourable terms.[74]

In the calculation of market discount Merrett, Howe and Newbould selected the market price ruling on the second day of dealings, 'this being the day closest to the date of issue when business in the share could be expected to be at a normal level'.[75] The analysis revealed substantial market discounts for offers and placings; the (unweighted) market discount on offers for the period 1959–63 was 17.2%, and on placings 25% of the proceeds of issue net of conventional costs. On average offers for sale generated lower market discounts than on placings. In contrast fifteen tender issues made in 1963 showed market discounts of only 6.46%.[76] They concluded that the issuing houses had tended to take inadequate notice of the effects of the upward movement in prices during the period studied in making their assessment of the likely reception for issues. Accordingly, on the basis of the lower market discount it displayed they advocated the wider adoption of the tender method. This would produce considerably lower total costs, for example, offers made in 1963 had average total costs of 60.8% of net proceeds, compared with only 17.2% for the tender method.

The appearance of a market discount for the period 1959–63 reflected not only excess demand for shares on a rising market, but also the practice of the market of pitching prices at attractive levels. The appearance of a premium (quite apart from the introductory discount) is deemed necessary to induce underwriters to participate in issues, and to attract applications from stags. For the underwriters an expected premium reduces the risks of getting left with a large block of stock which cannot be sold off in the short term. Also the fact that the issue price has to be fixed some time in advance of issue with the possibility that market conditions may change leads to the introduction of an element of caution in price fixing. Many issuing houses, therefore, aim at a premium in the region of 10–15%.[77] In the case of a good issue it is seldom the case that they give it away, but neither on the other hand does the market quickly forget a flop.

In connection with the above approach it is worth noting that R. F. Henderson did some similar calculations in his survey of issues for 1945–

1947. Indeed his calculation of placing costs included an element of market discount. He also analysed offers of under £250,000 and took the average price on the first day of dealings as the basis for calculating his costs of issue, defined as 'this price multiplied by the number of shares in the issue, less the sum received by the vendors of the shares from the issuing house, net of expenses'. On this basis the aggregate costs for fifteen offers worked out at 24%, compared with 11% conventional costs. However, Henderson argued against the use of the opening price basis (except for placings for 'want of anything better') since it is the prospectus price which represents the price paid by the public at their first and main opportunity to acquire shares. The opening price calculation is not a reliable guide to market valuation since by the time the market opens it is known whether the issue is over, under or just covered by the subscription. This knowledge is bound to influence the price level and such prices will vary widely in relation to prospectus price depending on the popularity of the issue.[78] The price is, of course, made in a market where only a portion of the issued total is traded.

Market institutions

Merchant bank new issue activity in the post-war period has been almost exclusively confined to the domestic front. There was little by way of surplus from the balance of payments for foreign lending, while given their wartime experience there was little inclination on the part of investors to lend abroad. On the home front there was the growing attraction of industrial equity issues. The members of the Issuing Houses Association, formed in 1945, is drawn largely from the ranks of the merchant banks, members of the Accepting Houses Committee, numerous investment banks, and from financial trusts who are dealers in securities and sponsors of new issues – the survivors of the 1920s flood of such creations. The composition of the acceptance houses has changed very little from the early post-war years, there being a few amalgamations and some new entrants.[79] The number of the other members of the Issuing House Association has increased somewhat since 1945. Shortly after its formation the I.H.A. had a membership of 52, 'which included every issuing house in the country'.[80] By 1970 the membership had increased to 58. The number of stockbrokers interested in the new issue field has remained very large; in 1963 147 brokers handled one or more issues without the participation of an issuing house, while the total number of issues handled by brokers amounted to 988. The comparable figures for 1969 were 97 and 1,112.

As to the work of the market agents the analysis by Merrett, Howe, and

Newbould of the information contained in *The Times Issuing House Year Book* for 1963 provides the most detailed picture available. In that year the issuing houses handled 549 issues, of which placings were the most numerous, 162; public issues and offers, 90; rights issues, 105; share exchanges, 112; bonus issues, 64; and introductions, 16. Of these 29 were handled by non-members of the I.H.A. Only seven issuing houses handled more than twenty issues. As to the volume of issues handled by brokers alone the figure of 988 was recorded for 1963. One broker handled over 100 issues, while 21 brokers handled over 11 issues, with 120 brokers being involved with between 1 and 10 issues. The majority of issues dealt with by brokers were capitalizations and exchanges (well over 350 of each) but these were seldom very complex capital re-organizations, 51 public issues and offers, 48 placings, 33 introductions, and 117 rights issues.[81]

The work done by an issuing house or broker, acting either as principal or agent for a company, in the issue process is quite considerable. In line with their now accepted responsibility to the public they ensure that the credentials of the client company are satisfactory and they pursue an accounting, legal and technical investigation of some depth. The issuing house/broker advise in all matters relating to the issue – the amount, the method, the type of security, the terms of the issue and the timing.[82] They endeavour from the public interest standpoint to ensure that an issue is made on the 'proper terms', while from the company's standpoint it reflects rather on the sponsors of an issue if within a relatively short space of time a company has to resort to a rights issue because it has run into liquidity problems. Contact is thus not confined to the issue but is close and continuous, and indeed the issuing house may support an issue if the price is seen to be weakening. On the market arrangements and pricing of the issue the broker is fully consulted, and it is through his offices that an approach is made to the Quotations Department of the Stock Exchange. Indeed, the latter in its own surveyance of applications relies heavily on the work of the sponsoring issuing house and broker.

Although the issuing houses are responsible for raising the money they do not provide more than a limited portion of any issue themselves. Essentially they are sponsors and underwriters. To this end they have at hand a well-developed underwriting network, and it is comparatively rare for an issuing house to underwrite wholly by itself. The bulk of the sub-underwriting is done by a large number of city institutions who come to this circle 'as they become established bodies' and as contacts are made as 'part of the general mechanism of the City'.[83] Insurance companies are by far the most important group: in 1959 they were reported as taking half the underwriting, but the proportion is now probably around a third.[84] Other important groups are the pension funds, investment trusts and charitable funds, and the very large investment funds managed by most merchant banks. The underwriting list is an important asset for the issuing house and stockbroker, just as to be on it is a great advantage for the institutions. Occasionally the broker to the issue may act as the agent 'who goes around and places the sub-underwriting on behalf of the issuing house', and for this he is paid an overriding commission.[85] The commission paid to the sub-underwriters varies with the number of shares they agree to take up and the length of time they are at risk.

The general impression appears to be that over the post-war period both issuing houses and brokers have increased their efficiency as issuing agents. *The Economist* commented rather acidly that during the 1950s the issuing houses were greedier and less conscientious, and that 'the sheer inaccuracy of judgement of the issuing houses and brokers has been reduced'.[86] The study of Merrett, Howe and Newbould for 1959–63 can offer little by way of long-term testimony. However, they found, contrary to what the I.H.A. asserted to the Radcliffe Committee, that there was no particular advantage in choosing an issuing house in preference to a broker in an effort to reduce either conventional costs or the market discount. There was, however, an advantage in selecting particular issuing houses and brokers as far as the pricing of shares was concerned. This would indicate that more work should gravitate to such houses, but it was pointed out that new companies to the market were usually ignorant of such disparities, and that anyway a heavy oversubscription is equated with success so that a high market discount is quite acceptable.[87] The assertion by the issuing houses to the Radcliffe Committee that they were more suited to new issue work than brokers, would no doubt hold if the comparison is with small brokers, but some broking firms are now larger than some of the issuing houses and can give equal advice and service.[88]

Notes

1 For detailed coverage of the Committee's work see Committee on the Working of the Monetary System, *Report*, Cmnd 827, paras 471, 965–77 (Radcliffe Committee, 1959); J. C. R. Dow, *The Management of the British Economy 1945–60*, Cambridge, 1964, pp. 242–4; 'Government Control over the Use of Capital Resources', *Midland Bank Review*, August 1950; 'Capital Issues Control: Dead or Dormant, *Midland Bank Review*, February 1960.

2 *Income from Companies and its Distribution*, Cmnd 6172, Report No. 2, pp. 16–17, Royal Commission on the Distribution of Income and Wealth, 1975.

3 *The Economist*, 9 June 1945, p. 776.

4 The figures for total manufacturing in the Bank of England (old series) are somewhat larger which is due to differences in compilation; see notes to table 6.1.

5 R. F. Henderson, *The New Issue Market and the Finance of Industry*, Cambridge, 1951, p. 126. These companies were new to the market, while the 'no money' category meant that the company itself received no new capital.

6 *The Economist*, 5 July 1952, p. 50.

7 *Midland Bank Review*, February 1947, p. 6.

8 B. Tew and R. F. Henderson (eds) *Studies in Company Finance*, Cambridge, 1959, pp. 64–8. They found that the amount of net investment in fixed assets was not of itself an important influence on the degree of recourse to the new issue market.

9 *Midland Bank Review*, February 1947, p. 6; February 1948, p. 8.

10 Tew and Henderson, op. cit., p. 73.

11 Only a small part of the increase in bank lending went directly to finance private investment, but no doubt some of the new deposits created seeped through to support the flow of new issues; P. B. Kenen, *British Monetary Policy and the Balance of Payments 1951–57*, Cambridge (Mass.), 1960, pp. 101–4.

12 By excusing tax on the amount of the allowance it gave a subsidy of about 10% and 5% on plant and buildings respectively; Dow, op. cit., p. 207; see also Chapter 8.

13 H. B. Rose, 'Monetary Policy and the Capital Market 1955–56', *Economic Journal*, 1957, p. 404.

14 See Chapter 11.

15 *The Economist*, 22 October 1960, pp. 388–390; *Midland Bank Review*, February 1961, p. 11.

16 *Midland Bank Review*, February 1966, p. 24.

17 *The Economist*, 14 October 1967, p. 222; 18 November 1967; 16 March 1968, pp. 107–108.

18 This figure includes the £123m. of rights issue by B.P., but only half of this came from the market.

19 Some of the rights issues made in 1975 were designed to overcome the restrictions imposed on dividend levels by the prices and incomes policy which limited increases per share to 10%, but total dividends could be increased in proportion to the number of shares. In October 1975 the Treasury required companies to seek prior approval for such issues which reduced the use of this device; *Midland Bank Review*, February 1976, p. 23.

20 *Midland Bank Review*, February 1953, p. 14.

21 *Midland Bank Review*, February 1955, p. 14; February 1956, p. 16.

22 *Midland Bank Review*, February 1968, p. 8; February 1969, p. 11. At the end of 1968 the redemption yield on debenture and loan stocks stood at 9.2%, and the earnings yield on industrial shares at 4.5%.

23 The large volume of debt issues in 1965, £426.5m., was aided by the buoyancy of the fixed interest market during the second half of the year. Most of the stock issued was debt with a small element of unsecured loan stock. The figure of equities for 1966 is swollen by the B.P. rights issue of £60m.

24 *Midland Bank Review*, February 1951, p. 10; February 1952, p. 13.

25 *The Economist*, 16 September 1950, p. 488. This method avoided stamp duty, and the other costs and complications of public issue. The institutions were happy to co-operate since they got blocks of high-grade stock, with acceptable yields, and the absence of public dealings was no hardship with such short-dated stock.

26 Stock Exchange rules state that 'In the absence of exceptional circumstances the issue for cash of equity capital, or capital having an element of equity, must be offered in the first place to the equity shareholders unless those holders have agreed in general meeting to other specific proposals', Stock Exchange Yellow Book, para. 22.

27 L. C. L. Skerratt, 'Convertible Loan Stocks 1958–1968: An Empirical Investigation', *Journal of Business Finance*, vol. 3, 1971, pp. 29–31.

28 ibid., p. 32.

29 J. Sparrow, 'Convertible Loan Stocks', *Journal of Business Finance*, vol. 1, 1969, p. 27.

30 ibid., pp. 27–8.

31 ibid., p. 26. L. C. L. Skerratt calculated that £82.3m. of convertibles were issued for acquisition purposes in 1962, an average per year of £40m. during 1965–7 and £107m. in 1968; Skerratt, op. cit., p. 29.

32 *Midland Bank Review*, February 1969, p. 11.

33 *The Economist*, 5 April 1969, p. 67. At this time several variations were offered to tempt subscriptions, e.g., dual currency stocks; for details see *Midland Bank Review*, February 1970, p. 4.

34 *The Economist*, 2 July 1949, p. 40; 7 January 1950, p. 40.

35 Rose, op. cit., p. 404.

36 P. R. A. Kirkman and J. Usher, 'Recent

Developments In Preference Share Finance', *Journal of Business Finance*, vol. 3, 1971, p. 44.

37 ibid., pp. 45–7, for a detailed discussion of these difficulties. The authors note that the brewing industry still retains a very high preference share level, despite the savings which possible exchanges with debentures might bring.

38 The figure for 1972 of £650m. of equities contains a large financial element. Issues by banking and finance amounted to £565m., of which £482m. went to investment trusts and finance houses while £100m. was used for investment in continental securities.

39 A. J. Merrett, M. Howe and G. D. Newbould, *Equity Issues and the London Capital Market*, London, 1967, p. 158.

40 F. W. Paish, *Business Finance*, 2nd ed., London, 1961, pp. 112–13.

41 *The Economist*, 20 October 1945, p. 573; 9 February 1946, p. 127. It should be noted that the prevailing paper shortage and other problems made offers a little difficult to organize.

42 *The Economist*, 8 May 1966, p. 1004.

43 *The Economist*, 23 July 1949, p. 210.

44 Merrett, Howe and Newbould, op. cit., p. 126.

45 *The Economist*, 30 March 1946, p. 506. The issuing houses defence of this practice was that they relied on professional support for issues which had poor public response, or when some unforseen 'external event queers the pitch'.

46 The Stock Exchange at this time was not prepared to use renouncible forms for new issues, which was a device used by one issuing house to curb stagging.

47 Although the placing method can be regarded as a form of underwriting, this does not rule out underwriting being done for such issues. One means of avoiding such an underwriting commission and still ensure a successful placing is the recently introduced technique of pre-placing. This involves approaching prospective placees to obtain some idea of their interest before the firm placing letters are sent out; favourable replies to such pre-placing letters effectively underwrite the stock.

48 Private placings are not recorded in the Bank of England series. Such placings involve unquoted shares. Against the cheapness of this method must be put the fact the price obtained may be below that of a quoted security so as to compensate the investors for lack of marketability.

49 G. W. Murphy and D. F. Prussman, 'Equity Placings on the New Issue Market', *Manchester School*, 1967, p. 174.

50 *The Economist*, 7 April 1945, p. 451. This delay of six months served to raise the cost of underwriting since the terms had to cover the additional risk of having to hold stock for that period. At the time of placing little information had to be made public, although this was later remedied when permission to deal was obtained.

51 *The Economist*, 20 July 1946, pp. 106–7.

52 In September 1966 the proportions to be placed were raised to 35% for equity and 30% for fixed interest. This higher figure was fixed in an attempt to prevent quoted companies from being classed as 'closed' companies under the terms of the 1965 Finance Act.

53 *The Economist*, 27 March 1965, pp. 42–6.

54 Merrett, Howe and Newbould, op. cit., p. 76.

55 The analysis was based on the price ruling on the second day of dealings in the share. 'Extensive analysis failed to reveal any feature other than the methods of issue itself to account for the significant difference in the average market discount on the two fixed price methods, offers and placings, and on the tender method of issue'; ibid., pp. 174–5. This finding was confirmed in a study of several tender issues made in the first half of 1964, see M. E. Lehr and G. D. Newbould, 'New Issues – Activity and Pricing Performance 1964 to 1967', *Investment Analyst*, October 1967, pp. 20–3.

56 Paish, op. cit., p. 120.

57 S. K. Edge, 'Shareholders' Reaction to Rights Issues', *Manchester School*, 1965, pp. 263–4; 'Sources of Funds from Rights Issues and their Cost', *Journal of Economic Studies*, 1966, pp. 30–51.

58 For a detailed description of the mechanics of the process and some examples see Merrett, Howe and Newbould, op. cit., pp. 52–3.

59 ibid., p. 56. *The Economist* reported that in the case of the spurt of rights issues in 1968 many were priced within 15–20% of the market value of the shares; 8 June 1968, p. 83.

60 ibid., pp. 54–5. For an account of the 1975 rights boom see P. S. Manley, 'The New

Issue Revival', *Moorgate and Wall Street*, Spring 1976, pp. 29–44.

61 Paish, op. cit., pp. 120–4.

62 *The Economist*, 17 August 1946, p. 265.

63 *Midland Bank Review*, 'Government Control over the use of Capital Resources', op. cit., p. 4.

64 Paish, op. cit., p. 122.

65 F. Lavington, *The English Capital Market*, London, 1921, p. 190.

66 Merrett, Howe and Newbould found for the period 1959–63 that the fixed element in issue costs rose, but that variable costs fell. Taking these two together, the total costs in the small issues tended to rise, and in the larger issues to fall. Consequently they concluded that some of the effects of inflation were offset 'perhaps by rising efficiency'; p. 128. In a more limited survey E. W. Davies and K. A. Yeomans found that while issue costs were falling in the 1960s, by 1971 the levels of 1959 had reappeared due, they suggest, to inflation pushing up service costs which militated against all issues but was particularly bad for small issues; *Company Finance and the Capital Market*, Cambridge, 1974, pp. 17–19.

67 The Radcliffe Committee estimated that a private placing of say under £100,000 cost between 2.5–3%; however, the real cost would be the high yield paid on unquoted stock; Radcliffe Committee, *Report*, para. 230.

68 Henderson, op. cit., pp. 144–7.

69 J. K. S Ghandi, 'Some Aspects of the Provincial New Issue Market', *Bulletin of the Oxford University Institute of Economics and Statistics*, vol. 26, p. 255.

70 Underwriting losses for the period 1959–1963, as calculated by Merrett, Howe and Newbould, were very low, being 14% of receipts; see p. 106. During the late 1960s heavier losses have been reported, and underwriters reacted by becoming more choosy.

71 Merrett, Howe and Newbould, op. cit., p. 109.

72 Henderson, op. cit., pp. 132–3. Expressed as percentages of gross offers.

73 ibid., pp. 133–4; Merrett, Howe and Newbould, op. cit., pp. 110–12.

74 Merrett, Howe and Newbould, op. cit., chapter 6.

75 ibid., p. 158. The conclusions were not changed if average prices for the first week or month had been used.

76 The average market discount for offers made in 1963 was 34.2%, and for placings 38.5%. Davies and Yeomans confirmed the findings of Merrett, Howe and Newbould in the broad distribution of revealed discounts. For their sample they found that issues by tender displayed the lowest average discount at 6.95%, offers for sale stood at 8.88%, and placings 19.08%. Also they found that there was an inverse relation between firm size and market discount in stable markets; Davies and Yeomans, op. cit., pp. 54–6.

77 Sir T. Hartford, 'Pricing a Flotation', *Journal of Business Finance*, 1969, p. 19. Assuming that the price is fixed on a Monday the prospectus usually appears the following Monday, the Allotment Letters are posted the Monday after that for dealing the following day. About a fortnight thus elapses from the fixing of the price to the commencement of dealings.

78 Henderson, op. cit., pp. 123–5. The range was smaller for placings where there is no certain knowledge of the state of over or undersubscription.

79 The most important amalgamation took place in 1965 when M. Samuel merged with Philip Hill, Higginson, Erlangers to form Hill Samuel & Co. Ltd. During recent years the commercial banks have displayed some interest in merchant banking activity and have done so by acquiring shares in merchant banks, or by recruiting expertise from such banks. The impression seeems to be 'that they have not yet found the knack' of handling new issues.

80 The Association was formed in 1945 to negotiate with the C.I.C. Its main objects are to 'represent the interests of Banking Houses and other institutions in relation to their activities as Issuing Houses and in particular to provide a medium for placing before H.M. Government, the Bank of England, the Council of the Stock Exchange and other public bodies, authorities and officials the views of the Association on matters affecting such activities'; *The Times Issuing House Year Book*, 1970, p. 13.

81 Merrett, Howe and Newbould, op. cit., pp. 21–6.

82 For a detailed description of the mechanics, see ibid., pp. 17–28. In the matter of timing the marshalling of the queue for large issues of over £1m. is done by the government broker; under that figure by the Stock Exchange. It has its origins in the 1930s with the informal restrictions placed on the market during the War Loan Conversion operations. The Treasury's memorandum of guidance to the C.I.C. merely carried established practice a stage further.

83 Radcliffe Committee, *Minutes of Evidence*, Qs 4035, 4031.

84 Radcliffe Committee, *Minutes of Evidence*, Qs 4029–36. A leading stockbroking firm stated that the normal proportion for insurance companies to take is around one third.

85 Radcliffe Committee, *Minutes of Evidence*, Qs 4032, 4033–5.

86 *The Economist*, 16 March 1968, p. 102.

87 Merret, Howe and Newbould, op. cit., pp. 211–12.

88 The issuing houses claimed that they had an advantage in terms of expertise and resources, especially if something went wrong; Radcliffe Committee, *Minutes of Evidence*, Qs 4020, 4023.

7 Banks and industry

The clearing banks were inhibited from taking a full share of the new business . . . and consequently lost ground, as a group, in the face of keen and successful competition from both domestic and foreign institutions.
                    THE MONOPOLIES COMMISSION
If the public provide not a bank, private bankers will take the advantage of this circumstance . . . .
                                DAVID HUME

The control of bank advances

For almost the entire post-war period commercial bank advances have been subject to varying degrees of official guidance. It has generally taken the form of requests, delivered on behalf of the Treasury by the governor of the Bank of England, but in the background there is the knowledge that statutory powers of direction could be invoked. For the most part such requests have been qualitative, with an occasional stiffening of quantitative controls. The looseness which characterized the qualitative guidance given arose from the wartime origins of the control. On the outbreak of war the banks were requested, in the interests of conserving real resources, to restrict advances 'to purposes which would assist the war effort or which were otherwise designed to meet national needs', that is, the 'needs of defence production, the export trade, coal mining and agriculture'. The banks thus had freedom of action with regard to the control of 'advances made in the normal course of banking business', and this exemption was continued after 1946 in the Borrowing (Control and Guarantees) Act. Such an informal method had its critics, but the prevailing physical controls made the strict working of financial ones less pressing. The banks themselves were at no loss to cut out extreme cases, and an official historian of the period observed that the 'easy and shadowy rein on which it was run was as good as the occasion demanded'.[1]

Throughout the immediate post-war period the banks were reminded on several occasions that they should conduct their lending according to the principles and spirit of the control exercised by the Capital Issues Committee. However, in the 1951 squeeze new and specific provisions were introduced regarding C.I.C. surveillance of certain bank lending practices. Traditionally, where banks sought a ruling from C.I.C. on applications for advances (as they had done in some cases) concern had been primarily with priority categories. Now the C.I.C. had to examine the terms proposed for repayment or refunding, and it was required to consider what stipulations should be made on these matters. The C.I.C. was instructed that when its permission was sought for a capital issue to refund bank advances previously granted, it must not concern itself with the fact that money had been lent and spent, but must be guided by the eligibility of the purposes for which it was spent. The C.I.C.'s practice was reported as being to insist that no advance should be granted for capital purposes unless there were firm arrangements for funding within six months.[2] In addition the banks were told that advances should not in general be made for capital expenditure purposes, but it was left to the banks to decide what was fixed or working capital purposes. Such procedures were not popular since banks could be put in a dilemma as to whether to accept a frozen advance, or else endanger a customer's business by calling in a loan; it also came at a time when more orthodox means of control were being introduced. Such C.I.C. shadowing of bank advances ended in 1953.

The general qualitative guidance given for most of the post-war period was, however, free from direct entanglement with C.I.C. The main import of qualitative guidance was that banks should scrutinize advances made in the ordinary course of business in the light of official policy as periodically made known to them. During the early post-war years the guidance given to the banks followed that given to the C.I.C., and requests for such co-operation were made in 1945, 1947 and 1949. These emphasized that credit policy should be such as to ensure that inflationary pressures would be kept in check, along with the familiar strictures to restrain lending for personal needs, speculative purposes, property deals and H.P. finance.[3] The goals towards which the banks were to steer their advances were set out more precisely in 1964 when the Bank of England laid down loan priorities for financial institutions and the tone amply indicates government intentions with regard to bank credit. It ran as follows:

Although continued restraint will be needed on the total of sterling credit granted to the private sector, lending to customers in the priority categories will not be restricted. The priority categories ... are the finance of exports, and lending in support of productive investment in manufacturing industry or agriculture. At the other end of the scale there should be no appreciable increase (other than seasonal) in lending for the finance of personal consumption, or for property development apart from housebuilding: credit that is facilitating payment for imports of manufactured goods for home consumption or for stockbuilding should continue to be restricted to the greatest extent possible.[4]

While the banks endeavoured, during periods when such cautionary behaviour was required of them, to shepherd advances 'to where they can assist directly or indirectly the export industries or necessary internal trade', they did not particularly like this discriminatory method of restraint. Banks and customers occasionally found that while long-term considerations might bring benefits to the national economy there was little by way of short-term gains to exports or through import saving. The banks reported that 'there have been instances in which failure to obtain credit from a bank for purposes which were officially regarded as standing low in the order of priorities, has been followed by resort to other largely unregulated and probably less economical, sources of finance.'[5] Added to these criticisms there were several others. Qualitative requests came into conflict with quantitative limits – the need to expand facilities for the highest priorities might come up against the ceiling imposed by quantitative restraint; customers kept coming to the banks without considering the validity of the purpose for which an advance was required; the requirements of many companies had to be assessed in relation to their total financial position and it was therefore not easy to deal with an application by reference to a particular requirement; while a bank might not allow an advance for some explicit purpose the customer might counter by using more fully overdraft limits already at his disposal for ordinary day-to-day business; and banks did not find it easy to classify industries as exporting or non-exporting so that any ruthless discrimination was bound to err – as one bank chairman put it, 'there is a vast range of accounts which simply cannot be classified in accordance with any simple schedule of sheep and goats'.[6]

The first quantitative restrictions were imposed in the mid-1950s. In July 1955 the banks were asked to make a 'positive and significant reduction' in advances. They agreed as a broad objective that the cut should be in the region of 10% of outstanding private sector loans which meant that they kept in step, but, of course, the cut did not apply equally to all customers. A year later a direct request came from the Chancellor asking the banks to pursue more resolutely a quantitative fall in advances.[7] The final request in this initial period of direct restraint was made in

September 1957, through the normal channels, that 'the average level of bank advances during the next twelve months . . . be held at the average level for the last twelve months.' This request was withdrawn in July 1958.[8]

During the next six years the banks were not hampered by quantitative limits. Admittedly from 1960 onwards they had occasionally to cope with calls for Special Deposits, but these were relatively small in amount while the burden of adjustment was made to fall on investments rather than the intended target of advances.[9] Quantitative targets then reappeared in May 1965 when the banks were requested to keep the growth, not only of advances, but also of acceptances and commercial bills, within a limit of 5% for the year from the end of March 1965. This 105% ceiling, due to end in March 1966, was continued until further notice in February 1966. The spring of 1967 brought a release from this unpleasant obligation, but the November devaluation led to the re-imposition of ceilings. With exceptions for shipbuilding, export finance, and public sector loans, the banks were asked to keep the total of all other advances down to their existing level. In May 1968 the exempted categories were brought within the ceiling which was raised to 104% of November 1967, but it was emphasized that non-priority lending would have to make room for increases in priority lending. Within a few months, however, the exceptions noted above were again excluded and the ceiling put at 98% of the November 1967 figure. Considerable difficulty was experienced by the banks in getting near this target and following several requests by the authorities they were ultimately 'fined' in June 1969 by a reduction in interest paid on Special Deposits. Continuing difficulties with the 98% ceiling led to the introduction in April 1970 of a 105% figure based on mid-March 1970.

In his Budget speech of 1971 the Chancellor noted that the existing arrangements for bank control were 'clearly defective on the score both of flexibility and of scope for competition'. Accordingly, in September, a more flexible system was introduced directed at regulating bank resources. Under the new arrangements the allocation of credit among customers was to depend primarily on interest rates and on the ability of borrowers of acceptable risk to pay the current market rate. Total official reliance on market rationing devices was, however, short-lived. Within a year qualitative guidance was again invoked and reaffirmed, the request being to restrict personal sector lending and insure priority for exports, industrial investment and other essential purposes. At the end of 1973 a further control was introduced in the form of the Supplementary Deposit Scheme, designed to aid control of bank lending and the money supply, a system known as the 'corset'. It continued in operation throughout

1974, but due to the weakness of demand for loans, and since most banks were well within the limits permitted under the scheme the Bank of England suspended its operation in February 1975. With the rapid growth in lending in 1976 the corset was re-applied in November.

Dislike of qualitative controls was very mild compared to the mounting frustration induced by successive quantitative embraces. Having already exercised a careful scrutiny of applications for the requirements of national policy the banks felt that there was little room for squeezing out advances, or for forcing customers to contract their operations. Severe difficulties arose from technical aspects. It was widespread banking practice to extend credit to customers in the form of overdrafts with an agreed maximum. Though such limits were formally open to be drawn upon throughout the year in most cases it was on the understanding that the customer would only run up to his limit for customary seasonal needs for a particular agreed purpose. According to the Radcliffe Committee it was rare for more than about two-thirds of total overdrafts to be used at any one time.[10] Thus in the initial stages of a squeeze there might well be an increase in advances as companies hastily drew on agreed facilities, while any cutbacks achieved took the form not of a reduction in advances already taken, but merely a reduction of borrowing limits; and even then large swings in borrowing could occur outside a bank's control. To bring about reductions in lending, which fell on non-priority borrowers, banks found that it could only be done 'by bearing down on borrowers with a degree of ruthlessness far beyond any reasonable concept of banker-customer relationship'.[11] It also involved the banks in a 'formidable administrative task'. All existing borrowing contracts had to be reviewed to see where reductions could be made, while the continuing flow of applications for new or increased advances had to be rigorously examined. In the personal and professional categories this amounted to several hundred thousand accounts and even large cuts in individual loans would only produce a modest overall reduction; an increase in accommodation to a few large customers could nullify such labours.[12]

Credit squeezes also tended to operate differentially against small firms in several ways. Firstly, small firms that did borrow from their bankers tended to be more dependent on such channels than large firms so that any cut would hit them more severely. Secondly, with relatively few small firms in the export business they fell outside that priority category. Thirdly, standards of creditworthiness tended to rise in a credit squeeze so that new or marginally small borrowers tended to be refused first. Finally, such restraints hindered the development of wider banking facilities which might have been of special benefit to small firms. Such disabilities were in general the consequence of size rather than conscientious discrimination by the banks.[13]

The figure for the ceiling was not so readily apparent if allowance was made for seasonal movements. In addition, no matter at what time of year a squeeze was introduced 'there will always be some advances which are building up to a seasonal peak and must be allowed to do so, regardless of general policy'.[14] It also fell somewhat hard if, at the time the ceiling figure was fixed, a bank had been particularly diligent in keeping lending down and as a result their base might be lower than that of their competitors. Particularly bitter criticisms were levied against the 98% ceiling because by 1969 it was a very dated target – with purchasing power falling companies needed a lot more finance for raw material purchases at post-devaluation prices. It was a nominal target, with no allowance for price changes as was often the case for public sector targets.

In more general terms the banks disliked such controls since they inhibited competition. It imposed a certain uniformity on the banks who claimed that they were 'caused to make a common front to our customers'. But this was not as stultifying as sometimes claimed since the banks asserted to the Radcliffe Committee that 'there is an understanding between us only in respect of occasions when one bank is trying to get an account down, or more probably refusing to make a new advance because of the credit squeeze'. In that case a bank would not grant credit if refused on 'Chancellor's grounds' by another bank.[15] Finally, the frequent changes in official policy in the mid-1950s and especially in the mid-1960s was deemed not to be the most conducive climate in which to develop better banking practices or advances management.

Bank advances to industry since the war

In February 1946 the total advances of banks reporting to the British Bankers Association amounted to £848m., of which £336m. was related to manufacturing and other productive activity. During the war the level of advances of the London clearing banks fell by some £230m. while their advances ratio declined from 44% to 15.5%. On the other hand the volume of deposits rose by £2,600m., of which 86% was represented by liquid assets, mostly in the form of Treasury Deposit Receipts, an instrument for direct short-term lending to the Exchequer.

While the First World War saw a rise in advances of some 20% the Second did not repeat that trend and for this there were several reasons. It was not that the banks played no part in the finance of industry but that other sources of working capital dwarfed those from the banking sector.

Banks were subject to informal controls on lending policy, that is, to make no loans save those that directly served the war effort. In practice, repayments due to the contraction of civilian industry exceeded lending for war purposes: the war produced considerable deferment of spending on repairs, replacement and rebuilding.

The main reason for the banks being replaced as suppliers of working capital arose from the introduction of progress payments by the government for work done. Prior to the war working capital needs (wages and raw materials) had been met by the banking system. But in the case of large armament orders involving long production periods special government provisions were made in the form of payments related to satisfactory progress and paid in proportion to the value of specific stages of work inspected and approved. For such contracts it was felt that the scale and type of accommodation needed was not a suitable area for bank advances.[16] With the outbreak of war the rate of expansion of contractors' production increased so straining their resources, and after consultations between the Bank of England and the government the banks were requested to look favourably on contractors' and sub-contractors' working capital needs, but asked not to lend to uncreditworthy customers or commit themselves imprudently, while further assistance was given through increased progress payments.[17] However, these accommodating additions were put aside once the 'phoney war' stage ended and production was stepped up by seven-day working and a three-shift system with its mounting wage bill. Banks were then requested to pay all contractors' wage bills 'without reference to the state of their banking accounts or to the safety of the needed banking accommodation'.[18] Consultations with the banks then produced a promise from government departments that they would ensure prompt and more liberal progress payments, thus alleviating the demand for bank funds while conditions for bank lending were set out more clearly. Though hastily assembled the progress payment system remained essentially unaltered for the war and provided considerable working capital needs; one estimate put it at £150–200m., which seems a conservative figure.[19]

The demand for working capital was also curtailed by the introduction of government holdings of raw materials. This arose naturally out of the practice of bulk buying and had the advantage that it greatly reduced idle stocks since contractors needed to carry stocks only to meet immediate needs, while significantly, most materials subject to bulk purchase were issued free to contractors. Working capital provision was also helped by the willingness of the government to accept delivery of completed stores at the earliest possible moment so that contractors did not need to lock up capital in stocks of finished goods.[20]

Towards the end of the war there were signs that bank advances were beginning to recover a little, partly because the injunctions on the banks to lend only for the war effort were not treated as strictly as in 1939. Further, even where firms had access to progress payments they occasionally preferred in later years to use bank advances for tax reasons. Bank overdrafts counted as part of capital employed and on the excess of this over the capital employed in the standard period 8% profit was allowed.[21] Although this involved interest charges it was worthwhile. This consideration was not important at the outset of the war when any capital was welcomed, but in the last two years it had an increasing influence.

When the war ended the banks were heavily underlent with an enormous volume of liquid assets to hand. They were confident that they could meet the post-war conversion needs of industry, and stated that they were prepared to be 'more liberal in our qualifying conditions as to repayment, without however departing from sound banking principles', and that they would consider 'applications for advances based as much on the character, integrity and business capacity of the borrower as upon the extent and nature of his own material resources'.[22]

Between 1946 and 1952 the volume of bank advances to manufacturing, as reassured by British Bankers' Association figures (see table 7.1 p. 200), trebled, while those to 'other production' increased from £135m. to £293m. Advances rose quickly in the immediate period of reconversion in 1946–7, levelled off in 1948, were boosted by the 1949 devaluation of sterling, and shot up during the Korean War boom. Two points, however, should be made. Firstly, the figures given reflect advances made, that is, they do not show the volume of applications by customers wishing to secure the right to draw on a bank so that some time would elapse before such accommodation appeared in balance sheets. The figures thus did not fully reflect the extent of the finance agreed for modernization and development. Secondly, the overall picture conceals variations in the experience of individual banks. For example, during 1946 the northern banks experienced a more rapid recovery in advances than the Big Five; further, the closer links of some banks with certain activities gave rise to large movements in individual bank advances, for example, the close ties of the National Provincial Bank with tobacco financing.[23]

The reasons for the rise in advances during 1946–7 are not difficult to discern, but they are many and will only be summarized here. It is convenient to generalize the demand for advances under two headings; those arising from positive needs due to increased expenditure and, secondly, negative ones due to deficiencies in other sources of company financing. On the positive side even before the war ended many businesses arranged overdraft limits to finance the switchover to commercial production and the idle period of retooling. Also, many branches of industry requested the restoration of pre-war credit facilities. The most important influence was probably the rise in production and the associated need to finance stocks of raw materials and finished goods, complicated by the problem of rising prices, particularly raw materials. The chairman of the Westminster Bank thought that the main influence on advances was the 'ever rising prices of materials which when held as stock obviously need greater financing'.[24] Stock financing was probably greater than it need have been since larger stocks were held than were necessary for the amount of work in progress. This arose because, faced with periodic shortages, many firms were unable to break the habit of acquiring, when given the chance, materials in demand. Such overstocking of essential commodities merely increased the scale of bank accommodation.[25]

On the negative side were the following influences. The arrival of peace meant that a large volume of production and distribution formerly covered by government progress payments now had to be privately financed. Also, taking over stocks previously held by the government required short-term finance. Further, the high level of financial liquidity which characterized business as it emerged from the war was soon absorbed by conversion and capital replacement.[26] Neither was it possible to build up reserves quickly by ploughing back profits, not even with the uninvited help of dividend restraint. The tax burden in the form of Excess Profits Tax, together with inadequate depreciation allowances, drew off a large proportion of profits thus restricting internal funds. In the prevailing capital market conditions with its own re-adjustment problems, and with the added restraint of a bonus tax, companies were reluctant to raise permanent capital through new issues.

However, the growth of advances was somewhat less than expected. While many firms sought assurances from their bankers that finance would be available when required, it was not fully used in the early period of reconversion.[27] In some instances companies received settlements of outstanding war contracts while others got cash compensation payments for physical war losses. Reduced demand for bank accommodation also arose from shortages of supplies and skilled labour which put a brake on re-equipment, and these supply bottlenecks on items of working capital delayed the impact of structural changes on the level of bank advances.[28]

The post-war expansion was checked in 1948, although in the 'other production' category advances continued to rise. The halt was probably due to deflationary influences in the luxury and semi-luxury trades. The easing of inflationary pressures also helped to reduce some of the bottlenecks which had been causing an accumulation of semi-finished goods, thus giving rise to a reduced demand for bank finance.[29] The break, however, was only of a temporary nature. The devaluation of sterling in September 1949 pushed up the cost of imported raw materials which quickly led to an increase in advances to those trades dependent upon such supplies. The outbreak of the Korean War and the accompanying boom merely served to accelerate these trends, coupled with a sharp rise of around 10% in the cost of capital goods.[30] The growth in output and activity, especially in industries benefiting from defence orders, increased the need for working capital, and this together with the extra cost of stockholding due to a rise of one-third in the price of raw materials in a year, required more bank funds just to carry normal stocklevels and for granting trade credit to customers, let alone for any expansion plans.[31] With heavy tax demands, together with limited non-bank sources, bank accommodation was put under some strain. Despite directives to restrain advances it proved difficult in the circumstances to keep them down. With the equity market somewhat depressed some customers needed accommodation pending the raising of new capital, 'whilst others need assistance until such time as they can decide whether their present volume of business will prove lasting enough to justify such a step'.[32]

The 1952 recession produced a fall in advances to manufacturing while those to 'other production' remained more or less unchanged at around £290m. The decline in advances to manufacturing was brought about by several factors. The introduction of stiffer monetary measures included a call to restrict advances more effectively to purposes essential to economic recovery and the defence of the country. This appeal worked more satisfactorily than was later the case, since banks found it easier to cut down lending to their worst customer risks – there was some fear of bankruptcies at the time and the fall in raw material prices made borrowers only too willing to run down stocks.[33] Import prices fell – by about half the amount they had risen in the boom – and this was reflected in the price of raw materials which declined by about 14%. On the volume side there was a reversal of the previous accumulation of stocks and the inventory recession caused a fall in output, a process which was particularly evident in the textile industry.[34] Finally, other sources of external funds were more readily available and companies were able to make new issues in order to fund bank advances.

Encouraged by an expansionary budget, low interest rates and the relaxation of physical controls, production recovered in 1953, a phase which lasted until mid-1955. Advances to the manufacturing sector, however, showed little signs of this recovery until the middle of 1954, the variations during 1953 and early 1954 being the usual seasonal ones with little or no underlying growth. That the sector was making less use of advances than previously might be attributed to the higher level of business profits, greater new issue activity and the sharp fall in raw material prices. Wholesale prices of raw materials fell by some 9% from 1952 levels, and relatively small price changes usually led to much larger swings in capital requirements. Although the government in 1953 continued the policy of progressively returning the importing of raw materials to private hands this did not lead to a sharp rise in financing requests for this purpose because of downward price movements and greater certainty led to reduced stock accumulation.[35] Judging by bank comment they were not altogether disappointed in the sluggish demand for credit. Recovery of the capital market and more internal funds relieved the banks who 'had willy-nilly to support industry with very large industrial lines of overdraft' which could not be too easily funded.[36]

The close of 1954 and the first half of 1955 brought a sharp rise in the demand for advances. It became clear by this stage of the boom that the needs of rising output and sustained high levels of activity exceeded the funds available from new issues, while business liquidity was also diminishing. The banks, although operating near to their liquid asset ratio requirement, obliged by selling gilt-edged. Towards the end of 1955 the pace of the rise in advances had been slowed by deflationary measures introduced to help with the balance of trade deficit, including two rises in bank rate which for the first time since the war took the advances rate over the minimum of 5%, and the July directive to the banks to bring about a 'positive and significant reduction in their advances over the next few months'. A year later came a more stern request 'that the contraction of credit should be resolutely pursued'.

During this period the level of advances to manufacturing stabilized, but there was no sharp fall. The policy pursued by the banks was to cut down on limits rather than pressure clients to reduce advances already taken. It was reported that there was a growing tendency among customers to borrow more closely up to their credit limits than previously, while it was suggested that the banks were eager to avoid responsibility for decisions that might lead to short-time working and falls in production.[37] The main impact of the restriction fell on prospective borrowers, since the banks scrutinized new applications very carefully, and the knowledge of tests applied by the banks reduced the number of applicants coming forward. It is hardly likely that controls would have brought, in manufacturing at least, any sharp drop in advances since the proceeding period had contained little by way of speculative borrowing or 'excessive building up of stocks of goods in traders' hands, against which orthodox measures had in past experience been directed'.[38] Anyway, manufacturing encompassed many activities coming within the national interest categories, particularly engineering.

Despite the continuation of the squeeze advances to manufacturing increased in the first half of 1957 due to the needs of exporting industries and for essential home purpose, while, even with the restrictions, other customers made greater use of agreed facilities. The surge was short-lived and in the final quarter advances fell, a trend associated with the 7% September bank rate and another call to restrict advances. Also important was the abrupt fall in commodity prices which had started before the September measures came in. The reaction to this drop began around May but became much more general with the introduction of the September measures, when businessmen quickly took stock of the situation.[39]

From the first quarter of 1958 to the end of 1960 advances to manufacturing increased by nearly 40%. This rapid rise followed on the relaxations of July 1958 when restrictions on bank lending were lifted, together with an expansionary fiscal policy carried further in the 1959 budget. In this conducive climate manufacturing production rose by an impressive 14·5%. Firms were quick to turn to the banking system for finance because the recent pause had not been onerous enough to make them hesitate to ask for more, or too poor a credit risk to be granted it. Even with the improvement in their advances by early 1959 the banks still felt a little bit out of it in that their advances contribution was small in relation to the volume of credit available to business. The expected balance of payments difficulties, higher bank rate and calls for Special Deposits appeared early in 1960. Despite efforts by the banks to push large borrowers to the new issue market, demands from big firms continued and banks faced the usual problem that despite the pressures of higher interest rates and those on liquidity, further growth was almost inevitable in view of commitments made before official restraint was applied. The first response of companies to restrictions seemed to be to increase overdrafts outstanding by drawing on existing limits. With deteriorating trading conditions working capital needs rose with growing stocks of finished goods. Business, it was felt, did not borrow at 7% unless they were pretty desperate for money. It was suggested that a further element in the demand for advances, given the restrictions and the downturn in activity, was that 'bank finance nowadays is geared to fixed investment as well as floating capital'; for 1960 this claim was probably a little exaggerated.[40]

Only modest changes in the level of advances to manufacturing took place in the stagnant period of production during 1961–2. The crisis of July 1961 brought in higher interest rates and calls for Special Deposits, but as the balance of payments improved and domestic activity fell further the authorities reduced rates and repaid Special Deposits. By October

1962 the situation was such that restrictions on the banks were withdrawn. The check in the rate of growth of advances during this period followed from the measures taken to slow down the economy. The fall in advances in the second half of 1961 was due to higher rates and the pressure put on customers in earlier months was showing through in the advances figures. Also the number of new issues for funding purposes increased. Advances recovered in 1962, but despite the cheapness of bank funds relative to other sources (rates elsewhere were described as extortionate) banks reported that while there were plenty of enquiries there was a reluctance to invest by certain customers.[41] Even when production rose sharply in 1963, with stock building following some six months later, advances continued to be rather docile. While many borrowers were granted higher overdraft limits these were negotiated more for future needs than present use. With reviving output industry found itself with better profit margins and an improved flow of internal funds. Although stock building was on the increase it was done cautiously and firms were reluctant to start new investment projects until later in the boom. Indeed, in mid-1963 some heavy borrowers were reported to be making large repayments of advances.[42]

Re-stocking and increasing production continued in 1964-5 and was accompanied by a substantial rise in advances. Over the period November 1963 to November 1965 advances to manufacturing rose by nearly £500m., and this in the presence of loan priorities, Special Deposits and the 105% ceiling of May 1965. Despite restrictions lending continued to rise because of the perennial problem of prior commitments being drawn upon and as companies postponed new issues on an uncertain market. The imposition in October 1964 of the import surcharge also brought additional demands for funds. However, during 1965 the effect of the restrictions and the slow down in activity dampened advances demand. Borrowers who used up their limits encountered resistance to further extensions. Under the discipline of the 105% ceiling banks became very selective, and they reported their position as 'being greatly helped by a number of substantial reductions in overdraft limits resulting from funding operations by customers in the market'.[43]

The high level of economic activity and the state of the balance of payments in 1966 induced a continuation of the advances ceiling until March 1967, and the banks were also asked to ensure that priority needs were met. Although the increase in advances in 1966 was below that of the two previous years the banks found keeping within the ceiling an uncomfortable trial. The problem was complicated over and above the usual customer/banker relationship by the introduction of selective employment tax and Schedule F payments on dividends withheld under the provisions of corporation tax.[44]

Although the start of 1967 was marked by the removal of loan ceilings it was, for balance of payments reasons, a short-lived freedom and in the autumn the by now familiar ceilings and loan priorities were all back again. Over the year advances rose fairly modestly with banks reporting that the demand for advances was firm, but that a large number of industrial customers had reduced their overdrafts for a number of unrelated reasons, including steel nationalization.[45] The level of advances remained fairly stable into 1968 (see table 7.2, p. 201) reflecting the effects of the credit squeeze and the reduced level of stock building in manufacturing. Despite the strictures which accompanied the November 1968 currency crisis the level of advances rose steeply in 1968, and well into 1969, with industry having to cope with the demands of the Import Deposit scheme and the pressures arising from reduced liquidity. By May 1969 the banks had breached the stipulated ceilings and consequently incurred a fine levied by reducing interest paid on Special Deposits, a move which the banks regarded as largely irrelevant since they were already carrying out the government's instructions to the best of their ability.

Advances to manufacturing picked up quickly in 1969 induced partly by a fear among some companies that further mandatory sanctions would follow so they hurriedly drew on unused facilities. In addition, conditions for getting non-bank finance were far from propitious. In the face of persistent demand the unrealistic ceiling of November 1968 was abandoned, a measure which helped to ease company liquidity, the intention thereafter being to permit a gradual rise in advances. In the event the demand for advances proved buoyant with much 'hard core' borrowing since capital expenditure ran well ahead of the supply of internal funds. A considerable incentive was present for firms to do this, since for some time there was a large differential in favour of bank rates compared to market rates.[46] By contrast 1971 proved a sluggish year for advances. The sharp fall reflected declining output, reduced fixed investment and stockholding. The banks felt all this keenly and they complained that their advances 'stuck to about half the total of limits when the normal ratio is over 60%'.[47]

The demand for advances from industry remained sluggish into 1972, and did not really pick up until the end of the year. With no revival in investment spending and adequate new issues companies had little need to go to the banks, while some were reported as running off previous borrowing in order to profit from suitable movements in market rates. In addition, with high borrowing rates at the year end many preferred to run down liquid assets. The increased borrowing that did occur in the early part of the year was partly linked with the recovery of output but the Bank of England also noted that 'some companies may have drawn on unused credit facilities with the banks to relend the funds at the exceptionally high rates obtainable in the money markets during and after the run on sterling'.[48]

The advances 'merry-go-round' became very active in the first quarter of 1973 and in this 'manufacturing companies seem to have been heavily involved'. However, the budget took away tax free capital gain on new certificates of deposits, and in December the clearing banks decided to relate their advances rate for certain customers to market rates rather than base rates, all of which reduced the extent of the re-cycling, but it did not entirely end it. Companies at this time were becoming increasingly dependent on bank finance to meet their *bona fide* activities and they received accommodation from both the London clearing banks and other banks on an unprecedented scale. Indeed, company indebtedness to the banking system would have been greater 'had not the Issue Department (of the Bank of England) purchased £226m. of commercial bills'.[49] At the end of 1973 bank accommodation constituted the outstanding source of funds for stock finance, capital expenditure, paying tax bills, and a little 'merry-go-round' activity. With the three-day week in 1974, intense pressures on company liquidity, and the inactivity of the capital market bank borrowing became the only source of external finance. During the year advances to manufacturing by the London clearing banks rose by some £1,500m., and by £550m. from other banks. With the depressed level of investment, reduced stockbuilding and stagnant production in 1975–6 companies required much lower levels of bank credit, while their liquidity was given a welcome boost by the low tax payments arising from stock relief. On the receipt side the record amount of funds raised on the equity market by way of rights issues enabled companies to reduce their short-term indebtedness to the banks and generally to strengthen their balance sheets.

The industrial classification of bank advances

Following the statistical blackout of 1939 figures of classified advances did not become available until 1946.[50] The British Bankers' Association series (1946–66; see table 7.1) relates to all advances made by member banks through offices in Great Britain, irrespective of the borrowers country of residence. Members of the Association comprised the London clearing banks, Scottish banks, most Northern Ireland banks, other deposit banks, and many dominion and overseas banks; the activites of several important banks were thus not included. The figures for the various banks are not on a uniform date, and the classification is based solely on the business of the borrower and does not take account of the object of the advance or the nature of the security held. There are 27 categories compared to only 15 in the pre-war clearing bank classification (see Chapter 3). In comparison with the clearing banks' total of bank advances this series was regarded as 'clean'. The figures did not include any nominal or internal accounts; in most cases (Lloyds being the leading exception) the clearers' figures included cheques in transit between branches of the same bank.[51]

From 1967 onwards a new analysis covering all banks which contributed to the banking sector statistics became available. The figures relate to the third Wednesday in February, May, August and November, and includes advances in sterling and foreign currency made to customers. As far as possible the analysis is based on the Standard Industrial Classification, with 25 categories. Advances are classified by industry, irrespective of ownership (i.e., private or public sector).[52] Table 7.2 gives the figures for the components within manufacturing.

In terms of general trends the pronounced feature is the increase in the percentage taken by manufacturing, rising from around 25% after the war to 40% of all advances in 1966, a proportion which also carries through in the clearing bank figures from 1969 to 1971. Thereafter the effect of Competition and Credit Control changes in 1971 caused a proportionate decline in manufacturing advances. The two broad categories which declined in relative importance were services and more markedly 'personal and professional', from around 28% after the war to about 15% in the late 1960s. Competition and Credit Control, however, revived the fortunes of the latter group, while inflation and stock market fluctuations have resulted in the clearing banks increasing their assistance to the rest of the financial system. The general post-war redistribution was, of course, encouraged by the ever present qualitative guidance. Throughout the 1950s the banks in their annual reports stressed that their lending policy was in accordance with official wishes. While they prided themselves in meeting the prior needs of export and other productive industries they were, however, conscious that the 'swing from personal lending where readily realisable security is generally taken, to the greater hazards of lending to commerce, industry and agriculture, frequently with nothing more tangible than an assessment of a balance sheet position, of necessity involves a greater measure of risk'.[53]

Throughout the post-war years engineering has more or less retained its position as the largest category of purely industrial borrowers. Although rivalled in the immediate post-war period, and especially in the Korean

Table 7.1   Bank advances to manufacturing industries : 1946–66 British Banker's Association series (£m.)

Year*	Food, drink, tobacco	Chemicals	Shipping & shipbuilding	Iron & steel & allied trades	Engineering, etc.	Textiles	Other manufacturing	Total manufacturing
1946	59	9	11	16	63	25	40	223
1947	75	15	15	14	82	31	60	292
1948	82	20	17	17	112	44	81	373
1949	101	19	16	24	110	48	92	410
1950	121	22	16	22	93	66	114	454
1951	143	26	16	17	110	99	149	560
1952	158	35	12	31	150	95	150	631
1953	133	26	16	55	154	81	127	592
1954	134	27	17	49	138	89	135	589
1955	163	31	22	30	159	100	160	665
1956	156	33	28	40	197	91	156	701
1957	151	32	35	56	233	115	158	780
1958	150	33	52	50	236	111	168	800
1959	185	36	74	67	284	117	203	966
1960	189	40	86	82	361	139	265	1,162
1961	215	52	106	96	482	159	293	1,403
1962	212	70	114	107	529	168	324	1,524
1963	228	81	102	133	536	179	377	1,636
1964	247	81	98	147	549	217	427	1,766
1965	283	93	91	163	679	227	499	2,035
1966	296	131	90	179	796	229	547	2,268

*Averages of quarterly figures as at February, May, August, November.

Source: Bank of England Statistical Abstract, No. 1, 1970, pp 68–70.

Table 7.2   Bank advances to manufacturing industries: 1967–7 London Clearing Banks series (£m.)*

Year†	Food, drink, tobacco	Chemicals	Metal manufacturing	Engineering	Shipbuild- ing	Vehicles	Textiles, etc.	Other manufacturing	Total manufacturing
1967	175	105	151	567	47	198	197	243	1683
1968	206	106	124	637	69	199	208	243	1792
1969	236	113	155	762	118	260	232	282	2158
1970	252	127	148	873	187	347	240	319	2493
1971	228	123	130	877	264	325	220	303	2470
1972	217	152	127	1130	441	348	225	316	3051
1973	354	209	173	1617	635	412	291	377	4066
1974	577	291	235	2144	732	589	392	560	5521
1975¶	501	265	230	1134	284	262	362	569	3601
1976	449	324	221	1035	292	211	395	585	3512

* Sterling and foreign currency.
† Averages of quarterly figures as at February, May, August, November. Figures relate to lending to U.K. residents. From 1975 medium-term export lending is excluded from the series.
¶ Average for last three quarters only due to compilation on a new basis.

Sources: Bank of England Statistical Abstract, No. 2, 1975, p. 73; Bank of England Quarterly Bulletin, recent issues.

War boom of 1951–2, by the food, drink and tobacco industries, it has increased its claim on advances from about 7% of total advances to around 14% in recent years. The rapid increase in engineering advances from the mid-1950s was helped by the bias in the successive policies of restraint which particularly favoured industries involved with capital goods. Much of the output of engineering was also exported and export finance was usually excluded from the various ceilings and given preferential interest treatment (see pp. 207–8).

A noticeable feature of table 7.1 is the short-term fluctuation in the size of advances to some industries. This happened most noticeably in food, drink and tobacco, and textiles during 1951–2, these being among the industries most exposed to the steep rise in commodity prices. Other industries were affected by defence orders which brought additional working capital needs. The effect of the 1952–3 price fall was to reduce demand for commodity stock building finance, while the revival of consumer demand permitted a reduction in holdings of finished goods. The steep rise in advances to iron and steel in the early 1960s arose because the impending change in the ownership of the industry made it inappropriate to approach the capital market.

Most of the bank advances granted were done on the usual short basis at prevailing market rates. However, there were two interesting exceptions to this pattern, shipbuilding and export finance. British shipbuilding took a diminishing share of world production in the post-war years and by 1955 it had lost its premier position, with the accompanying problem of new orders falling below output. In this period British shipowners found it beneficial to order abroad because of better delivery dates, and particularly to obtain advantageous credit facilities by way of lower interest rates and longer repayment periods. Measures were therefore taken in the early 1960s to improve the structure of the industry and its financial arrangements. Traditionally the banks had always been important sources of finance for shipbuilding, most of it lending in the ordinary course of business. From 1961 onwards special provision involving the banks became available in order to help gain orders for British yards.

The special needs of the industry were recognized as early as 1957 and limited financial assistance was introduced at the time with the setting up of the Ship Mortgage Finance Co. This company provided finance for ships built in Britain for British and foreign owners, and it also financed reconstructions and modifications of foreign built vessels in British yards. Funds were lent for periods of up to ten years on security of first mortgage in amounts of up to 50% of building costs for new ships, and up to one-third for existing ships. Its initial capital of £1.0m., later increased to £4.0m., was subscribed by I.C.F.C., and various financial and shipbuilding interests. Additional funds were obtained by debenture issues and bank borrowing. By 1969 it had helped about 100 vessels involving over £24.0m. and found participants for a further £17.0m.[54]

Following negotiations with interested parties the commercial banks agreed in 1961 to provide medium-term export credit with E.C.G.D. guarantees for ships at 5.5%, the banks financing the first five years and the longer term finance coming from a group of insurance companies at 6.5%. In 1965 the insurance companies withdrew, leaving the banks to provide credit for the whole period at 5.5%. Overseas shipowners ordering British ships could secure 80% credit on a contract price, repayable over eight years or so from delivery and at a fixed rate of 5.5%. Domestic shipowners at the time had to pay considerably more or go abroad for similar concessionary terms. However, with the 1967 Shipbuilding Industry Act such facilities were made available to British shipowners placing orders in home yards. Normally, such loans were repayable over eight years, but they could be extended to ten to meet foreign competition. Buyers were charged a 1% commitment commission on the amount of each loan contract, and promissory notes maturing half yearly were issued. Such loans in 1969 were guaranteed by the government up to a limit of £400m.[55]

While the nature of the assistance offered has remained very much the same there have been several important changes in two matters, the refinancing of loans and the rate of interest charged. To enable the banks to extend these additional facilities to home shipowners the Bank of England agreed to provide, as in the case of export credits, refinancing facilities covering if necessary the whole of any advance made under the scheme, thereby protecting the banks' liquidity position. With the growth of this form of credit the banks in 1969 were accorded automatic access to refinance facilities, if fixed rate lending absorbed more than a defined share of total bank resources.[56] It was found, however, that the growing volume of such fixed rate finance led to concern in the Bank of England at the possible amount of re-financing paper in its portfolio and that this might impair market management. Accordingly in 1972 new refinancing provisions were brought in relating the banks' refinancing facility to their current accounts, that is, any lending beyond 18% of current account balances was to be refinanced with the E.C.G.D. or the Department of Trade and Industry as appropriate.

When fixed interest rate lending for ships was introduced 5.5% was more or less in line with prevailing market levels. But as market rates moved upwards in the 1960s banks became concerned with the low return received on a growing volume of commitments. Thus in 1970 the rate was raised to 7%, while in 1972 arrangements were introduced so that the return received by the banks would not necessarily be the same as that paid by the borrower. Rates varied with market levels and were calculated on the basis of an agreed formulae; the 'observed rate' was made up of the average of the Treasury Bill yield and the clearing banks' lending rate to the nationalized industries, and to this was added a margin of 1.25% to allow for operating costs and the long-term nature of the banks' commitment. The rate for the borrower was fixed by the government in the light of competitive rates abroad and general economic considerations.[57]

As well as shipbuilding finance the banks have also greatly expanded the provision of export facilities, ranging from the traditional coverage of short-term orders via bills or overdrafts to long-term credits of up to seven years given on special terms. This arose largely because the pre-war channels for capital projects needing finance for several years were no longer available. Foreign buyers could not borrow freely in London to finance capital imports, while exporters faced heavy internal demands, so leaving them with little margin to provide long-term credits to buyers. The insufficiency of long-term capital relative to demand, coupled with the competition offered by foreign exporters, made it essential that U.K. exporters should be able to offer competitive credit terms for a large proportion of capital exports. For the early post-war years the duration of such credit was limited by the desire of the authorities to minimize the repayment period, thereby boosting the reserves, but after 1954 Exchange Control allowed exporters of capital goods to give whatever length of credit they thought necessary. However, the period of guarantees given by the Export Credits Guarantee Department has generally been limited to a period of around five years. The shorter post-war credit period meant that such business had little appeal for most institutional channels and the burden of supplying credit to fill the gap in facilities fell largely on the shoulders of the commercial banks.

Prior to the mid-1950s the banks provided a considerable amount of finance, largely with overdrafts, for short-term and intermediate contracts of up to about three years for light capital equipment. In the case of longer term credit of about five years duration, for heavy capital equipment, the banks did some business, sometimes alone or by consortium arrangements and generally in the form of supplier credit.[58] The importer generally repaid the bank, who held his promissory note as security, in half-yearly instalments over the term of the credit. These contracts carried E.C.G.D. guarantees but these were not made directly to the banks, they merely had the guarantees assigned to them.[59] Under these arrangements the banks were understandably reluctant to expand credit greatly since the risk of buyer default was certainly present and they were not prepared to commit funds indefinitely without transfering risks to an outside agency of undoubted strength. Therefore, in order to help capital goods exporters it was announced in the 1954 Budget that the E.C.G.D. would provide direct guarantees to the banks for a large proportion of the amounts in question. The special scheme for bank finance for export credits thus grew out of established arrangements.

Accordingly it was announced in 1954 that, in parallel with the credit insurance guarantee given to exporters, E.C.G.D. would be prepared to provide a guarantee direct to the financing bank. Such specific guarantees, for which exporters paid an additional premium, promised unconditional payment to a bank if the buyer did not pay up for any reason. Regardless of the circumstances in which a default arose a bank thus had complete security. Initially guarantees were available for contracts with a minimum value of £500,000, for three-year credits or longer from the date of shipment and up to 85% of value. Later the minimum value was removed, credit cover raised to 100% and the minimum period cut to two years.

With growing demands for credit, especially for large projects, and an increased volume of officially supported foreign competition in long-term credit, further provision was made in 1961 when the E.C.G.D. introduced financial guarantees to cover business financed on a buyer credit basis. In this case E.C.G.D. guaranteed loans made by banks directly to an overseas buyer or borrower (normally 80% of the cost of U.K. goods or services), thus allowing payment to be made to the supplier on cash terms. Exporters were thereby relieved of all financing and recourse problems which was a return to the pre-war pattern of export finance. The financial guarantee covered the full amount of the capital and interest against non-payment for any reason on projects of over £2m. The buyer credit facility was further expanded in 1969 when guarantees were extended to cover medium-term credit, two years or more from shipment and the minimum contract value was reduced to £1m.[60]

The other main financial facility was the extension in 1966 and 1967 of guarantees to banks for short-term contracts, which was an important development since most export credit falls into this category involving either bills or overdrafts. The Comprehensive Bill Guarantee, introduced in 1966, covers 30-days to 2-year credit and the buyer gives a promissory note or accepts a bill of exchange. E.C.G.D. then undertook to guarantee fully the exporters bank for any sum three months overdue on a bill or note. The second type of guarantee came a year later, the Comprehensive Open Account Guarantee, and covered exports on open account unsupported by bills or notes on terms of up to six months credit or 'cash against documents overseas'. In this case the guarantee is of a loan for 90% of the net invoice value of insured exports. To borrow against the

Table 7.3   Guarantees and refinancing (£m.)

Date	Specific guarantees to banks and financial guarantees (Medium- to long-term bank advances to exports outstanding)					Comprehensive guarantees to banks (Short export credits)		
	Guarantees issued during yr	Guarantees current at end of yr	Net bank finance outstanding at end of yr	Of which refinanced[a]	Of which eligible for refinance under Part I/Refinance Facilities (as since revised)	Guarantees issued during year	Guarantees current at end of yr	Net bank finance outstanding at end of year[b] (mid-Dec.)
End yr								
1961	28	178	85		42			
1962	44	223	109		54			
1963	98	309	124		59			
1964	145	433	140		68			
1965	123	532	171		81			
1966	197	686	236		107	65	61	n.a.
1967	252	874	347		146	117	93	45
1968	442	1279	500		208	201	141	95
End March								
1968	266	932	372		153	140	133	94
1969	449	1339	538	(-)	217	241	163	134
1970	737	2010	758	(33)	337	297	259	196
1971	1468	3335	1051	(194)	460	418	362	221
1972	719	3744	1404	(395)	—	471	406	228
1973	689	4097	1699	(604)		492	442	273
1974	1100	4814	1955	(792)		607	555	389
1975	1850	6253	2408	(1173)		723	818	494
1976	2367*	8293*	3082	(1679)		n.a.	n.a.	591
1977	3473*	11143*	3748	(2160)		1488	1627	n.a.

*Estimated

[a] Relates to the clearing banks and Scottish banks only; finance extended by other participants is probably small.

[b] Refinance under the new scheme introduced in March 1972.

Source: Bank of England; Export Credits Guarantee Department.

guarantee the exporter gives the bank a promissory note to cover repayment of his loan shortly after payment is due from the buyer. If the exporter does not repay, E.C.G.D. pays the bank.[61]

Table 7.3 gives the amounts of guarantees issued and outstanding over the period 1961–8 (calendar years) and 1968–77 (end March years), along with bank participation and the degree of refinancing used to 1977. The growth in volume and the short-term fluctuations reflect the behaviour of exports, with devaluation and price rises affecting the figures for later years. The long-term nature of the specific guarantees is reflected in the large total of amounts outstanding. The increased demand for this sort of accommodation has also been due to the decided interest rate advantage it offered compared with other forms of finance available at market rates. It should be noted that the banks have traditionally provided a large part of short-term export credits outside these special schemes, but since this has usually formed part of company working capital it cannot be separately identified.

Before 1962 the banks provided export finance at rates linked to bank rate, the overdraft rate for short-term finance and a somewhat higher one for longer loans with definite repayment dates. Bank customers, however, were not too keen on paying this additional premium as protection against a call for quick repayment.[62] Although more financial facilities were made available from 1961 onwards it became apparent that overseas buyers were reluctant to commit themselves to fluctuating interest rates. To meet this difficulty the clearing banks and the insurance companies agreed in 1962 that the former would provide fixed rate finance up to seven years at 5.5%, while the latter would provide funds at 6.5% (up to £100m.) where longer term finance was requested. A commitment fee of 1% was payable on both the medium and longer term lending. Since these arrangements were not free from practical problems the clearing banks agreed in 1965 'in the national interest to take over the financing hitherto provided by the Insurance Export Finance Co.', and provide funds at 5.5% for the entire period where this exceeded seven years. These fixed rate arrangements applied to all credits of two or more years, and covered those guaranteed directly by E.C.G.D. to the banks. The rate was an estimate 'based on past experience of an average lending rate appropriate, given the E.C.G.D. guarantee and the liquidity arrangements ..., to the whole term of a credit'.[63]

It was soon apparent that 5.5% was low in relation to market levels but the banks agreed to provide finance at fixed rates to the benefit of exporters. From the banks' standpoint 5.5% was a low rate when market levels were rising quickly and concern about increased future commitments led to a new scale of charges in 1972. No longer was the rate paid to the banks necessarily to be the same as the fixed rate paid by the borrower; it was to vary with market rates in accordance with an agreed formula.[64] Any difference between the agreed rate of return to the banks and the fixed rate was to be settled through an adjustment in the interest payable by the banks on the refinancing loans.

In the event these arrangements did not work out as smoothly as was hoped. A big gap appeared between the agreed rate and the fixed rate due to the rapid rise in interest rates, while the growth of fixed rate credit elegible for refinance was less than expected. As a result the sums due to the banks under the above formula were greater than the sums due to the government as interest on refinanced loans. After prolonged consultations in 1974 the general framework of the arrangements were retained, but the agreed rate of return to the banks on unrefinanced lending is tapered so that the margin over the observed rate falls as the latter increases.[65]

In reviewing financial facilities for exports the Radcliffe Committee had concluded that they were adequate (in 1959) but foresaw that growth might bring problems for the banks, firstly, on liquidity grounds, and secondly, that fixed rate lending would absorb a large proportion of their resources.[66] The first problem soon appeared in 1961 and the Bank of England relieved the pressure by introducing a refinance facility. The transactions eligible were export credits of over two years with an E.C.G.D. guarantee. The Bank of England was ready to refinance the amount of an outstanding credit repayable within the next eighteen months or 30% of the total amount outstanding whichever was the greater. Coverage was extended in 1965 to longer term credits when the Insurance Export Finance Co. dropped out of longer term financing. Such refinanceable amounts could be treated as part of the banks' liquid assets, thus relieving the liquidity position, whether or not refinance was sought. In fact it was not used, but it was available to provide cash to meet any sudden deposit withdrawal.[67]

More rapid growth in the provision of export finance by the banks brought the second problem to the forefront. To ease the prospect of fixed rate lending absorbing too large a part of a banks' resources, the Bank of England agreed in 1969 to provide access to refinance where fixed rate lending for exports and shipbuilding absorbed more than a defined share of total bank resources. Part I of the scheme retained the liquidity provisions of the original refinance scheme; the sums eligible for refinance are given in table 7.3. Part II applied to lending at fixed rates. To the extent that such lending was not treated as liquid under Part I, the Bank of England was ready to refinance an amount in excess of a defined percentage of a banks' total resources. Very shortly, however, the clearing banks became increasingly concerned with the growing volume of future financing to which they were committed, while the Bank of England was worried about the prospect that refinance facilities might impair the management functions of the Issue Department through its acquisition of eligible paper. To deal with the clearers' anxiety a limit was set on their commitment, that is, 18% of current account deposits (instead of the previous 10% of gross deposits). Eligible paper held by any bank in excess of this figure is refinanced with the authorities. All new refinance for exports would from 1970 onwards be provided by E.C.G.D. The sums refinanced under the 1972 arrangements are given in table 7.3.[68]

Lending rates

From 1945 to 1971 advances were made at rates linked to bank rate. Rates charged changed automatically with bank rate, unless the minimum was in operation, with most lending done between 1% and 5% above bank rate.[69] In terms of agreements between the banks the most important was that establishing a minimum figure of 0.5% over bank rate for 'blue chip' industrial and commercial borrowers, but although it was an agreed minimum, it was up to each bank to decide to which of its borrowers it should apply. Where uniform rates applied to certain categories of borrowing, e.g., exports and shipbuilding, it was done at the request of the authorities.

The only major change in the above arrangements occurred in 1964 when the clearing banks took steps towards 'more economic pricing of their loans'.[70] They did this in response to increasing pressure on the deposit side – higher rates induced switching to deposit accounts – while the heavy demand for loans made it desirable to add an element of price rationing to more arbitary methods. The banks therefore raised the floor for the minimum rates – 'blue chip' from 4% to 5.5%, the next category of good business and personal clients from 5% to 5.5%, and others to 6%. Also a wider spread of rates between various types of borrowers was negotiated leading to higher rates for most new overdrafts. The minimum levels were later revised, in 1969, to bring bank rates more into line with other rates and to reduce pressure on bank facilities. With Bank of England approval rates were increased by 0.5% so that the lowest rate charged to first class borrowers was 1% above bank rate, with a minimum of 5%.[71] Another important development in the early 1960s was the more widespread use of commitment fees of up to 1% on agreed overdraft facilities. Previously these were applied to large medium- and long-term export credits, but they were now extended to standby credits opened for big companies more or less as an insurance to help corporate treasurers job in and out of the London market. Not only were they levied at bank boardroom level but also increasingly by branch managers handling smaller facilities.[72]

With the introduction of Competition and Credit Control in September 1971 the clearing banks abandoned the interest cartel and from October rates for advances were no longer linked to bank rate (replaced by the minimum lending rate in 1972) but rather to a base rate determined by each bank in the light of market conditions. The practice has been to retain the differentials associated with risk over and above 1% plus the base rate. The level of base rate is not changed daily but the banks watch the range of market rates and change the rate when all the indications of cost and competition point firmly to a shift of 0.5%. However, following the 'merry-go-round' activities of 1973 the clearing banks announced that in order to curtail arbitrage transactions by their customers they proposed to indicate to certain clients that advances could in future be related to market rates instead of base rates.

A noticeable feature of bank loan rates was their narrow range, and although it tended to fan out somewhat with greater discretion on the part of individual banks and with higher interest rates, most of their business is restricted to lending to low risk borrowers. Since the early 1960s the leading banks have adopted a wider spread as a move to recognize differences in creditworthiness between blue chip and marginal small business loans. The narrowness of the margin became particularly evident in periods of credit restraint when banks, unwillingly, had to choose the best among acceptable risks and ignore the rest. Rates were probably too low to clear the market of creditworthy projects. The traditional view of the banks is that the range of lender risks they are prepared to accept is narrow and that if they charge higher rates it would put them into another type of market.[73] On occasions, however, they seem to have pushed out the margin, but usually at the safe end. The practice was reported in the 1950s that some banks were usually prepared to 'shade' the rate for large accounts, while the Radcliffe Committee stated that 'a bank will on occasion trim its rate to keep or attract a particularly valuable customer'.[74] While the imposition of commitment fees added a further element of cost, it would appear that there has been no consistent attempt to use interest rates as a rationing device at the margin.

On the demand side few industrial customers seem to have been dissatisfied with the terms of bank borrowing. In a survey conducted by the Monopolies Commission in 1968 it was reported that of the sample of 183 large companies only 2 had broken ties with a bank over terms.[75] Although many large companies keep accounts with more than one clearing bank very few do so for the benefits of competition or to compare costs and charges; the practice has largely arisen from tradition, convenience, the geographic spread of business, and mergers. Very few companies switch banks because of a refusal to obtain a loan or overdraft. In practice, in the 1960s at least, it was not all that easy to cross the street since no bank would accept an application for an advance if the Head Office of another bank had turned it down for any reason, and this was particularly true during credit squeezes. Banks, of course, are not eager to lose customers since it presents a bad image in getting new ones.

Non-clearing bank finance

In 1961 there were some 80 foreign banks operating in London, about half of which were British overseas banks, and their activities were, according to the Radcliffe Committee, of 'relative unimportance in the domestic financial scene'. By October 1976 the secondary banking sector numbered 312 banks, including the Accepting Houses and 'Other British Banks'.[76] As to the provision of finance to U.K. residents, sterling and other currency advances increased from £92m. for 1951–4 (annual average) to four times that amount by the early 1960s. While there were some advances to customers who are resident in the U.K. 'domestic business was mainly incidental; but the American banks did not limit their banking business in the U.K. in this way and . . . ventured rather further and more actively into such business than the other overseas banks'.[77] During the 1960s sterling lending rose from £804m. at the end of 1964 to just over £1,400m. in 1971. Following the introduction of Competition and Credit Control arrangements, sterling advances increased to £9,488m. at the end of 1976, and lending in foreign currencies to U.K. residents to £8,501m.

In general overseas banks played an important role in the financing of overseas trade, and their lending to U.K. companies (more often than not subsidiaries of foreign firms) was limited and related to trading needs. In the 1950s this pattern prevailed and the volume figures (see above) support this generalization; the overseas banks who gave evidence to the Radcliffe Committee asserted that although they held sterling resources by virtue of trade requirements, they did not compete with U.K. banks for purely domestic business. In the 1960s, however, all banks increased their domestic activity, as reflected in the growth in their sterling advances, but two groups displayed very rapid expansion in this sphere, namely, the American banks and the category 'Other British Banks'.

Sterling advances by American banks increased from £194m. in December 1964 to £2,537m. twelve years later, along with an equally rapid growth in lending in other currencies. The big expansion occurs after the 1971 changes and will be discussed further below. As to the 1960s, in this period the United States banks were heavily involved in financing the needs of American subsidiaries in the U.K. The relative cheapness of sterling finance, the problems of the United States balance of payments, and the desire to limit currency exposure were all factors tending to encourage the local financing of such companies; in 1967 some 80% of their advances were related to subsidiaries or branches of United States companies in the U.K.[78] The 'Other British Banks' group grew rapidly in the 1960s and by 1970 rivalled the Accepting Houses and the British Overseas and Commonwealth banks in the level of its sterling advances; after 1971 it quickly became the largest provider of sterling funds. Among this group were the subsidiaries set up by the clearing banks in the mid-1960s to attract large deposits at market rates and to lend on terms and conditions outside the normal range of the parent banks' activity. However, many of these subsidiaries were set up when quantitative limits on advances operated which greatly restricted their lending to manufacturing and other categories so that most of the funds collected were placed in the parallel money markets.[79]

The distinctive feature of secondary banking from the point of view of the finance of industry is that it specialized in term lending on a matching principle against term deposits. In making advances secondary banks tailor their loan terms and conditions to particular circumstances. Loans are given lasting from a few years to periods of up to seven years, some being repayable in instalments, others on maturity. While the clearers tended to stay with the overdraft approach, which they believe to be the most useful form of short-term accommodation available for industry, the secondary banks have offered term loans which proved very popular. The American banks, of course, had considerable experience in term lending, and in the practice of making up suitable financial packages for clients. The increased popularity of term loans probably stemmed from their greater security at a time when overdrafts were liable to be cut, they tied in more suitably with newer forms of investment appraisal and financial budgeting, and they were linked not so much to asset backing but rather to the cash flow prospects of a company, which was an extension of creditworthiness. While the early varieties of term loans were little more than 'rolled-over' overdrafts, more formal contracts on the American pattern gained ground. As to their lending in other currencies mainly for trade purposes, this channel was used by companies when restrictions were placed on sterling advances in the mid-1960s. Several overseas banks were reported as accommodating new demands for funds by lending foreign currencies to U.K. residents who had obtained the necessary exchange control permission to borrow.[80]

Little detailed information is available on the rates charged for advances. Since the secondary banks are not involved in the payments' mechanism and their business is largely wholesale, the margin added to the cost of deposits is probably narrower than that of the clearers, but they tend to pay more for their deposits. Generally their lending rates are higher than those of the clearers, and it is not likely that they undercut them even for their best borrowers, since the 'blue chip' customers of the clearing banks get trimmed rates. In 1967, in their evidence to the Monopolies Commission, the United States banks indicated that their margin over the clearing bank blue chip rate, then at 8.5%, was 1.5%. With increased competition since 1971, and with the clearing banks obtaining deposits in the parallel money markets the differential between the two sectors has probably narrowed.

It is since 1971 that sterling lending by the secondary banking sector has increased very rapidly; between 1964 and 1970 the volume scarcely doubled, but from 1971 to 1976 it increased fourfold. Prior to 1971 official ceilings severely restricted lending capacity, especially for new arrivals on the scene, while dollar business tended to dominate their business. After the changeover American banks were reported as keenly bidding for sterling loan business, making the 'rounds of big company offices to offer a chunk of cash at the equivalent of as little as $\frac{1}{2}$% over base rate'.[81] New arrivals on the scene were reported to be offering loans at no profit at all in order to get business.[82] Despite their specialist techniques, entering the domestic loan business proved an uphill struggle for many foreign banks since companies tended to remain loyal to British banks. Attitudes were, however, beginning to change and more companies now employ foreign banks, while the American banks in particular have capitalized on the relationships developed in the Eurodollar market with the larger British firms as a foothold for expanding their sterling business.

Of their total sterling lending 27% goes to manufacturing and 9% to 'other production', while the percentages for foreign currencies are 17% and 9% respectively. Within the manufacturing sector it is noticeable that the foreign banks are heavily involved with the chemical and allied industries, with bigger commitments than the clearers. In addition, the loans made to engineering and vehicles, food drink and tobacco are large, reflecting the presence of several important foreign subsidiaries. The largest rise in borrowing after 1971 has however been to the 'financial' category and has been due to increased lending to property companies and other financial institutions, while the 'merry-go-round' no doubt had some effect as well.

Notes

1 R. S. Sayers, *Financial Policy, 1939–45*, London, 1956, pp. 185–7.

2 *The Economist*, 15 December 1951, p. 1486; *The Economist*, 26 December 1953, p. 977.

3 'Government Control over the Use of Capital Resources', *Midland Bank Review*, August 1950, p. 6.

4 *Bank of England Quarterly Bulletin*, June 1967, pp. 164–5.

5 Midland Bank, Annual Report, 1958. The Clearing Banks stated to the Radcliffe Committee; 'There are several concerns with resources of up to £10m. or £15m., who are doing our normal type of business for our customers which we have had to decline; of course they are charging them much more.' These were the 'so called industrial banks'; Committee on the Working of the Monetary System, *Minutes of Evidence*, Q. 3559 (Radcliffe Committee, 1960).

6 Sir Oliver Franks, 'Bank Advances as an Object of Policy', *Lloyds Bank Review*, January 1961, p.9.

7 J. C. R. Dow, *The Management of the British Economy 1945–60*, Cambridge, 1964, p. 240.

8 The banks agreed amongst themselves on a formula by which the limitation of total advances was to be applied individually, which apparently took some account of each bank's performance in the earlier freeze; *The Economist*, 31 December 1957, p. 1075.

9 In May 1965 the banks were told by the Bank of England that the call for Special Deposits should be fully reflected in the banks' lending policies and that it should be mitigated as little as possible by the sale of investments; *Bank of England Quarterly Bulletin*, June 1965, p. 111.

10 Radcliffe Committee, *Minutes of Evidence*, Qs 3625–29: 'If you took availments and limits, availments would be somewhere about 50% of limits.' Three of the clearing banks stated to Radcliffe that in their experience over recent years (pre-1958), the credit squeezes had not caused any important fluctuation in the ratio between availments and limits; *Minutes of Evidence*, p. 962.

11 *Banker's Magazine*, February 1969, p. 144.

12 In June 1958 98% of borrowers had advances of less than £10,000 which accounted for only ⅓ of the money lent; Franks, *op. cit.*, p. 7. On the problems of implementing the squeeze at branch level see 'Bank Managers – Squeezed and Squeezing', *The Banker*, July 1965, pp. 460–3.

13 Committee of Inquiry on Small Firms, *Report*, Cmnd 4811, para. 12.17 (Bolton Committee, 1971).

14 Franks, op. cit., p. 11.

15 *The Economist*, 11 February 1956, p. 426.

16 W. Ashworth, *Contracts and Finance*, London, 1953, p. 182.

17 ibid., p. 185. Advanced payments for work was not usually used. The government refused to weaken its purchasing position to the extent involved in making such payments.

18 ibid., p. 185.

19 *The Economist*, 27 January 1945, p. 118.

20 Ashworth, op. cit., p. 194. At end of March 1945 the Raw Materials Department had some £409m. of stocks.

21 ibid., p. 190.

22 Lloyds Bank, Annual Report, 1945; Midland Bank, Annual Report, 1946.

23 *The Economist*, 22 January 1949, p. 155.

24 Westminster Bank, Annual Report, 1948. Industry also had new burdens by way of social security contributions.

25 District Bank, Annual Report, 1949.

26 This was not as rapid as might have been the case since controls and scarcity slowed up maintenance and replacement; see A. Luboff, 'Some Aspects of Post-war Company Finance: An Analysis of Tabulations of Company Accounts published in *The Economist*', *Accounting Research*, April 1956, p. 179.

27 The gilt edged contribution should not be ignored. 'A large part of the bank finance for industry took the form of purchases of industrial holdings of gilt edged'; *The Economist*, 12 February 1949, p. 292. During 1946–8 the clearing banks had an investments-deposit ratio of just under 50%. They did not start to unload gilts until 1949.

28 Barclays Bank, Annual Report, 1947; *The Economist*, 18 May 1946, p. 808; 27 July 1946, p. 147; 31 August 1946, pp. 341–2.

29 *The Economist*, 25 September 1948, p. 512.

30 In his analysis of *The Economist*'s returns Luboff found that for 1427 companies in 1951 that there was a 'general one-way' movement in advances owing to the spectacular rise in commodity prices, indicating that a large number of companies had recourse to their banks; see Luboff, op. cit., p. 182.

31 Midland Bank, Annual Report, 1952;

Barclays Bank Chairman noted, 'it is surprising not that bank advances inclined upward but that they did not do so more sharply'; Annual Report, 1951.

32 District Bank, Annual Report, 1950.

33 *The Economist*, 25 September 1955, p. 1008; National Provincial Bank, Annual Report, 1953.

34 *The Economist*, June 1952, p. 839; Dow, op. cit., pp. 72–3.

35 Midland Bank, Annual Report, 1953.

36 Lloyds Bank, Annual Report, 1955. That the banks reported few bad debts was due as much to rising prices as to any deliberate avoidance of risky commitments by the banks.

37 *The Economist*, 11 February 1956, p. 426.

38 Midland Bank, Annual Report, 1956.

39 Barclays Bank, Annual Report, 1959.

40 *The Economist*, 30 July 1960, p. 490; July 1961, p. 71.

41 Barclays Bank, Annual Report, 1963. The Midland Bank in its report for 1962 noted that competition from 'other financial institutions' was on the increase which may have been an influence upon sluggish advances.

42 At this time trading concerns were reported to be using spare cash to buy Treasury Bills; Westminster Bank, Annual Report, 1964. There was also a tendency to hold lower cash-asset ratios than in the early 1950s due to amalgamations and the reluctance to show liquid positions due to take over threats; District Bank, Annual Report, 1964.

43 Lloyds Bank, Annual Report, 1966.

44 The big leap in advances between November 1965 and February 1966 was due to companies wanting to make interim dividend payments to shareholders before the April deadline for Corporation Tax.

45 District Bank, Annual Report, 1968.

46 Lloyds Bank, Annual Report, 1971; Midland Bank, Annual Report, 1971.

47 Barclays Bank, Annual Report, 1972. A spot check of 20 industrial customers of one bank showed that they had taken up only 20% of their limits; *The Economist*, 18 December 1971, p. 74.

48 *Bank of England Quarterly Bulletin*, September 1972, p. 320.

49 *Bank of England Quarterly Bulletin*, September 1973, pp. 300–1.

50 *The Economist* maintained that the banks had figures for the new basis prior to August 1946 but they were not released; 26 October 1946, p. 675.

51 The effect of including this item was that a rise or fall in the volume of cheque payments produced artificial changes in the advances figure. Even when all banks, in 1958, showed the transit item the advances figures continued to be swollen by certain extraneous items, including balances with banks abroad.

52 For full description of the series see *Bank of England Quarterly Bulletin*, March 1967, pp. 48–51. On the seasonal adjustment of this series, and the B.B.A. series, see *Bank of England Quarterly Bulletin*, June 1972, pp. 220–5, and *Bank of England Statistical Abstract*, No. 2., 1975, pp. 80–1. On modifications made in 1975 see *Bank of England Quarterly Bulletin*, December 1975, notes to Table 10.

53 Lloyds Bank, Annual Report, 1955.

54 'Shipbuilding in Britain', *Midland Bank Review*, May 1969, p. 7.

55 The guarantee covered the total finance provided together with interest. Examining the suitability of contracts was undertaken by the Ship Mortgage Finance Co.

56 *Bank of England Quarterly Bulletin*, September 1969, pp. 292–3.

57 *Bank of England Quarterly Bulletin*, March 1972, p. 48.

58 Under 'supplier credit' the exporter extends credit to the buyer and arranges finance where he cannot provide it from his own resources.

59 Guarantees were of two main types: (a) comprehensive guarantees covered a range of exporter's business over a period of time; and (b) guarantees on individual contracts on major capital items. While the standard guarantees given to exporters by E.C.G.D. could be assigned they did not cover the bank against losses for which the exporter was to blame. Banks, although they had doubts, always met the needs of respectable customers, but they were unhappy about recourse to the exporter.

60 *Bank of England Quarterly Bulletin*, December 1969, p. 429.

61 ibid., p. 428.

62 Barclays Bank, Annual Report, 1960.

63 *Bank of England Quarterly Bulletin*, December 1969, p. 430.

64 *Bank of England Quarterly Bulletin*, June 1972, p. 206.

65 *Bank of England Quarterly Bulletin*, March 1975, pp. 48–9.
66 Committee on the Working of the Monetary System, *Report*, para. 896.
67 For details see *Bank of England Quarterly Bulletin*, December 1969, p. 431.
68 Under the 1972 arrangements the Bank of England agreed that at its own discretion it would be prepared to provide refinance facilities along the lines of the Part I Scheme to meet any sudden and unexpected demands upon the banks.
69 In the early post-war years falling interest rates brought a gradual reduction of charges. In 1947 the Midland Bank asserted that no one paid an interest rate as high as 5% on borrowings. Earlier, in 1946, the banks had, however, ceased to pay interest on current accounts and introduced a uniform rate on deposit accounts as against the pre-war practice of a London and a country rate.
70 See *The Banker*, 'Levering up Bank Lending Charges', September 1964, pp. 551–4.
71 *Bank of England Quarterly Bulletin*, December 1969, p. 395.
72 *The Economist*, 22 August 1964; Midland Bank, Annual Report, 1965. It is a fairly common European practice to levy further charges on top of the basic interest charge, either on the limit of the facility or the sum actually outstanding and this varies from 1% to 3%; see *The Banker*, 'Short Term Borrowing in Europe', May 1967, p. 410.
73 The Chairman of the Committee of London Clearing Bankers put it to the Radcliffe Committee in these terms; 'A man is either credit-worthy or not credit-worthy: if he is credit-worthy, he gets his accommodation ... on the terms I have stated'; *Minutes of Evidence*, Q. 3698.
74 Radcliffe Committee, *Report*, para. 138.
75 *Report on the Proposed Merger of Barclays Bank, Lloyds Bank and Martins Bank*, H.C. 319, July 1968, pp. 69–73.
76 There were 30 Accepting Houses, 70 other British banks, 58 American banks, 19 Japanese banks, 107 other overseas banks, and 28 consortium banks; for a complete list of banks see *Bank of England Quarterly Bulletin*, December 1976.
77 Radcliffe Committee, *Report*, para. 201.
78 Monopolies Commission, *Report*, H.C. 319, op. cit., p. 75. In 1967 about 48% of their sterling deposits came from British companies, compared with 38% in 1964. The proportion of sterling advances stayed at around 15%.
79 For example, the Midland Bank Finance Corporation started operations in 1967 but since it had no lending outstanding on which to calculate a ceiling its aggregate advances remained for sometime a fraction of the resources available; Midland Bank, Annual Report, 1968.
80 *Bank of England Quarterly Bulletin*, June 1968, p. 164.
81 *The Economist*, 18 December 1971, p. 74.
82 These newcomers were criticized for rate cutting, while their rates of return on assets in 1972 indicated that many United States branches were a drag on their United States parent's profitability.

8 Internal finance

*the regular annual investment by individuals in
their own businesses or properties ... must always
be the most important form of saving – far more
important than the visible public investments.*

SIR ROBERT GIFFEN

The volume of internal funds available to a company depends on the
stream of gross trading profits and other current income, and on the sums
distributed from this total in interest, dividends and taxation. The residue
consists of two components: first, depreciation allowances which represent
funds retained for the purpose of keeping capital assets in good working
order (capital consumption), and second, net savings which represents
funds available for adding to the stock of capital assets. In the case of
industrial and commercial companies (see Chapter 11 for further
description of this sector) the volume of internal funds available for
financing working and fixed capital requirements over the post-war period
has been influenced by periodic changes introduced by governments in
relation to dividend payments, taxation policy and depreciation allowances. The other major influence on savings has been fluctuations in
company profits associated with the regular post-war cycles.

General trends in company income and its appropriation 1948–1976

Table 8.1 gives the main sources of funds for industrial and commercial
companies for the post-war years, expressed as percentages of total
sources, and in annual averages; the figures for 1948–51 relate in the main
to companies excluding those in insurance, banking and finance, and
should be treated with a degree of caution. Gross trading profits are

presented after deducting stock appreciation, thus removing the influence
of stock price changes from the profit figures.[1] Other internal funds are
derived from rent and non-trading income in the U.K., and from income
earned abroad. External funds comprise capital grants made by the public
sector, overseas investment in U.K. companies, and borrowing from the
banks, other financial institutions, and the capital market, while a decrease
in liquid asset holdings is treated as a source of funds, and an accumulation
as a reduction of funds available for financing capital expenditure (see
Chapter 11).

Table 8.1   Sources of funds: Percentage of total sources

Year	Internal			External
	Gross trading profits†	Other current income	Total	Total External
1948–51*	65	23	88	12
1952–55	72	22	94	6
1956–60	69	21	90	10
1961–65	64	20	84	16
1966–70	59	22	81	19
1971–76	45	35	80	20

* Estimated from N. I. B. B. figures for all companies *less* financial companies
   where available.
† Less stock appreciation.

Source: For 1952–76, table 11.1 (p. 310).

   Taking a broad view of post-war experience as presented in table 8.1
internal funds as a proportion of total sources fell from the 90% level in
the late 1940s and early 1950s to 84% in the early 1960s, and to 80% in
recent years. The corresponding increase in importance of external funds
took the form of greater recourse to the banks and the capital market,
along with a run down of liquid assets. Also in later years overseas
investment in U.K. companies has grown, but the totals involved, apart
from a few years, were relatively modest. The reduced importance of
internal funds is mainly attributable to the record of gross trading profits.
The decline in the latter as a proportion of total sources is apparent in
table 8.1, falling continuously from 72% in 1952–5 to 45% in 1971–6. This
fall is to some extent reflected in the lower share of total domestic incomes
taken by industrial and commercial companies, and the increased share
taken by income from employment. Broadly, this probably reflected the
easier trading conditions of the 1950s when higher costs could be passed

on in higher prices, changing to the more competitive climate of the 1960s both in the markets for finished goods and in factors of production, while the increasing rate of inflation in recent years has ushered in price restraint policies which tended to squeeze profits. Other income, in contrast, has grown appreciably, sufficient to maintain its proportion of total sources for most of the period and to increase it markedly over later years. Since about 1968 this trend has been sustained by the rise in income earned abroad, that is, profits of U.K. companies operating abroad and of foreign subsidiaries of U.K. companies, together with non-trading income from abroad.

Within these trends there have been marked cyclical patterns. While other current income has climbed gradually, with some minor variations, gross trading profits on the other hand have fluctuated considerably. Generally fluctuations in profits have followed those of output. In an expansionary period output and selling prices tended to rise faster than costs, giving higher profits. In the retreat from such booms the slow down in output tended to squeeze margins with rising unit costs so that profits grew less rapidly, and on occasions they fell. It was in years when profits rose most rapidly that their contribution to total sources diminished, the reason being that capital expenditure rose sharply necessitating resort to external funds. During periods of recession, profits tended to maintain their share of total sources due to the falling off in the volume of fixed investment expenditure by companies and reduced external borrowing (for detailed description of these changes see Chapter 11).

The appropriation of the gross income of companies is given in figure 8.1 on an annual percentage basis for the period 1948–76. The figures for 1948–51 are for companies excluding those in insurance, banking and finance, and for 1952–76 for industrial and commercial companies. The main items which bear upon the determination of savings are dividend and interest payments, sums due in taxation, and depreciation policy. While the latter is not indicated separately in the chart it will be treated below as an important influence on the behaviour of company savings.

Taking dividends and interest payments certain distinct phases are apparent. In the immediate post-war years they absorbed a falling proportion of current expenditure, a feature linked with nationalization, but far more influential was the dividend limitation practised at the time. During the early and mid-1950s the proportion paid out in dividends remained quite stable, as does that of interest on debentures and other borrowing. Over these years dividend payments rose gradually reflecting the upward trend of profits, but since companies were reluctant to allow dividends to fall, and usually wished to avoid sharp changes in payments from year to year, fluctuations in profits around the trend were not reflected in aggregate dividend figures. The small rise in the item interest reflects the rise in interest rates, the gradual increase in bank borrowing and the enlargement of fixed interest borrowing by debenture issues. From 1958 onwards, however, the proportion of income going to dividends rises sharply, and stays well above the 20% level until the late 1960s. Only a small part of this increase is attributable to new equity issues since these rose broadly at the same pace as total expenditure by companies. The most important influences were probably the removal in 1958 of the discriminatory treatment of distributed profits, and the reaction of companies to the high incidence of take-overs in the late 1950s which made directors reluctant to retain large reserves of liquid assets. The introduction in 1965 of corporation tax, which favoured profit retention and the issue of fixed interest capital rather than equity, brought a reversal of the trend with the share of income taken by dividends falling from around a quarter to about an eighth in the early 1970s. The other noticeable change is the rapid rise in the item 'other interest' from the late 1960s onwards, which is associated with the growth of borrowing from financial institutions.

While the allocation of funds to dividend and interest payments changes relatively slowly over time, the item tax payments and profits due abroad presents a contrasting picture. In figure 8.1 the latter items are presented together for industrial and commercial companies, since they are not given separately prior to the early 1960s (separate figures are available only for *all* companies). Although there have been fluctuations in profits due abroad this figure has grown apace with profits and has little effect on the percentages given in figure 8.1, apart from a few recent years. Taxation due abroad has fluctuated in much the same way as U.K. tax. Generally such fluctuations have been in the opposite direction to those of profits because the tax figures represent payments rather than accruals of tax liabilities for each year. Broadly speaking there was a delay of some eighteen months, so that low tax payments in say 1960 related to the low profits of 1958. Conversely tax on rising profits in 1960 and 1964 did not have to be paid immediately, thus enabling the funds to be used temporarily for financing purposes. The general pattern was for companies to add to tax reserves in boom periods and run them down in depressed periods, which no doubt discouraged them from undertaking other expenditure.

As can be seen from figure 8.1 taxation remittances in the period to the early 1960s absorbed a declining proportion of company income. Whereas in the early post-war years tax took about one-quarter to one-third of income, by the late 1950s this fraction had fallen to one-fifth and by the mid-1960s to well below 10%. The fall in the post-1959 period is associated with the more generous distribution policy of companies which transferred to the shareholders a bigger share of the total tax liability on income. Also up until the changeover to corporation tax rates were generally falling, while tax allowances against investment expenditure were increasing. Following the introduction of corporation tax the proportion of income going in tax rises to around 16% in 1970, but by 1973 had slumped to just over 8% and to 5% in 1976.

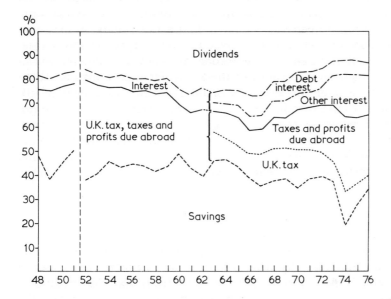

Figure 8.1   Appropriation of company income 1948–76 (%).

During the 1950s profits due abroad (profits earned in the U.K. by foreign-owned branches and subsidiaries) grew gradually, with some minor fluctuations, averaging around £200m. in the late 1950s, and remaining at this level into the late 1960s, increasing to over £580m. in 1972–6. Taxes paid abroad (taxes paid to overseas governments by U.K. companies operating abroad), on the other hand, grew appreciably faster and were subject to larger fluctuations. From around £200m. in the early 1950s the figure doubled by the end of the decade, and by 1974–6 amounted to nearly £3,800m. a year, the rapid rise dating from 1970. In terms of the percentage of total allocations the two items increased significantly from 1968 onwards, from 14% to 30% in 1974, falling back to 27% by 1976.

The remaining item, savings, is the sum available to meet capital and other expenditures. It consists of retained profit plus depreciation allowances, the former for asset expansion, the latter for asset replacement. In practice, however, it is often difficult to distinguish clearly between the needs of replacement and those of expansion, particularly in periods of significant price and technical changes. Savings thus may be regarded as funds for general purposes drawn upon to pay for stocks of raw materials, increases in the volume of work in progress and to finance capital development and plant replacement. With regard to the savings ratio some clearly defined patterns emerge in figure 8.1.[2] Firstly, in the boom years the savings ratio rises noticeably, e.g., 1954–5, 1959–60, and 1963–4, while it falls off in the ensuing depression. Secondly, the ratio remains at a relatively high level for most of the 1950s, far higher than anything displayed in the inter-war years (see Chapter 4). From 1964 the ratio falls continuously to the 1970 low of 34%, the main factor in this being not increased distributions but the increased proportion taken in taxation. The ratio in 1974 fell to a very low 20% largely due to a sharp rise in the proportion of income absorbed by 'other interest' and by taxation and profits due abroad at a time when gross trading profits fell by 12% on the previous year.

Depreciation allowances

Since the last war it has been a generally accepted principle that capital expenditure undertaken by firms to generate income should be entitled to certain capital allowances to provide relief from tax. The traditional purpose of such allowances as a means of apportioning annually the depreciation in the capital employed has, however, been considerably altered so that the concept of recognizing wear and tear in material assets has been greatly extended to provide varying incentives to industrial investment. Such a policy of granting investment relief kept the effective rate of tax below the statutory rate and thereby increased the cash flow available to firms. Such capital allowances provided relief from tax on a large scale; allowances reduced the amount of income and corporation tax payable by taxpayers of all kinds by about £1,000m. in 1970–1.[3]

The broad system of commercial depreciation is to decide upon the various methods of depreciation (for example, straight line – buildings; reducing balance – plant and equipment), the percentage of the original cost that is to be written off, and the number of years over which this is to be done.[4] But while a business may adopt any system of depreciation that it likes it is only allowed to offset against tax on an agreed scale. In the U.K. the Inland Revenue (often criticized for taking a very long-term view) in conjunction with industry determined the normal life of particular assets, which in turn produced the appropriate rate of depreciation to be applied to the written down value of the assets. It was a basic principle that firms were permitted to write off the total cost, but no more than the cost of the asset. The procedure for plant and machinery, however, produced a multiplicity of rates. The Inland Revenue fixed the life of the asset, then the rate of depreciation was calculated that would produce a written down value of 10% of the original cost by the time the item was expected to be suitable for scrap. The operational rates were then 80% of this calculated rate.[5] However, in 1962 it was decided to simplify the administration of what had become a rather complicated system of allowances. The multiplicity of rates of annual writing down allowances was reduced to three; where, for a particular class of asset the rate had been less than 15% (on the reducing balance basis) it was increased to 15%; rates between 15 and 20% were increased to 20%; and those between 20 and 25% were raised to 25%. Before this change most of the annual rates had been below 15%, with the result that 15% became the commonest annual rate; about $\frac{3}{5}$ of the capital expenditure incurred on plant and machinery between 1962–70 qualified for that annual rate.[6] A further modification was introduced in 1970.

The above simplification of rates for annual writing down allowances involved a weakening of the link between commercial depreciation on plant and machinery and the rates of tax allowance. But the decisive breakaway from commercial amortizing as the basis for measuring depreciation rates occurred much earlier in 1945 when the system was substantially recaste from the pre-war arrangements in order to stimulate industrial investment in the reconstruction period.[7] The introduction of initial allowances was designed to increase finance, and as an interim solution to the observed trend that the prevailing depreciation allowances assessed on original cost was insufficient to cover replacement cost at post-war prices.[8] There was also the general opinion that additional depreciation was superior in its economic effects to a system of replacement cost depreciation.[9] Thus, in addition to the proportion normally allowable, a further proportion of the cost was allowed free of tax in the year of purchase and this rate of initial allowances was unrelated to commercial depreciation. In the later years of an asset less was allowed, so that over its agreed life the same aggregate depreciation was granted, which effectively meant an interest free loan from the government, equal to about half the allowance given at the prevailing rate of tax.[10] Its purpose, therefore, was to defer tax, not to compute income. For any single asset the loan had to be repaid but so long as a firm's investment outlays did not fall the loan was retained. Perhaps a more apt portrayal was given by A. R. Prest, that initial allowances amounted to 'a free gift if insufficient income is earned to repay them, a larger gift if the business continues to grow, and a growing gift if the business grows at an increasing rate'.[11]

The legislation of 1944–5 created six types of depreciable assets – plant and machinery, industrial buildings, buildings and equipment used in scientific research, patent rights, agricultural buildings and works, and mining assets; only minor additions have since been made. Capital expenditure on any of the above assets could be written off by way of an annual depreciation charge as a cost for taxation purposes. Expenditure on other capital assets did not attract any concession for tax purposes. The additional allowance introduced in 1945 was 20% for plant and machinery and 10% for building works.

Table 8.2 gives the main changes in initial allowances during 1945–76. Changes in initial allowances were generally meant to act as an encouragement or otherwise, to investment. To encourage investment in 1949, by giving help when capital equipment was installed, Sir Stafford Cripps doubled the allowances on plant and machinery. Two years later Mr Gaitskell suspended these arrangements as from April 1952, permitting the interval, because investment planning and execution took some time. It was felt that the heavy calls which the defence programme would make on the engineering industry made it desirable to reduce the pressure of civilian demand for plant and machinery. Mr Butler restored the concession in 1953, but at the original rate of 20%, while a year later he brought in investment allowances as a more powerful stimulant. The 1955 boom and the ensuing balance of payments crises led to the withdrawal of investment allowances early in 1956, with the old initial allowances coming back into use. To encourage expansion in 1958 modest increases were made in the rates, while in 1959 investment allowances were again brought in but this time with initial allowances on a reduced basis. When cash grants replaced investment allowances in 1966, capital expenditure items not eligible for such grants were deemed eligible for initial allowances at 30% for plant and machinery and 15% for buildings. While initial allowances continued to apply to buildings they were replaced in 1970 for plant and machinery by a system of first year allowances (see p. 227).

In 1954, as a more powerful stimulus to investment, investment allowances were substituted for initial allowances. These allowances, introduced at 20% of expenditure on plant and machinery, and 10% on industrial and agricultural buildings, were added to the normal depreciation provision as a deduction against taxable profits in the first year. Thus, while initial allowances gave help in the first year at the cost of reduced allowances in later years, the new system also gave similar help in the first

Table 8.2   Rates of initial and investment allowances, 1945–76 (% of investment expenditure allowed under *A* 'initial' or *B* 'investment' allowances)

Effective date	Plant and machinery		Industrial buildings	
	A	B	A	B
April 1944	20	–	10	–
April 1949	40	–	10	–
April 1952	0	–	0	–
April 1953	20	–	10	–
April 1954	–	20	–	10
Feb. 1956	20	–	10	–
April 1958	30	–	15	–
April 1959	10	20	5	10
Nov. 1962	10	30	5	15
April 1963	10/f.d.ᵃ	30	5	15
Jan. 1966	30ᵇ	–	15	
April 1970	30ᵇ	–	30/40ᶜ	–
Oct. 1970	–	–	30/40ᶜ	–
March 1972	–	–	40	–
Nov. 1974	–	–	50	–

ᵃ f.d. free depreciation allowed in development districts and Northern Ireland.
ᵇ Initial allowances on new plant and machinery which did not qualify for investment grants.
ᶜ Forty per cent in development and intermediate areas and Northern Ireland.

Source: Inland Revenue Reports.

year, but with no reduction in later years. Firms' liquidity thus benefited, and by excusing tax on the amount of the allowance it gave a subsidy of about 10% and 5% on plant and machinery, and buildings respectively.[12] Another feature of the scheme was that some new categories of assets were included, e.g., agricultural works and buildings, and plant and machinery dealt with on a renewals basis. It was also considered a more powerful stimulus because after the year of expenditure investment allowances carried relief that would not have been available under initial allowances, in that annual allowances computed on a reducing balance basis would be larger than under the system of initial allowances.[13]

When a restrictive monetary policy was introduced in 1956 investment allowances were withdrawn and were not re-instated until 1959 (at the 1954 rates) but this time with initial allowances (see table 8.2). In 1966 investment allowances were replaced by a system of cash grants, the benefits of which were independent of the tax situation of the firm making the investment.

Although welcomed by business and frequently used by Chancellors as a means of influencing the pace of investment, especially in manufacturing, the allowances system was open to several criticisms, some general, others of a specific nature. To take the former first. As early as 1955 the Royal Commission on the Taxation of Profits and Income had concluded that as a means of selection 'in separating ranking from non-ranking investment, the categories of assets are so widely embracing that the process, judged as a method of selection, appears conspicuously imprecise for an instrument of taxation'.[14] This was repeated in the 1966 White Paper on *Investment Incentives*; the benefits were too widely dispersed to be fully effective, while some items which were eligible had little or no relation to productive investment.[15] A further criticism was that the system tended to discriminate 'in favour of less relative to more profitable investment, as well as in favour of short relative to long investment'.[16] Long-term investment with a three-to-four year planning process was usually done independently of the uncertain availability of such concessions, while small-scale expenditure done at relatively short notice could easily avail itself of such advantages, which tended to give an impetus to ready made improvements rather than long-term planned investment. British businessmen often complained bitterly about frequent changes in the system. On more specific points the practice was criticized because benefit was dependent on the tax rate (which varied), the availability of other income, and that the lag of the realization of the tax incentive behind the investment decision was too long; tax relief was dependent on the decision to invest, but had to wait upon the investment itself. Industry preferred speedy embursement but the initial effects of investment allowances were not felt until about eighteen months (on average) after the expenditure had taken place. Although not a fault of the system a C.B.I. survey observed that while firms were increasingly taking account of tax provisions, a substantial number did not take tax allowances fully into account in their investment decisions, focusing attention on gross rather than net yields.[17]

To meet some of the above criticisms and to provide more powerful incentives, investment allowances were replaced in January 1966 by investment grants. To assist investment in manufacturing, grants were paid in respect of expenditure on new plant and machinery used for carrying on certain qualifying processes. It was argued that such payments could be more 'readily taken into account by individual firms when making their investment decisions; they can provide help for new enterprises which have not yet begun to earn profits; and after a transitional period they will provide a swifter re-imbursement to firms of the expenditure they have incurred.'[18] An additional reason for change arose from the introduction of corporation tax in 1965 which reduced the value of existing allowances to companies. It effectively reduced the rate of tax against which capital allowances could be set from 56.25% to 40%. Compensation for this loss could have taken the form of increasing the size of allowances but it was decided to opt for grants instead.[19]

At the outset manufacturing and extractive industries received investment grants of 20% on new plant and machinery, with different rates for newly redefined development areas. The depreciable base of an asset in receipt of a grant was reduced by the amount of the grant. Industries not qualifying for investment grants continued to get initial allowances but at a higher rate of 30%, while new industrial buildings and structures obtained initial allowances at higher rates, with buildings in development areas in certain circumstances obtaining grants. The level of grants changed in later years, plant and machinery going up to 25% in 1967 and reverting to 20% in 1969 with other rates changing in step. By 1969–70 investment grants totalled about £500m., sums which the government of the day, in 1970, felt involved 'a high public expenditure cost' without achieving the objectives aimed for when the system was introduced.

The disadvantages of investment grants cited in 1970 were, of course, the points of criticism made at the time of their introduction. Such grants were beneficial to firms whether they made a profit or not, and could therefore on that definition lead to the inefficient use of resources; it might be acceptable to give benefits to firms temporarily in difficulties but not if they were permanently unprofitable. The scheme was designed to discriminate between manufacturing and service industries, an object which by 1970 was felt to be unwise in view of the latter's contribution to growth and the balance of payments. It was also costly and burdensome to administer. The new administration in 1970 therefore replaced grants with tax allowances and took the opportunity to simplify the system. Accelerated depreciation (for long favoured by industry but disliked by the Exchequer for revenue reasons) again represented the principle incentive to invest in plant and machinery. The system involved a high first year allowance with writing down allowances for subsequent years standardized at a single level. Thus from October 1970 expenditure on plant and machinery was eligible for a first year allowance of 60% and a standard rate, whatever the life of the asset, of writing down of 25%, the reducing balance to be written off successively in later years. Capital expenditure on plant and machinery in development areas qualified for free depreciation, and compared to the practice in 1963–6, when free depreciation also applied, a wider range of assets was included.[20] Ships continued to benefit from free depreciation as they had done since 1965. In September 1971 the rate for plant and machinery was raised to 80%, and as a further stimulus to investment to 100% in March 1972.

In general terms the granting of various types of investment incentives kept the effective rate of profit tax below the statutory rate and thereby increased cash funds available to firms. The beneficial effects on firms' position may be indicated by the broad ratio of tax accruals and capital allowances to gross trading profits given in table 8.3.[21] The ratio of tax accruals to gross trading profits falls from the early 1950s to the mid-1960s. With the change to corporation tax and the introduction of investment grants the ratio rises over the period 1966–70, but falls again in the next few years with the reversion to capital allowances. The ratio of capital allowances to gross trading profits shows an opposite general trend, rising from the 20% level in the early 1950s to over 40% in the early 1960s. In the period 1966–70 it falls to under 40%, but with the return of allowances climbs steeply to over 74% in the period 1971–6.

Table 8.3   Tax accruals and capital allowances as percentage of gross trading profits (annual averages)

Annual averages	Tax accruals*	Capital allowances
1952–55	50.2	19.0
1956–60	41.5	29.1
1961–65	37.1	41.8
1966–70	50.4	38.8
1971–76	40.5	74.8

* Equal taxes paid plus additions to tax reserves.

Source: National Income and Expenditure Blue Books.

The various investment incentives outlined above placed substantial funds at the disposal of companies. One estimate put the value at around £48m. in 1954 rising to £450m. in 1964, which represented 5.8% of fixed investment in the former year and 19.0% in the latter.[22] Liberal tax incentives combined with periodic penalties on distribution policies meant that companies were given a basis for building up liquidity, which might or might not have encouraged investment; at least they could not feel impeded by capital shortage.[23] There can be little doubt that such enlargement of internal flows was important, especially for firms who did not have ready access to outside funds. As to the general effects of allowances on investment there has been considerable debate. The Royal Commission of 1955 felt that 'allowances do not operate so much by encouragement as by making feasible that which might otherwise be infeasible.'[24] A later investigation came to the tentative conclusion that 'alterations in initial and investment allowances since 1951 have had some discernible effects on investment in the correct direction.'[25] However, the opinion seems fairly widespread that private investment has fallen short of the desired level. Viewed in general terms and taking the ratio of gross fixed capital formation in manufacturing to gross domestic product the pace was very stable. The ratio ranged around 3.7% in the late 1950s and early 1960s, rising to 4.4% at the end of the decade, but then slumping below 4.0% in the early 1970s and to 3.0% in 1975–6.

Company taxation policy

For the greater part of the post-war years company profits were subject to income tax, which on distributed profits was treated as a withholding tax and credited to the shareholder against his tax liability, and profits tax, a two-tier system which in 1965 was replaced by a single corporation tax. The origin of profits tax, which only applied to companies, is to be found in the National Defence Contribution introduced in 1937 to help raise funds for armament expenditure; the government with its purchases had helped to create a business revival so it felt justified in claiming some fiscal benefit. It therefore imposed a tax of 5% on company profits and 4% on those of partnerships and individuals carrying on a trade or business. In April 1939 provision was made for levying an armaments profits duty but with the outbreak of war a more general profits tax was introduced at a rate of 60% on the amount by which profits exceeded 'standard profits', as defined by reference to an earlier period, but it was imposed so that all undertakings paid either excess profits tax or the National Defence Contribution, whichever was the larger.[26] In the following year excess profits tax was raised to 100% on gains above standard profits and remained at that level until 1945. An estimated 80,000 companies paid this tax during the war, the yield from it rising from £72m. in 1940–1 to £477m. in 1944–5. While it may have been a good short-term tax for revenue purposes there is little doubt that by its very nature it encouraged extravagant and wasteful outlay.

From the pre-war standard rate of 5s. 6d. in the £ income tax was raised to 10s. in 1940, to remain so for the war. In 1941 it was decided to treat 20% of excess profits tax as a reserve to be made available to industry for post-war reconstruction, and for several years after 1945 such refunds occurred; £167m. in 1946, £80m. during 1947–50 and £33m. over 1951–9. With the repeal of excess profits tax in 1946 the provisions of the National Defence Contribution became operative and as from January 1947 it became a permanent levy and was renamed profits tax.

In its new form profits tax applied only to companies and was chargeable by reference to profits and distributions of profits for each 'chargeable accounting period', which was the yearly accounting period of the business, while a differential rate was applied to distributions. Profits of less than £2,000 were not subject to tax, while those between £2,000 and £12,000 were allowed an abatement.[27] The rate of 25% was charged on distributed profits, and 10% on undistributed (see table 8.4 for post-war tax rates). The rate on undistributed profits remained unchanged until 1952, but the rate on distributed profits was raised to 30% in 1949 and to 50% in 1952. The object of increased discrimination at this time was to discourage dividend increases which were seen as contributing to consumption expenditure and inciting wage claims, and to encourage companies to plough back more into the business.

Up until 1952 profits tax had been a deductible item in computing the profits of a company for income tax, but from then on the deduction was withdrawn so that companies paid higher income tax on profits than

Table 8.4   Rates of tax on income and profits 1947–75*

Financial years	Standard rate of income tax (%)	Profits tax		Corporation tax (%)
		Distributed %	Undistributed %	
1947–48	45	25	10	
1949–50	45	30	10	
1951–52	47.5	50	10	
1952–53	47.5	22.5	2.5	
1953–54	45	22.5	2.5	
1955–56	42.5	27.5	2.5	
1956–57	42.5	30	3	
1958–59	42.5	10		
1959–60	38.75	10		
1960–61	38.75	12.5		
1961–62	38.75	15		
1964–65	41.25	15		
1965–66	41.25			40
1967–68	41.25			42.5
1968–69	41.25			45
1969–70	41.25			42.5
1970–71	41.25			40
1971–72	38.75			40
1973–74	30†			52
1974–75	33†			52
1975–76	35†			52

* The timing of these changes often did not coincide with the beginning of the fiscal year.
† Basic rate.

Source: Inland Revenue Reports.

previously. However, rates on profits tax were cut to 22.5% on distributed profits and to 2.5% on retained profits, but this represented a greater penalty on distribution. While these new rates produced an effective reduction in profits tax, they were accompanied by the imposition of a temporary tax in the form of an excess profits levy whose purpose was to cream off profits arising from the Korean War rearmament boom. Thus from January 1952 to January 1954 there was an excess profits levy of 30% on profits in excess of a 'standard' rate of profits subject to a limit of 15% of total profits.[28] In October 1955 the rate on distributed dividends was raised to 27.5% largely to restrain excess demand in the economy, and in 1956 both rates were increased, on this occasion simply to raise revenue.

The Royal Commission on the Taxation of Profits and Income in its final report in 1955 recommended the abolition of the differential rate of profits tax, which was done in 1958 with the introduction of a single rate of 10%. The rate was subsequently increased to 12.5% in 1960, to check rising dividends, and to 15% in 1961, in this case mainly to shift the burden of taxation from persons to companies with the increased receipts from profits tax comfortably covering the remission of surtax. Companies continued to pay income tax on both retained and distributed profits, the rate standing at 7s. 9d. between 1959 and 1964; changes in the standard rate were of course mainly determined with reference to the individual income tax.

Although the Royal Commission rejected the idea of a single corporation tax, and as late as 1963 the then Chancellor of the Exchequer considered it impracticable, the divorce of personal and company taxation was made in 1965 in the form of the somewhat hurried introduction of corporation tax. Thus the uniform profits tax became corporation tax with the rate raised to 40% to maintain yield, while income tax on retained earnings was abolished and limited to dividends where it continued to operate as a withholding tax. Companies deducted income tax on distributions made to shareholders and had to account to the Inland Revenue for the income tax.[29] Among the benefits accorded to the change were that it would divorce company and personal taxation, reduce tax avoidance and evasion, and lead to more company saving, permitting increased investment. Savings would be encouraged, since undistributed profits were granted relief from income tax, thus the tax charged on the marginal £ of retentions was reduced relatively to the tax charged on the marginal £ of distributions. At the same time a fully fledged capital gains tax was introduced (unrealized gains however found an attractive tax shelter), while company profits were defined to include capital gains on chargeable assets.[30] Finally, a significant feature of the new system was that interest on debt borrowing was an allowable expense before corporation tax was levied, which led to a marked change in the relative proportions of debt and equities issued over the next few years (see Chapter 6).

In April 1973 a further change was introduced whose aim was the reverse of those arising from corporation tax as it had operated from 1965 onwards. The new system encouraged companies to distribute profit, and market conditions permitting, to raise new funds by equity issues rather than fixed interest. The Chancellor claimed that discrimination had distorted the working of market forces and so tended towards the 'misallocation of scarce investment resources'. Under the 1965 corporation tax scheme a company paid tax at a specified rate, 40% for most of 1965–73, on all its profits whether retained or distributed, but in addition it was required to deduct income tax at the standard rate on dividends paid. Thus, undistributed profits were taxed at a lower rate than those distributed. In contrast the imputation system introduced in April 1973 is neutral as between retained and distributed profits. Companies pay corporation tax at 52%, small companies at 42%, but deduction of tax from dividends ceased.[31] When a company pays a dividend or makes some other qualifying distribution it is required to make a payment of advance corporation tax (ACT) at a specified rate of the distribution, for example, in 1974–5 it was 33/67ths.[32] The advance payment is then set against the corporation tax assessed on the profits of the accounting period so as to reduce the amount of tax then payable on income. The U.K. recipients of a distribution in respect of which ACT is payable is entitled to a tax credit.[33]

The most recent change in taxation provisions relates to stock appreciation. From a level of around 14% of gross trading profits in 1970–2 stock appreciation rose to 25% in 1973 and, helped by the depreciation of sterling, reached a high of 43% in 1974. The requirement to pay tax on this increment of profit threatened to worsen the already serious liquidity position of the company sector, and in the autumn of 1974 the Chancellor announced a scheme to defer corporation tax on profits arising from the abnormal rise in stock values. The temporary relief, introduced in the first Finance Act 1975, applied to increases in stocks and work in progress for certain large companies with stocks in excess of £25,000. If the value of stocks increased in the 1973 account, tax was deferred on that part of profits equal to the amount of the increase less 10%, raised to 15% in 1976, of the trading income of that period. The second Finance Act 1975 extended the relief to apply for two years, and widened the range to cover all businesses. The relief applies to changes in book values of stocks (whether due to price changes or stock building) so that at the margin stock building effectively attracts free depreciation just as most fixed assets do.[34] As a result of the relief, companies were provided with funds to replenish stocks at higher current prices, with the tax accruals of industrial and commercial companies as recorded in the Blue Book falling very appreciably by 1975. With the later continuation of stock relief and the prevailing system of capital allowances almost the whole of any profits which a manufacturing company reinvests is effectively relieved from corporation tax.

A distinctive feature of company taxation during the period 1947–58, and from 1965–73, was the differential rate of tax with distributed profits carrying a relatively higher level. While many other countries have experimented with differential taxes on profits, universally they imposed heavier tax burdens on undistributed profits than on dividends. It was a canon of progressive taxation to tax especially severely such parts of company profits which escaped surtax or its equivalent. Thus a relatively higher tax on retained profits is advocated since retentions provide shareholders, through the enhanced capital value of shares, with net capital gains which either escape income tax or are taxed at a lower rate than that applicable to the higher brackets of personal income.[35] For example, from 1958 onwards distributions in Germany have been taxed at a much lower rate than retentions; the distributed profits of a company are charged at a rate of 15% and the undistributed profits at a basic rate of 51%. In view of Britain's relative uniqueness in this respect it is as well to outline the reasons put forward from time to time in support of the practice.

It was generally agreed that punitive rates on dividends were not imposed to raise revenue but rather to discourage the distribution of profits. The tax was an alternative to using statutory limitation of dividends and as an additional support to appeals for voluntary dividend restraint. By limiting dividends the hope was to dampen wage rises. Such arguments were used by Chancellors from both major political parties (higher dividends led to higher wage claims) and firmly supported by union and management organizations alike.[36] But, as was often pointed out, the ability of a company to pay higher wages is measured by profits before tax rather than by the relatively small fraction of such profits paid out in dividends.

A further basis for approving the practice was that of equity. The differential tax was widely supported by a wide range of academic, political and industrial opinion who believed that it was an instrument for the redistribution of wealth, while some urged even further progression of the differential. Even the Minority Report of the 1955 Royal Commission contrived to argue in its defence on this point, on the grounds that a differential profits tax depressed dividends which then acted as a countervailing factor to the formation of tax free capital gains.[37] By contrast foreign opinion did not regard as fair and equitable the harbouring of retained profits from the full rigour of profits taxation.

The practice also received support as a useful anti-inflationary device on the grounds that it reduced consumption demand by squeezing dividend income. However, this particular argument found little support from the Royal Commission;

> except as a strictly short term measure, there is an obvious weakness in the power of the tax to check inflation. Indeed given that profits are in fact retained or are ploughed back, there is no safe inference that this is less inflationary in its effects than the distribution of a corresponding amount by way of dividends. Some part of a larger distribution may be saved, even by an individual receiver, on the other hand, it does not follow that smaller distributions will reduce consumptive demand.[38]

Perhaps the most important reason for the persistence with the differential feature of profits tax was that of encouraging investment. Certainly when corporation tax was introduced in 1965 one of the declared intentions was to encourage companies to 'plough back profits for expansion'. While such a policy had quite respectable parentage in the evidence given by Keynes and Dalton to the Colwyn Committee on National Debt and Taxation in 1927, more recent verdicts were highly critical of the effectiveness of such a stimulant. The *Majority Report* of the 1955 Royal Commission questioned the foundations of the 'longer-term objective of encouraging productive investment in the form of ploughed back profits'; the profits tax 'does not encourage companies to plough back profits, so much as to retain them'.[39] A similar view came from the *Minority Report*:

> the artificial encouragement of the retention of profits by companies is not necessarily an advantage. Beyond a certain point it does not in itself stimulate the rate of capital formation – as is shown by the fact that in the last few years the net amounts retained by companies have greatly exceeded their financial requirements, both on account of capital expenditure and of investment in working capital.[40]

Indeed both Reports were critical of the notion that mere retention was an economic advantage. In the words of the *Minority Report*:

> the system of financing capital expenditure so largely out of the undistributed profits of companies does not ensure the best use of the community's savings. It makes it more difficult for fast expanding

firms to raise capital in the capital market; it strengthens the monopolistic tendencies in the economy; and it encourages wasteful expenditure on behalf of those firms who have more money than they can use and who are yet prevented (by custom and tradition as well as by the instruments of public control) from channelling these funds to their most profitable use.[41]

The belief that there is a close dependence between growth and retained earnings received a damaging blow from the investigation conducted by I. M. D. Little. In his famous paper on 'Higgledy Piggledy Growth' he asserted that in the majority of cases examined there was no evidence to indicate that retained profits had a significant effect on the growth of earnings. In a regression of the rate of change of pre-tax earnings on lagged retentions and asset size for 13 groups of British companies for 1951–9, it was found that only in the case of one group was the sign of the regression coefficient for ploughback positive and significant.[42] An earlier enquiry by B. Tew and R. F. Henderson into the saving and investment intentions of quoted companies covering 1949–53 found that there was little evidence of any connection between intentions to save and to invest. However, they were conscious that the enquiry covered an abnormal period of cheap money, of dividend restraint, and when investment intentions were often frustrated by controls and shortages.[43]

A major objective of policy for the period 1947–58, and 1965–73, was to encourage the retention of company income through the tax system. Opinion as to the success of this policy is very divided. The Majority Report of the 1955 Royal Commission doubted the effectiveness of the tax differential: 'It has not prevented the increase in amounts distributed by way of dividend which has been noticeable since 1953 and we are disposed to think that, even with the present big difference between distributed and undistributed rates it can have only a minor influence on distribution policy when other influences combine to pull in the opposite direction.'[44] The Minority Report disagreed, asserting on the basis of a comparison of 1938 and 1953 figures (gross profits up four times, dividends up by less than half, while savings rose eight times) that the existence of the differential tax had undoubtedly been a major cause of the relative modesty of dividend distributions as compared with the rise in earnings.[45] This view was supported by a later investigation which concluded that differential tax rates had been a prime factor influencing dividends between 1949–53.[46]

However, a survey covering a longer period, 1957–61, by A. Rubner, resulted in the categorical insistence that while for 1947–51 the pay-out ratio dropped as compared with earlier years, for years after 1951 the percentage of company profits going to dividends rose consistently; 'Between 1951 and 1958 . . . there is no correlation between the widening of the differential rates of the profits tax and the pay-out ratio; in fact, the opposite can be observed, that is, the heavier the tax burden on distributed profits, the higher the percentage of total profits which are declared as a dividend.' In Rubner's view the repeal of the differential tax in 1958 should have led to a 'flood of increased dividend distributions'. As it turned out the 'remarkable feature is not the rise in the pay-out ratios but the relatively small rise'.[47] He maintained that the fall in the pay-out ratios between 1947–54 was due not to the increasing burden of the differential tax, but rather because gross company profits contained a large proportion of 'illusory profits in the form of stock appreciation'. Adjusting for this, the range within which pay-out values fluctuated narrowed considerably. Also, the key influence on fluctuations in pay-out ratios was not the structure of profits tax but the general level of all direct taxation. While the joint rate of profits tax did not fluctuate greatly (see table 8.4, p. 230) it is evident from table 8.3 (p. 228) that tax liabilities constituted a sharply declining proportion of gross profits, due in no way to the differential tax but rather to the influence of investment allowances. On the basis of his figures Rubner found that between 1951–3 and 1959–61, the proportion of company profits going to taxes fell from 49% to 35.8%, and that 7.3% of this fall went to swell savings, while 5.9% increased the fund out of which higher dividends were paid.[48] The same point was made much earlier in 1954 by a lone voice in the academic world. D. Walker argued that British companies had a highly inelastic policy of distributing profits, and that larger profits were rarely transmitted into higher dividends, so that the punitive taxation of dividends would not lead to a reduction in dividends but would fall on the planned volume of company savings. A two-tier profits tax did not lower dividends, it merely transferred 'savings out of the control of Boards of Directors (via taxes) into the hands of the government'.[49]

While the rise in the pay-out ratio after 1958 was influenced by the removal of the differential, it was also decisively stimulated by the incidence of take-over bids which led directors to distribute profits and reduce liquid assets to minimize the 'bait' for the 'raiders'. What is surprising about the rise in the pay-out ratio is its smallness; had there been a pent up demand the rise should have been much greater.[50] The average pay-out ratio (dividends/earnings, including depreciation) for 1961–2 was 37% compared with 30% in 1958–9, while in 1963–4 the ratio fell back to 33%. In terms of the appropriation of company incomes (see figure 8.1, p. 221) the proportion distributed in dividends rose from 18% in 1958 to 25% in 1961. Apparently, the proportion of profit so distributed by quoted companies did not rise as rapidly, suggesting that the greatest increase in distributions occurred among unquoted private companies.[51]

The restoration of the incentive to retain earnings with the adoption of corporation tax in 1965 produced, over the period 1966–70, a pay-out ratio in the range 33% to 36%, somewhat above the ratio for the years immediately following the ending of discrimination in 1958. However, over these years aggregate dividends remained stable, and declined significantly as a percentage of total income, from 24% in 1966 to 17% in 1970. Company savings in this period also remained very stable and, as with dividends, recorded a distinctive fall as a percentage of total income from 40% in 1966 to 33% in 1970 (see figure 8.1). During 1971–6 dividends continued to fall as a percentage of income reaching a low of 10% in 1974, when savings slumped to 21% of income. The sharp drop in the pay-out ratio in 1973, to 25%, arose because of the big rise in savings in the boom, nearly a quarter on the year, while in 1976 it declined to 23% as income recovered and dividends were controlled. It would appear that corporation tax had some 'tax shelter' effects on the level of dividend payments, while the decisive factor determining changes in the pay-out level was the fluctuation in earnings associated with changes in gross trading profits. The stability of dividends over this period was arguably attributable in some degree to various schemes for dividend limitation and the fall in equity issues, but probably the most influential factor, as in the 1950s, was that large British companies had a highly inelastic policy of distributing profits.

Dividend payments

Among the factors which affect the amount of dividends distributed by a company are the level of past profits, the proportion distributed and the expected level of profits. Presumably companies will not increase distributions unless they have confidence that the level can be maintained, while if they envisage opportunites for expansion they may well restrain current distributions for larger future dividends. The influence of these general considerations may be tempered by two others which operated frequently and with varying degrees of severity during the post-war years. As related above, taxation may be adjusted through differential rates, and other means, so as to encourage retentions. The volume of dividends may also be affected by the imposition of compulsory or voluntary limitation. The main arguments in favour of control centre on increasing company savings to encourage investment, and the social one, that higher dividends might be sustained by higher prices; against these are the arguments that control might lead to falling share prices so increasing the cost and difficulty of obtaining new capital from the market, and that with rising prices real dividends decline leading to disenchantment with investment in industry. Over the post-war period there are very few years when some kind of dividend control has not operated and when the above arguments have not been rehearsed.

Although in the immediate post-war years of 1946–7 there was wide acceptance of 'moral dividend limitation', and despite Dr Dalton's request in 1945 that funds should go to development rather than increased dividends, higher payments were made. It was in no sense a breakaway, but the increases were quite noticeable, involving companies over a wide industrial field. Such rises were paid out of increased profits, although some companies increased actual earnings by bringing into credit earlier provisions which they no longer needed. Other companies, notably those in the nationalization groups had, for obvious reasons, decided to treat their shareholders generously; after many years of restraint directors felt that higher profits should benefit others apart from company reserves.[52]

The introduction of dividend limitation in 1948 was associated with the policy aimed at restoring external stability and narrowing the trade gap. Along with prices and wages restraint the Federation of British Industries agreed with the Chancellor that subject to 'exceptional cases' the 'gross amount distributed by a business by way of dividends in the current year should not exceed the gross amount distributed on the same capital in its last financial year'. The restraint did not apply to new companies, or to companies suffering from concentration, war damage or enemy occupation.[53] Though simple, and preferred to any rigid or complicated scheme, it meant that in the first instance companies were the judges of their own eligibility for exceptional treatment. It also meant that companies, who up to that time had ploughed back profits, would have to withold distributions from future increased profits accruing from such reinvested earnings, while companies who had distributed to the hilt would be given a further brief to do so. Voluntary restraint was carried through into 1949, but by then many firms were in no position, due to falling profits, to indulge in a dividend spree even if they were free to do so. The Chancellor was anxious that restraint should continue but the enthusiasm of industry was waning with a growing number of reservations from large companies, and rather than continue with the 1949 scheme they preferred to pursue a policy of 'moderation and restraint'.[54] However, in the aftermath of devaluation, when industry found increasing difficulty in getting finance, the employers' organization agreed to continue with the practice of restraint, no doubt encouraged by the Chancellor's limited lifting of the ban on bonus issues.[55]

With the rise in profits in 1950 restraint was applied far less strictly by companies; they felt that the government's pledge to stabilize wages had not been fullfilled, which made them freer with their dividend policy. Following this perceptable spurt in dividend payments the Chancellor in his next Budget raised the rate of undistributed profits tax from 30% to 50%, hopefully as 'a powerful incentive to companies to put profits to reserve rather than increase dividends', and in preference to a more cumbersome statutory control of dividends. Yet in the summer came a bill to control dividends. Mr Gaitskell's change of heart arose because 'practically every morning there is news of a company increasing its dividend in a pretty substantial way', which, he argued, 'inevitably acts as a continual irritant on the great majority of the population who are not equity shareholders ... [and thus the] psychological consequences of sharp increases in dividends are far greater than their direct monetary effect'.[56] This was almost certainly so; *The Economist* reporting on 877 company accounts which appeared in the period April–June 1951 found that gross trading profits rose by 27.5%, and out of this, after tax, dividends rose by £10m., less than one-tenth of the profit increase. The White Paper *Control of Dividends* (Cmd 8318) proposed a limit on the gross amount of equity dividends distributed by public or private companies during the period covered by the three accounting years from 27 July. The limit for the majority of companies was to be the average amount distributed or declared in respect of the two accounting years to 26 July. Companies who had paid no dividend in the previous two years could do so to the amount of 5% of their issued capital, and new companies would be limited to a 7% distribution, while those distributing less than £10,000 were to be exempt. Since it was overtaken by a general election and a change of government its main effect was to 'throw the Stock Exchange into complete disorder', which according to Dr Dalton 'is good fun anyway'.

The effect of the various phases of dividend limitation during 1948–51 on the level of distributed payments is by no means easy to identify. Taking companies which were in private ownership throughout the period 1938–51 (which removes the effect of nationalization) the proportion of gross trading profits distributed amounted to about one-fifth for the years 1948–51 compared with nearly three-fifths in 1938, a fall made mainly to accommodate increased taxation. Thus after the short burst of 1946–7 the percentage distributed remained low; the total distributed during 1948–51 rose by 18% but gross trading profits went up by 42%.[57] Without restraint distributions would probably have been larger were it only to maintain real income. Further evidence of its impact was the series of bonus issues which appeared in 1949, considerably enlivening the market. In many cases this was merely a revival of the pre-war practice of paying a scrip bonus along with the dividend. At this time they were invariably capitalizations of reserves by free scrip issues or by restoring the par value of previously written down shares. Companies did not, however, conform to dividend limitation if they maintained their previous percentage dividend payment. Thus, in 1949 a ban was introduced on free bonus issues due to the allegation that they were being used to evade restraint; the Chancellor colourfully referred to the 'capitalisation of large profits and their distribution as bonus shares to shareholders'.

Although a comparatively small number of companies made increased distributions for which reasonable justification could not be found in the agreement on voluntary dividend limitation, apart from the fact that they had recorded 'bumper earnings', for most of this period there were other pressures acting as a curb on dividends in addition to the tax shelter advantage of differential profits tax. Firstly, there was a clear need to plough back profits to maintain fixed and working capital and in 1949 most leading company chairmen were aware that this took precedence over dividend payments. Secondly, falling profits brought its own brake on distributions. Thirdly, some companies tended to regard their shareholders not as an equity interest but rather as lenders who were satisfied with a more or less fixed rate of return. Such a view was possible until the advent of the first take-over bids in the early 1950s. Certainly, dividends were not adjusted downwards given the prevailing prospects of dividend limitation. The dividend policies of companies tended to be quite stable so that if income fluctuated with tax levels unchanged, the impact fell on savings rather than dividends.[58] The much-voiced fears of a dividend spree and the ensuing psychological dangers were, on the evidence, much overdrawn.

The new government of 1951 continued with the 'secondhand garment that was so hard worn' by its predecessor, the Chancellor advocating a policy of 'modified dividend restraint' mainly on the grounds that its psychological effects would help dampen wage demands. However, during the period of Mr Butler's investment boom industry paid out higher dividends and increased slightly the percentage of income allocated for that purpose, not at the expense of savings but from higher profits and a fall in the proportion going to tax (see figure 8.1, p. 221).[59] While the thaw was helped by high profits and a fall in stockholding, what really freed companies from the bonds of voluntary restraint was the growing incidence of take-over bids. These early bids, aimed at financial pickings, indicated the dangers of accumulating liquid reserves, and that shareholders' resistance and bidders' eagerness increased and diminished respectively as share prices responded to higher dividends. Even in some official quarters the view gained ground that it was to the 'advantage of the national economy that profits should be released as dividends, to add to the supply of capital available for useful investment elsewhere'.[60] With increased institutional shareholding it could no longer be forcibly argued that all distributed dividends would go to sell current consumption, and that if invested it would be misguidedly or rashly made. In this period therefore dividends were increasing broadly at about the same rate as earnings for the whole company sector, and they were accompanied in many instances by scrip issues. The 1956 credit squeeze produced a slowdown in distributions and the Chancellor had little need to preach caution or the virtues of limitation; declining profits brought conservative actions with some companies fearful that they might not be able to maintain existing rates.

Following a gradual rise in dividends in 1957–8, reflecting a similar trend in profits, the 1959–60 boom produced a sharp movement in distributed dividends. As a percentage of income appropriated dividend distributions rose from 18% in 1958 to 22% in 1960, and 25% in 1961, the highest level of the period (see figure 8.1). While gross trading profits increased by over 20% in the boom, dividends rose by some 43%. This was the general picture, and while many firms and industries had similar patterns of distribution there was some variation. Firms in the consumer goods industries, like drink and tobacco, clothing and footwear, miscellaneous metal goods, and retail distribution, paid out much higher proportions of their income and retained less as depreciation provisions.[61] From the level of 15% to 18% of income in the 1960s the boom increase in dividends shifted the share into the 20% to 25% range for the whole of the 1960s. Only a small portion of the 1958–60 rise is attributable to new equity issues, which rose broadly in line with total expenditure by companies. The change in pace probably owed a great deal to the high incidence of take-overs which, as in previous episodes, made companies less inclined to hold large reserves of financial assets.[62] Financial institutions also took a greatly increased interest in equities for growth and income, while with an increased volume of new issues companies wanting to come to the market frequently sought to maintain the status of their shares by dividend 'sweeteners'. Finally, the abolition of the differential profits tax, with its discriminatory rate for distributed dividends, and the removal of the 'tax shelter' position of retained income, was an important ingredient.

The balance of payments crisis in 1961 ushered in a 'pay pause' and as part of the general measures companies were asked to exercise restraint in dividend distributions, but the policy only lasted for a short time. Thereafter dividends continued to rise slowly, spurting upwards in 1965 to nearly 25% of company appropriations due to the impending introduction of corporation tax. Thus the figure for 1965 was high, largely at the expense of that in 1966; the reverse happened in 1972 when companies delayed dividend payments to take advantage of the new imputation tax system which came into effect in April 1973. Dividend levels for the rest of the 1960s, as recorded for quoted companies, or for industrial and commercial companies, remained relatively stable, but with a discernible fall as a proportion of company appropriation.

It was not only the 'tax shelter' effect of corporation tax which produced constancy of dividends. From July 1966 to December 1969 a form of dividend restraint was in operation. The 1966 restraint held that 'no increases in dividends were to be paid for twelve months except where no dividend had been paid for several years and the business had become profitable, or where an increase was necessary to combat a take over bid.'[63] Severe restraint was lifted for a brief period in 1967–8 and replaced by a request to companies to exercise 'moderation in distributions', but then replaced by the imposition of a 3.5% ceiling on dividend increases which lasted until 1970.[64] Even in its absence companies would probably not have paid out much more in dividends, since the rate of corporation tax was increased and the special surcharge on unearned income made them reluctant to distribute more. After two years of voluntary restraint, which meant 'keeping dividend increases in line with the general rise in other incomes', the Counter Inflation Act of 1972 imposed an immediate standstill on prices, pay and dividends. Under this legislation companies were forbidden to declare dividends in excess of the corresponding dividends paid in the previous year. A year later a more permanent measure of control was brought in which gave the government powers to regulate prices, pay and dividends for a three-year period, and which set up the Prices Commission and the Pay Board. Curiously, the power to control dividends was entrusted to the Treasury, with some exceptions. The basic requirement was that no company incorporated in the U.K. could raise the sum distributed in any account year by more than 5%, later amended to 12.5%, over that for the preceding year.[65]

The payment of fixed interest by companies has, of course, never aroused any political concern. However, it is worth noting that following the introduction of corporation tax in 1965, and the increased amount of fixed interest debt issued subsequently, that debt interest rose from some £400m. in 1965 to over £650m. in 1970. Part of the increase was attributable to rising interest rates in the period. More startling has been the very sharp rise in the item other interest payments, particularly since 1971. In 1965 it absorbed about 6% of company income, increasing to 8% in 1970, but by 1974–5 it had reached nearly 18% (see figure 8.1). It reflected the very heavy short-term borrowing indulged in by companies in the difficulties of 1974–5, the funds coming from banks and other financial institutions.

Notes

1 Stock appreciation is regarded by the Inland Revenue as profit for the purposes of tax. Prior to the war there were instances of exceptions to this practice, but their quantitative importance is unknown; L. T. Barna, 'Valuation of Stocks and the National Income', *Economica*, 1942, p. 349.

2 There is considerable variation in the proportion of retained income. In their survey of 1948–54 Tew and Henderson found nine industrial categories which fell within the range 31–7%; among the exceptions were iron and steel, 41%; chemicals, 40%; breweries and distilleries, 23%; and tobacco, 25%; B. Tew and R. F. Henderson, *Studies in Company Finance*, Cambridge, 1959, p. 168.

3 *Report of the Commissioners of H. M. Inland Revenue*, Cmnd 4838, 31 March 1971, p. 10.

4 In the past the charge for depreciation appearing in company accounts, at least for plant and machinery, was often used on the declining balance method at rates also used for calculating tax allowances. More and more companies are now using in their published accounts only the straight line basis for calculating depreciation allowances on all the classes of fixed assets, having regard solely to expected life and obsolescence. The progressive advancement of high initial allowances, investment grants, and recently the first year tax allowance of 100% have contributed towards this change in practice; J. L. Walker, 'Estimating Companies' Rate of Return on Capital Employed', *Economic Trends*, November 1974, p. XXXI.

5 Industrial buildings were depreciated on a straight line basis and assumed to last 50 years; D. Walker, 'Depreciation Problems and Taxation' in J. L. Meij (ed.) *Depreciation and Replacement Policy*, Amsterdam, 1961, p. 184. In November 1962 the writing down allowance for industrial buildings was increased from 2% to 4%.

6 *Report of the Commissioners of H.M. Inland Revenue*, Cmnd 4615, 1970, p. 12.

7 The recommendations arose from an Inland Revenue enquiry in 1944 into business taxation and the treatment of capital expenditure.

8 At the time numerous commentators were worried about inflated replacement costs. They expressed the view that a debilitating seepage of capital was taking place, since a system of depreciation allowances based on original cost instead of replacement value led to an overstatement of taxable profits and the erosion of business capital. In some countries depreciation allowances were calculated after multiplying the cost of the fixed asset by an officially computed index that expressed the fall in the value of money since the date of acquisition; see *The Economist*, 26 July 1952, p. 244.

9 F. W. Paish argued, using capital consumption estimates, that while normal depreciation only covered some three-quarters of depreciation at replacement cost, the addition of initial allowances during 1949–51 adequately covered replacement costs; F. W. Paish, *Studies in an Inflationary Economy*, London, 1962, pp. 266–7.

10 The introduction of accelerated depreciation required more attention to be given to equating the capital allowances given in respect of an asset with the net capital expenditure incurred upon it (original cost less scrap). The 1945 Code therefore provided for a system of balancing allowances and charges designed to equate the net capital expenditure with the total of allowances given over the life of the asset; *Report of the Commissioners of H. M. Inland Revenue*, 1971, op. cit., p. 11.

11 A. R. Prest, *Public Finance*, London, 1970, p. 341. Few businesses reflected the 'loan' in their accounts by transferring the amount of tax deferred to some kind of suspense account: for the most part it merged with net profits to be distributed at will; *The Economist*, 2 July 1949, p. 34.

12 J. C. R. Dow, *The Management of the British Economy 1945–60*, Cambridge, 1964, p. 207. The rate of income tax plus profits tax on undistributed profits was then 47.5%. Each remission was complete in itself and the withdrawal of the allowance did not affect that remission.

13 Royal Commission on the Taxation of Profits and Income, *Final Report*, Cmnd 9474, 1955, para. 413.

14 ibid., para. 415.

15 *Investment Incentives*, Cmnd 2874, 1966, para. 14. For similar points see *Conditions Favourable to Faster Growth*, N.E.D.C, 1963.

16 R. A. and P. B. Musgrave, 'Fiscal Policy' in R. E. Caves (ed.) *Britain's Economic Prospects*, London, 1968, p. 60. See also J. Black, 'Investment Allowances, Initial Allowances and Cheap Loans as Means of Encouraging Investment', *Review of Economic Studies*, 1959, pp. 44–7.

17 *Investment Incentives*, op. cit., para. 15. See also R. S. Ashton, 'Investment Policy in Private Enterprise', *Lloyds Bank Review*, October 1962, pp. 24–6.

18 *Investment Incentives*, op. cit., para. 17. Applications were made to the Board of Trade and grants were payable within six months of the presentation of claims. The arrangement was administratively complex and costly; on the government side alone it involved a staff of about 1,000 at an annual cost of £2m. In comparison the allowances system was administered by the Inland Revenue.

19 Roy Thomas, 'The change in corporation Tax and the Incentive to Invest', *Journal of Business Finance*, vol. 5, no. 1., pp.69–75.

20 With investment grants development areas attracted 40% rates, compared with 20% elsewhere. 'The cost of the regional differential in this form has been unduly high in relation to the benefit provided'; *Investment Incentives 1970*, Cmnd. 4516, para. 10. However, in March 1972 direct cash grants were restored to expenditure on plant and machinery in development areas but unlike previous grants they did not affect a company's eligibility for capital allowances.

21 The use of liability rather than collection figures is based on the assumption that the effect on company behaviour stems from liability rather than collection changes: see Musgrave, op. cit., p. 38.

22 ibid., pp. 58–9.

23 For the controversy as to whether the liquidity effect or the profitability effect (by raising the rate of return) was the most important influence on investment; see D. C. Corner and A. Williams, 'The Sensitivity of Business to Initial and Investment Allowances', *Economica*, 1965, pp. 32–47.

24 Royal Commission, 1955, op. cit., para. 424.

25 R. M. Bird, 'Depreciation Allowances and Counter Cyclical Policy in the U.K. 1946–60', *Canadian Tax Journal*, vol. XI, 1963; see also R. M. Bird, 'Countercyclical Variations of Depreciation Allowances in the U.K.', *National Tax Journal*, 1963.

26 The 'standard profits' were normally based on the profits of a pre-war period (ordinarily the calendar year 1935, or the calendar year 1936, or the average of the calendar years 1935 and 1937, or the average of the calendar years 1936–37); *Report of the Commissioners of H.M. Inland Revenue*, 1947, pp. 31–2.

27 Due to these exemptions the number of companies which paid profits tax was not as high as the total number of companies might suggest. In 1960–1 some 100,000 companies were assessible to profits tax, of which 46,000 received some measure of abatement. About 200,000 companies were completely exempt from the tax, but their total profits, around £50m., represented less than 2.0% of the total profits chargeable to profits tax; *Report of the Committee on Turnover Taxation*, Cmnd 2300, para. 130 (Richardson Committee, 1964).

28 The net receipts from the Excess Profits Levy for the period 1952–3 to 1955–6 was £163.7m., the total number of assessments being 29,877; *Inland Revenue Reports*.

29 In the case of companies trading before the 1965 Finance Act tax was payable on 1 January following the end of the fiscal year in which the companies accounting period ended. For companies not so trading the tax was payable within *nine* months of the end of the accounting period for which it was assessed. Such companies lost the long 'lag' which had been found useful – the payment of tax on high profits could be postponed for well over a year; see R. S. Sayers, 'The Timing of Tax Payments by Companies', *The Three Banks Review*, September 1967, pp. 24–32.

30 For a full discussion of the change see A. R. Prest, 'Corporation Tax', *District Bank Review*, 1965; M. Crawford, 'The 1965 Reforms in the British Tax System', *Moorgate and Wall Street*, Autumn 1965.

31 Small companies are charged a lower rate since they rely more heavily on retained earnings, finding it more difficult to raise capital than large companies; see *Reform of Corporation Tax*, Cmnd 4955, 1972, para. 26.

32 Payments of ACT are mainly made in the first month following the end of the quarter in which dividends are paid.

33 See *Report of the Commissioners of H.M. Inland Revenue*, Cmnd 5168, 1972, and *Reform of Corporation Tax*, op. cit., pp. 4–7.

34 *Inland Revenue Report*, Cmnd 6302, 1976, pp. 8–9; *Bank of England Quarterly Bulletin*, December 1974, pp. 397–9. In the 1976 Budget it was announced that relief will be calculated by reference to the amount of the book value increase less 15% of trading profits after deduction of capital allowances.

35 A. Rubner, 'The Irrelevancy of the British Differential Profits Tax', *Economic Journal*, June 1964, p. 350. British shareholders in companies with low ratios of distribution escaped the major burden of the profits tax and the payment of surtax.

36 The *Minority Report* of the Royal Commission of 1955, felt that there was an 'undoubted psychological link between dividend payments and wage claims'; para. 102.

37 Royal Commission, *Minority Report*; 'an increase in dividends would have had the most undesirable effects . . . because of the far greater untaxed benefit which shareholders would have obtained in the form of capital gains'; para. 100.

38 Royal Commission, *Majority Report*, para. 535. Certainly, the Treasury lost revenue through the differential rate, particularly in the area of surtax; see Rubner, op. cit., p. 351.

39 ibid., para. 536.

40 Royal Commission, *Minority Report*, para. 103.

41 ibid., para. 103.

42 I. M. D. Little, 'Higgledy Piggledy Growth', *Bulletin of the Oxford University Institute of Economics and Statistics*, November 1962, pp. 408–11.

43 Tew and Henderson, op. cit., pp. 49–51.

44 Royal Commission, *Majority Report*, para. 537.

45 Royal Commission, *Minority Report*, para. 99.

46 S. J. Prais, 'Dividend Policy and Income Appropriation' in Tew and Henderson, op. cit., pp. 34–40.

47 Rubner, op. cit., p. 354.

48 ibid., pp. 355–6.

49 D. Walker, 'Some Economic Aspects of the Taxation of Companies', *Manchester School*, 1954, pp. 27–9.

50 M. Feldstein maintained that the abolition of the split rate had resulted in net dividends increasing by 40%; 'The Effectiveness of the British Differential Profits Tax', *Economic Journal*, 1967: F. W. Paish concluded that the effect of the change was 'hardly perceptible'; quoted by Caves, op. cit., p. 55.

51 Gross ordinary and preference dividends represented 28.6% of the gross income of quoted companies in 1960, compared with 25.5% in 1958; 'Income and Finance of Quoted Companies, 1949–60', *Economic Trends*, April 1962, p. vi. A. Williams concluded that the increased flow of distributions must have come from 'static firms with excess liquidity'; see his chapter on Great Britain in *Foreign Tax Policies and Economic Growth*, Columbia, 1966, p. 419.

52 *The Economist*, 12 October 1946, p. 596.

53 *The Economist*, 20 March 1948, pp. 466–7. When excess profits tax was announced in 1940 a measure for 'Limitation of Dividends' had gone a considerable way towards the Statute Book, while in 1946 there had been talk of an 'excess dividend tax', as a means of preventing inflationary spending; *The Economist*, 9 March 1946, p. 385; 6 April 1946, p. 546.

54 *The Economist*, 9 February 1949, p. 342.

55 After the 1949 devaluation distributed profits tax was raised from 25% to 30%. The effect was that companies maintained dividends so putting less money to retentions.

56 *The Economist*, 28 July 1951, p. 229. The *Economist* estimated that the average rate of ordinary dividend as a percentage of ordinary capital was around 15%, but expressed over ordinary capital and reserves the return was only about 5%. The direct effect on consumption depended on

the size of the net dividend, while nothing was known as to the sum paid in surtax, or how much relief was granted from the standard rate of income tax.

57 Using *The Economist* data A. Luboff found that up to 1951 dividends increased less rapidly than profits, 5% and 18% respectively, reflecting dividend limitation, and the tendency of many companies to regard part of the high profits earned in 1950–1 as due to price rises and stock appreciation which they ploughed back to meet future needs; A. Luboff, 'Some Aspects of Postwar Company Finance: An Analysis of Tabulations of Company Accounts published in *The Economist*', *Accounting Research*, April 1956, p. 1.

58 Cuts in dividends as a result of falling profits were very uncommon. A conservative attitude towards raising dividends in good years made cuts unnecessary in bad years; see Luboff, op. cit., p. 174.

59 Luboff found that during 1953–4 dividends increased more rapidly than profits, 24% compared with 14%. This was due not only to higher dividends but also to a smaller extent to dividends on newly issued capital; Luboff, op. cit., p. 173.

60 *The Economist*, 5 February 1955, p. 483; statement by Lord Kenet, Chairman of the C.I.C.

61 'Income and Finance of Quoted Companies 1949–60', *Economic Trends*, April 1962, p. vii.

62 Apart from bona fide take-overs there were a number aimed solely at 'dividend stripping' which cost the Inland Revenue about £4.0m. a year. It was a device whereby a company could strip off the industrial profits of another company it had purchased, in a dividend to itself and then set that payment off against its own tax loss, which often enough it acquired by buying a company that had accumu-

lated one. The practice was stopped by the Finance Acts of 1958 and 1959, while earlier dividend stripping by finance companies had been put down by the 1955 Finance Act; *The Economist*, 19 April 1958, p. 233; 11 April 1959, p. 149; Royal Commission, *Minority Report*, paras 144–6.

63 'The Use of Prices and Incomes Policies in Britain; The Search for a New Instrument', *Midland Bank Review*, August 1973, p. 13.

64 Companies which had previously reduced their dividend levels could return to the old level, subject to Treasury approval and examination. Such cases were largely in the retailing and allied trades; *The Economist*, 23 March 1968, p. 88.

65 In its *Report on Income from Companies and its Distribution*, Cmnd 6172, 1975, the Royal Commission on the Distribution of Income and Wealth noted for quoted companies that the 'best estimate we have been able to make of the growth of dividends over the period (1963–74) adjusted for changes in the capital base is 82%, an average of 7.5% p.a. or 5.6% compound; para. 142. Some of the rights issues made in 1975 were intended to circumvent the restriction on increased dividends imposed by the prices and incomes policy. This limited the increase in dividends per share to 10% but total dividends could be increased in proportion to the number of shares. By making the right to buy additional shares available at a large discount companies were able to raise their shareholders dividend yield by more than 10%. In October the Treasury required companies to seek approval before making such issues; *Midland Bank Review*, 'The Year of The Rights Issue', February 1976, pp. 22–3.

9 Trade credit, short- and medium-term finance

*In their passage from the soil to the consumer
goods pass through the hands of a series of owners,
creating as they pass a train of debts, a series of
trade credits.*

F. LAVINGTON

Trade credit

Credit involves the provision of goods or services in exchange for payment which is deferred, or it may take the form of a payment in advance for goods to be received. It can arise from transactions between firms, or from exchanges between firms and households, or domestic and overseas companies, and so on; the main concern here is with domestic trade credit. In company balance sheets it generally appears as 'trade and other creditors and accounts', and 'trade and other debtors and payments in advance', the former appearing on the liabilities side as sums owed by the company, the latter as an asset representing sums due to the company. Trade credit given is the amount of money owed to the firm by its customers; trade credit taken is the amount the firm owes to its suppliers. The credit period relates to the time, a few days or several weeks, between the delivery of goods and payment for them. Thus the total credit provided by a firm to its customers may be taken as the product of sales over the credit period and the credit period itself, so that it may alter with changes in either item. Normally, the amount of trade credit given varies with the volume of turnover, while trade credit taken tends to be sensitive to changes in stocks and work in progress. That is, sales are assisted by extending credit, while short-term stock acquisition is financed by obtaining credit from suppliers.

On the use of trade credit in the inter-war years very little information is available. As in the post-war period it was certainly an important part of company finance, net trade credit probably exceeding the volume of bank and external funds available to companies. Lavington, writing about the years immediately after the First World War, states that trade credit was widely used in trades where the seasonal method of payment was common, but that with the gradual demise of this type of settlement the volume of extended trade credit diminished. More generally he observed that few accounts were paid promptly. The volume of trade credit depended on many elements, including changes in the organization of trade and in the financial situation of sellers or buyers. While there were forces making for the expansion of trade credit, such as the increased volume of goods and greater specialization of trade, there were others making for a reduced volume. With many products direct marketing by manufacturers was cutting out retailers, while improved communications brought new ways – 'the old custom of buying heavily two or three times a year is now obsolete, and clever trades now buy from hand to mouth, weekly or even daily'. In addition there was a deliberate effort on the part of some trades to use less trade credit, preferring the superior marketability of short-term trade bills. No doubt wartime pressures, increased state participation, and changing financial conditions reinforced the tendency to shorten trade credit.

The terms of trade credit varied greatly between trades. Generally, discounts for prompt payment were the most popular usage. For example, with wool piece goods it was '$3\frac{1}{2}\%$ discount if payment was made by the first of the following month, net prices if paid for within three months'. Iron and steel manufacturers were reported as giving Yorkshire engineering firms one month's credit, and they in turn granted similar credit to their customers. In the car industry, however, Lavington reported that manufacturers sold to retailers for cash only. Since the security of the credit granted depended on the reputation of the customer it was to be expected that conditions would be onerous, with very short periods for some and longer for others.

> The recognised terms were: 3d in the £1 discount for payment within fourteen days and net prices for payment at the end of two months. This corresponds to an interest charge of about 10 per cent per annum, for two months' credit, as compared with about 14 per cent per annum for three months' credit in the drapery trade and about 7 per cent per annum for credit up to six months granted by woollen and worsted manufacturers in the sale of piece goods to merchants.

Costs were thought of as being heavy, and this, according to Lavington, was 'borne out by the general opinion that it is greatly to the advantage at any rate of retailers, to be in a position to pay cash to the wholesalers and manufacturers with whom they deal.'

As to cyclical pattern Lavington noted that in times of active business in shipbuilding 'suppliers stiffen their backs' and granted shorter terms to customers so that more business was done for cash because of the greater profitability from increased turnover. More generally, however, he argues that rising confidence in anticipation of further sales was a powerful counterforce, so that trade credit tended to expand during active periods and 'does so by means of resources obtained from the banks'.[1] The evidence on liquid assets presented in Chapter 4 lends some support to this claim in the period of recovery from the depression when the volume of trade credit granted by a sample of firms increased significantly during 1932–5, in this case financed largely from internal funds.

In the post-war world trade credit continues to occupy a significant role in the short-term financing arrangements of industry. In relation to other current assets and liabilities trade credit taken and received are usually large items, but even so little precise information is available apart from that relating to the aggregate figures for quoted companies whose defects for short-term analysis are readily apparent. While the granting and taking of trade credit continues throughout the year a great deal is seasonal and varies with the volume of stock purchases and sales of finished goods. Such seasonality cannot be reflected in annual balance sheet figures. As to changes, compared with pre-war practice, few firm conclusions can be offered but the following impressions have been suggested. It has been claimed that the average period of trade credit reported is distinctly shorter, a development linked not only with institutional changes, that is, industrial and marketing structures, but also with war-time experience of scarcity coupled with adequate liquidity on the part of firms. In periods of tight monetary policy it is also maintained that better techniques in budgetary control, stock control and credit management brought shorter credit periods. Due to greater prosperity and sustained demand discounts are less used than in pre-war years. In addition, it is claimed that for most of the post-war period trade credit was a less vulnerable part of the general credit structure of industry, and less likely than in pre-war years to collapse under the impact of a check to trade expansion. Until the 1974–5 crisis it was also suggested that outside sources of funds would be available to meet trade credit needs, while company capital structure in general, before 1965 at least, was less geared than the pre-war level, and there have been no sudden bursts of insolvences due to the total collapse of selling prices. These overall impressions are probably correct, but the experience of the early 1970s may lead to some future qualifications.[2]

While trade credit is largely given and received within the sector comprising manufacturing and distribution it is not entirely so. Retailers give credit to persons, while the unincorporated sector, the nationalized industries, and the overseas sector are also important users. Probably an important part of the net trade credit given by the quoted company sector consists of assistance to exports, and in transactions with the unquoted sector.[3] It is also probable that the figures for the quoted sector (see below) understate the amount of trade credit given within each group of companies since it is thought that the companies involved had several thousand subsidiaries.

Much of the trade credit granted is automatic and largely reflects changes in 'industrial factors'. In some industries where it is a clearly established custom to grant trade credit for a certain period an expansion of output will lead to more trade credit. But the amount may also be modified by financial considerations. While the value of turnover may remain unchanged trade credit given might contract in the face of a credit squeeze. The receipt of trade credit is more likely to be a source of funds subject to financial considerations in that it is always possible to pay cash immediately for goods.[4]

Table 9.1 Trade credit: Quoted companies 1948–71 (Balance sheet at end 'year' £m.)

Year	Trade and other debtors	Trade and other creditors	Ratio of debtors/creditors
1948	985	776	1.26
1950	1222	933	1.30
1955	1985	1498	1.32
1960	2882	2199	1.31
1961	3745	3035	1.23
1963	4346	3561	1.22
1964	5147	4078	1.26
1969	8362	7000	1.19
1971	8759	8439	1.03

* Linked series 1949–60, thereafter assorted series, the coverage of which differs due to changes in the minimum size of company included.

Sources: 1948–60: Economic Trends, April 1962, p. xv; 1961–71: assorted series from Financial Statistics.

Table 9.1 gives the amount of trade credit granted (debtors) and that taken (creditors) by the quoted sector, along with the ratio of debtors to creditors. The coverage is for quoted manufacturing companies during

1948–60 and for quoted companies from 1961–71 (various years). The growth in total and net trade credit over the entire period is consistent with the increase in industrial turnover, but the degree of change in net trade credit is smaller than expected given the cyclical variations during these years. The ratio of debtors to creditors remains quite stable throughout the 1950s, and indeed the 1960s; it falls sharply in the period 1969–71 but this probably reflects the changed composition of the companies in the table (see note to table 9.1). Taking debtors and its relation to total assets, it appears to remain relatively stable during the 1950s as did the creditors/liability ratio. The ratio of net trade credit to net assets rose slightly from 5% to 6%. Taking similar figures for the 1960s some greater changes are apparent. Between 1964 and 1971 the ratio of debtors to assets rose from 21% to 23%, while that of creditors to liabilities rose from 17% to 22%. This meant that the ratio of net trade credit to net assets fell from 6% to nearly 1%. However, the total number of companies is much smaller for 1971 than for earlier years, and they are larger companies, which suggests that they were not the generous givers of trade credit they were once claimed to be.

Within the general pattern of trade credit for the company sector as a whole there are interesting and sharp contrasts in relation to different industrial sectors, those which exhibit different rates of growth, and companies of different size. For most of the post-war period the ratio of debtors to creditors for the manufacturing sector has been in the region of 1.2 to 1.3 (see table 9.1), suggesting that overall trade credit was granted. Tew and Henderson in their investigation found that in most manufacturing industries 70%–85% of companies were giving more trade credit than they were receiving, particularly heavy givers of trade credit being electrical engineering, electrical goods, wholesale distribution and tobacco, the latter giving credit to leaf-buying organizations and distributors.[5] Among industrial groups which had a majority of companies receiving more trade credit than they were giving were those where the common element was cash sales to the consumer. For example, entertainment and sport, drink, retail distribution and miscellaneous services came within this category. The building and contracting industry was another instance where receiving trade credit was an important facility; for a third of the companies involved net trade credit received amounted to more than 10% of their net assets.

In their analysis of rates of growth of companies (measured in terms of increases in net assets) Tew and Henderson found that the use of trade credit varied with activity. In the case of rather static companies trade credit was often a net source of funds; in as many as 54% of slow-growing companies net trade credit was a source of funds, and many of these firms were in distribution. Fast-growing companies, on the other hand, were users of funds for trade credit purposes and often substantial ones. The granting of trade credit by fast-growing companies stems partly from the industrial nature of trade credit, that is, it tends to expand with turnover. In general these companies had high investment-income ratios and borrowed heavily from the banks and the market to finance such provision, and for them trade credit represented a substantial use of funds. Many such companies may well have used the offer of exceptionally liberal trade credit terms as one method of increasing their share of the market.[6]

For the small corporate and unincorporated companies the role of trade credit is obviously important but there is no agreement as to its precise contribution. The Radcliffe Committee was of the view that trade credit was more important for small firms than large, and that small firms were more likely than large to be net receivers of trade credit.[7] The suggestion being that in periods of restraint large firms adopted a benevolent attitude to smaller customers by running down their more ample liquid assets, or by bank borrowing. Unincorporated companies, in particular, often have insufficient assets to induce a bank to provide a loan, while the quality of the management may be doubtful. Other sources of finance are therefore exploited, so that net trade credit received is likely to be important in trades with easy entry and where businesses operate at the margin of profitability, unless there is a vigorous boom. But in the case of small firms debtors are also likely to be an important item, larger than for large firms. In 1954 H. B. Rose found that debtors as a percentage of total assets for quoted manufacturing companies was 17.1%, for 197 private companies it was 22.6%.[8] More recently the Bolton Committee reported that in a sample of small firms (unquoted firms employing under 200) the debtors to total asset ratio was 27% for 1968–9, compared with 23% for quoted companies in 1967. The percentage of creditors to liabilities was 26.7% and 18.5% respectively.[9] On the whole small companies seem to be net givers of trade credit and a possible explanation of this inverse relationship between debtors and size may be that small concerns are less strict in the collection of debts, that legal action is probably too costly, and finally because large customers may take credit (a 'coercive' view of trade credit) during periods of liquidity strain if the small company is not a monopoly supplier of goods to the large one.[10]

The terms on which trade credit is made available varies a great deal. Sometimes they are recommended by trade associations, while many are the 'accepted custom of the trade'. While discounts are less common than in the inter-war period they continue to be fairly widely used. They are, however, expensive to administer, and the low proportion of customers who take advantage of such terms, or who are influenced by them, is leading to a slow decline in their use. Manufacturers in such trades as building materials, paint, boots and shoes, light engineering products, ironmongery and fertilizers were reported as offering discounts.[11] There is considerable variety in the level of discounts, but the most common is about 2.5% for payment within one month. Normally these discounts do not vary when other rates of interest are altered. Special rates are sometimes offered for payment made within 7 to 10 days, and the rate of interest here on an annual basis is high (e.g., 2% within 10 days, net 30 days gives an annual rate of 36.7%) which reflects the sellers assessment of the risk of a longer credit period and the cost of debt collection when a slow payer has to be pressed for payment.[12]

Discounts are used mostly where the buyers and sellers are small firms. Prompt payment discounts are offered on sales in order to conserve liquidity, while a large firm offering discounts to a small firm may do so to reduce the risk of default. Activities where working capital requirements are large also offer cash discounts, or request prompt payment; their desire to secure the latter is understandable if they want to replenish stocks before expected price rises appear.[13] On the other hand, why buyers do not take advantage of say a 2.5% discount for payments made within a month (if the discount is not claimed it amounts to obtaining finance at an annual rate of 29.4%) is not exactly clear since cheaper sources of funds have always been available. The following reasons have been put forward; firstly, a firm may be reluctant to reduce its trade indebtedness by putting stronger pressure on its debtors; secondly, firms may run close to the limit on their overdraft and increased trade credit may be easier to get than extra limits; thirdly, borrowing from a bank may seem more onerous than trade credit since the former is usually secured by a charge on a firm's assets and the loan obtained may be small in relation to the security represented by the charge; finally, trade credit is a far more flexible means of financing.

In the case of the sale of basic materials between large firms for example, steel, oil, coal, food products, chemicals, etc., no cash discounts are offered. Generally these are net cash terms with payment within a specified date following the month of delivery or invoice so that the maximum credit period may be up to about eight weeks. However, many companies require payment within one month, and most require payment within 45 days; longer periods are generally associated with small companies slow in despatching invoices.[14]

To echo the Radcliffe Committee, while it is possible to make some broad generalizations on the financing of trade credit, 'the pattern is by no means clear cut'. Trade credit given (debtors) may be financed from retained profits, or by external funds from banks or the capital market.

The most obvious starting point is by a reduction in holdings of cash and liquid assets, a decrease which may be remedied by seeking additional funds from the banks or elsewhere, or the firm may take more credit from its suppliers.[15] Takers of trade credit can, of course, use this channel to boost their cash position. Some firms, especially small ones, may not be able to resist an increase in the amount of trade credit they give, and they may also be unable to pass on the pressure by taking more credit. Such 'stretching' of accounts payable ('leaning on the trade') may cause serious short-term liquidity problems for small firms, and others, who are forced to run down cash positions, or seek help from the banks. The extension of credit may be permitted by the supplier with the compensation of higher prices, but that can only be used if demand for the product is inelastic.

In their investigation of trade credit Tew and Henderson found several divergent patterns. Companies who were net givers of trade credit seemed to rely heavily on bank overdrafts. But they also noted that 'financial' pressures were present in that some companies drew on both bank credit and trade credit as a source of funds during periods of easy money. In addition, they found that some companies combined highly illiquid positions at the end of the period (1948–52) with a large excess of debtors over creditors, while another group of companies were in a highly illiquid position with a large excess of creditors over debtors, that is, despite receiving a lot of trade credit over the period they were highly illiquid at the end of it.[16]

Granting trade credit, while it is a use of funds, may also give access to funds, since the debt obtained may be used as security for a loan in that it may be covered by credit insurance which is assigned to a bank. Over recent years commercial credit insurance underwriting has increased greatly in volume as more companies experienced liquidity problems. In the pre-war years it was estimated to be around £75m., by value of domestic business turnover, and in the late 1950s it was put at about £1,000m.[17] No recent figures are available as to the total volume of domestic trade debts which are insured, but one of the leading companies in the business, Trade Indemnity Co. Ltd, reported that in 1976 it had insured transactions of £7,687m. with a gross premium income of nearly £15.0m.[18] It has been in common use in the fashion trades, consumer goods industries, and the building industry for many years, while more recently the increasing uncertainty of the business climate led to a wider demand for credit insurance. Companies with a rather narrow spread of customers find such cover useful, more so than large companies who have well-spread order books which effectively provides self-insurance. This latter feature would not apply to companies who are obliged to give trade credit.

Usually an insurance company will cover a proportion of the total outstanding invoice value, normally 75–85%, the amount varying with the degree of risk. In principle the whole turnover has to be offered, although individual policies are drawn up to cover a transaction with specific customers.[19] The insured submits a list of customers' names and notes the maximum amount of credit required on each. Provided the insured has taken all reasonable steps to collect debts the insurance company will pay any claim up to the percentage agreed. The cover is confined to the risk of the customer failing to pay within a specified period after the due date for payment. Often the insurers will also offer a debt collection service on overdue accounts.[20] The cost of cover is roughly of the following order; in a safe trade on short-trade credit terms it may be less than 0.125% for 85–90%, and in a hazardous trade 0.75% for 50% cover. Special terms are quoted for long-term credits or markets with special credit risks.[21]

The general developments in the use of trade credit gave rise to interest in the question of whether it was being used to frustrate the desired restrictive effects of monetary policy. The possibility that this might happen had been noted by Lavington (and earlier writers) who analysed the prospects in terms of the transport of capital from units with surplus funds to those with deficits, and in terms of the expansion of trade credit supplying purchasing power so that goods could be purchased without the immediate use of any form of currency.[22] Interest centred on two interpretations. The Radcliffe Report drew attention to the importance of gross trade credit, arguing that lengthening the term of trade credit could easily swamp restrictive bank lending. Other commentators concentrated on the volume of net trade credit as a means whereby idle balances were transferred to firms who may have been denied access to bank accommodation. Little agreed evidence emerged. The Radcliffe Committee concluded that there was 'undoubtedly some redistribution of liquidity between business because of changes in trade credit; but we are not able to say to what extent this redistribution was in favour of less liquid concerns'.[23] Looking at the experience of a large number of companies for 1949–60 G. Whittington concluded that in general weak firms receive more net trade credit in squeezes than in ease periods.[24] There is, however, no grounds for assuming that changes in net trade credit received will always come to the aid of weak firms in squeeze years, although this may be the case in individual industries in particular years.

Factoring

From the standpoint of short-term sources of funds factoring is a means whereby a firm can obtain finance on the security of its trade debtors, i.e., accounts receivable. In essence the operation consists of a factor purchasing a client firm's debts (title is transferred to the factor) from a list of the client's approved customers. The factor collects all debts from the customers and outstanding balances are remitted to the client. Frequently a proportion of the value of the debts factored is advanced to the client at an appropriate rate of interest. The advantages of the service, especially for small firms, is that it can provide ready funds at the time of delivery of goods, rather than wait anything from 30–90 days, and it relieves the client firm of the expense of handling the sales ledger and dealing with debt collection. Thus companies can improve their cash flow from the trade debtors item, and obtain savings on the collection of debts. Factoring is thus not a lending operation but one which seeks to use existing company assets more effectively.

Factoring was introduced to the U.K. around the early 1960s, but it has been well established in the United States with a turnover of about £3,000m. But:

> like so many good things, factoring appears to have originated in the U.K. textile industry before an American textile industry developed. Firms selling to the U.S.A. appointed factors to take deliveries and deal with customers, and some of these began also to act as guarantors. The developing U.S. industry found it convenient to take advantage of the factors' knowledge of markets, etc., but their role in handling the product declined in favour of guarantee, finance and special service functions. In the U.S.A. factors of this kind are still referred to as 'old line' factors and call their clients 'mills', whatever their trade might be.[25]

The adoption of factoring services by companies in the early 1960s was due largely to the problems they faced by granting extended credit to customers during credit squeezes. Not only did this require considerable efforts in getting invoices paid, but it also locked up capital in trade debts. Experience in the United States clearly indicated that factoring could free funds for working capital needs without in any way diluting equity capital. Early factoring facilities tended, therefore, to concentrate on the financial provision and debt collection, which raised memories of the strong-arm debt collecting methods and the exhorbitant rates of the immediate post-war years.[26] Essentially industry tended to see factoring as a 'last ditch' method of raising funds which brought quick business to some early factors. The administration of sales ledgers was regarded as of secondary importance so that credit rating techniques in these early days were not as efficient as they were later to become. The race to get high turnover figures often led to business which was not suitable to factoring. Losses followed and clients' firms and their customers expressed dissatisfaction with the service rendered.[27]

The basic aim is to make cash available to clients in exchange for book debts. This is done on two bases; without recourse and with recourse factoring – only one firm does a large amount of the latter type. Without recourse factoring means that, except in trading disputes, the factor has no claim on the client firm up to an agreed credit limit if he fails to obtain payment from the customer. Approved debts therefore obtain full credit insurance compared with only proportionate cover by conventional insurance channels. The basic procedure for without recourse factoring is usually as follows:

> Copies of invoices [are] sent by the client to the factor daily in schedule form and an agreed percentage of the net value of these invoices, usually about 80 per cent, is advanced to the client on the same day. A monthly accounting is made to the client, itemising the net value of sales factored during the month, including the total amount of advances released, service charges and the credit balance in the client's favour at the end of each month. The factor's credit department investigates the customers' creditworthiness and fixes agreed limits of credit on each customer. Each customer is notified that the invoice is payable to the factor by a 'factoring legend' fixed to the original sales invoice which is despatched to the client. Where an account becomes seriously overdue the collection department will follow up to obtain settlement.[28]

Thus the factor provides finance, accounting services, and in the above case takes the credit risk on all approved debts, which requires careful credit appraisal to reduce the possibility of bad debts.[29] Where customers are not considered fully creditworthy factoring services may be obtained on a with recourse basis. In this case the factor retains the right to obtain from the client money advanced against invoices if payment is not forthcoming from the client's customer. Very few factors offer this type of service, arguing that their main function is to take credit risks. About 20% of factored turnover is handled on this basis, while the importance of such recourse is small since factors estimate that less than 0.25% of all debt recovery is from clients.[30]

Depending on the terms of the agreement the factor may either agree to make payment, less commission, for the value of the invoices received at the end of an agreed period – this representing the average debt turn – or settle for the amount involved when each customer pays his account. In the former case the client has the advantage of a predetermined cash flow in relation to his own sales.[31] In addition the client company can have a most useful financial facility (especially in the absence of bank accommodation) which enables him to draw up to an agreed percentage – usually 75% to 80% – of the value of the invoices passed to the factor, while the balance will be paid over at an agreed date. This prepayment facility provides immediate cash resources against sales and is reported as being widely used. Further immediate financial facilities can be obtained where there is a close link between a factor and a bank. The factor agrees to pay to the client's bank the sums due on invoices at the agreed dates, and on the strength of this the bank will make an advance to the firm. The bank may advance up to 80% of the net amount of the factored debts, and receives payment direct from the factor near the maturity date of the invoices. Thus the client gets a bank advance, while the standing of a company's book debts are increased in the eyes of the banks when guaranteed by the factor.[32]

For the detailed work of handling the sales ledger, collecting payments, credit rating, assuming risks, and so on, the factor levies a service charge. This is a percentage of turnover and ranges from 0.75% to 2.5%. The actual charge made to a client is assessed by reference to such considerations as the volume of business, the size of the average invoice, the average period of credit taken, and so forth. A separate interest charge is levied for advances, that is, the prepayment facility. Typically this is 2% to 3% above bank base rates, depending on the state of competition and whether the factor is prepared to trim his rate to get the account. It is made on the day-to-day balance outstanding with the client. Once the interest rate for advances is agreed it does not vary with the size of the actual loan, or the credit rating of the client firm. Finance for prepayment is normally raised by the factor from its associated bank. Thus, the total cost of obtaining finance by means of factoring may be high, but it is not possible to compare it with other costs due to the inclusion of the service charge. Whether or not such costs are regarded as high by the client firm depends on the efficiency of their own accounting and debt collection procedures, while some may have little option in resorting to factoring if access to other sources of short-term funds is restricted.

Due to the nature of the costs involved factors generally impose a minimum turnover condition on client firms. There is no set figure but the minimum tends to be in the region of £100,000 to £250,000, with a minimum invoice value of about £100. Individual factors will vary their floor depending on their assessment of the state of the credit market, but some are prepared to go down to a turnover figure of £50,000 if they consider that there is growth potential. Factors, however, are perhaps more concerned with the size of the client's customers than with the client himself; they prefer small clients with several large customers to a large client with many small customers. What they look for are firms with a high growth rate who have financially sound customers dealing on normal credit terms and whose business is repetitive in character. Indeed from a small firm's point of view it is easier for a factor with several claims on a large group to make an impact than for the small supplier, particularly in difficult credit times.

The main appeal of factoring is for firms in the £100,000 to £5m. turnover class who find running a sales ledger on a computerized basis uneconomic. According to the Bolton Committee factoring services were of substantial value to the larger small firms, and that these accounted for a high proportion of factoring turnover, some $\frac{2}{3}$ in 1971.[33] As to industrial usage it is mainly confined to manufacturing activity but there is no dominant industrial user as is the case of textiles in the United States. This wide spread is seen as a point of strength, and the gradual expansion towards the service industries is being encouraged. An important area of recent growth has been in the export trades which offers clients protection against bad debts and immediate sterling against sales. Formerly this service was provided by foreign agents but it is now increasingly done through factors' own branches.

Companies who do not wish to use the full service of factors may obtain finance against debtors by confidential invoice factoring. However, factors generally do not regard the provision of funds against invoices as very profitable since it merely involves a financial facility whose use tends to reflect changes in the cost and availability of funds from normal channels. Most factors do not offer the service, and some do but do not advertise the fact; the estimated annual turnover in 1971 was £140m. In this type of service the factor purchases book debts but the sales ledger stays with the firm, while the client's customer is unaware that the debt has been transfered. The client collects the debts and the factor has recourse to him. There is no commitment on the client's part to do any particular volume of business, he may use it irregularly or keep it in reserve. If used the invoices are discounted on acceptance at up to about 75% of the total value of the bills, the balance later being paid when the client, acting as an agent, obtains payment of the invoices from his customers. Since the factor has no control over the sales ledger and accepts considerable risks, interest charges tend to be in the 15%–18% region. For reasons of cost and security large clients are preferred; when credit is tight it is reported that small clients are crowded out when big companies request increased facilities. The interest charge does not vary with the size of the loan or the credit rating of the borrower, and overheads (initial investigation and subsequent monitoring) are at least as high for small as large firms. A minimum turnover of £100,000 is looked for, while credit is not provided in excess of the paid up capital of the borrower. There is a minimum loan size of £10,000, with a maximum of about £250,000, while the average made is around £30,000.[34]

By 1967 factoring had an estimated turnover of around £100m., the outstanding credit being about £20m.; estimates for 1971 put the turnover at about £200m. However, over the next two years it climbed quickly to around £700m. in 1974, a surge associated with the rise in commodity prices which led companies to factor debts to obtain much needed cash, while interest rates on bank accommodation had the same impact. Factoring services are offered by a dozen companies, in addition to those made available by finance houses. About half the factoring companies date from the early 1960s, the remainder were set up in 1970. All are subsidiaries of banking or financial concerns. The clearing banks entered the field in 1970, although before this they had worked closely with various factors. Home banks at this period were anxious to offer a wide range of financial facilities to customers, and they were conscious that United States banks in London had considerable experience of factoring. The quickest solution was therefore to acquire an interest in existing factors.[35]

Commercial bills

When the members of the Radcliffe Committee came to write their report in 1959 they were able to state fairly confidently that 'the business in commercial bills is vestigial [and that there was an] ... irreversible shrinkage in the relative supply of commercial bills.'[36] Although the Committee noted the expansion which occurred in bills in the 1957 credit squeeze and that 'the discount houses must still be reckoned with as one of the sources of short term finance to which industrial and commercial borrowers turn if they are prevented from borrowing from their banks', they were of the opinion that the 'feeling on the part of the discount houses that they live partly by the goodwill of the banks militates ... against any extended efforts to rebuild (against the historical trend) the commercial bill business'.[37] Since then this 'historical trend' has been substantially reversed and the commercial bill business is anything but 'vestigial'.

A bill of exchange, as defined by the Bills of Exchange Act 1882, is 'an unconditional order in writing, addressed by one person to another, signed by the person giving it, requiring the person to whom it is addressed to pay on demand or at a fixed or determinable future time a sum certain in money to or to the order of a specified person, or to bearer.'[38] Normally a bill is drawn by the seller of goods (the drawer) with a maturity of three months (where no goods are involved the bill is drawn by the person raising finance). The person receiving the bill (the drawee) may either accept it himself (by signing) or pay commission to a bank or accepting house to do so on his behalf; a bill is judged not on the name of the drawer but on that of the acceptor. Generally bills with one acceptance signature (ranging from that of a large international company to an individual trader) are known as trade bills, those with the additional guarantee of a bank or accepting house as a bank bill. There is, however, a limit on the amount of any one bank's acceptances which a discount house will take. Once accepted a bill becomes a negotiable instrument changing hands by endorsement. If the acceptor fails to meet the bill the holder has recourse against the endorsers and the original drawer. Thus the lender of money against a bill has the security of at least two names, one of which is often an 'undoubted' one. Some of the advantages of bills are that since the issuance can be varied it is a flexible instrument, that the drawer may discount a bill according to his needs, and those who lend against bills may hold them to maturity or discount, and that it imposes good 'financial discipline', since failure to pay a bill is regarded more seriously than 'stretching' trade credit.[39]

Inland bills of exchange are either involved with the movement of goods into the possession of the purchaser, or they are finance bills. The former are generally referred to as 'self-liquidating paper' since on the sale of the goods funds will be available to meet the bill on maturity. Normally 91 days is sufficient to cover the time the underlying goods are in transit. While there are some 60-day bills and others longer than 91 days, some 85% of bills are of three months duration; the market naturally resists any changes in issuance based on expectations of interest rate movements. Bills without an underlying transaction of this kind are referred to as finance bills, a type of paper which has increased greatly in volume since the Radcliffe period and represents about 40% of commercial paper. Since it is not linked to any specific underlying transaction or movement of goods its quality is dependent on the names of the drawer and the acceptor. There are three main types of finance bills: (1) paper drawn by finance companies where the accepting banks are given a general charge on the underlying merchandise that has been sold; (2) bills whereby export manufacturers borrow against a general charge over goods in transit at a given moment in time; and (3) bills such as those drawn by financing stocks of raw materials, e.g., tobacco companies raise money by drawing against stocks of leaf in warehouses. In this type of arrangement an accepting house agrees to accept drafts up to a specified amount drawn upon them by the manufacturer, usually payable three months after date. The manufacturer agrees to put the accepting house in funds at or before the maturity date of the drafts. Since it is accepted the manufacturer has no difficulty in discounting it.[40]

Until the Finance Act 1961, it was possible to estimate from stamp duty receipts the total value of bills in circulation, but with the changeover to a flat rate this was no longer feasible. The estimated total of commercial bills outstanding in 1951 was £575m., falling to £395m. in 1952, and increasing to £726m. in 1959.[41] Of this latter figure the Bank of England estimated that about half were bank bills, held for the most part by the banking system and the discount market. They also held some trade bills, but the bulk of these, around £380m. in 1959, were held by drawers, or perhaps lodged as collateral for bank loans. As to the use of commercial bills since 1959 the only readily available indicator is the identified holdings of such paper by the banks and the discount market, given in table 9.2; also given are figures for acceptances by the banking sector. The appreciable growth in the discount houses portfolio of bills, to become by the end of 1976 their most important asset, and in that of the clearing banks, and other banks, reflects the increased use of bill finance over the period, as does the accompanying rise in the volume of domestic acceptances by the banking sector.

Several reasons may be advanced for the resurgence of commercial bills and their use by large public companies. They may be treated under the headings of the cost of bill finance, availability of alternative finance, and the supply of assets to the discount houses. To turn first to the cost elements. In the Finance Bill 1961, the *ad valorem* stamp duty of 1s. per £100 was replaced by a flat rate duty of 2d per bill. Thus, on a three months bill, this represented a saving of $\frac{1}{3}$ of 1% per annum, not a great deal, but it did reduce costs and increased flexibility especially on shorter bills which became popular afterwards. The 2d flat rate was finally removed in 1971. The other significant cost reduction occurred with acceptance commissions. This took place due to increased competition in the banking sector with the arrival in London of so many foreign banks, especially American banks. In 1952 acceptance commissions were between 1.5. and 2% p.a., but by the mid-1960s they were reported to be a good deal lower, perhaps by as much as 0.75%, with a few being done at 0.5%. Although acceptance by a foreign bank does not constitute 'eligible paper' it did mean that the market was prepared to absorb large amounts of bills at best rates.[42]

In the case of restriction on alternative forms of finance, it was not until 1965 that the authorities took definite steps to limit the amount of bill finance. Before this date credit squeezes on bank advances drove frustrated borrowers, often with the clearing banks blessing, to the bill market if the business was suitable and the price not too high. However, in the 1965

Table 9.2   Commercial bills and acceptances* (£m.: end year)

	1960	1965	1970	1974	1976
Commercial bills					
London clearing banks	133	356	305	675	551
Discount houses	117	339	697	1,182	940
Accepting houses	22	18	7	44	111
Other banks	81	81	62	347	664
Total	353	794	1,071	2,248	2,266
Acceptances					
U.K. residents	n.a.	486	581	1,963	2,172
Overseas residents	n.a.	241	382	721	287

* 1960 to 1974; apart from the figures for the London clearing banks for
  1960, 1965 and 1970 coverage is for 'other bills' or 'other U.K. bills',
  which for the most part comprise commercial bills; 1976 figures relate
  to 'other bills' within the reserve assets of the above institutions and
  'bills' other than reserve asset holdings.

Source: Bank of England Quarterly Bulletin.

credit restrictions the Bank of England requested that lending to the
private sector should not increase by more than 5% over the level of
March 1965; commercial banks were requested to limit their acceptances
and purchases of commercial bills, and the Accepting Houses and the
Discount Market were asked to observe a comparable degree of restraint.
The target was not met despite the policy of the discount houses of
increasing their rates of discount for trade bills in relation to bank bills,
and for the latter in relation to Treasury bills.[43] The removal of this limit
in April was quickly followed by another in November 1967. Credit
available through commercial bills and leasing was to observe the same
ceiling as advances, based on the November level. While commercial bills
escaped specific mention in the 1968 measures, they were subject to the
105% limit of April 1970, in so far as the guidance applied to credit made
available by the discounting of commercial bills extended directly by the
banks.[44]

Finally, in the case of demand from the banks and the Discount Market,
the period since 1960 has seen phases when the supply of Treasury bills
was sharply reduced so that they represented a very low proportion of
their total assets. This reduced volume of Treasury bills was associated
with reductions in the borrowing requirement, calls for Special Deposits,
and balance of payments deficits which put sterling at the disposal of the
Exchequer. The effect was to drive down Treasury bill yields so that the

traditional differential with other bill levels was greatly increased. The discount houses could, therefore, offer to their customers on such occasions commercial bills at attractive yields over Treasury bill levels.[45]

Most of the bills discounted by the market are bank bills, which also predominate in the bill portfolios of the clearing banks since they constitute eligible paper at the Bank of England. In addition, the banks prefer paper which has evidence on it that it has been drawn against actual shipments. Most trade bills are held by the drawer until maturity, or are used as security for loans; the clearing banks hold some fine trade bills. While the Bank of England discounts and lends against bank bills quite readily, it exercises careful surveillance on the quality and quantity of trade bills through its connection with the discount houses and the accepting houses.[46] In order to monitor the trade bill market the Bank of England since 1963 regularly takes parcels of trade bills, and will only take a limited amount of finance bills since the Bank is anxious to discourage the growth of this type of finance.[47]

The use made of bill finance depends on the habits of users, the availability of alternative funds, and the cost of the funds. There are two elements in the cost; the acceptance commission charged by the acceptor and the rate of discount at which bills can be sold. The level of acceptance commission varies with the credit standing of the drawee and for commercial borrowers of good standing who will have no difficulty in meeting a bill at maturity it will be around 1.25%. If the drawer wants to obtain funds by discounting a bill the cost will vary with the standing of the firm, general credit conditions, and the level of market rates, of which the most important is the Treasury bill rate. Fine bank bills will generally be discounted about 1–1.5% above the Treasury bill rate, but occasionally the differential may vary due to changes in market forces. The margin between trade bills and Treasury bills is much more variable depending as to the credit standing of the firm involved. Generally, the margin is about 2.5 to 3% over the Treasury bill rate.[48] While they are profitable for the discount houses there is only a limited demand for such paper from the banks. The purchaser of such bills will pay particular heed to the quality of the endorsements and the purpose for which the credit is being raised, bearing in mind the attitude of the Bank of England to such paper.

Firms may use bill finance in three main ways. They can themselves obtain acceptance credits and thus have bills easily drawn against them for goods supplied, they can draw upon customers who have acceptance credits, and they can draw and then discount trade bills. The facilities of a discount house may be made available in the following way. A company makes an application for a discounting facility and after appropriate examination the discount house will agree a limit to the value of bills which it is prepared to discount at any one time. Often a discount house will only discount bills from an agreed list of acceptors. Thus, a company may bring bills for discount on a running basis, that is, as old ones mature new ones may be brought in. If the bills are in order cash is paid in to the borrower's bank.

The bulk of the increase in the use of bills since 1960 has originated from large public companies, as well as the nationalized industries who use bills to finance inter-industry purchasers of goods. Companies have used the facility extensively for the purpose of raising working capital, that is, by the issue of finance bills. They feel that there is little risk attached to their bills, and their ability to bargain hard means that they can generally obtain bill finance at rates equal to overdraft rates. In the case of large company needs merchant banks syndicate together on acceptances, taking agreed proportions of the total. The use made by smaller companies of bill discounting is limited, although the Bolton Committee, like others before them, urged greater use of this flexible and traditional facility. The Committee estimated that in 1971 about £10m. of finance was made available to small firms through the Discount Market.[49] For the most part discount houses are not prepared to deal with small companies, a reluctance which extends to Accepting houses as well. In addition some large companies dislike having bills drawn on them by small companies, since they do not like committing themselves to payment on a fixed date; 'stretching' trade credit seems preferable. Where large firms are prepared to accept bills drawn by small firms it generally enables such bills to be discounted.

Leasing

Leasing, that is the divorce of ownership from the use of assets, has long been practised in the U. K. in respect of property and a limited range of other assets. Similarly, real estate leasing has a long history in the United States. The leasing of industrial equipment, however, has a comparatively modern origin. In America it was the aircraft industry in the years after the war which gave equipment leasing its first fillip, under the inducement of rising costs and technological change.[50] While the technique crossed the Atlantic in the 1950s and was used in computers, copying equipment and telephone installations, the lessors of such equipment were normally specialist companies with close ties to the manufacturers, again American-owned. There appears to have been some reluctance to apply leasing more widely and the effective start of leasing in the U. K. does not take place until 1959. In 1963 some five houses started leasing, and thereafter the number grew steadily so that the value of assets leased rose from an estimated £56m. in 1965 to around £200m. in 1972.[51] The progress of the industry since 1971, the date of the formation of the Equipment Leasing Association, is given in table 9.3. By 1973–7 annual assets leased by the Association represent about 10% of investment in plant and machinery by the company sector.

Table 9.3   Survey of leased assets (£m.)

	1971	*1972*	*1973*	*1974*	*1975*	*1976*
Original cost before grant of assets purchased for lease in each year by E.L.A. members	159	130	288	321	340	421
Original cost before grant of leased assets owned by E.L.A. members at end of each year.	402	516	761	1,078	1,425	1,669

Source: Equipment Leasing Association.

The relatively rapid growth of leasing over recent years has been due to a number of causes. Under the pressure of competition firms in the 1960s began

> to find an increasing need to replace their existing assets by more modern equipment, but found also that the cost of replacement . . . was a growing obstacle due to the increasing sophistication, and consequently the increasing cost, of plant and machinery. The attractions of spreading payments over a period, and paying for a new machine out of its earnings, began to assume greater importance, particularly with the increase in the rate of inflation.[52]

The subsidiaries of American companies led the way in that when the Treasury imposed restrictions on their sterling borrowing they turned to leasing, a well-developed alternative for them. More generally, the successive restraints on customary credit lines forced companies to look for other ways of finance, and the leasing facility once arranged was permanently available whatever measures were later introduced. Finally, a considerable attraction arose from the system of tax allowances and investment incentives introduced in the early 1960s. Capital allowances on new plant and equipment made it worth while for a group earning large profits to enter the leasing business or form a leasing subsidiary. The lessor as owner claimed the appropriate allowances which could be set against tax due on group profits, and thereby reduced terms could be offered to the lessee. It was for this particular reason that leasing rather than some form of deferred payment finance became popular.

Unlike a mortgage or a hire purchase agreement a leasing arrangement is not a contract for financing the purchase of an asset, but a means of financing its use. Title does not pass to the lessee but remains with the lessor; the former has the use of an asset, the latter its ownership. Normally, the business wanting the equipment would approach a leasing company, or the manufacturer's salesman could initiate the leasing arrangement. The leasing company purchases the equipment and then it is leased to the business concerned after its credit status has been checked. The lessee supplies information about its operations usually providing accounts for the previous two or three years. The leasing company thus finances an item of equipment which the lessee has the use of, in return for the payment of specified rentals over an agreed period of time. At the end of the period the asset is either sold or re-leased to the customer at a nominal charge. For some leasing companies skill in disposing of equipment at the termination of a lease is of considerable importance, whereas leasing with a manufacturer's guarantee as to repurchase relieves the leasing company from such a problem.

Two main types of leases are used. Financial leases involve a contract with payment being made over an obligatory period of specified sums sufficient in total to amortize the capital outlay of the lessor and give some profit. The obligatory period is less than, or, at the most, equal to, the estimated useful life of the asset. The lessee maintains the asset. Normally, a financial lease cannot be cancelled during the primary period so that where a firm's cash flow is irregular or other uncertainties are present, an operating lease may be more appropriate. In the case of an operating lease the asset is not wholly amortized during the non-cancellable period (if any) of the lease, while the lessor does not rely entirely for his profit on the rentals. Under an operating lease maintenance is provided, the cost being built into the lease payments.

The terms of a lease, that is, the price for the use of an asset, takes into account not only the original cash value of the asset and several other financial considerations (tax changes and the availability of allowances), but also the life of the asset. Most leases provide for a primary and a secondary period. In the case of a financial lease the primary period is negotiated between the lessor and the lessee and relates to the useful life of the asset, and the rental will enable the lessor to recover the capital outlay, net of any grant received and after taking into account the benefit of any allowances. While the primary period may vary from between 1 to over 10 years, some 86% of leases are up to 5 years, 10% between 5 to 10 years, and only 4% over 10 years.[53] Normally, the primary period for fixed equipment is 5 years, and for mobile equipment 3 years. The secondary period is at the option of the lessee, and is often of indefinite length, the reduced rentals being little more than nominal. With an operating lease, where the rental is not intended to amortize the capital outlay, a second lease may be negotiated or the asset sold.

The charge made for the use of equipment is expressed as a percentage, but it is not an interest charge as such, rather a composite fee. All costs to the lessor are recovered in the rental charge, which is arrived at by adding to the cost of the asset, net of any investment grant, a flat percentage ranging between 6.75 to 7.5% (giving approximately a true rate of 13–15%), and dividing by the term of the agreement, usually 5 years. The general view seems to be that the net percentage return to the lessor has been the same for some time, which implies that prevailing rates reflect the higher cost of credit as well as fiscal changes.[54] The leasing company is repaid in equal instalments, which involves taking a view as to the behaviour of interest rates over the leasing period. Until recent years this tended to lock them into existing contracts but now it is common practice to insert variation clauses into leasing agreements to take account of changes in the cost of borrowed funds for the lessor. In fixing its charges the lessor is able to take advantage of any capital allowances an asset may attract, since for tax purposes the purchaser of the asset may offset such allowances against taxable profits. This gain from 'initial write-off' can be passed on in lower charges to the lessee, subject to a tax adjustment if the asset is ultimately bought by him. This provides an immediate benefit in the rental to the lessee, while his profit position may preclude any benefit from tax allowances.

A few other considerations also relate to charges and terms. The size of the lessee only enters into consideration indirectly as a limit on the total value of the equipment leased. Some lessors, for example, will not wish to have outstanding assets of any kind valued at more than about a half of the commitment of the owners themselves. The lessors main worry is the ability of the borrowing company to meet the fixed payments, and the ease or difficulty of disposing of assets in the event of failure of the lessee. Generally, leases to small companies, regarded as less satisfactory business, are preceded by more testing inquiries, while the lessor may request advance payment of rentals to reduce uncertainty.

Several advantages are claimed for leasing arrangements over the purchase of an asset. The latter involves an immediate charge on capital, or on credit lines, while leasing makes no charge on capital. Neither does it disturb existing borrowing powers, or impose a charge on other assets. Under company law there is no requirement to show the leased article as an asset, and the lease rentals as a liability; it is a means of 'off-balance sheet' financing. However, where a note of such liability is not rendered the concealment is of little value, since it is unlikely that a company can borrow more than is normally considered safe by adding a lease to an already extended debt-gearing position because most leasing companies, like the banks, are aware that the rental is a fixed obligation which only the creditworthy can meet.[55] Thus, the income of the lessee must be deemed adequate to meet the agreed series of rentals, while at the end of the lease the commitment is self-liquidating. During the 1960s leasing also provided an inflationary hedge. Since payments were in fixed amounts and made out of future earnings in fixed money terms then the real costs of a lease fell over time with rising prices. Finally, the ability of the lessor to claim tax allowances which are reflected in reduced rentals means that, especially for equipment intensive companies who could not buy assets outright, this is a useful form of finance, while the rental is allowable against income subject to corporation tax. Such firms may not have sufficient profits to benefit fully from tax allowances, but they can benefit immediately from reduced rentals.

The precise number of lessors in the U.K. is not known, but it is thought to be somewhere in the region of 130. Most of these have connections with a finance house or banking organization. The bulk of the remainder are probably subsidiary leasing companies of manufacturers and suppliers who found it advantageous to form their own leasing service. In 1974 it was estimated that totalled leased assets at original cost was around £1,400m., of which nearly £1,100m. was held by members of the Equipment Leasing Association. Very little information is available as to the sort of firms who employ leasing facilities; the general impression is that up to around 1970 it was mainly used by larger enterprises, but that since then the facility has been drawn upon by smaller firms needing expensive equipment. There was certainly a reluctance on the part of firms to turn to it regarding it as a last resort means of financing. Nowadays it is increasingly viewed by medium to large companies as an automatic second choice, after the banks, as a source of outside finance. However, for many firms it continues to be treated with some reserve.[56]

While finance houses were subject to periodic restraints from 1965 onwards leasing was not singled out for mention until April 1967, when the Bank of England requested that credit given by way of 'leasing of industrial plant should be treated as subject to the same priorities and restrictions as credit given in the form of loans and overdrafts'.[57] At the time finance houses had spare capacity in the car hire business, within the ceiling, with which to accommodate leasing demand. This specific restraint was invoked in later directives, but in 1969 the Bank of England agreed that if banks and finance houses transferred the business to separate subsidiaries the restrictions would not apply. When in force the restrictions were felt more by small firms, since they tended to be treated as marginal borrowers, whereas large firms' custom was more highly valued. In addition, leasing done by individual manufacturers tended to be limited because they suffered from a reduced flow of bank accommodation.

The inter-company loans market

This is a market in sterling deposits between companies. Although a few large companies had lent to each other in the mid-1960s' credit squeezes, it was not until 1969 that an organized market appeared. The impetus came from industrial companies who found it increasingly difficult to get funds by way of bank overdraft owing to the operation of strict monetary controls. In November 1967 the authorities tightened the existing credit restrictions by asking the clearing banks to reduce their private sector lending to the level ruling just prior to the date of the sterling devaluation. By mid-1969 the banks were still short of the target, which led to the imposition of a fine by way of halving the interest on Special Deposits as encouragement for the banks to fall in line. This form of quantitative control, linked with the long-standing qualitative requests, hit certain companies particularly hard since bank accommodation was an important source of outside funds for them.

In the same period companies needing to import were required to make payments under the short-lived Import Deposit scheme. Over the first six months of 1969 this involved a sum of £436m., which was a considerable drain on liquid funds. To alleviate part of this strain a market was organized by some provincial and London money brokers in import deposits, but the bulk of the burden was taken up by a run down of bank deposits by the company sector.[58] Thus, allied to the restriction on access to bank funds came a pressure on liquid funds. On the supply side there were many company treasurers eager to obtain higher rates than on more secured lending.

Certain organizational changes also took place, and these proved conducive to the market's expansion. This concerned amalgamations among many of the dealers in the market so that they brought together groups covering a fairly wide range of interests. From the brokers' standpoint this was beneficial, since it enabled them to offer prospective clients a comprehensive assessment of a whole range of possible short-term investments. In terms of arranging inter-company loans it meant easing the problem of matching willing lenders and borrowers at the right maturity and price. Also, at the outset, the authorities had some doubts as to the propriety of certain practices since they were unhappy about the activities of some of the fringe operators in the market who were prone to persuade firms to overcommit themselves with borrowing; stronger broker units lessened official fears on that front.

The market involves lending by firms with surplus liquidity (in the form of sterling deposits) to those in deficit through the agency of a broker. A certain amount of direct lending takes place between companies but very little is known about this aspect of company activity; one estimate puts it at about 10% of the inter-company market total. As for the dealer market, the amounts placed range from a minimum of £50,000 up to a few million; most loans are over the £250,000 mark. Brokers naturally prefer large blocks since handling costs absorb less of the commission, which is generally charged at the rate of 0.063% to 0.25%, depending on the standing of the company. The term of the loans range from around three months to three years in some cases, and very rarely up to five years. Accepting loans at call or very short notice is not popular with borrowers owing to the inconvenience of frequent renewal and the accompanying uncertainty.

In addition to the funds which were placed in the market arising from a build up of bank deposits by a company, funds were also generated for the market, particularly in the 1970–1 period. One practice which found quick favour with some company treasurers, and reportedly encouraged by brokers, was the drawing of bills of exchange which were then discounted. The proceeds were then on-lent in the inter-company market at a margin sufficient to yield a profit on the transaction for the company concerned. The turn varied with circumstances, but it was in the region of 1.25%. Companies also engaged in the 'merry-go-round' by using the market, that is, borrowing on overdrafts and placing the deposits in the market at 2% above the interest cost of the funds. Both practices were disapproved of by the authorities.

The bulk of the business executed through the market is confined to transactions between the top 200 or so companies in industry and commerce. Not infrequently *The Times* 'Thousand' list is used as a reference by companies interested in participating in the market. The conditions of each loan are agreed between lender and borrower, but the distinctive feature of the market is the absence of formal documentation. More often than not the debt instrument merely takes the form of an exchange of letters, particularly in the case of the most creditworthy names. These are companies with large quoted capitalizations, good profit records and management, with regular and consistently good dividends. Longer term loans tend to be backed by a banker's guarantee (which were not subject to official restraint), or else loans can be backed by collateral in the form of some claim on a company's assets, e.g., debentures or a mortgage. Short loans are generally unsecured, which carries dangers of illiquidity in quickly changing financial markets. The onus is very much on the lending company to assess the loan period very carefully since it has to assume that funds will be locked in for a fixed term.

The practice of securing a bank guarantee for a nominal commission at least gave the market some semblance of a last resort facility. Some brokers estimated that as much as 20% of the total business was backed by bank guarantees, but this is probably on the high side. It was reported, however, that several United States banks in London openly advertised such services to would-be borrowers. The practice was welcomed by many banks at the time since it meant that they could provide links between their customers and brokers when they had reached their lending ceiling, and so maintain customer goodwill. Also, it brought the banking sector into an area of transactions which by their nature had largely by-passed them, and which had aroused some doubts among clearing and merchant bankers. Under restraint from official requests they felt that their function was being usurped by brokers in no way so inhibited. Their animosity was greatly roused on occasions when companies borrowed from the banks to lend in the market at a profitable margin.

Estimates of the size of the market are very rough indeed. Those made in early 1970 put it at around £50m. to £100m. of loans outstanding, while towards the end of 1971 various observers gave a wide range of from £100m. to £300m. More recent verdicts on the market's size have ranged from the assertion that it was dead, to under £100m. There are no estimates of the volume of funds placed directly between firms. It is perhaps reasonable to suppose that the market experiences certain seasonal variations, with loans increasing towards the end of the financial year with pending tax payments. Also, during the year a firm may alternate between lending and borrowing depending on its liquidity position, and a few companies made it a practice to be seen to be both lenders and borrowers in the market, thus ensuring the primacy of their name. Little is known about whether the market is composed of an equal number of lenders and borrowers of roughly equal size, or whether, which seems more likely given the size distribution of top companies, lenders tend to be concentrated among big concerns and are fewer in number than borrowers. As to the distribution of lenders and borrowers between industries it is known that insurance groups have on occasions been large lenders along with certain banks, whilst the spread of companies operating in the market covers a broad spectrum of industry, including oil, chemicals, fibres, paints and cars.[59]

The level of rates are related to those in the inter-bank market, the margin depending on the state of the market, the duration of the loan, and the presence of a banker's guarantee. Without a guarantee a risk premium is added varying with the quality of the borrowers. The spread of rates over the maturity structure of the market varies depending as to the availability of funds, and expectations regarding future liquidity.

Since 1972 the inter-company market declined in significance, which arose from several causes. One of the basic factors in its growth was the restriction on bank accommodation to the private sector. The introduction of the new credit controls in the autumn of 1971 removed the curbs on bank lending, thereby reducing the need to resort to such a degree to the loans market or more directly to borrowing from other firms. Secondly, the new policy also brought greater freedom of interest rates movements so that company treasurers were increasingly inclined to place funds in some form of marketable instrument to provide maximum mobility for their liquid assets. Bills and certificate of deposits seemed preferable to loans in uncertain markets. Thirdly, company treasurers, following the collapse of some leading companies and fringe financial institutions, became more cautious with shareholders' funds, seeking security along with good yield.

Notes

1 F. Lavington, *The English Capital Market*, London, 1921, pp. 263–73.
2 For a full discussion see H. B. Rose, 'Domestic Trade Credit and Economic Policy', Committee on the Working of the Monetary System, *Memoranda of Evidence*, vol. 3, pp. 219–27 (Radcliffe Committee, 1960).
3 The Radcliffe Committee was of the opinion that the bulk of net trade credit granted by the quoted sector went to exporters; Radcliffe Committee, *Report*, Cmnd 827, 1969, p. 105.
4 B. Tew and R. F. Henderson, *Studies in Company Finance*, Cambridge, 1959, p. 93.
5 ibid., p. 96.
6 ibid., pp. 101–3.
7 Radcliffe Committee, *Report*, para. 306.
8 Rose, op. cit., p. 220.
9 Committee of Inquiry on Small Firms, Cmnd 4811, p. 13 (Bolton Committee 1971).
10 In a recent work, *Company Finance and the Capital Market*, 1974, E. W. Davies and K. A. Yeomans studied the effects of the 1968–70 squeeze and found that in general 'the smaller firm gave substantially more credit under squeeze conditions yet had little control over his own trade creditors

and was apparently less able to take credit than the large firms'; p. 101.
11 Rose, op. cit., p. 223.
12 ibid., p. 223.
13 In contrast to European and American practices British companies are reluctant to charge interest on overdue accounts; it is however slowly becoming more acceptable.
14 *Credit Management Databook*, 1973, pp. 3–10. In recent years a number of companies have offered extended credit terms as a means of clinching contracts; longer terms may well be an alternative to price reductions.
15 In the early 1950s United States companies with large cash balances increased the length of credit extended in tight money periods; see A. Metzler, 'Mercantile Credit, Monetary Policy, and Size of Firms', *Review of Economics and Statistics*, 1960, pp. 429–36.
16 Tew and Henderson, op. cit., pp. 103–4.
17 Rose, op. cit., p. 223.
18 At present about seven companies provide credit insurance, and of these two date from pre-war days; Credit Insurance Association (1912) and Trade Indemnity (1918).

19 For details of the many kinds of policies available see J. C. Vann, 'Credit Insurance Expansion', *The Banker's Magazine*, October 1972, pp. 157–60.

20 In 1974 Trade Indemnity reported a sharp rise in the number of accounts received for collection, involving a total of 8,756 to the value of £5.86m. The number of failures notified rose to 1,911, much above the previous year, and the gross claims paid (less salvages) increased substantially to £2.4m. (Annual Report for 1974).

21 See *Credit Management Databook*, op. cit., pp. 59–63; also T. G. Hutson and J. Butterworth, *Management of Trade Credit*, London, 1968, ch. 10.

22 Lavington, op. cit., ch. 43. For a useful summary of earlier references to trade credit see M. S. Levitt, 'Monetary Theory and Trade Credit, An Historical Approach', *Yorkshire Bulletin*, 1964, pp. 88–96. See also R. S. Sayers, 'Monetary Thought and Monetary Policy in England', *Economic Journal*, 1960, pp. 710–24.

23 Radcliffe Committee, *Report*, para. 311.

24 G. Whittington, *The Prediction of Profitability; and Other Studies of Company Behaviour*, London, 1971, p. 147. The debate in the early 1960s generated several interesting contributions; F. P. Brechling and R. G. Lipsey looked at the experience of 75 companies in the 1950s and concluded that the firms felt the 'quantity effects of monetary squeezes and that they react to them by ... lengthening their credit periods', and that net credit changes were 'potential frustrators of monetary policy'. In a reply to these results W. H. White asserted that the analysis was defective and when corrected it indicated that the role for trade credit was reduced to 'negligibility'; see 'Trade Credit and Monetary Policy', *Economic Journal*, 1963, pp. 618–41, and 'Trade Credit and Monetary Policy: A Reconciliation', *Economic Journal*, 1964, pp. 935–45. A somewhat later investigation of the accounts of 50 companies for the period 1956–63 showed that in credit squeezes there had been 'little evidence of a marked expansion or contraction of either trade credit given or taken'; J. B. Coates, 'Trade Credit and Monetary Policy: A Study of the Accounts of 50 Companies', *Oxford Economic Papers*, 1967, pp. 116–32.

25 Committee of Inquiry on Small Firms, Research Report No. 4, *Financial Facilities for Small Firms*, p. 186. In their evidence to the Radcliffe Committee the London Discount Market Association stated that 'On the fringe of the money markets there are houses that do this kind of thing (deal in accounts receivable) but nothing to do with the Discount Houses'; *Minutes of Evidence*, Q. 3400. See also M. Westlake, *Factoring*, London, 1975, ch. 3.

26 P. O'Brien, 'Factoring's Breakthrough Year', *The Banker*, 1968, p. 139.

27 R. A. Pilcher, 'Factoring—A New Banking Service', *The Banker*, 1972, pp. 675–6.

28 O'Brien, op. cit., p. 139.

29 Some 40% of factoring staff are involved in the important matter of assessing creditworthiness of customers. This is what determines whether a firm will be accepted and the credit limits which are applied, as well as the detailed charges to be levied.

30 *Financial Facilities for Small Firms*, p. 186.

31 J. D. Burton, 'Factors for Consideration', *Journal of the Institute of Bankers*, 1973, pp. 283–4.

32 P. A. Pilcher, 'Banks and Factors: Partners in Finance', *The Banker*, 1968, pp. 147–8.

33 Bolton Committee, *Report*, para. 12.28.

34 ibid., para. 12.29.

35 Pilcher, op. cit., pp. 149–50. For a list of factors and their parent companies see *Credit Management Databook*, op. cit., pp. 51–8. See also Westlake, op. cit., ch. 6.

36 Radcliffe Committee, *Report*, para. 584.

37 ibid., para. 165.

38 On the technicalities of bill operations see Gilletts' *The Bill on London*, London, 1952, the standard work on bills of exchange. See also *This is Bill-Broking* by Allen Harvey and Ross Ltd.

39 The incidence of failure to meet a bill is fairly low; few houses go in for risky business at high rates.

40 It would appear that this
    sort of bill which came into force in Liverpool in the cotton warehouses in about 1932, and then spread to other trades. With this type there is no genuine movement of goods corresponding to the bill; it is a bill drawn on goods in a warehouse which are going to be sold. That is the sort of bill which tends to increase if banking accommodation in respect of certain classes of customers is being restricted; Evidence of Mr A. W.

Tuke to the Radcliffe Committee, *Minutes of Evidence*, Q. 3548.

41 'Commercial Bills', *Bank of England Quarterly Bulletin*, December 1961, p. 31.

42 A bill of exchange drawn and accepted outside the U.K. – 'Foreign domicile bill'; there is no market for these in London.

43 *Bank of England Quarterly Bulletin*, June 1967, p. 155.

44 In the new controls introduced in 1971 commercial bills eligible for rediscount at the Bank of England were regarded as a reserve asset but only 'up to a maximum of 2% of eligible liabilities'. Since 1973 credit control has been applied to the discount market through a limit on each house's aggregate holding of 'undefined assets', among them commercial bills, to a maximum of 20 times its capital and reserves.

45 Richard Law, 'The Resurgence of the Commercial Bill', *The Bankers' Magazine*, December 1965, pp. 343–4.

46 The policy of buying commercial bills varies with the Bank's assessment of credit control needs. Throughout most of 1974 the Bank stopped buying eligible commercial bills because it did not wish to finance private sector transactions which escaped the supplementary deposit scheme; *Bank of England Quarterly Bulletin*, June 1974, p. 144.

47 *Bank of England Quarterly Bulletin*, June 1967, p. 153.

48 These are discount rates, the yield is higher; the difference increases as interest rates rise, for example, 5% discount on a yearling bill yields 5.26%, 10% discount yields 11.11%.

49 Bolton Committee, *Report*, p. 164. See also *Financial Facilities for Small Firms*, pp. 199–206.

50 I am indebted to Dr Brian Terry, University of Warwick, for information on the early development of leasing in the U. K.

51 Estimates for the years 1965–70 relate to the activities of finance houses and Accepting Houses in leasing, but these omit leasing conducted by several other parties. The volume of leased assets by the finance houses is published regularly in *Financial Statistics*, and amounted to £26m. at end 1975. Several finance houses are members of the E. L. A.

52 *Equipment Leasing* (E.L.A., 1974), p. 10.

53 ibid., p. 8.

54 *Financial Facilities for Small Firms*, pp. 182–3. Also A. Hichens, 'The Cost of Equipment Leasing', *Investment Analyst*, December 1966, pp. 28–30.

55 Hichens, op. cit., p. 33.

56 R. A. Fawthrop and B. Terry, 'Debt Management and the Use of Leasing Finance in U. K. Corporate Financing Strategies', *Journal of Business Finance and Accounting*, vol. 2, no. 3, Winter 1975, pp. 295–300.

57 *Bank of England Quarterly Bulletin*, June 1967, p. 164.

58 Hamish McRae, 'London's Shifting Money Markets', *The Banker*, January 1970, pp. 36–7.

59 On the Australian inter-company loan market experience see H. Ross, 'An Examination of the Short Term Money Market in Australia', *Economic Monograph No. 321*, Economic Society of Australia.

10 The public corporations

*although the industries have obligations of a
national and non-commercial kind, they are not,
and ought not, to be regarded as social services
absolved from economic and commercial
justification*

CMND 1337, 1961

Public corporations have two main characteristics; firstly, they are publicly controlled in that Ministers, directly or indirectly, appoint the whole or most of the boards of management, and secondly, they are usually free to manage their affairs on basically commercial lines without detailed scrutiny by an elected body. Such a corporate body has considerable financial independence, including the power to borrow, within specified limits and usually on fixed interest terms, and to maintain reserves. The second characteristic does not apply to some public corporations, for example, the Royal Ordnance, and the Forestry Commission, which are treated as part of the central government sector, while other public corporations will be excluded from detailed comment below because they are not involved in productive activity, for example, the Bank of England and the B.B.C. While the figures presented in *National Income and Expenditure* under public corporations also covers activities outside the range of industries commonly understood as 'nationalized industries', for example, housing corporations, the main emphasis here will be upon the financial aspects of the fuel and power industries, iron and steel, and transport.[1] These are the main contributors to the Gross National Product.

As to their place in the economy it is obviously important, but not as predominant as sometimes supposed, at least, when viewed quantitatively. The coverage of the nationalized industries has, of course, changed over time. Up to 1952 it expanded continuously so that by then it was responsible for about 10% of G.N.P., compared with a mere 1% in 1945. During 1952–60 the sector diminished somewhat with the de-nationalization of steel and road haulage. With the transfer of the Post Office to the public enterprise sector in 1961 the previous level of contribution to G.N.P. was attained. The setting up of the British Steel Corporation in 1967 brought the percentage of G.N.P. up to 11%, taking net output as a percentage of G.N.P. By 1973 the figure had fallen back to 9% of G.N.P. but increased to 12% by 1976. The bulk of this contribution to G.N.P. comes from the coal, gas, electricity and the publicly owned portions of iron and steel, and transport and communications; the part played by other public corporations in the generation of the G.N.P. is relatively small. In the area of investment activity their role is more dominating. In 1952 public corporations were responsible for 19% of gross fixed capital formation, increasing to 22% in 1967, but which declined to 16% in 1974, and then rising to 20% in 1976 following the slow rate of increase of private sector investment.

The present public enterprise sector is largely the product of the years 1945–51. By comparison, the pre-war public corporations sector was miniscule (see table 10.1), and in 1939 consisted of the Port of London Authority (formed in 1908 and modelled on the Mersey Docks and Harbour Board, but it was more of a local authority than a modern public corporation), the B.B.C. (1928), the Central Electricity Board (1926), the London Passenger Transport Board (1938), and B.O.A.C. (formed in 1939 to absorb Imperial Airways and British Airways, but which did not become operational due to the war). The Central Electricity Board was probably the first public corporation in the modern sense of having been created by public authority, with defined functions and powers, and financial independence; it was set up to 'promote and control the bulk generation of electricity and to construct and maintain the bulk transmission lines'.[2]

The main post-war acts were passed between 1946 and 1949. In 1946 acts were passed nationalizing the Bank of England, setting up the National Coal Board, the two air corporations, B.O.A.C. and B.E.A., and the very short-lived British South American Airways Corporation. Under the Transport Act of 1947 several transport undertakings, including railways, were nationalized; the electricity supply industry was also taken over in that year, and a year later the gas industry. A major part of the iron and steel industry was taken into public ownership in 1949 but in 1953 it was largely de-nationalized, only to be re-nationalized in 1967 by the Labour Government.[3] In 1961 the Post Office was given a new status and became an independent public corporation, while a year later London Transport ceased to be nationalized and the Greater London Council assumed responsibility.[4] In 1975 the National Enterprise Board was established (its subsidiaries continue to be classified to the companies sector), while the most recent addition is the British National Oil Corporation, established on 1 January 1976.

The process of nationalization involved the acquisition of property and the payment of compensation, the terms of which were determined by parliament. However, no standard approach was adopted. Sometimes compensation was based on the market values of acquired assets as recorded by Stock Exchange prices, an easy procedure to apply. In others it was related to the net 'maintainable revenue' that would have been realized without nationalization, and occasionally the annual debt charge of the acquired undertaking was simply taken over.[5]

Stock Exchange valuations were used as the basis of compensation in the case of railways, iron and steel, and certain gas and electricity undertakings. Under the Transport Act 1947, which set up the British Transport Commission, railway securities were acquired at their average value in the Stock Exchange Official List for six business days in November 1946, or at the average mid-month quotations for February to

Table 10.1   Public corporations: Investment and financing (£m.)

Year[a]	Gross fixed capital	Undistri- buted income[b]	Loans from central gov't (net)	Public dividend capital	Stock issues (net)	Other bor- rowing (net)[c]	Miscel- laneous sources[d]	Deprecia- tion[e]
1938	10	4	—	—	—	—	—	3
1946	16	11	3	—	6	—	1	5
1950	288	118	29	—	163	—	11	109
1955	570	182	142	—	367	—	−3	181
1960	794	304	485	—	1	15	1	310
1966	1,458	653	843	—	−13	17	49	552
1967	1,669	666	1,145	18	—	−17	−18	607
1968	1,624	818	1,087	13	—	−29	−141	716
1969	1,487	884	892	4	−215	43	204	767
1970	1,679	831	852	9	−8	144	−11	843
1971	1,862	810	1,145	—	−72	135	147	920
1972	1,774	930	1,039	40	−183	120	53	1,069
1973	2,061	1,196	710	31	−349	848	143	1,185
1974	2,815	1,347	685	59	—	720	531	1,431
1975	3,949	1,596	1,762	403	—	486	830	1,661
1976	4,730	2,749	1,139	480	—	1,591	89	2,032

[a] The Post Office became a public corporation in 1961; steel was de-nationalized in 1953 and re-nationalized in 1967.
[b] Before providing for depreciation and stock appreciation.
[c] Includes borrowing from banks, abroad and superannuation funds.
[d] Includes adjustments for subsidies some minor capital transfer items, and other identified financial transactions (net).
[e] At historic cost as given in published trading accounts.

Source: National Income and Expenditure Blue Books.

July 1946, if the latter were higher. Net maintainable revenue was not used in this case since it would have involved too many difficult judgements about the circumstances in which the railways would operate in the post-war period. Total compensation was put at £927m. of government stock at 3%, yielding annually £28m. This was somewhat below the figure of interest and dividends previously paid out, which had been inflated by war-time traffic, but the B.T.C. had to face a fixed interest burden compared to the variable dividend of the railway companies. In the case of iron and steel securities quoted on the Stock Exchange Official List, they were valued at average prices for the period 1-25 October 1948, or, an average of the mean of the quotations on certain days, whichever was the higher. Unquoted securities were valued by an arbitration tribunal set up under the Act. Quoted electricity securities were taken over on similar lines to those outlined above, but gas and electricity undertakings acquired from local authorities were simply transferred with the new Boards taking over the annual debt charges. Such a procedure penalized those local authorities who had redeemed debt or ploughed back profits.

For the coal industry compensation was determined on the principle of net maintainable revenue, that is, by assessing what the assets might reasonably be expected to earn in the future if not nationalized. The assets were assessed at £164.6m. and stock to this sum, Treasury 3.5% 1977-80, was given in compensation. In this case it was a direct liability of the Exchequer, though the debt is being repaid by the Board to the Exchequer on an annuity basis. The yield from this stock was below the average net profits of the private coal companies but it was pointed out that certainty of income would compensate for the reduced return. Finally, in one rather specialized activity, road haulage, a different basis was employed. Few, if any, of the road hauliers involved had quoted capital, and therefore the physical assets were acquired at replacement costs, less a compounded 20% p.a. reduction for depreciation. A separate allowance was made for goodwill due to the self-employed nature of many operations, and this was equal to not less than two and not more than five times the annual net profit.[6]

The interest and principal of all compensation stock was guaranteed by the Treasury, with the quoted value at the time of issue being equal to the agreed values of the securities acquired but at a lower gilt-edged yield. These guaranteed issues were particularly large, some £2,200m. being raised between 1949-51, with only £200m. for cash-raising purposes.[7]

General trends in financing capital requirements

Most of the industries taken into public ownership after the war had very large arrears of ordinary maintenance and of renewal of capital assets arising from the war and the depressed state of some of the industries during the inter-war period. Under their respective Acts, therefore, authority was given for sustained programmes of heavy capital spending for replacement and modernization in coal, gas, railways, and electricity. Gross fixed capital formation by public corporations thus rose swiftly from £42m. in 1947 to over £350m. in 1951, and by the mid-1950s averaged over £600m. a year.[8] Subsequent expansion continued to be quite rapid, although it was concentrated on the needs of the electricity industry and the telecommunications services of the Post Office. In recent years, from 1970 to 1974, expenditure on investment in transportation and communications (mainly railways, airways and the Post Office) increased by nearly one-third, whereas that of fuel and power (mainly coal, gas and electricity) remained fairly stable. More recently the scale of annual investment in these sectors has been similar. Gross domestic fixed capital formation by public corporations increased from £1,458m. in 1966 to £4,730m. in 1976, while at constant prices there is a steady increase from £1,738m. to £1,946m. respectively; between 1974 and 1976 real investment increased by 13%. In manufacturing, investment at current prices rose from £1,518m. in 1966 to £3,957m. in 1976, while at constant prices it fell from £1,774m. to £1,659m. respectively; between 1974 and 1976 real investment fell by 18%. Public sector investment has been less volatile than that in manufacturing since the former has been shielded from several policy measures designed to restrain private sector demand.

The capital requirements of the nationalized industries are considerable, averaging about one-fifth of U.K. gross fixed capital formation, compared with one-third for companies. The general pattern for private industry is that about three-quarters of the finance needed for capital expenditure comes from funds generated internally. The nationalized industries, however, have not been able to rely so greatly on a high self-financing ratio and borrowing has been used to fill the gap.

The general trends in the capital receipts of public corporations during the years 1946–76 are reflected in the figures given in table 10.1 and which represents predominantly the activities of the fuel and power industries and those in transport and communications. The important entries and exits of industries into the sector are noted at the foot of the table. The main trends are readily discerned.

In the early phase about one-third of capital needs came from savings (undistributed income before providing for depreciation and stock appreciation). Government loans constituted a relatively small proportion of all funds, between 10% and 20%, while market borrowing by stock issues brought in about one-third to one-half of all needs. The abrupt change of policy in 1956 whereby all the requirements of the industries were met from the Exchequer, with no further issues of guaranteed stocks by individual corporations, was occasioned by problems of monetary policy and debt management. In addition some boards were encouraged to meet their capital requirements by Exchequer borrowing rather than by price rises and more self-financing. In the period 1957–9 the self-financing ratio of public corporations fell to around 20%, the rest of their capital budget coming almost entirely from the Exchequer. This sharp deterioration was associated with several heavy deficits in the transport and communications industries, while fuel and power continued to show an improving record of self-financing.

Since 1960 there has been decreased reliance on the Exchequer for investment funds. The reasons for this trend are not simple. An important ingredient was the stipulation of more precise financial objectives in the 1961 White Paper, *The Financial and Economic Obligations of the Nationalised Industries*. In particular, the obligation to earn sufficient revenue to meet costs 'taking one year with another' was made more precise, and henceforth deficits were expected to be matched by surpluses over a five-year period. By setting financial targets for each industry it was anticipated that revenues would exceed running costs and that larger savings would accrue to replace current assets and finance capital developments. A further review came in 1967, which indicated that investment should be directed to those activities where the expected returns were greatest. As part of the more specific guidelines industries were expected to cover fully their accounting as well as operating costs, and so avoid deficits. With greater freedom to adjust prices, and in pricing policy, it was hoped that more efficient investment would yield larger surpluses for financing. Overall, the self-financing ratio since the 1967 review has fluctuated quite widely, but looking at individual groups it is noticeable that the ratio for fuel and power rose quite sharply after 1970 (for the period 1970–4 it averaged 60%), while that for transport and communications had fallen from an annual average of 57% for 1965–9 to 45% for 1970–4. This was partly attributable to the levelling off of investment expenditure in the former group, while with the latter a rapid rise in investment expenditure coincided with a stable volume of savings, at a time when nationalized industries could not operate outside official price restraint policies. During 1975–6 subsidies and price rises improved the savings ratio of the fuel and power sector and raised that of transport and communication to 70%.

Other reasons may also be put forward for the improved ratio in the 1960s. Some industries had by then passed their investment peak; the figures for the fuel and power group suggest this. In the transport and communications group it is only since 1971 that their investment expenditure has reached a level above that of the fuel and power industries; the growth in importance of the Post Office is matched by the reduction in investment by the electricity industry. Finally, during the period various corporations have been the beneficiaries of capital write-offs of some importance which yielded savings on current accounts (see p. 291).

Sources of funds

(1) *Internal funds*

Although the industries nationalized between 1945–50 had different histories, economic strengths and prospects, nevertheless their economic and financial powers and obligations as laid down by the relevant statutes followed a fairly standard pattern. This was based on the view that they were to be a combination of social services and commercial concerns, and 'perhaps on the hope that the ability to borrow at Government rates would enable them to meet the limited financial obligations prescribed by statute and also to carry out their non-commercial obligations'.[9] In general terms the undertakings were expected to pay their way and most of the regulating statutes contained requirements to that end. Their statutory obligations prescribed that their revenues should 'on an average of good and bad years (or some similar phrase) be not less than sufficient to meet all items properly chargeable to revenue, including, interest, depreciation, the redemption of capital and the provision of reserves'.[10] The Acts thus set out a minimum performance, not a maximum financial requirement, and it was defined in terms of a surplus or deficit. This differed from the ordinary definition of profits (or loss) in as much as provision had to be made from revenue for all the items given above before a surplus in the statutory sense arises. Some profits were thus anticipated in the ordinary sense in order to accumulate reserves from them.[11]

Apart from operating surpluses (which include subsidies received) the main sources of internal finance have been the provisions for the depreciation of fixed assets and plant, for the redemption of capital debt and for general reserves. Of these, the former has been by far the most important. It is worth noting that for the post-war years depreciation represented around 50% of the gross trading surplus for the public corporations sector; the item stock appreciation, which is so large for private industry, is trivial, apart from 1974–6. However, the *net* trading surplus has only covered interest payments (the main item charged against income in the appropriation account) in three periods, 1952–4, 1963–8, and more recently in 1976.

The regulating statutes have not laid down the specific lines along which depreciation should be implemented. Different methods and standards have been used by the various industries, but in general it has been done on a straight line basis using the historic cost of their assets. In the airlines industry they also used the concept of obsolescence for aircraft, while depreciating other plant and equipment in the conventional manner. In the case of the electricity industry the allegation has been made that depreciation policy was too prudent thus depressing profits and the financial rate of return shown; United States conventional generating stations were written-off over 35 years, U.K. ones over 25 years.[12]

Most of the Boards noted in their annual reports that following the practice widely adopted in industrial concerns some additional provision should be made out of revenue to meet the difference between historic cost and replacement cost depreciation, a margin caused by rising prices, and which can also be used as a reserve against obsolescence. After the 1961 White Paper the supplementary provision for depreciation at replacement cost was made specific, in that an allowance had to be made from revenue for 'such an amount as may be necessary to cover the excess of depreciation calculated on historic cost'. In the case of the Post Office this sort of supplementary charge is arrived at by applying current price indices to the historical cost of certain asset groups and computing depreciation at appropriate rates on the added values. For assets where technical advance occurs no charge is made, or where there are large sale proceeds. The practice in the steel industry differed somewhat. At the vesting date, 1967, the Corporation adopted a basic 15-year life (i.e., 6.66% p.a. depreciation rate) for nearly all of its fixed assets. This level was intended to take account of both obsolescence and replacement so that no separate reserve was kept. While actual replacement and obsolescence proved slower than the planned rate, construction costs mounted rapidly and lately the Corporation decided to make separate provision for replacement.

After looking at their performance in the late 1950s the 1961 White Paper concluded that the 'total retained income of all [the nationalized] industries taken together (including supplementary depreciation provisions, capital redemption of funds and reserves) has not been sufficient to provide for the replacement of assets used up in the production process, and this is also the case in most of the individual industries.'[13] One calculation put the deficiency of historic cost depreciation below replacement cost at £1,100m. for the period 1948–57. Taking figures for recent years the discrepancy between replacement cost, as reflected in the estimates of capital consumption provided in the National Income Blue Book, and depreciation provisions for public corporations averaged around £170m. a year in the early 1960s, rising to about £500m. for the early 1970s and to over £1,000m. in 1975–6. The implication of this shortfall should not however be treated as seriously as the figure might indicate. As the Central Statistical Office warn, capital consumption estimates 'should be valued at the cost of replacing capacity but so far it has only been possible to value it at the estimated cost of replacing existing fixed assets with identical assets'.[14] Thus, they make no allowance for technological change, which in some of the nationalized industries has been extremely important so that the cost of replacing capacity need not be above the cost of the original plant even with inflation, although with its quickening pace in recent years this disclaimer must be losing some of its force. In the case of electricity, gas, and airlines there have been large technical advances with associated economies of scale which have tended to reduce replacement cost below what it otherwise would be.[15]

The Acts required nationalized industries not only to provide out of revenue for the payment of interest on capital and depreciation, but also to make provision for the redemption of capital. Industries were required to repay their capital indebtedness over a period of years, and most of the stocks issued had very long redemption dates. Also, advances made by the Ministry of Fuel and Power to the fuel and power industries and to the British Transport Commission were to be redeemed over a period of fifty years. Redemption fund provisions vary between industries, some being on a straight line basis and others compound, while in the case of the National Coal Board terminable annuities were issued with small payments in relation to revenues. The sums set aside annually for the redemption funds are, with Treasury approval, left in the industry temporarily to finance further capital expenditure rather than being invested externally. In practice, with the agreement of successive governments, the industries 'have not been required (nor have they sought)' to make provision on the scale initially indicated.[16]

The third source of internal funds are general reserves. Industries are required to build up such reserves and Ministers have powers to issue directions as to their size. In practice, relatively small reserves have been accumulated for the various purposes to which they might be put, for example, stabilizing prices in periods of inflationary trading conditions, or offsetting a deficit in any one year. Apparently, little attention has been given to building up reserves as part of price policy. Although some of the undertakings showed general reserves in their balance sheets in the 1950s they were in some cases 'entirely obliterated by accumulated deficits on revenue account'.[17]

In the period up to 1961 the proportion of capital receipts which came from savings (before providing for depreciation and stock appreciation) fell from the range 30–8% in the early 1950s to a disturbingly low 22%

during 1957–9, although by 1960–1 it recovered somewhat to 38%. For the main nationalized industries the increase in savings in this period was only about a half of the increase in the level of investment, which meant that the dependence of the public enterprise sector on the rest of the community doubled over the period. However, in the case of the fuel and power group the ratio of savings to capital formation remained fairly stable at between $\frac{1}{3}$ and $\frac{2}{3}$ for the 1950s; in transport and communications savings by the late 1950s were negative.

Comparisons were, and continue to be, made of the nationalized industries financial performance with that of the private sector, in particular, manufacturing industries. It was stated in the early 1950s that quoted companies financed around three-quarters of their investment from internal funds. Further comparisons were made in terms of the relative rates of return on capital. Although the return on capital in one or two of the nationalized industries was calculated at around 8% (net income as a percentage of net assets) most of them in the 1950s earned considerably less than 5%.[18] By contrast similar yardsticks for manufacturing and distribution yielded figures of around 15% for 1957–9, with results of a similar order of magnitude for a large sample of iron and steel companies. Such a basis of comparison for private and public sector industries must, however, be treated with some caution because the valuation of assets cannot be obtained on a uniform basis, there is a wide divergence between undertakings in the nature of their assets, and accounting practices vary.

After making such comparisons the 1961 White Paper went on to assert that the proportion of internal funds or rates of return on capital achieved in the private sector could not be copied by the nationalized industries. Straightforward comparisons ignored the important fact that the latter were not fully commercial in their nature, or engaged in similar types of activity.[19] Many of the industries were 'akin to public utilities where a lower return on capital employed is traditional, partly because of the absence of risk in the business and partly because the earnings of such utilities are normally subject to public regulation owing to the advantages of monopoly which they are believed to enjoy.' In this period the 'Boards have been continuously subject to pressure from public opinion [and Ministers] to keep their own prices down even when costs and prices elsewhere have been rising.' Their financial position correspondingly reflected these 'onerous national and commercial obligations' which forced them to rely more heavily on the Exchequer 'than is healthy either for themselves or for the economy as a whole'.

The above deficiencies prompted a major assessment of the policies which guided the overall conduct of the nationalized industries and led to the 1961 White paper *The Financial and Economic Obligations of the Nationalised Industries*. The government concluded that there would be no advantage in altering the basic financial and economic principles which the industries by their statutes were required to pursue, but in order to provide a more satisfactory basis for operation these principles needed 'to be interpreted more precisely in the form of financial objectives for the nationalized undertakings generally'. The obligation to earn sufficient revenue to meet costs 'taking one year with another' was made more precise; in future deficits were expected to be matched by surpluses over a *five-year period*. In arriving at the surpluses and deficits for each year there should be charged against revenue those items normally deducted, including interest and depreciation on historic cost basis, while provision was also to be made for reserves to enable assets to be replaced at current prices and to finance future capital development.

Each industry was set a target for a specified period and which was subject to annual review. The financial objectives in force in 1967 are given in table 10.2. In some cases the objective was expressed in terms of progress towards a break even point, for others in terms of a rate of return on capital employed. The assets of undertakings were used as a denominator, since they were readily comprehensible and also took some account of changes in the scale of an undertaking. The objectives set were different for each industry and for the various area boards. This was done so that they would reflect different statutory and social obligations, conditions of demand, domestic costs and other factors peculiar to individual undertakings. Industries with considerable non-commercial obligations were given lower rates of return, while the rate for electricity exceeded that for gas since the Treasury wanted to encourage the more capital intensive electricity industry to be as self-financing as possible.

The general need, then, was for undertakings to increase their *net* revenues and the principal means whereby this was to be done was by reducing costs and improving efficiency. It was accepted that Boards must have freedom to increase prices if necessary where they believed them to be artificially low, but overall pricing policy was still the object of official scrutiny. If costs were raised due to the imposition of commercially unprofitable activities, then Boards could seek an appropriate adjustment to their financial objectives. On the capital account Ministers would continue to monitor expenditure while endeavouring to enquire closely into any spending in excess of approved ceilings.

From the standpoint of the self-financing ratio the six years after 1961 were a distinct improvement on the previous record. The ratio of savings to total capital receipts for public corporations was consistently above 40%, and reached 53% in 1963. The improvement in the savings ratio of

Table 10.2   Financial objectives in force in 1967

Industry	Objective	Period covered
Post Office	8% net[a]	1963/4–1967/8
National Coal Board	To break even after interest and depreciation, including £10 million a year to cover the difference between depreciation at historic cost and replacement cost[b]	
Electricity Boards (England and Wales)	Average 12.4% gross[c]	1962/3–1966/7
Gas Boards	Average 10.2% gross[c]	1962/3–1966/7
B.O.A.C.	12½% net[a]	1966/7–1969/70
B.E.A.	6% net[a]	1963/4–1967/8
British Railways Board	Have the statutory obligation of reducing their deficit and breaking even as soon as possible	

[a] Income before interest but after depreciation at historic cost, expressed as a percentage of average net assets.

[b] The N.C.B. were relieved of their objective temporarily in April 1965, but it was later restored.

[c] Income before interest and depreciation, expressed as a percentage of average net assets.

Source: Nationalised Industries: A Review of Economic and Financial Objectives, Cmnd 3437, p. 16.

the transport and communications industries was particularly marked, attaining 72% in 1966, but the increase in investment was comparatively modest compared with a twofold increase in the fuel and power industries. In terms of the ratio of net income to average net assets the Post Office had almost achieved its 8% target by 1966–7; during 1964–7 B.O.A.C. was continuously above its target; the N.C.B. between 1961–8 earned a small surplus in some years; both electricity and gas were very much below target.

Although, on the score of savings there had been an improvement, for several reasons a further review of the financial objectives of nationalized undertakings was needed. For some industries the time periods within which targets were set in 1961 had expired, and others would soon be in the same position. There had been important technological changes and discoveries of new natural resources which had significant long-run implications for the fuel industry, whilst demand patterns in the transport and aviation industries were constantly changing. Again, the role of the nationalized industries price policy within the government's prices and incomes policy needed to be precisely stated. Finally, the overall capacity of the nationalized sector had been expanding to meet increased demand, which required an investment programme on a bigger scale than had been contemplated in the 1961 review; their annual investment was equivalent to the whole of that for private manufacturing industry. This meant heavy demands on manpower and capital, 'and the need to measure these calls, to assess priorities, and to allocate resources upon an economically and socially rational basis has become even more important.'[20]

The 1967 White Paper, *Nationalised Industries, A Review of Economic and Financial Objectives* set out specific guidelines for investment and pricing policies. In future sums of money for internal financing would be residually determined after taking hopefully correct pricing and investment decisions; accordingly it was not 'intended to express financial objectives in terms of self-financing ratios'. The target rates of return were kept, although in a more flexible form, with the prospect of different figures being set for different periods for the various parts of an industry. However, the objective of obtaining an acceptable rate of return on new capital could not be seen to be achieved merely by maximizing the financial returns for an industry. The efficient allocation of resources required the direction of investment to those activities where the return was expected to be greatest and judged according to a common measure of return on new investment. For this purpose all nationalized industries were expected to use discounted cash flow techniques in assessing their investment projects with a common test discount rate of 8%. Some industries had already used such an approach, now it was to become general. The 8% figure, later revised, was held to be broadly consistent, having regard to different circumstances in relation to tax, investment grants, etc., 'with the average rate of return in real terms looked for on low risk projects in the private sector in recent years'.[21] Essentially the general adoption of the test rate of discount was a device to ensure that the calls of the private and public sector upon resources did not get out of line with each other in the long run. If some easing of public sector investment was judged to be necessary then although projects satisfied the required criteria, short-term relief could be obtained by postponement; if in the long term the nationalized industries investment programme was thought to be excessive then the test rate of discount could be suitably adjusted.

Correct methods of investment appraisal could only prove effective if the nationalized industries pursued pricing policies which were relevant to their particular economic circumstances. While these differed between industries certain general considerations held; prices should be fixed so that revenue should normally cover their accounting costs in full, thus avoiding deficits, and that prices 'if they are to contribute towards a more efficient distribution of resources must also attract resources to places where they can make the most effective contribution to meeting the demands of users'. Thus, while prices should cover overall accounting costs they should also be set to reflect the costs of the particular goods and services provided. Unless this is so there is the risk of cross-subsidization and consequent misallocation of resources.

The nationalization Acts were rather vague when defining the obligations of the various industries in setting prices. They ranged from indications that reasonable prices should be charged, to suggestions that reductions should be made. Generally, however, it was understood that prices should be such as to yield sufficient revenue to cover expenditure properly chargeable to revenue 'taking one year with another'. Most of the undertakings began by basing their prices on average costs, a practice later modified in some industries by the introduction of differential tariffs. Considerable debate occurred over the merits of the practice of pricing on average or marginal costs, the advocates of the latter claiming that such pricing reflected the actual cost of providing each individual service, so allowing consumer preference to operate. The former maintained that provided aggregate revenue covered total expenditure plus interest charges the question of whether individual components of goods and services supplied was run at a loss or profit was not a dominant consideration. Although some concessions were made by way of a reduction for large customers, little attempt was made to charge the full economic cost of supplying small quantities at some remove from the sources of supply. Behind all this debate was the need to justify price changes to the appropriate minister. Such a procedure meant delay, so that when applications were granted revenue had in the meantime been lost. At worst approval could be (and was) withheld, even though the proposals were regarded as in the interests of an industry, but they were deemed to conflict with the general economic and social policy of the government.

While the 1961 White Paper had conceded that there should be greater freedom of price movement by boards its successor went a great deal further. Prices should be related to the true costs of providing the goods and services consumed 'in every case where these can be sensibly identified'. In the long run, therefore, prices were to be related to 'the cost of supplying on a continuing basis those services and products whose separate costing is a practical proposition (i.e., long run marginal costs)', such long-run marginal costs to include provision for replacement of fixed assets along with an adequate rate of return on capital employed.[22] If excess demand or spare capacity should emerge then short-run costs might be more appropriate for price fixing; curtail the former by higher peak-time charges, and deal with the latter by lower off-peak prices to encourage consumption.

In the period after the 1967 White Paper the public corporations sector achieved a reasonable degree of self-financing; by 1973 the undistributed income of public corporations amounted to 54% of total capital receipts. Thereafter, with a substantial increase in capital expenditure and the effects of price restraint the ratio deteriorated to 32% in 1975, recovering to 50% in 1976 when nationalized industries were allowed to raise prices. However, in terms of attaining the target levels of rates of return set out in the 1967 White Paper, and later revisions, the performance of the main industries has been disappointing. From 1969–70 to 1973–4 the electricity industry was set a new target of 7% *net* (which applied to the whole industry), but during the period price restraint prevented this objective from being reached. Heavy cost increases were only matched by moderate price rises, so that, for example, in 1971–2 profit was £180 m. less than expected. However, with price increases in 1975–7 the industry attained a 10.4% rate of return for 1976–7. A similar story applies to the gas industry. For the period 1969–70 to 1973–4 it had a target of 7% *net*, but the average return for the period was 6.5%. After two years of losses the industry realized net rates of return of about 9% in 1975–7. The Gas Council estimated that in the period 1967–74 price restraint policy, pursued at government request, involved them in a loss of revenue of £110m., and even after compensation of £74m., paid under the Statutory Compensation (Financial Provisions) Act of 1974, they still had a balance of £35m. to carry. For the Steel Corporation the target set for 1973–4 to 1976–7 is 8% net; in recent years it fell way below this but for 1974–5 it reached 8.9% and in the following year it slumped to zero, recovering slightly in 1976–7 to 2.1%. The N.C.B. target over this period has been to break even but since 1969 it has not been required to earn £10m. a year to provide for the excess of replacement over historic cost. Even so, large deficits occurred when pricing took place on underestimated costs but recent price increases produced operating profits in 1976–7.[23] The N.C.B. has also aimed at an internal financing ratio of 50%, and in 1976–7 managed to reach a 40% level.

According to the Select Committee on Nationalised Industries the government accepted the fact that targets fixed in the past 'had in some cases gone by the board'. Price restraint policy was regarded as more important than nationalized industry policy. It was estimated by the Treasury that the combined deficits of the nationalized industries, as a result of price restraint in 1972–3 was something of the order of £150m. Admittedly, compensation was paid, but such short-term remedies to the effects of semi-permanent price restraint render medium- to long-term planning difficult. Given freedom the industries could have done much better. Low prices creates a demand on sources and for increased investment; it would therefore seem desirable to return to economic pricing as soon as possible to avoid over-investment and a repetition of large compensation payments from the Treasury. While a return to a system of workable long-term financial objectives is planned by the Treasury it has been considerably delayed because the nationalized industries were required to help in restraining inflation.

The internal flow of funds of some corporations has been given spasmodic boosts by way of 'gifts' arising from capital reconstructions which have been adopted as a solution to a problem of recurring and accumulating deficits. This state of affairs usually resulted from changes in economic circumstances, technological change, or management failure in the enterprise concerned. Since the early 1960s they have become not an uncommon feature of a changing economy, and while they are put into practice with some reluctance little disgrace is attached to their adoption. This is possibly because of a confusion between commercial failure and running into the red to meet social obligations, because it has been argued in some instances that the terms of compensation at the time of nationalization were too generous, and despite the extra burden on the tax payer a capital write-off 'appears to work like a magic wand'.[24]

Capital reconstructions can take various forms, 'including a reassessment and consequent write-off of part of an industry's capital liabilities to the Exchequer, a suspension of interest charges on part of a capital debt, a transfer to the Exchequer of an industry's liabilities in respect of market stocks, or the write-off of an accumulated deficit which has previously been covered by borrowing.' In all cases the effect is to reduce interest payments, and as with subsidies, to place an additional burden on the Treasury. A capital write-off then is equivalent to a continuing subsidy paid by the Treasury which is equal to the interest on the capital written-off, and does not involve the minister concerned in further detailed management. A straight subsidy, however, can be adjusted year by year in accordance with an industry's needs and eventually ended but a write-off or transfer of capital implied a permanent subsidy. Between 1962–8 capital write-offs had involved the Treasury in the loss of some £70m. a year of interest.[25] The loss since then has probably been twice this amount.

The sums involved in write-offs since 1962 are given in table 10.3. The net figure of £487m. in 1963 relates to the write-off of loans to the British Transport Commission, and the very large figure for 1969 to the liabilities of the nationalized transport bodies covered by the Transport Act 1968. The figure of £350m. in 1972 represents a reduction of £200m. in the Public Dividend Capital of the British Steel Corporation, plus a write-off of £150m. of loans; the latter brought an interest saving of £6.7m. during the year.[26] Those for 1973 relate to the N.C.B. and the Post Office, while British Rail benefited from most of the 1975 figure.

In recent years internal funds have been greatly supplemented by the receipt of government subsidies. Prior to 1960 subsidies amounted to a few million a year; throughout the 1950s the figure was around £4m. They became important in 1960 when the revenue deficits of the nationalized transport undertakings were covered by central government assistance. The annual sums involved for the public corporations sector are given in table 10.3 for the years since 1960, and as is readily noticeable it is only since 1972 that the amounts paid have increased dramatically, being almost equal to the volume of savings in 1974 and 1975.

Table 10.3 Public corporations: Capital write-offs and subsidies 1960–1976 (£m.)

Year	Capital write-offs	Subsidies
1960	—	121
1961	—	143
1962	10	148
1963	487	142
1964	—	132
1965	525	151
1966	—	156
1967	—	192
1968	19	205
1969	1,258	155
1970	255	175
1971	—	176
1972	350	444
1973	543	654
1974	—	1,337
1975	227	1,225
1976	—	984

Source: National Income and Expenditure Blue Books.

Three main categories of subsidies are paid to the nationalized industries. Up to 1968 most of the total subsidy paid was on account of the nationalized transport undertakings and involved grants to cover revenue deficits, grants towards the costs of unremunerative services and other specific payments in support of the inland transport bodies. In 1968 over 80% of the total subsidy paid went to transport. During 1969–72 the sum involved amounted to an average of £110m. a year, rising to £317m. in 1974 and £476m. in 1976. Assistance to the coal industry has been made under the various Coal Industry Acts passed between 1965 and 1973 and provides for grants in connection with pit closures and for operational purposes, and for reimbursements to the Electricity and Gas Boards in respect of the cost of additional coal consumption. Grants made in 1972–1973 and 1973–4 have also been paid to cover revenue deficits. During 1966–71 the total grant payable to coal was only £70m., rising to about £170m. annually in 1972–4, and falling to £65m. in 1976. The most recent component is that for compensation for price restraint on the part of the public corporations. Such sums are payable under the Statutory Corporations (Financial Provisions) Act of 1974 to the Gas, Electricity and the Post Office in compensation for the effects of price restraint from 1970 onwards. During 1970–2 the payment ran at about £45 m. a year. In 1973 it amounted to £230m., rising to a massive £606m. in 1974, but by 1976 it fell to a mere £10m., since the sector was permitted to put up prices sharply in line with the 'proper market level'.

(2) Borrowing

The original nationalizing Acts set out various ways in which money could be borrowed, and laid down limits on that facility. Thus, for each industry a statutory limit is prescribed for borrowing to finance capital expenditure and within that limit ministerial approval is required. However, with a few exceptions such as the N.C.B., temporary borrowing for working capital purposes does not need prior consent. Up until 1976 ministerial control of borrowing was secondary to control of investment and, once approved, the government did not restrict the supply of capital to finance projects. If industries could not finance investment from internal funds then Exchequer advances were a natural consequence of investment decisions, or resort to outside borrowing with Treasury guarantee. Table 10.4 lists the existing statutory limits, increases permissible by order, and the amount outstanding at 31 March 1977. In 1976 cash limits were introduced, the estimates of their external capital requirements serving as a sort of control figure.

Under the Borrowing Acts the normal pattern is that they make provision for the expected requirements of the industry for a period of from 4–7 years, which is divided into two parts by an intermediate limit which may not be exceeded without the passing of an Affirmative Resolution of the House of Commons. Parliament thus has an opportunity every two or three years to review and control the borrowing of the nationalized industries. As the statutory limits are approached legislation is passed providing new limits to meet estimated future needs. The

Table 10.4 Nationalized industries: Borrowing powers (£m.)

Nationalized industries	Existing statutory limit	Increase permissible by order	Amount outstanding at 31 March 1977	Relevant statute
National Coal Board	1,100	300	912	Coal Industry Act 1976
Electricity Council and Boards	6,500	—	5,309	Electricity Act 1972
North of Scotland Hydroelectric Board / South of Scotland Electricity Board	1,500	450	1,090	Electricity (Financial Provisions) (Scotland) Act 1976
British Gas Corporation	2,500	200	2,100	Gas Act 1972
British National Oil Corporation	600	300	340	Petroleum and Submarine Pipeline Act 1975
British Steel Corporation	3,000	1,000	2,284	Iron and Steel (Amendment) Act 1975
Post Office	4,800	—	4,090	Post Office (Borrowing) Act 1972
British Airways Board	700	—	477	British Airways Board Act 1977
British Railways Board	600	300	386	Railways Act 1974
Other Boards*	747	100	508	Airports Authority Act 1975, Transport Act 1968, Stat. Corps. (Financial Provisions) Act 1975

* British Airports Authority, British Transport Docks Board, British Waterways Board, National Freight Corporation, National Bus Company, Scottish Transport Group.

Source: The Treasury.

borrowing powers conferred on the Electricity Council and the Post Office are by far the largest, followed by British Steel and British Gas.

Table 10.5 gives an account for the main corporations of the amounts outstanding against statutory financing limits as at 31 March 1977. Five categories are given, borrowing by stock issues, net government advances, temporary borrowing, public dividend capital and borrowing abroad. It is apparent that electricity, gas, and the Post Office have the biggest net government advances, and that over recent years these corporations have been the largest borrowers overseas. Whereas in the years ending 31 March 1972 and 1973 foreign currency borrowing outstanding amounted to an average of around £310m., in 1977 it amounted to £3,949m. or 22.6% of the total outstanding borrowing of the nationalized industries as taken for the purposes of the National Loans Fund.

(a) *Borrowing by stock issues*   The first stocks issued by the newly formed corporations after the war were for compensation purposes, but up to 1956 they also made several issues to finance capital expenditure programmes. The electricity, gas and transport undertakings were authorized by their various statutes to borrow by issues of stock; the N.C.B., however, borrowed from the Exchequer from its inception. In practice, new capital expenditure was financed by bank overdrafts as it was incurred which were then repaid from the proceeds of a stock issue, usually in sums of around £150m., while their timing was dictated by the fact that an undertaking had reached its limits with the banks. All issues, which had fixed maturities and interest, were guaranteed as to capital and interest by the Treasury. The liability to meet interest charges and capital repayment rests with the industry not on the Exchequer, unless the guarantee is invoked. These stocks were, and still are, treated as gilt-edged securities so that their terms of issue and subsequent marketability reflected government credit rather than any commercial assessment of the industry.

Some of the issues were made direct to the National Debt Commissioners. In that instance the effect was to reduce the amount which the Commissioners could lend to the Treasury, so that it had to increase its market borrowing, and, in effect, borrow to finance the industry concerned. Most issues, however, came direct to the market, formally issued by prospectus in stated amounts. As with ordinary government securities amounts not subscribed by the public at the time of issue were taken into the portfolio of the Issue Department of the Bank of England and later 'peddled out' on the market by the government broker as demand arose. In proportion to the unsold stock taken in by the Issue Department, the Bank of England reduced its lending to the Exchequer, who then increased its market borrowing through issues of Treasury Bills. In so far as these bills were taken up by the banking system they merely replaced the nationalized industries' bank borrowing.

Following the difficulties which the authorities had in 1955 in selling nationalized industries' stocks a succession of issues had to be 'taken in' by the Issue Department. The Bank of England was afraid that it might soon be 'cluttered up with a lot of unsaleable stock', while the effect of financing Treasury needs by Treasury Bill issues was greatly impeding the authorities declared aim of restricting credit by reducing bank liquidity. In the 1956 Budget it was therefore announced that the issue of stock by the nationalized industries would end and that their needs, like that of the N.C.B., would be met directly from the Exchequer. The Finance Act 1956 gave the Treasury power to make advances for long-term capital purposes to the nationalized industries and authorized it to borrow for that purpose. Introduced as a temporary expedient it has become a permanent system.[27]

Over the period 1947–55 the electricity industry made by far the largest amount of issues; it made fifteen issues and raised £926m. In the same period the British Transport Commission raised £302m. with four issues, and the Gas Council £295m. with the same number of issues. The figures of annual issues made for various years by all public corporations are given in table 10.1 (p. 278) and the total volume outstanding is given in table 10.5.[28]

The necessity of raising large sums to meet the capital needs of the corporations brought forth various proposals that funds could be attracted by the issue of some kind of equity. The Herbert Committee in 1956 thought that the Electricity Boards should be allowed access to the market since it would have 'considerable psychological value' in justifying actions on pricing and investment to the public.[29] The market would no doubt assess and produce funds, at a price – which might include severe surgery on corporations to produce viable units.[30] The Radcliffe Committee took a different view on the matter. The nationalized industries could not by their nature offer a share of the ownership of the business to the private investor, they could not pledge their own assets, and neither were they free to determine their own prices. It did not seem likely that a 'nationalized industry equity with a fluctuating yield (and perhaps in some years no yield at all) and without a Government guarantee would attract much money'.[31] It was also doubtful whether it would ever be possible to get such large issues underwritten, along with the problems of timing which plagued fixed interest stocks. The 1961 White Paper agreed that unguaranteed borrowing from the market on an industry's own credit was not a realistic alternative to the prevailing arrangements, and the 1967

Table 10.5 Nationalized industries: Analysis of amounts outstanding against statutory financing limits at 31 March 1977 (£m.)

Nationalized industry	Net government advances	Borrowing by stock issues	Temporary (and other domestic) borrowing	Borrowing abroad	Public dividend capital	Total
National Coal Board	501	—	43	368	—	912
Electricity Council and Boards	3,396	520	6	1,387	—	5,309
North of Scotland Hydroelectric Board	208	69	6	155	—	438
South of Scotland Electricity Board	462	—	4	186	—	652
British Gas Corporation	1,438	214	34	414	—	2,100
British National Oil Corporation	340	—	—	—	—	340
British Steel Corporation	712	—	173	520	879	2,284
Post Office	3,344	—	—	733	13	4,090
British Airways Board	83	—	—	134	260	477
British Railways Board	331	—	3	52	—	386
Other Boards*	495	—	13	—	—	508
Total	11,310	803	282	3,949	1,152	17,496

* British Airports Authority, British Transport Docks Board, British Waterways Board, National Freight Corporation, National Bus Company, Scottish Transport Group.

Source: The Treasury.

White Paper went along with this opinion.[32] However, in their evidence to the Select Committee on Nationalised Industries in 1968 some industries, notably electricity, expressed a desire to raise equity or fixed interest capital on the market, arguing that it would provide greater flexibility in timing and in the terms of issue so as to meet their special requirements. In practice this has not materialized along such lines but since 1973 a considerable portion of their capital finance has come from market sources (see pp. 300–4).

(b) *Exchequer advances*   The change over from direct access to the market to borrowing from the Treasury, brought about by the Finance Act 1956 was not as abrupt as appears since most of the market issues made just before this had been taken up by the authorities and financed by issuing Treasury Bills to the banking system. Under the Act the Exchequer was authorized to lend to the main nationalized industries in addition to the N.C.B. and the Post Office, while the power of undertakings to borrow were set out by their own legislative basis. Later on, this rather complex arrangement was simplified so that for each corporation one Act governs its borrowing powers (which some boards regarded as too inflexible) and authorizes the Exchequer to make advances to it. The Statutory Limits which applied at 31 March 1977 are set out in table 10.4. From its inception the N.C.B. borrowed for capital purposes from the Exchequer, but from 1965 it was empowered to borrow 'from any other person' with the Minister's consent.

Issues are made to the nationalized industries as payments from the National Loans Fund, that is, from the general financial resources of the government. Usually they take the form of long-term loans, the period for which each advance is made depending on the average life of the asset which is to be financed. In the case of electricity, gas, transport and the Post Office, loans are normally for 25 years, which is about the average life of their assets, and the funds are taken up when needed. Loans to the N.C.B. are generally for periods of 15 years, except for loans related to the provision of coal stocks which are for periods of 1–5 years only. The Coal Board also obtains temporary loans from the Treasury for the purpose of financing day-to-day transactions. Due to the pattern of payments and receipts there is a peak of temporary borrowing mid-month, while due to the seasonal nature of the coal trade more temporary money is needed in the first half of the Board's financial year. Loans are repayable in instalments or at maturity, and in the case of those subject to sinking fund provisions the funds so earmarked are left with the industry to meet financial needs.

The rate of interest, which is payable half-yearly, is fixed for the duration of a loan, and is determined at the time of the advance in relation to the rate paid by the Exchequer for market funds of comparable maturity, with rates being adjusted upwards to the nearest 0.125% to cover the costs of debt management. Interest on temporary money is related to Treasury Bill rates.[33] In the mid-1960s long-term loans were made at around 6.625–7.375%, while with the general rise in interest rates, those in 1974–5 were between 13.5%–17.375%. This upward drift, coupled with the increase in government loans outstanding from £6,510m. in March 1966 to £10,530m. in March 1974, and to £11,310m. by March 1977, caused the interest paid to the central government by public corporations to rise from £385m. to £1,024m. between 1966–74 and to £1,490m. in 1976. Interest paid to the government in 1966 was around 37% of the operating surplus of corporations, rising to 41% in 1974 but then falling back to 33% in 1976.

One problem with fixed interest loans is that if a corporation fails to earn a surplus sufficient to cover interest payments, then in the absence of a capital reconstruction, further fixed interest borrowing has to be used to pay the interest due, which merely creates greater future burdens to be placed against likely earnings. A method of avoiding this is to cease to carry forward automatically all debts on capital. This involves the creation of a form of equity capital similar to that of ordinary share capital in a limited liability company. Treasury consideration of non-redeemable Exchequer Dividend Capital dates from 1963 but the first opportunity to use it arose with the reconstruction of B.O.A.C.'s capital structure in 1966. Under this scheme the Corporation's outstanding liabilities in respect of Exchequer advances were cancelled and responsibility for B.O.A.C. stock transferred to the Exchequer. The capital eliminated was replaced by a fixed interest loan of £31m., and £35m. of Exchequer Dividend Capital on which B.O.A.C. would pay an annual dividend rather than fixed interest. The dividend was to be 'such amount as may be proposed by the Corporation and approved by the Minister with the consent of the Treasury, or such other amount as the Minister may, with the approval of the Treasury after consultation with the Corporation determine.' Indeed, in 1966–7 a dividend of 15% was paid, more than would have been due on fixed interest loans.[34] Under the Civil Aviation Act 1971 all capital amounts outstanding in respect of B.E.A. and B.O.A.C. were extinguished and an equivalent sum was advanced to the British Airways Corporation. Of this, £65m. was in the form of Public Dividend Capital, which was increased to £136m. in 1973–4 and on which a 4.5% dividend was paid; at 31 March 1977 British Airways had £260m. of Public Dividend Capital.[35]

Other industries, especially B.E.A. and British Railways, expressed an interest in getting some sort of equity capital, but the government at the time took the view that it was only 'suitable for those nationalised industries which are fully viable but which are especially subject to fluctuating returns as a result of their trading conditions, the nature of their assets, etc.'[36] It was certainly felt to be unsuitable for undertakings in regular deficit since they would never pay a dividend and Public Dividend Capital would for them be little more than an interest free, non-repayable advance.

In 1968 the British Steel Corporation proposed to the government that part of its fixed interest debt should be reconstituted as Public Dividend Capital. The Steel Corporation pointed to the fact that the fluctuating character of the industry has the consequence that

> while over the years [it] ... would be fully viable and reward the Exchequer with a good return, in some years the surplus of income over expenditure would not be sufficient to meet the full interest burden on a capital composed entirely of debt, especially if interest were charged at the high market rates now current.[37]

The main fear was that current earnings might not cover interest charges and in the absence of reserves the Corporation would then need to borrow to pay the interest. Thus, in 1969, £700m. of the Corporation's commencing capital debt of approximately £834m. was reclassified as Public Dividend Capital. The effect of the conversion was that it reduced the amount which the Corporation needed to borrow to finance its interest liability to the National Loans Fund by some £60m. in 1968-9 and £50m. in the following year.[38] No dividend was proposed by the Corporation in the next few years, while in 1972 the total of Public Dividend Capital was amended to £500m., but additions have since been made to it through Exchequer loans bringing its total of Public Dividend Capital outstanding to £879m. in March 1977. A modest gross dividend of 2% was paid in 1974-5, but since then no dividend has been paid.

(c) *Temporary borrowing* There are two main sources of domestic temporary borrowing; bank advances and loans by superannuation funds to the parent organization. All the nationalized industries possess powers to borrow temporary funds from banks and other financial institutions in order to meet day-to-day fluctuations in cash requirements and for short-term working capital needs. During recent years they have been encouraged by the Treasury to exploit all suitable private sector sources, both at home and abroad.

Up to 1956 bank borrowing by the nationalized industries was allowed to rise to the limits agreed with the banks, and then it was funded by a stock issue. This led to wide swings in bank borrowing over short periods of time. For example, at the end of August 1955 nationalized industry bank borrowing amounted to £196m., but then fell to £49m. in February, rising to £123m. in August, and finally falling back to £54m. in May 1957; thereafter it stabilized below £90m.[39] Up to about 1967 clearing bank lending to nationalized industries was around £80m. a year, but with the addition to their ranks of the Steel Corporation the demands for bank finance probably doubled. The Steel Corporation obtained credit facilities for 364 days which allowed it flexibility to repay and redraw depending on needs and market conditions. In recent years of the temporary borrowing outstanding at 31 March as given in *Loans from the National Loans Fund*, about half has been on account of steel; this has been required to finance large stock levels, sharp increases in raw material prices, and a greater reluctance on the part of debtors to settle. The peak of bank lending to the public corporations was reached in 1974 with a figure of £772m. and it arose from the liquidity problems of price restraint and reduced assistance from the central government. By 1975 the sector had become a net repayer of loans, but this creditor status only lasted for one year since it borrowed over £450m. in 1976.

Lending to the nationalized industries has always been exempted from the numerous ceilings on bank advances which applied to private sector borrowing. Short-term loans are made at 0.5% or 1% over the Syndicated Base Rate (a rate agreed by the banks from time to time in the light of their declared base rates), and are covered as to principal and interest by government guarantee, which is renewed periodically up to a stated limit for each undertaking. Generally each industry maintains accounts with more than one bank, while their borrowing requirements are shared between banks in agreed proportions.

Borrowing from superannuation funds, within prescribed limits, was generally around a few million pounds a year in the 1960s, but by 1974–6 the amount involved had increased to about £35m. per year for all public corporations. Other less important sources of funds noted in the statement *Loans from the National Loans Fund* include loans from short-term money markets, for example, the local authority loan market and the inter-bank market (where money is also put out occasionally) and savings bank deposits. Acceptance credits are used by the Steel Corporation, with a Treasury guarantee attached, and these are in the form of 90-day bills of exchange being used for export transactions. For payment of inter-industry deliveries of products bills of exchange have been used, increasingly since 1967, which are discounted in the London Discount Market.[40] Finally, British Rail accommodate a large part of their investment requirement by leasing, and short-term loans are raised for this purpose by a subsidiary of the Railways Board. Between 1972 and 1974 the majority of new stock acquired by British Rail was leased from the private sector, while the total leasing activity of the nationalized industries in 1976–7 was in the region of £120m. worth of equipment.

(d) *Borrowing abroad*   While B.O.A.C. had borrowed from the International Bank for Reconstruction and Development and the Export–Import Bank of the United States for financing purchases of American aircraft and spares, it was not until 1968 that the main nationalized industries were given power to borrow foreign currencies for long periods to finance their investment programme and for the repayment of domestic debts. Following a review of public corporations and local authorities borrowing put in hand in 1967, and with the defence of sterling very much in mind, the government early in 1969 introduced forward exchange cover on medium- and long-term borrowing abroad (loans of five years or more). With the floating of sterling in 1972 it was withdrawn, but brought back again in 1973. Under the scheme both interest and principal are 'irrevocably and unconditionally guaranteed by the Treasury', which means that if the pound falls on the foreign exchange market the extra cost of repaying the borrowed currency will be met by the Treasury. The Bank of England controls the timing and terms of borrowing under the scheme.[41] Where such cover is taken the loans are included in the balance sheets at the amount of their sterling proceeds; in other cases they are included in the accounts at the rate of exchange prevailing at the end of the financial year.

Electricity and gas made their first borrowing in 1970, the Post Office in 1971 and the N.C.B. in 1974 (financial years). Such borrowing was encouraged by the authorities since the self-financing ratio showed little signs of rising sharply in the face of the declared policy of price restraint. They were also anxious to keep down lending from the National Loans Fund, while borrowing abroad could be serviced more cheaply than domestic loans due to the interest margin in favour of external rates. Also, since 1973 the authorities are reported to have encouraged foreign borrowing by both public corporations and local authorities as a means of boosting the foreign exchange reserves; during 1973 and 1974 the nationalized industries foreign currency borrowing amounted to $2,010m. and $1,840m. respectively.[42] Total borrowing outstanding increased from £2,256m. in 1975 to £3,949m. in March 1977 (for details of the industries involved see table 10.6), while the total borrowing outstanding with exchange cover as at 28 February 1977 amounted to $9.6b. In addition the corporations themselves were eager to achieve greater flexibility as to the terms and conditions of borrowing since economic financing was increasingly important when they were pressured to pursue a more commercial approach.

The volume of foreign borrowing during the financial years 1968 to March 1977 is given in table 10.6; the end column gives the amounts outstanding for the main corporations as at 31 March 1977. From 2% of outstanding borrowing in March 1971, borrowing abroad increased sharply to represent 22.6% of total borrowing at 31 March 1977. Electricity has been the largest borrower, followed by the Post Office, steel and the gas industry. Most of the borrowing in the period 1969–73 was done in Germany, Luxembourg, and Switzerland, with public issues and placings being used. More recently use was made of the Euro-dollar market where the British Steel Corporation raised $240m. in 1974. In 1976 $175m. was raised for three industries by issues on the Euro-dollar bond market, while the Electricity Council, Post Office, and the National Water Council arranged a medium-term syndicated bank credit amounting to $1.0b. Some of these foreign loans have maturities of up to 25 years, but the bulk of the borrowing has been done on a short- to medium-term basis.

A significant feature of such loans is that the interest cost is below that of comparable funds from the National Loans Fund. Under the initial scheme in 1973 the charge made for the exchange cover was such as to allow an interest rate advantage of 0.5% compared with National Loan Fund money. Later the scheme was modified with the object of inducing borrowers to secure the finest terms so that the interest benefit to the

Table 10.6 Borrowing abroad: Amounts borrowed during financial year and sums outstanding at 31 March 1977 (£m.)

Nationalized industries	1968 to 1972	1973	1974	1975*	1976*	1977*	Amount outstanding at 31 March 1977
National Coal Board	—	—	26	35	122	184	368
Electricity Council and Boards	36	24	587	114	100	530	1,387
North of Scotland Hydroelectric Board	3	—	16	10	77	40	155
South of Scotland Electricity Board	6	14	66	59	16	45	186
British Gas Corporation	88	21	110	—	162	20	414
British Steel Corporation	—	—	47	218	178	215	520
Post Office	11	4	210	209	37	245	733
British Airways Board	117	−16	7	2	−22	22	134
British Railways Board	20	17	−6	−1	6	44	52

* Figures of 'Provisional out-turn' given in *Financial Statement and Budget Report*.

Sources: Loans from the National Loans Fund, Financial Statement and Budget Report, H.M.S.O.

borrower was about 1%. For example, the National Coal Board reported for 1974–5 that it made several foreign currency borrowings on which the average rate of interest was 8.9%. Even after the addition of an element to cover the Treasury charges for exchange guarantees and underwriting, bringing the total cost of servicing the loans to 11.2%, there was still a saving of approximately 1% compared with rates from the National Loans Fund. The Board estimated that by borrowing from abroad rather than the National Loan Fund it reaped a saving of £3.6m. on interest costs. In the case of a large Euro-dollar loan made by the British Gas Corporation in 1973–4 an additional feature was incorporated whereby the loan was made at a floating credit rate subject to prevailing interest rates in the short-term Euro-dollar market, but also embodying a maximum average interest rate of 10.5%. The Gas Corporation estimated that the use of foreign funds achieved savings of 'several million pounds'.[43]

Notes

1 A full list of public corporations in existence at 31 December 1966 is given in Rita Maurice (ed.), *National Accounts Statistics; Sources and Methods*, London, 1968, pp. 249–50. For the purpose of the annual *Financial Statement* and *Loans from the National Loans Fund* the term nationalized industry embraces the following boards: N.C.B., Electricity Council and Boards, North of Scotland Hydro-Electric Board, South of Scotland Electricity Board, British Gas Corporation, British Steel Corporation, Post Office, British Airways Board, British Airports Authority, British Railways Board, British Transport Docks Board, British Waterways Board, Transport Holding Company, National Freight Corporation, National Bus Company, and the Scottish Transport Group; the British National Oil Corporation and the National Enterprise Board are now also included.

2 E. Davies, *National Enterprise; the Development of the Public Corporation*, London, 1946, p. 24. See also W. A. Robson (ed.), *Public Enterprise*, London, 1937.

3 The British Steel Corporation acquired 14 major companies and 200 subsidiaries, including about 40 overseas.

4 For details of these legislative changes see W. A. Robson, *Nationalised Industry and Public Ownership*, London, 1962, ch. 2.

5 For pre-war compensation practices see Davies, op. cit., ch. 8.

6 H. G. Webb, *The Economics of the Nationalised Industries*, London, 1973, pp. 5–7.

7 Full details of all the issues made are given in the *Finance Accounts* for 1952. This large programme of issuing required considerable official support since the institutions were not very enthusiastic. The National Debt Commissioners absorbed well over £300m. during 1948–51; see Pember and Boyle, *British Government Securities in the Twentieth Century*, London, 1950, for details of individual stocks and holdings of the N.D.C. at various dates.

8 Gross fixed capital formation consists of investment in vehicles, ships and aircraft, dwellings and other new buildings etc., and plant and machinery. During the period 1954–8 plant and machinery comprised some 53% of annual investment by public corporations; in the early 1970s the average annual figure had risen to 63%.

9 *The Financial and Economic Obligations of the Nationalised Industries*, Cmnd 1337, para. 4 (1961 White Paper).

10 ibid., para. 5.

11 For a discussion of this practice in comparison with commercial methods see

R. W. S. Pryke, *Public Enterprise in Practice*, London, 1971, pp. 178–9.

12 ibid., pp. 194–6. In the United States depreciation is not charged until the investment has come to fruition and the plant is in service.

13 1961 White Paper, para. 9.

14 Maurice, op. cit., pp. 383–4.

15 For details see Pryke, op. cit., pp. 186–8. Both air corporations reported in 1970 that their historic cost depreciation exceeded the amount which it would be necessary to set aside if they were working on a replacement cost basis.

16 1961 White Paper, para. 7.

17 ibid., para. 9.

18. ibid., para. 10. Only the Post Office and B.E.A. produced rates of over 6% in 1959.

19 For a discussion of this point see Pryke, op. cit., pp. 197–9; more useful comparisons might be with similar activities in the private sector, where they are discernible, or with similar private sector activity abroad.

20. *Nationalised Industries: A Review of Economic and Financial Objectives*, Cmnd 3437, para. 4 (1967 White Paper).

21 ibid., para. 10. The test rate of discount was different from the rate of interest which the nationalized industries paid on borrowing from the Exchequer, since they borrowed at rates reflecting government credit. See also Select Committee on Nationalised Industries, 1967–8, *Ministerial Control of the Nationalised Industries*, vol. iii (H.C. 371–III), App. 7, pp. 27–8.

22 1967 White Paper, para. 21.

23 For detailed comments on targets and results see the Annual Reports of the industries, and also Select Committee on Nationalised Industries, 1973–4, *Capital Investment Procedures* (H.C. 65) pp. xxiii–xxviii. Recent targets have been expressed on a *net* rather than *gross* basis so as to avoid the complications arising from different depreciation practices at a time of rapidly rising prices.

24 Select Committee on Nationalised Industries, 1967–8, *Ministerial Control of the Nationalised Industries*, vol. 1 (H.C. 371–2), paras 602–10; see also C. D. Foster, *Politics, Finance and the Role of Economics*, London, 1971, pp. 149–62.

25 ibid., paras 604–5. In the Capital Account of the Central Government Sector capital reconstructions appear as capital grants, i.e., notional payments to public corporations in order to repay government loans which have been formally written-off.

26 Full details of write-offs are given in the Annual Reports of the corporations affected; they are also given in the Notes to the Central Government Capital Account in the Blue Book.

27 Committee on the Working of the Monetary System, *Report*, Cmnd 827, paras 86–7 (Radcliffe Committee, 1959).

28 For details of individual issues see the annual *Finance Accounts* and Pember and Boyle, op. cit.

29 Webb, op. cit., pp. 138–9.

30 Foster, op. cit., ch. 14.

31 Radcliffe Committee, *Report*, para. 593.

32 The Select Committee on Nationalised Industries, 1967–8, op. cit., agreed that unguaranteed borrowing would be unrealistic. With government credit involved there would always be an implied guarantee. They estimated that unguaranteed borrowing would be 0.5% higher. Several corporations had powers to borrow on such terms but none had done so since the war. In the inter-war years the Central Electricity Board issued £53.5m. of stock without Treasury guarantee. It did this to obtain greater independence of the Treasury but it was compelled to offer 0.75% more interest and the stock was issued at discount. Large amounts of its early issues were left with the underwriters; 5–5.5% morally backed by the State but unguaranteed by the Treasury, was not enough for investors; Davies, op. cit., pp. 140–2.

33 Select Committee on Nationalised Industries, 1967–8, op. cit., vol. 2, Treasury Evidence, p. 6.

34 Select Committee on Nationalised Industries; 1967–8, op. cit., vol. 1, paras 611–13.

35 Select Committee on Nationalised Industries (Sub-Committee A), 1974–5 (H.C. 389–i), British Airways, *Minutes of Evidence*, pp. 8–9.

36 Select Committee on Nationalised Industries, 1967–8, op. cit., vol. 2, Treasury Evidence, p. 11.

37 British Steel Corporation, *Annual Report*, 1967–8, para. 1.10.

38 *Loans from the National Loans Fund, 1969–70*, Cmnd 3995, p. 4.

39 Bank of England, *Statistical Abstract*, no. 1, 1970, table 11. See also *The Economist*, 20 June 1953, p. 867.

40　In 1974 the Gas Corporation used trade bills to finance payments to natural gas suppliers whenever favourable conditions prevailed in the money market. In 1976 public corporations borrowed over £60m. using commercial bills.

41　See Bank of England, Annual Report and Accounts, February 1974, p. 20, for details of the schemes of exchange cover.

42　*The Times*, 27 January 1975. Detailed lists of borrowings are periodically given in Written Answers in *Hansard*.

43　British Gas Corporation, Annual Report 1973–4, March 1974.

11 Sources and uses of funds 1952–1976

one should not push too far the association between specific uses and sources of funds.
SIMON KUZNETS

The purpose of this chapter is to present a survey of the main trends in the sources and uses of funds over most of the post-war years for industrial and commercial companies. The period covered by the tables 11.1 to 11.5 is 1952 to 1976; 1952 is taken as the starting point since estimates for several components in the tables are only available from that date onwards.[1] An additional reason is that by then most of the major nationalization schemes had been implemented and the effects on the size of the company sector resolved. The figures used are derived from the National Income Blue Book series for industrial and commercial companies, although some items are only available for all companies. The sector consists broadly of all corporate bodies other than public corporations, banks and other leading financial institutions, and agricultural companies. That is, it covers bodies which have the features of corporate status, private control and a policy of making profits. However, some fringe activities are included in the sector figures, for example, trade associations, and certain central government, grant-aided bodies serving industry, such as the British National Export Council, British Travel Association, and industrial training boards.[2] Coverage has changed over time due to nationalization, the reclassification of companies to the banking sector, and liquidations, etc. The most significant change was the enlargement of the sector in 1953 with the de-nationalization of steel, and later, its reduction by the re-nationalization of the industry in July 1967.

In principle the national income account figures relate to all industrial and commercial companies resident in the U.K. The accounts are consolidated for such companies so that inter-company payments do not appear in the figures. Also the figures relate only to the U.K. activities of companies and do not include overseas operations; certain transactions between parent companies and overseas subsidiaries, such as unremitted profits, direct investment, etc., are shown explicitly. For the purposes in hand this series has several advantages in that domestic activity is shown separately; all industrial and commercial companies are included, although it is estimated that the 4,000 largest ones probably account for about three-quarters of total company profits; the figures relate to calendar years as against a variety of accounting data; and estimates are available for depreciation at current replacement cost and for stock appreciation.[3]

Some of the drawbacks should be briefly noted. Information is not drawn from a common source so that quality is variable. In some cases estimates are only available for all companies (including financial companies), so that items for the industrial and commercial group are residuals after identifying the financial companies' component. Even then, the identified financial group figure is not comprehensive, so that some financial activities remain reflected in the industrial and commercial figures. Changes in some financial assets and liabilities are estimated, being residuals for the company sector after deducting identified transactions by all other sectors, and for earlier years the errors are greater. Not all financial assets and liabilities are covered by the statistics, the most important omission being the item for domestic trade debtors and creditors. The unidentified item is occasionally quite large reflecting partly errors and omissions. For all that the broad outlines are probably correct and there is consolation in one official comment that they 'would not be much changed even if the statistics were complete'.

The other main series for the post-war period is that for large quoted and unquoted companies prepared by the Department of Industry. This is compiled from the published accounts of listed and unlisted companies and is confined to companies operating mainly in the U.K. in the areas of manufacturing, distribution, construction, transport and certain other services. Since the analysis is based on the consolidated accounts of groups of companies it thereby includes the activities of overseas subsidiaries. By being drawn from the comprehensive source of company accounts it is possible to construct a balanced picture of the sources and uses of funds. However, certain drawbacks apply to the series. Firstly, some degree of window-dressing may creep into some of the items, for example, bank loans and overdrafts are reduced temporarily at balance sheet dates. Secondly, figures relate to accounting years so that the time period covered ranges over nearly two years. Thirdly, various adjustments are made to the figures due to consolidation which may render them not entirely precise. Finally, a further complication is that the population of companies covered by the analysis changes from year to year.[4]

The broad features portrayed by both series are very similar and this follows since large quoted and unquoted companies dominate the sources and uses of funds by all companies; they are thought to account for something like $\frac{1}{2}$ to $\frac{2}{3}$ of the net assets of all industrial and commercial companies. Due to differences in detail precise comparison between the two series is not possible, but some references will be made below to changes recorded in the Department of Industry series where such movements have been in marked contrast to those displayed by the national income series.[5]

The component parts of sources and uses

On the sources side (see table 11.1), the following constitute the main internal items. Gross trading profits represent earnings from production and trade in the U.K. Rent and non-trading income covers only such income as arises in the U.K. and is drawn from rent on property used by other sectors (intra-company rent is omitted) and interest on financial assets such as public sector debt. Income from abroad, estimated from balance of payments returns (and net of depreciation provisions) includes the following; income on portfolio investment, that is, remitted interest and dividends; other investment income which comes largely from the earnings of U.K. oil companies and interest obtained by companies on trade credits granted; and income from direct investment, that is, the profits of non-resident branches and subsidiaries, whether remitted or not. However, since unremitted profits of U.K. subsidiaries abroad are not available for the finance of fixed assets at home this part of foreign income is treated as an outflow and in table 11.2 it appears, therefore, as an item of capital expenditure, that is, as an outflow in intra-company investment overseas in the finance accounts.

As to external funds the following are the important items. Capital grants in the 1950s consisted largely of receipts of war damage compensation, while in the early 1960s they were mainly central government grants to assist industry. From 1967 receipts of investment grants became the largest component within this item. The entry 'overseas investment in U.K. companies' may be taken as a measure of the unremitted profits of overseas branches and subsidiaries in the U.K. and appears as an inflow in the finance accounts of the company sector representing long-term investment in this country. In the appropriation account it forms part of profits due to overseas parent companies.

Table 11.1   Industrial and commercial companies: Sources of funds (£m.: % of total sources; averages of periods)

Year	Internal					External						Total sources
	Gross trading profits[a]	%	Other current income[b]	Total	%	Capital grants	Overseas investment in U.K. companies[c]	Borrowing/liquid assets	Total	%		
1952	2,271	78	749	3,020	103	32	8	−135	−95	−3		2,925
1953	2,438	77	720	3,158	100	42	13	−62	−7	−1		3,151
1954	2,612	73	753	3,365	94	23	50	150	223	6		3,588
1955	2,884	64	807	3,691	82	26	97	678	801	18		4,492
	(2,551)	(72)	(757)	(3,308)	(94)	(31)	(42)	(157)	(230)	(6)		(3,538)
1956	2,922	70	912	3,834	92	18	114	185	317	8		4,151
1957	3,115	72	971	4,086	94	11	96	149	256	6		4,342
1958	3,183	69	1,072	4,255	92	10	143	211	364	8		4,619
1959	3,443	68	1,112	4,555	89	7	117	412	536	11		5,091
1960	3,869	66	1,092	4,961	85	15	155	707	877	15		5,838
	(3,306)	(69)	(1,032)	(4,338)	(90)	(12)	(125)	(333)	(470)	(10)		(4,808)
1961	3,734	65	1,145	4,879	85	9	141	698	848	15		5,727
1962	3,708	64	1,226	4,934	85	12	138	694	844	15		5,778
1963	4,072	66	1,338	5,410	88	9	200	514	723	12		6,133
1964	4,602	62	1,419	6,021	81	17	116	1,239	1,372	19		7,393
1965	4,795	63	1,590	6,385	83	20	200	1,049	1,269	17		7,654
	(4,182)	(64)	(1,344)	(5,525)	(84)	(13)	(159)	(839)	(1,011)	(16)		(6,537)
1966	4,654	64	1,463	6,117	85	26	253	816	1,095	15		7,212
1967	4,819	66	1,553	6,372	88	236	316	327	879	12		7,251
1968	5,157	60	1,916	7,073	82	454	378	729	1,561	18		8,634
1969	5,573	56	2,268	7,841	79	598	380	1,155	2,133	21		9,974
1970	5,558	51	2,578	8,136	75	526	600	1,626	2,752	25		10,888
	(5,152)	(59)	(1,956) (22)	(7,108)	(81)	(368)	(385)	(931)	(1,684)	(19)		(8,792)
1971	6,353	59	2,882	9,235	86	595	656	218	1,469	14		10,704
1972	7,098	57	3,348	10,446	83	409	423	1,237	2,069	17		12,515
1973	7,498	44	5,574	13,072	76	373	1,022	2,748	4,143	24		17,215
1974	6,571	32	7,684	14,255	70	364	1,630	4,131	6,125	30		20,380
1975	7,315	47	6,650	13,965	89	442	1,418	−122	1,738	11		15,703
1976	9,255	44	8,117	17,372	82	401	1,605	1,852	3,858	18		21,230
	(7,348)	(45)	(5,709) (35)	(13,057)	(80)	(431)	(1,126)	(1,677)	(3,224)	(20)		(16,291)

[a] Net of stock appreciation, but before capital depreciation.
[b] Rent and non-trading income in U.K., plus current income from abroad.
[c] This item is derived from balance of payments account figures of *private* direct investment in the U.K.; since only part of the sum relates to the unremitted profits of industrial and commercial companies it is not possible to subtract it from Gross Trading Profits, thus leaving a very small element of double-counting.

Source: National Income Blue Books.

In tables 11.3 and 11.4 borrowing (from banks, the capital market and other sources) is given net of acquisition of identified liquid assets (as presented in the financial accounts for the industrial and commercial companies sector). The former is a source of funds, while the acquisition of liquid assets may be taken as a use of funds, or a run down as a source of funds. In this case it has been treated as a (negative) source of funds for the following reasons. Companies accumulate liquid assets to finance short-term fluctuations in their total payments and receipts, and increases on that account constitute a use of funds. However, during the 1950s companies in aggregate seem to have drawn down their liquid assets to meet the needs of long-term capital expenditure so that reductions in liquid asset holdings became an important source of funds at a time when internal funds declined in relative importance.[6] Further, over recent years, especially 1971–4, it was very apparent that company borrowing, particularly from the banks, was used to build up liquid assets to an unprecedented degree. Thus, the increase in the flow of external funds into the company sector was accompanied by the expansion of financial assets held by companies thereby increasing their claims on other sectors. It would seem desirable, therefore, in order to measure the net absorption of funds by companies from other sectors, to take external borrowing net of their financial asset expansion. On the above grounds borrowing is presented net of the acquisition of liquid assets.

To turn to the uses of funds. Dividends and interest are self-explanatory items; the latter includes not only interest on capital but also that on short-term borrowing as well. Intra-company dividend and interest payments are excluded. It should be noted that prior to the introduction of corporation tax in 1965 dividends were given in the national income accounts as net of tax, while companies did not have to account to the Inland Revenue for the tax withheld. After the 1965 changes companies continued to pay dividends net of tax but they had to account to the Inland Revenue for the amount of tax deducted, and the amounts thus given are on a gross basis. With the 1973 changes income tax is no longer charged on dividends and companies are again recording dividends net of tax. Profits and taxes due abroad, both items of current expenditure, relate to the activities of U.K. branches and subsidiaries of foreign firms, and to overseas branches and subsidiaries of U.K. firms. Profits due abroad net of U.K. tax are the counterpart of overseas investment in U.K. companies in the sources of funds table. Taxes paid abroad are those paid to overseas governments and authorities on the income of overseas branches and subsidiaries of British companies and on the income from overseas portfolio investment.

The figures of U.K. taxes given in table 11.2 relate to tax payments on

Table 11.2 Industrial and commercial companies: Uses of funds £m: % of total uses; (averages of period)

Year	Current expenditure						Capital expenditure			
	Dividends %	Other interest %	Profits and taxes due abroad %	U.K. taxes[a]	Total	%	Identified capital expenditure	%	Unidentified items	Total uses
1952	476	135		1,283	1,894	65	692	24	339	2,925
1953	543	143		1,173	1,853	59	930	30	368	3,151
1954	601	150		1,059	1,801	50	1,280	36	507	3,588
1955	662	188		1,235	2,054	46	1,482	33	965	4,492
	(570) (16)	(154) (4)		(1,187) (33)	(1,911) (54)		(1,096) (31)		(545)	(3,552)
1956	682	214		1,176	2,072	50	1,750	42	329	4,151
1957	729	235		1,304	2,268	52	1,915	44	159	4,342
1958	769	249		1,410	2,428	53	1,829	40	362	4,619
1959	878	267		1,398	2,543	50	2,215	44	333	5,091
1960	1,096	332		1,071	2,499	43	2,821	48	518	5,838
	(831) (17)	(259) (5)		(1,272) (26)	(2,362) (49)		(2,106) (44)		(340)	(4,808)
1961	1,232	378		1,130	2,740	48	2,806	49	181	5,727
1962	1,223	388		1,355	2,966	51	2,451	42	361	5,778
1963	1,300	408	527	678	2,913	47	2,670	44	550	6,133
1964	1,339	612	678	566	3,195	43	3,686	50	512	7,393
1965	1,586	738	735	486	3,545	46	3,672	48	437	7,654
	(1,336) (20)	(505) (8)	(1,231)	(18)	(3,072) (47)		(3,057) (48)		(408)	(6,537)
1966	1,509	896	658	625	3,688	51	3,220	45	304	7,251
1967	1,463	912	720	941	4,036	56	3,244	45	-29	7,212
1968	1,434	1,036	1,016	919	4,405	51	3,729	43	500	8,634
1969	1,554	1,187	1,078	1,013	4,832	48	4,208	42	934	9,974
1970	1,378	1,268	1,363	1,297	5,306	49	4,665	43	917	10,888
	(1,468) (17)	(1,060) (12)	(967) (11)	(959) (11)	(4,453) (51)		(3,813) (43)		(525)	(8,792)
1971	1,530	1,286	1,731	1,104	5,651	53	4,388	41	665	10,704
1972	1,524	1,474	2,141	1,082	6,221	50	5,224	42	1,070	12,515
1973	1,638	2,328	3,024	1,156	8,146	47	8,895	52	174	17,215
1974	1,469	3,303	4,536	2,022	11,330	55	9,274	46	-224	20,380

Table 11.2 Industrial and commercial companies: Uses of funds £m.:% of total uses; (averages of period) *continued.*

Year						%		%		%	
1975	1,608	3,272	3,861	1,263	10,004	64	6,402	41	−703	4	15,703
1976	1,895	3,735	4,671	887	11,188	53	10,258	48	−216	4	21,230
	(1,611)	(10) (2,566)	(16) (3,327)	(20) (8) (1,252)	(8,756)	(54)	(7,407)	(45)	(128)		(16,291)

a Less additions to tax reserves.

Source: National Income Blue Books.

Table 11.3 Industrial and commercial companies: Financing of capital expenditure (£m.: % of total capital expenditure; averages of periods)

Year	Capital expenditure					Financed by:					
	Gross fixed investment	Stock building[a]	Other identified[b]	Unidentified items	Total	Savings[c]	%	Borrowing/liquid assets	%	Other[d]	%
1952	605	−63	150	339	1,031	1,126	109	−135	−13	40	4
1953	640	65	225	368	1,298	1,305	101	−62	−5	55	4
1954	750	200	330	507	1,787	1,564	88	150	8	73	4
1955	920	352	210	965	2,447	1,646	67	678	28	123	5
	(729)	(138)	(229)	(545)	(1,641)	(1,410)	(86)	(158)	(10)	(73)	(4)
1956	1,160	235	355	329	2,079	1,762	85	185	9	132	6
1957	1,335	185	395	159	2,074	1,818	88	149	7	107	5
1958	1,370	64	395	362	2,191	1,827	83	211	10	153	7
1959	1,426	134	655	333	2,548	2,012	79	412	16	124	5
1960	1,622	569	630	518	3,339	2,462	74	707	21	170	5
	(1,383)	(237)	(486)	(340)	(2,446)	(1,976)	(81)	(333)	(14)	(137)	(5)
1961	1,886	270	650	181	2,987	2,139	72	698	23	150	5
1962	1,873	43	535	361	2,812	1,968	70	694	25	150	5
1963	1,833	189	648	550	3,220	2,497	77	514	16	209	7
1964	2,288	654	744	512	4,198	2,826	67	1,239	30	133	3
1965	2,436	457	779	437	4,109	2,840	69	1,049	26	220	5
	(2,063)	(323)	(671)	(408)	(3,465)	(2,454)	(71)	(839)	(24)	(172)	(5)

Table 11.3 Industrial and commercial companies: Financing of capital expenditure (£m.: % of total capital expenditure; averages of periods)—*Continued*

Year	Capital expenditure					Financed by:					
	Gross fixed investment[a]	Stock building[a]	Other identified[b]	Unidentified items	Total	Savings[c]	%	Borrowing· liquid assets	%	Other[d]	%
1966	2,423	270	527	304	3,524	2,429	69	816	23	279	8
1967	2,362	208	674	−29	3,215	2,336	73	327	10	552	17
1968	2,614	343	772	500	4,229	2,668	63	729	17	832	20
1969	2,985	358	865	934	5,142	3,009	59	1,155	22	978	19
1970	3,350	441	874	917	5,582	2,830	51	1,626	29	1,126	20
	(2,747)	(324)	(742)	(525)	(4,338)	(2,654)	(61)	(931)	(22)	(753)	(17)
1971	3,468	−74	994	665	5,053	3,584	71	218	4	1,251	25
1972	3,900	−126	1,450	1,070	6,294	4,225	67	1,237	20	832	13
1973	4,825	1,211	2,859	174	9,069	4,926	54	2,748	30	1,395	16
1974	6,078	1,206	1,990	−224	9,050	2,925	32	4,131	46	1,994	22
1975	6,983	−1,862	1,281	−703	5,699	3,961	70	−122	−2	1,860	32
1976	7,745	−137	2,650	−216	10,042	6,184	62	1,852	18	2,006	20
	(5,499)	(36)	(1,871)	(128)	(7,534)	(4,301)	(57)	(1,677)	(22)	(1,556)	(21)

[a] Value of physical increase in stocks and work in progress.
[b] Investment abroad, purchases of U.K. company securities, and changes in hire purchase credit extended.
[c] Net of stock appreciation: includes dividend and tax reserves.
[d] Government grants to, and overseas investment in, U.K. companies.

Source: National Income Blue Books.

income less additions to tax reserves. The latter is the excess of accruals in the year over the tax payments, and has been credited to company savings. The other main financial item relates to the purchase of U.K. company securities (included in 'other identified' in table 11.3), which involves cash payments to other sectors of the economy so as to acquire control of other companies. Also included with it is the item 'changes in hire purchase credit extended', but it is of a very small order. Omitted from the tables by way of precise figures are subscriptions by companies to charities, but it has been included in the unidentified item as a use of funds; the sums involved are relatively small, the annual average for 1966–76 being £37.5m.

The remaining item in the uses of funds is capital expenditure covering gross fixed investment and stockbuilding. Fixed capital formation represents additions to physical productive assets, such as, machinery, equipment, buildings and land. These assets yield a continuous service and a stream of returns beyond the period of account in which they are acquired by the firm. Stocks and work in progress represent additions to completed goods not yet sold, materials and fuel not yet used, and partly finished products awaiting completion. In table 11.3 the figures are for the value of physical changes in the volume of stocks and work in progress. The item is not given on the basis of book value changes since it is deemed that appreciation in stock value does not arise from trading activity in the period given. Companies in their accounting procedures strike profits after valuing opening and closing stocks at the lower of cost or market value, and generally assume that stocks are used on a 'first in first out' basis. As a result the valuation of opening and closing stocks may reflect price increases. Stock appreciation thus represents capital gains from holding stocks when prices rise, presenting companies with an additional tax liability. Adding back stock appreciation would merely enlarge the savings item on the sources side, while on the uses side it would be balanced by taking book values of changes in stocks and work in progress rather than changes in physical quantities.

Trends in the sources of funds

As can be seen from table 11.1 total internal funds as a percentage of total sources fell from 94% (annual average) during 1952–5 to 80% in 1971–6. There was a corresponding increase in the amount of external funds used, which largely took the form of borrowing from banks and the capital market. While grants declined in importance up to the mid-1960s, from 1966 they increased greatly in size. Much larger increases took place in the item 'overseas investment in U.K. companies', which rose faster than total sources in recent years, reaching 7% of all sources in 1971–6 (see p. 322).

Within internal funds, other current income increased in volume and in relative importance from the mid-1960s. In the period from 1952–5 to 1961–5 it represented around 21% of total sources. By 1976 it rose fivefold on the 1964 level, constituting 35% of total sources for 1971–6, part of this increase arising from the depreciation of sterling. On the other hand, the trend in the contribution of gross trading profits to total sources has been distinctly downwards, from 72% in 1952–5 to 45% in 1971–6. This reflects the smaller share of total domestic income taken by industrial and commercial companies over the period as a whole. For example, during 1952–5 gross trading profits represented 16.5% of total domestic income (before adjusting for stock appreciation), while after the adjustment it was 16.6%. However, in the 1971–6 period the percentage had fallen to 14%, but taking the figures less stock appreciation the portion falls to 10% while for 1975 it fell to 7.8% (calculated on the basis of profits less depreciation the figures make very depressing reading; the share of net profits in net domestic income fell from 12.9% in 1965 to 4.5% in 1976). The counterpart to this development is the rise in the proportion of total income taken by employment which increased from 66% for 1952–5 to 67.8% for 1971–6. This may be taken as an indication of a change from the relatively easy conditions of the 1950s and early 1960s to the more competitive atmosphere of the late 1960s and 1970s, coupled with the operation latterly of price restraint policies.

While the trend of the portion of internal to total sources is downward for the entire post-war years, there have been marked cyclical patterns within it. Such fluctuations occurred in other current income, but they are much more pronounced in the case of gross trading profits. The behaviour of profits follows from that of output. In an expansionary phase of a production cycle output and selling prices have tended to rise faster than costs, particularly labour costs, and correspondingly profits have grown rapidly. As shown in table 11.1 (p. 310) between 1954–5, 1959–60, 1963–4, 1967–8, and 1972–3 the growth of profits was large with rises of £272m., £426m., £530m., £416m., and £400m., respectively. (One of the largest profit increases took place in 1970–1 and 1975–6, periods of stagnant production when prices rose at faster rates than material costs.) In periods when there has been a slowing down of the growth of output with consequent rising unit costs, profit margins have declined and the rate of profit increase has suffered, while on occasions profits have actually fallen. This happened in 1961–2, 1966, 1969, and most spectacularly in the severe recession of 1974 when gross trading profits represented less than a third of total sources of funds.

Taking the percentages of gross trading profits to total sources (see table 11.1) it is noticeable in periods when profits have risen that their contribution to the total supply of funds has contracted most. With the exception of 1974 this pattern can be seen in 1954–5, 1959–60, 1963–4, 1967–8, and 1972–3. It arises because expenditure in such years has risen more rapidly than profits and hence the resort to more external financing. In periods when profits have been stagnant or falling their share of total sources was more or less maintained, with the exception of 1974. Apparently at the end of a recession in output profits tend to increase somewhat as a proportion of total sources probably because with depressed expectations expenditure on fixed investment moves very slowly with a sluggish response to rising output.

It is worth noting that the decline of profits as a proportion of total domestic income is matched by a similar trend in the rates of return on capital employed by industrial and commercial companies. The measures taken are those of net trading income at historic or replacement costs (gross trading profits plus rent less capital consumption at historic or replacement costs), with further adjustments for stock appreciation. The denominator is net capital stock (fixed assets) at historic or replacement costs plus book value of stocks.[7] The rate of return at historic costs fell from 18.8% in 1960 to 16% in 1965 and to 14.1% in 1970, and following a short recovery to 17.6% in 1973 it fell to 16.3% in 1976.[8] The fall in the rate of return in the 1960s, which contrasts with the rising trend of the inter-war years (see Chapter 1), may have been the result of several influences. It is possible that firms engaged in excessive investment induced by very generous investment allowances, with an accompanying exhaustion of profitable opportunities. The periodic cycles of reflation and deflation may have prevented the economy from expanding in line with business expectations, giving rise to costly overcapacity. In addition, it might have proved difficult for firms to obtain the necessary supplies of skilled labour to use available capacity to the fullest extent. It is also possible that firms did not secure increases in average productivity, which technical progress promised, because of the failure to obtain the full co-operation of the labour force in adopting new equipment and methods. Abroad, industry faced stronger international competition as tariff barriers were taken down. It is also conceivable that there may have been a willingness on the part of savers to accept lower returns.[9] The rise in recent years, however, is somewhat illusory. Rates of return based on book values overstate the rate when prices are rising, since assets valued mainly at historic cost do not fully reflect changing prices, with a similar bias in profits. However, if rates of return are calculated at replacement cost the trend is downwards throughout the 1960s, from 13.5% in 1960 to 10.1%

in 1970 with a minor recovery in 1973 to 10.8%, falling to 7% in 1976. With further adjustment for stock appreciation rates of return fall sharply from 1968 onwards, dropping to 3.3% in 1976, a performance linked to depressed home demand and the persistent attempts made to keep down prices despite rising costs, initially by an appeal for voluntary restraint and later by the imposition of statutory control (see Chapter 8).[10]

Trends in the uses of funds

The main trend discernible in table 11.2 (p. 312) is that current expenditure as a proportion of total uses declined during the 1950s and early 1960s, while the percentage of resources committed to capital expenditure correspondingly rose. From 1966 the trend is reversed. The main reason for the pattern of events in the former period is that a declining share of current expenditure was absorbed by tax. In table 11.2 profits and taxes due abroad and U.K. taxes are given together for 1952–62, and as a percentage of total uses these fall during the periods from 1952–5 to 1961–5 due to the reduction in U.K. tax liability. This arose because internal income (net of interest) upon which tax is levied did not rise as fast as total sources. Also, in the early 1960s companies distributed a larger percentage of income so that the tax liability was transferred to shareholders. But most important of all, tax rates fell over the period and substantial concessions by way of various allowances were accorded to companies, U.K. taxes declining to 8% of total uses for the period 1971–1976.

While tax concessions continued into the 1970s, other items of expenditure grew faster than total uses, in particular, 'other interest' which includes debenture and loan interest. This rose after the 1965 tax changes following the surge of fixed interest borrowing, at rising interest rates, and as a result debenture interest increased from £400m. in 1965 to £650m. in 1970, and later rising to £880m. in 1976. More influential in raising current expenditure after 1970 has been the sharp rise in loan interest associated with heavy bank borrowing aided by higher rates. Loan interest rose from £585m. in 1971 to £2,424m. in 1974, three times the level of debenture interest, and accounting for nearly one-third of current expenditure. Profits and taxes due abroad, of which the latter is the largest component, tended to rise at the same rate as total profits for most of the recent period, but in 1972–4 it more than doubled compared with the stagnant performance of trading profits.

Tax payments display considerable short-term fluctuations, mostly in the opposite direction to those of profits. The figures given in table 11.2 relate to payments and not to accruals of tax. Thus, the tax payments of

1960 relate to low profits in 1958, and again that of 1972 relates to 1970 profits. Conversely, the lag may not be so helpful the other way round, since for example, during 1961–2 when profits were stable, companies had to discharge the high tax liability of the previous boom, and the same relates to 1969–70 following on the 1967–8 boom. Such pressures probably reduced capital spending by bringing about reduced savings.

Share dividends over the period displayed a somewhat mixed performance. Increases in the 1950s were gradual, mainly reflecting fluctuations in profits. Generally, companies allowed payments to fluctuate far less than profits, not wishing to pay out sharp increases; and they were even more reluctant to cut dividend levels. Throughout the 1950s company dividends as a percentage of total uses was very stable at the 16–17% level (table 11.2). However, in the ensuing period, 1961–5, the percentage rose sharply to 20%. Only a small part of this rise can be attributed to new equity issues which in the period increased broadly in line with total company expenditure. Several influences probably contributed to the change. Directors increasingly feared, in an active period of take-overs, that accumulations of liquid assets would attract a bid. It was also the period when the growth prospects of equities were highly regarded, while companies planning to come to the market sought to sweeten the path with dividend rises. The 1958 change in the structure of company tax, with the removal of the discrimination against distributed profits, no doubt exerted an influence.

With the adoption of corporation tax in 1965 the volume of equity issues declined sharply, with the tax structure favouring retentions rather than distributions. As a result during 1966–70 aggregate dividends remained very stable with the proportion of total uses reverting to the 17% level. The introduction of price restraint policies and dividend limitation from 1970 onwards kept the level of aggregate dividends more or less at a constant level, the surge of 1973 being due to companies delaying dividend payments until April 1973 so that they could take advantage of the provisions of the imputation system of tax.

Capital expenditure

Throughout the post-war period well over half of total capital expenditure has been on fixed investment (see table 11.3, pp. 313–4). Gross fixed investment displays a marked cyclical pattern which shows up clearly in all the post-war cycles. Investment activity is closely related to the level of demand and the associated state of business expectations which is greatly influenced by prevailing and anticipated monetary and fiscal policies. Increases in output from greater capacity utilization tend to produce sharp profit rises and the prospect of continuing this trend tends to encourage investment in or shortly after the peak of a boom, for example, in 1955–6, 1960–1 and 1968–9: 1974 to 1976 figures at current prices show large increases but at 1970 prices investment reflects the worst post-war recession, with manufacturing investment falling by 18%, and with *net* investment for manufacturing standing at the lowest level in the past ten years and half the level of the late 1960s. When demand declines and stocks rise, then profits tend to increase less rapidly or fall, with investment following the same path. Fluctuations in investment have also been brought about by changes in taxation and especially by the frequent changes in initial and investment allowances, and investment grants, and to a much lesser extent by changes in interest rates.[11]

Throughout the 1950s and 1960s stock building (represented by the value of physical changes in stocks and work in progress given in table 11.3) amounted to about 8% of total capital expenditure, while in 1971–4 the proportion fell to just over 5%. Of greater interest are the quite marked cyclical fluctuations which occur in the level of stock building (seasonal fluctuations are present but the annual figures mask these). During post-war cycles stocks have been built up rapidly when output increases, and generally before expenditure on fixed investment reached a peak. This is evident in the 1954–5, 1959–60, 1963–4 and 1967–8 cycles. Although there is a sharp rise in stocks during these booms it is noticeable that the ratio of stocks to output falls, to be re-established in the downward phase as production levels off. As the growth of output slackens stock building then falls off when industry has re-built its desired level of stocks. This pattern can be seen in the levelling-off years of 1957–8, 1961–2, 1966–7, and with a rundown of stocks in 1971. In the latter cycle the run down of stocks continued into the upward phase of the production cycle in 1972–3. In the early phase of the recovery the reduction arose from a running down of stocks of materials and fuels and to a lesser extent of work in progress, while in the later period of the boom in 1973 both of these items were rebuilt but holdings of finished goods fell sharply over eight quarters. The overall effect was a net reduction in 1972, followed by a build up in 1973 so that stocks amounted to 13% of total capital expenditure and continued stock building of finished goods and materials and fuel in 1974 sustained that level.[12] In the next two years manufacturers reduced their stocks of materials and fuel substantially, together with running down stocks of finished goods.

The figures of stock changes given in table 11.3 are of the value of physical increases in stocks and work in progress. On the basis of book values the changes take on a totally different magnitude, particularly from 1970 onwards. For industrial and commercial companies stock appreciation during 1964–9 averaged around £330m., but from £909m. in 1970 it swiftly climbed to an enormous £4,800m. a year for 1974–6. Such a rise presented companies with two serious problems. Firstly, stock appreciation was taxable so that tax bills rose, and secondly, companies had to find finance to maintain the physical value of their stocks in a period of rising prices. Under the tax system stock appreciation was treated as taxable income so that the nominal capital gain made on stock holdings in a period of rising prices was subject to company tax, which meant from about 1969 onwards that the real tax burden increased greatly. Having usually been of the order of 5% of gross trading profits before 1968, stock appreciation rose sharply to 38% of gross trading profits in 1974–6; the main influences here were the rise in commodity prices and depreciation of sterling. In order to reduce the liquidity pressures induced by such a tax liability the Budget of November 1974 provided temporary relief (now extended to the 'indefinite future') by deferring corporation tax on profits arising from abnormal increases in the value of stocks. Under the relief scheme the maximum amount of profit represented by increases in stock values on which tax was payable in the financial year 1974–5 was limited to 10% of trading profit in the accounting period which ended in the financial year 1973–4 (see Chapter 8). It was estimated that the relief reduced company tax payments by some £800m. in the financial year 1974–5.

In order to concentrate on fluctuations and trends arising from trading activity the figures in tables 11.1 (p. 310) and 11.2 (p. 312) were presented net of stock appreciation. Adding back stock appreciation would increase gross trading profits and accordingly savings, which would then be balanced by the item changes in book value of stocks rather than the value of physical changes in stocks. From the financing standpoint the presumption would be that price increases would be financed out of savings. In the main, however, company finance is not so neatly earmarked. In practice companies had to raise money to finance stocks and the extent of stock appreciation required unprecedented borrowing by companies from external sources, predominantly from the banking system.

The item 'other identified' capital expenditure in table 11.3 consists of three items, investment abroad, purchases of U.K. company securities, and changes in hire purchase credit extended. It increased from around 14% of all capital expenditure in the early 1950s to 19% in 1961–5, then fell back a little, to rise to 24% in the years 1971–6. The last of its three components is normally quite small, tending to fall in boom years and rise in the troughs, the timing of such fluctuations being further influenced by changes in hire purchase terms arising from official regulation. Investment abroad (that is, unremitted profits of U.K. subsidiaries overseas) averaged around £200m. in the 1950s, rising to £400m. in 1965. Following the introduction of government restrictions in 1965 the level fell off somewhat but recovered sharply in the 1970s, running at over £1,400m. a year in 1973–6. Cyclical patterns are present but they are not synonymous with those in other items of capital expenditure due to the fact that they are susceptible to more volatile elements than domestic activity.

The growth of this item, and in that of overseas investment in U.K. companies (see table 11.1), reflects the increasing activity of U.K. subsidiaries and multinationals abroad, and by overseas subsidiaries and multinationals in the U.K. market. Such rapid expansion, particularly in the last ten years, has been prompted by a variety of motives, including tariff avoidance, reducing transport costs and other delays, improving access to raw material supplies, responding to foreign competition in home markets and the search for wider markets. As a result the volume of United States investment in the U.K. grew from $0.8b. (book values) in 1950 to $8.0b. in 1970, most of the increase taking place since 1960. U.K. investment in the United States rose from $2.4b. in 1962 to $4.4b. in 1971, and this expansion accelerated in recent years as companies, following domestic mergers, felt themselves large enough to take on United States corporations, while the devaluation of the dollar and the ease of obtaining Euro-dollar finance all helped.[13]

Generally speaking the initial investment in foreign subsidiaries is financed by parent equity and some local financing, but when trade improves internally generated funds and local external sources take over as the main providers of funds. For example, U.K. subsidiaries in the United States rely heavily on short- and medium-term bank finance. In the case of U.K. multinationals, such as I.C.I. and B.P., sterling finance raised domestically cannot be used abroad so that for expansion purposes foreign currency borrowing is the main source of funds. Borrowing where a project is undertaken reduces the exchange rate risk involved, but the size and nature of local capital markets may greatly limit such matching. Some multinationals, however, prefer to raise their foreign currency funds centrally, especially on the various type of Euro-dollar markets, and they do so for tax reasons, the usual economies arising from a central pool: better terms are obtained on interest rates and maturities, debt servicing is easier, overall group gearing is more easily managed, and so forth. While it has been relatively easy to make large borrowings on the Euro-dollar markets, which are then converted to the required currency, dollar assets for servicing and redemption purposes are not always so readily attainable.[14]

The third item, purchases of U.K. securities, represents for the most part take-overs and mergers. The motives for these are many but for the post-war years they may be grouped into two. First, the main aim in the early phase was to get quick financial pickings by taking over companies with large liquid asset holdings, accumulated because of the tax discrimination against dividend distributions. Second, later activity has revolved around marketing and industrial matters; in the former case it could protect market shares and improve competitive strength, and in the latter, a take-over procures productive assets quickly, thus providing a rapid expansion of output with possible economies of scale (take-overs do not of course increase the total stock of productive assets, but they may lead to their more efficient use).

The merger movement of the late 1950s and early 1960s was concentrated largely on the quoted sector, involving mostly firms in the same industries. About 300 companies were acquired annually in the 1950s, valued at around £120m., with both number and value doubling in the 1959–60 boom. Over the next few years the number of acquisitions rose from 600 to over 1,000 a year, a rise in value terms from £370m. to around £500m. Although the actual number of acquisitions fell in the 1967–8 merger boom, there was a substantial increase in value to £1,650m. This represented some 32% of the use of funds for the quoted sector compared with 15% for earlier years. Large firms were particularly active, some 70 of the 100 largest U.K. companies being involved and representing about 10% of private sector company assets. However, the most salutory factor about the boom was that rational assessment of internal versus external growth played little part, the main considerations were those of speed, defence, sheer fashion, and the fear of missing out on short-term valuation discrepancy on the stock market.[15] Subsequent activity (for a time encouraged by the ill-fated Industrial Reorganization Commission) has been far less hectic, rising during periods of expansion as in 1972, and falling sharply away in the 1974–5 recession.

The 'unidentified items' in the tables is treated as a use of funds. It is apparent that it rises sharply in boom periods, falling off in the ensuing downturn. This pattern is consistent with regarding most of the item as attributable to trade credit granted by the company sector to other sectors, that is, to the unincorporated business component in the personal sector, and to the overseas sector by way of export credit.[16] The large negative figures for 1974–6 would seem to indicate that in a period of credit difficulties and falling output, industrial and commercial companies were receiving trade credit from other sectors (see Chapter 9). The rest of the item is attributed to errors in the various estimates, and to the difficulty of dividing certain items between the corporate sector and unincorporated businesses.

In terms of financing total capital expenditure table 11.3 (pp. 313–4) shows that savings became steadily less important as a source of funds, falling from 86% for 1952–5 to 57% in the early 1970s. Within that general downward trend there have been some marked cyclical fluctuations. In boom periods the contribution of internal funds declined sharply because capital expenditure outpaced available funds, forcing greater reliance on external sources, which up to 1967 came predominantly from banks and the capital market. Such cyclical swings are very apparent in 1954–5, 1959–60, 1963–4, 1967–8 and 1972–3. With the slackening of investment activity in the downward phase of the cycle the contribution of internal funds is rebuilt, although 1974 proved an exception due to the very sharp fall in the level of savings. Since 1967 'other sources', that is, capital grants and overseas investment in U.K. companies, greatly increased their contribution to total capital financing, the former due to the introduction of investment grants in that period, while the latter has stemmed from the increased importance of foreign subsidiaries operating in the U.K.

Up to 1969 the savings figure exceeded gross fixed capital formation, the surplus depending on the rate of growth of profit, which tended to increase faster than the rate of investment. The picture changes in 1969–70, when savings declined absolutely, but by 1972–3 the pattern was re-established, but then replaced in 1974–6 by large negative gaps. Taking savings as a percentage of gross fixed capital formation it falls from 193% in 1952–5 to 96% in 1966–70 and to 78% in 1971–6 (1974 produced the record low figure of 48% reflecting the enormous financial deficit of that year). On the basis of such a generalization it is tempting to conclude for most of the post-war years that internal funds financed plant and equipment expenditure while external funds were needed for relatively small investments in items such as stocks and securities. However, one cannot justifiably match individual sources with individual uses, but it is interesting to observe that for industry as a whole savings covered expenditure on the most important items.

Within the borrowing total there have been significant changes over the period.[17] The main sources in table 11.4 are market issues (ordinary, preference, and debenture) and funds from the banking system. 'Other sources' (from other financial institutions and the public sector) remained relatively small, apart from spurts in 1964–5, 1969–70 and 1973, which occurred at the top of the cycle as more conventional sources were closed off. The picture for 1952–5 is somewhat unusual due to the heavy run-off of bank advances associated with the stock building of the Korean War. The broad picture for the 1950s is that borrowing is about equally divided between market sources and the banking system, but from 1962 onwards an increasing proportion of borrowed funds is obtained from the banks, which in 1971–6 reached the unprecedented level of 79% of all borrowing, with the contribution of the capital market dwindling to 15%, compared with 38% in 1966–70.

By common agreement the volume of market borrowing in the 1950s was not in any significant way affected by the scrutiny of the Capital Issues Committee which lasted until 1959. In periods when bank advances were subject to direct restraint companies sought funds in the capital market either for expenditure purposes or to fund bank advances, for example, in 1961 and 1965, while in 1975 companies used rights issues to fund their extended resort to the banks. The volume of issues were closely related to the state of share prices; in periods of rising prices it was easier to make large equity issues, for example, in the rising and buoyant markets of 1959–61, 1968, and 1971–2 (see table 11.4). From 1962–7 equity issues averaged only £114m. a year, a time when the market was only on a slight upward course. In the largest equity collapse of the century in 1973–4 the volume of equity issues slumped to £43m. in 1974, while after allowing for the redemption of £56m. of fixed interest stock the contribution of the capital market became negative.

Prior to the 1965 tax changes the volume of fixed interest issues was mainly determined by interest rate and gearing considerations, and these induced relatively minor fluctuations during 1954–63: the average annual volume of fixed interest issues being £123m. The introduction of corporation tax in 1965, with its attendant advantages for fixed interest loans, brought a surge of debenture borrowing, much of it in the form of unsecured loan stock, in the next few years, completely reversing the previous dominance of equity issues. Heavy dependence on fixed interest borrowing affected the gearing ratio of companies, a fact about which they became increasingly concerned as interest rates rose and profits stagnated. From 1968 onwards dependence on debentures lessened somewhat since many companies felt that they had reached an appropriate level of gearing. Borrowing could only proceed up to a certain point in relation to internal funds.[18] In the period 1973–6 the fixed interest market only provided a very marginal amount of funds (see table 11.4), while in 1974 redemptions exceeded issues. This virtual cessation of debenture and loan stock borrowing arose mainly because of the very high levels of nominal interest rates. In the prevailing inflation considerable uncertainties in the calculation of cash flow made companies reluctant to finance new capital expenditure by issuing long-term debt carrying very high fixed rates of interest.

Bank borrowing grew absolutely and in relative importance during 1952–70, while in recent years its behaviour became highly volatile. In early cycles it tended to fall away when direct controls were stringently

Table 11.4 Industrial and commercial companies: Borrowing and liquid assets (£m.: % of capital expenditure; average of periods)

Year	Capital issues		From banks	Other[a]	Total	%	Net acquisitions of liquid assets	%	Borrowing less net acquisitions of liquid assets[b]	%
	Ordinary	Preference debentures								
1952	135		−200	41	−24	−2	111	11	−135	−13
1953	115		−20	11	106	8	168	13	−62	−5
1954	60	98	152	56	366	20	216	12	150	8
1955	117	119	59	78	373	15	−305	−12	678	28
	(161)		(−2)	(47)	(206)	(13)	(48)	(3)	(158)	(10)
1956	125	64	52	54	295	14	110	5	185	9
1957	127	154	23	51	355	17	206	10	149	7
1958	73	118	197	82	470	21	259	12	211	10
1959	139	111	429	83	762	30	350	14	412	16
1960	238	81	411	71	801	24	94	3	707	21
	(140)	(106)	(222)	(68)	(536)	(22)	(204)	(8)	(333)	(14)
1961	321	108	205	92	726	24	28	1	698	23
1962	152	164	300	60	676	24	−18	−1	694	25
1963	123	212	537	45	917	28	403	13	514	16
1964	158	254	752	152	1,316	31	77	2	1,239	30
1965	63	345	497	204	1,109	27	60	1	1,049	26
	(163)	(217)	(458)	(111)	(949)	(27)	(110)	(3)	(839)	(24)
1966	124	451	187	107	869	25	53	2	816	23
1967	65	350	333	41	789	24	462	14	327	10
1968	303	183	569	154	1,209	28	480	11	729	17
1969	183	335	664	171	1,353	26	198	4	1,155	22
1970	44	159	1,126	286	1,615	29	−11	—	1,626	29
	(144)	(295)	(576)	(152)	(1,167)	(27)	(236)	(5)	(931)	(21)
1971	160	215	732	87	1,194	24	976	19	218	4
1972	326	290	2,988	4	3,608	57	2,371	38	1,237	20
1973	107	51	4,504	694	5,356	59	2,608	29	2,748	30
1974	43	−56	4,411	−88	4,310	48	179	2	4,131	46
1975	966	71	418	164	1,619	28	1,741	31	−122	−2
1976	769	22	2,494	388	3,673	37	1,821	18	1,852	18
	(395)	(99)	(2,591)	(208)	(3,293)	(44)	(1,616)	(21)	(1,677)	(21)

[a] From other financial institutions and from the public sector.
[b] See table 11.5, p. 329.

Source: National Income Blue Books.

applied to advances, to expand again when relaxation followed. In such circumstances it formed a useful alternative to capital issues when interest rates were high and expectations persisted of a future fall in rates. However, during the years 1970–6, bank borrowing constituted 79% of total borrowing. This mammoth surge in bank financing, especially during 1972–4, was due to the sharp decline in the supply of internal funds, while companies were not able to raise much in the capital market due to falling share prices and sharply rising interest rates. Heavy reliance on the banks followed. Part of the accommodation was used to meet the needs of stock appreciation, and to build up liquid assets, and perhaps in anticipation of less favourable borrowing circumstances in the foreseeable future. But towards the end of 1973 it was observed that, while bank advances continued to be the 'outstanding source of funds' for the company sector, a large part of the accommodation so obtained was channelled back to the banks in the form of interest-bearing deposits. This arose because the prevailing structure of interest rates offered scope for such arbitrage. The Bank of England was of the view that in the early stages of this activity the strongest desire on the part of companies was to accumulate reserves.[19] The pattern of bank borrowing was not, however, uniform as between the national income series and that for quoted companies. In the case of the latter there was only a modest rise in advances in 1971–2, the big increase occurring in 1973. The discrepancy may have arisen because the increased demand for advances in the early phase of the cycle came largely from small companies who tend to be more heavily reliant on bank finance.[20] But in the 1973–4 increase the quoted sector took a prominent part in the celebrated 'merry-go-round'

Changes in liquid assets

In view of the preference of companies for internal finance the level of, and changes in, liquid assets is important for the pattern of financing. Companies tend to resort to outside sources, such as bank borrowing and capital issues, to the extent that internal liquidity is deemed inadequate relative to the level of expenditure, including that on investment. If companies have built up liquid assets expenditure can proceed unhindered; and if they restrain the rate of acquisition of such assets they are better placed to accelerate expenditure on capital items or other current expenditure.

Table 11.4 includes a figure for net acquisitions of liquid assets and that item expressed as a percentage of total capital expenditure; table 11.5 gives the identified components of liquid assets and their net acquisition. Its most notable feature is the cyclical pattern in the total column.[21] It would appear that companies in the aggregate build up assets at a fast rate before the expenditure peaks take place, and this pattern is clearly visible in 1954–5, 1959–60, 1963–4, and 1972–3 (see figure 11.1). In the peak expenditure year the acquisition of liquid assets falls markedly, and coincides with a sharp increase in borrowing (see figure 11.2). It is evident from table 11.4 (and figures 11.1, 11.2) that part of the build up of liquid assets, in anticipation of future spending, was heavily financed by borrowing, for example, in 1954, 1959, 1963 and, very much so in 1972.

The main identifiable liquid assets are bank deposits, other deposits, Treasury bills and local authority debt.[22] Over the years bank deposits have been by far the most important asset by which companies have accumulated liquid assets. Up until the mid-1960s clearing bank deposits predominated, but with the growth of the secondary banking sector, especially after the 1971 banking changes, deposits with 'other banks' grew in importance. Indeed, a survey of company liquidity among 200 large U.K. companies for the second quarter of 1970 showed 47% of total current assets in the form of deposits with 'other banks' and only 17% with the clearing banks. However, this was probably not very representative of industrial banking behaviour since most medium and small companies would concentrate deposits with the domestic clearing banks. Following the difficulties which some of the 'fringe' secondary banks experienced in 1973 there was some shift of deposits to the London clearing banks, the deposit banks holding 27% and 'other banks' 37% of total current assets at the end of 1976.[23]

The 1971–3 build up in deposits was quite unprecedented. As already noted there were several reasons for it: prevailing uncertainty induced liquidity accumulation; the favourable margin between bank lending rates and market rates for deposits; there was a marginal shift into deposits from certain security holdings due to uncertainty; and the cheapness of credit encouraged borrowing rather than using liquid assets to pay tax bills. Included in the deposit total given in table 11.5 is the item sterling certificates of deposit (introduced in 1968) and holdings of such assets by industrial and commercial companies rose sharply during 1971 and again in 1972. In the second quarter of 1970 some 5% of the total current assets of 200 large companies consisted of certificates of deposit, and by the third quarter of 1972 holdings rose to 18%, falling to about 8% at the end of the second quarter of 1974.[24] High interest rates, easy transferability in the secondary market, and favourable advances rates made such assets very attractive at certain times.[25] In the 1974 squeeze on company liquidity there was a large run-off of certificates of deposits so that by the close of the year total banking sector holdings of such assets had fallen by about a quarter.

Large companies probably predominate as holders of finance house

Table 11.5 Industrial and commercial companies: Acquisitions of liquid assets (£m.: averages of periods)

Year	Notes and coin	Bank deposits	H.P. deposits	Building society profits	Tax reserve certificates/Tax dep. acct.	Treasury bills	Local authority debt	Import deposits	Total
1952	36	94	4		-64	41	—	—	111
1953	55	49	8		32	-3	27	—	168
1954	64	34	28		103	-35	22	—	216
1955	48	-233	12		-84	4	-52	—	-305
	(51)	(14)	(13)		(3)	(2)	(1)	—	(84)
1956	38	-41	-10		-17	1	139	—	110
1957	27	18	28		-1	-1	135	—	206
1958	26	57	23		6	-4	151	—	259
1959	67	118	64		-34	-30	165	—	350
1960	50	-88	47	-6	24	—	67	—	94
	(42)	(13)	(29)		(-4)	(-7)	(131)	—	(208)
1961	48	-58	20	-5	-11	-15	49	—	28
1962	-73	95	-28	—	-54	15	27	—	-18
1963	31	278	47	5	-61	-30	133	—	403
1964	138	-30	28	2	-42	-82	63	—	77
1965	111	127	52	-6	-119	-25	-80	—	60
	(51)	(82)	(24)	(-1)	(-57)	(-27)	(38)	—	(110)
1966	77	87	-1	-2	-16	-11	-81	—	53
1967	62	321	—	9	29	—	41	—	462
1968	142	318	30	5	-20	-38	-32	75	480
1969	76	-214	55	2	-28	-12	-84	403	198
1970	208	121	4	-3	-6	9	-119	-225	-11
	(113)	(126)	(17)	(2)	(-8)	(-10)	(-55)	(51)	(236)
1971	166	919	-19	69	69	—	25	-253	976
1972	255	2,039	—	48	-76	-20	125	—	2,371
1973	70	2,430	49	-28	-67	-10	164	—	2,608
1974	355	-263	-43	-28	-26	43	141	—	179
1975	408	1,070	44	3	-14	276	-46	—	1,741
1976	502	1,065	39	-9	2	31	191	—	1,821
	(293)	(1,210)	(11)	(9)	(-18)	(53)	(100)	(-42)	(1,616)

Source: National Income Blue Books.

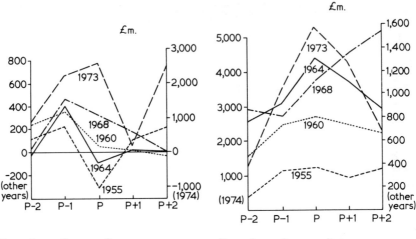

P   peak year for expenditure.

Figure 11.1   Liquid assets

P   peak year for expenditure.

Figure 11.2   Borrowing

deposits, while deposits with building societies are made mainly by small companies due to the restrictions imposed. Local authority temporary debt, including bills and call money, is much more important in the case of large companies. Treasury bills were a much more significant item in the early 1960s when the volume of bills issued was greater and rates more attractive; in later years bill shortages depressed rates causing companies to switch to more profitable alternatives. Up until December 1971 tax reserve certificates were issued to companies and were widely used as a method of earning interest on tax payments pending; if cashed the interest was lost. In April 1973 tax deposit accounts were introduced instead and are used to pay main, but not advanced, corporation tax.[26]

Some international comparisons

While it is difficult to make detailed and reliable comparisons of the way business is financed in different countries, due to such problems as the scope and nature of the information available and the differences in business organization, nevertheless it is illuminating to draw some general comparisons. For the purposes of this brief account a useful yardstick is the relative importance of internal and external finance; internal consisting of depreciation and retained profits, external of government grants and funds from capital market institutions. Table 11.6 presents sources of industrial finance for the U.K. and four leading countries, expressed as a percentage of gross physical investment with mean annual percentages for the years 1964–73 and for two sub-periods.

Taking the period 1964–73 the U.K. has the lowest percentage of net

Table 11.6   Source of finance for selected countries: 1964–73 (percentages of gross physical investment: mean annual percentage by period.)

Source of finance	U.K.	France[a]	West Germany[b]	Japan[c]	U.S.A.[d]
1964–7					
Ordinary shares	3.8	4.8	3.6	7.5	1.6
Bonds (including preference shares)	13.2	3.1	0.8	3.1	8.5
Long-term loans	14.5	16.7	11.0	60.9	10.6
Others (net)	−25.1	2.3	−1.7	−35.9	2.9
Net external finance	6.4	26.9	13.7	35.6	23.6
1968–73					
Ordinary shares	5.3	5.0	2.7	6.0	5.3
Bonds (including preference shares)	5.9	3.2	1.5	2.8	12.0
Long-term loans	18.2	16.2	16.8	74.9	15.1
Others (net)	−9.0	0.9	3.8	−52.7	0.6
Net external finance	20.4	25.3	24.8	31.0	33.0
1964–73					
Ordinary shares	4.8	5.0	2.8	6.2	4.6
Bonds (including preference shares)	8.4	3.2	1.4	2.9	11.4
Long-term loans	16.9	16.3	15.9	73.0	14.3
Others (net)	−14.6	1.2	2.9	−50.5	1.0
Net external finance	15.5	25.7	23.0	31.6	31.3

[a] Long-term loans include medium-term loans.
[b] Period 1 (1964–7) includes 1966 and 1967.
[c] Long-term loans include short-term loans.
[d] Period 1 (1964–7) includes 1964 and 1966.

Source: Finance for Investment, N.E.D.O., 1975, p. 56.

external financing, while the other countries had roughly an equal order of magnitude, with Japan and the United States showing the highest figures. Taking the sub-periods there is a discernible trend towards convergence in the second one, those with the smaller percentages increasing, while France and particularly Japan declined. In most countries, therefore, the demand for savings by the company sector seems to have been increasing. It has been suggested that the low figure of external funds used in the U.K. during 1964–7 stemmed partly from the high cost of such finance leading to its relatively low use. A far more important reason was the stagnation in gross fixed investment during these four years. In the second period the U.K. continued to lag behind the other countries, reflecting the lower rate of investment in plant and machinery.[27] A further feature, already noted in table 11.1, is the variability in the use of external funds. For the U.K. in the period 1968–73 net external finance ranges between 4.5 to 38.5%; in Japan from 27–40%, United States from 28–38%, West Germany 11–29%, and France 21–30%. The fluctuations in the U.K. case are closely linked with the business cycle.

Breaking up the sources of external finance into two broad groups, funds from the capital market and the banking sector, it is apparent that both the U.K. and the United States are basically market orientated, while the other countries given in table 11.6 are bank orientated. In the case of the U.K. 13.1%, and the United States 16%, of net external finance came from the capital market; the figures for the other countries being France, 8.2%; West Germany, 4.2%; and Japan, 9.1%. This contrast holds for the two sub-periods. Japan seems the most heavily dependent on bank finance, with most medium- and long-term loans coming from the banking system. Term lending is, of course, commonly used in most of these countries.

The general fall in the percentage of funds derived from internal savings may be ascribed to influences on both demand and supply. Falling profitability, together with increased tax burdens, reduced the flow of internal savings, thereby prompting a search for additional external funds; the figures presented in table 11.6 understate the trend since newer methods of finance such as leasing, and inter-company lending, have become more widely used. On the supply side there has been an increased flow of assistance from the public sector in the form of government grants and various types of regional aid. More generally the pursuit of full employment and easy money conditions have possibly reduced the assessment of risk on the part of lenders who are prepared to commit funds on a lower basis of internal participation, that is, as measured by the ratio of internal funds to fixed assets.[28]

In the case of British industry it has been suggested that one of the main constraints on investment and output is a scarcity of long-term capital. This assertion seems to be founded on two observations. Firstly, that those foreign countries which displayed the fastest rate of growth relied heavily on external funds, for example, Japan. Secondly, that external funds abroad were obtained predominantly from the banks which provided medium- to long-term funds. While it is possible to agree that fast rates of growth lead to higher percentages of external financing, the link is decidedly that way and not the other, and even fast-growing firms in the U.K. testify to that. On the basis of the second, the claim is made that the provision of external funds in the U.K. should be increasingly bank orientated with an injection of continental practices on the part of the suppliers.

The traditional criticism of British bank lending practices is that they are too cautious, being over-concerned with security and paying too little attention to the flow of income generated by the projects which are financed. While the predominant form of advance is still the overdraft all the clearing banks are now prepared to make medium-term loans to creditworthy customers, each bank looking at the balance sheet position in deciding on its total loans. One leading bank recently stated that lending over a term of years accounted for about one-third of its total advances. In practice overdrafts often revolve to become medium-term loans, and the burden of illiquid advances carried by the banks in the past has probably been greater than they have been willing to admit. On the demand side there is little evidence to suggest that companies prefer fixed loans to the overdraft; the latter has the distinct advantages of low cost and considerable flexibility. If the banks are to offer more long-term accommodation to industry they would need to attract deposits of roughly comparable maturity, even with an accompanying bolstering of capital ratios. The prospects of doing this with certificates of deposits with a term in excess of say three years is remote, while most certificates fall due within two years, and the horizon is more likely to contract with changing interest rates than it is to lengthen. Alternatively, on the asset side the central bank may oblige with rediscount facilities (and discussions to this end have taken place) but while this would reduce the matching problem for the commercial bank it would probably compound the problem of monetary management for the former. Given the range of liabilities presented to savers by financial institutions in the U.K. it is unreasonable to expect the banks to put their assets greatly out of step with their liabilities when the size and composition of these depend on public preference. Public taste is capable of manipulation but it is not easily done in the short run and would be of doubtful value in the longer term.

Prior to the movement of the banks into the term loan area some additional financial facilities for medium-term funds had been available from the Finance Corporation for Industry set up in 1945. It was intended to fill the gap between bank accommodation for working capital and longer term funds from the capital market. The medium-term loans provided had a minimum size of £200,000 and were made available where finance could not be obtained on reasonable terms elsewhere, and where the 'national interest' was served. Its capital was held by the major financial institutions and its lending resources came mostly from the London clearing banks at rates varying with bank interest rates. Throughout the 1950s and 1960s the scale of operations was very modest and at 31 March 1971 loans and investments outstanding amounted to £70m. Its most active involvement occurred when the steel industry was returned to private hands, but had the threat of re-nationalization hanging over it.

In 1974 the resources available to the Finance Corporation for Industry (since 1973 part of Finance for Industry Limited) were considerably increased to enable it to grant medium-term finance for large companies 'pending a restoration of a flow of funds through the wider capital market'. The funds are 'available mainly in the form of medium term loans at variable or fixed rates of interest subject to strict criteria of commercial viability'. Up to £1,000m. was made available by the leading financial institutions to the Corporation for this purpose. Since the depressed conditions of 1974 it has obtained sufficient business for it to become established as an effective medium-term lender in the 7- to 15-year range. Its portfolio in March 1977 comprised £241m. invested in 45 large companies, nearly half of its lending being advanced on an unsecured basis.

The above scheme widens the variety of choice of finance that is available, but it did not involve dilution of the conditions. A later scheme, an 'equity bank', sets out to provide equity funds in excess of what the market will provide on commercial criteria, and which are regarded as having favourable prospects. The suggestion here is that less than full returns are expected, but it seems unlikely that any appreciable gain will accrue to the quality of investment by allowing investment criteria to be softened. Equity Capital for Industry Ltd was set up at the initiative of the British Insurance Association in 1976, and most of the major institutional long-term investors are shareholders. It, like Finance for Industry, is developing an ability to monitor closely the progress of companies which receive loans; indeed, both have been involved in joint financing schemes where medium-term loans and equity capital have been required.[29]

For borrowing from the capital market two main instruments are used, fixed interest obligations and ordinary shares. Whether fixed interest bonds are marketed or placed the view has been expressed that institutional demand should be stimulated by prescribing asset ratios of some kind. Set ratios would not, in all probability, lead to a surge in demand from large institutional investors since they would prefer to select assets which best serve their liabilities management, while their receptiveness to further industrial fixed interest would be cool owing to the fear that high gearing would lead to default. While the Chancellor finally abolished stamp duty on fixed interest stocks in 1976, and thereby lowered dealing costs which improved the secondary market, attention could also be given to the favoured capital gains positions of gilt-edged, which could be extended to industrial bonds, while in some countries all bond interest is taxed at a preferential rate. Such concessions might well provide a powerful stimulus to the provision of finance.

The above argument against prescribed ratios holds also for equities, while the suggestion that banks should hold equities is hardly worth contemplating; where it operates abroad special historical circumstances apply and capital markets are very underdeveloped. Equity capital is properly to be acquired in the capital market and its availability is particularly dependent upon the state of the secondary market. A strong underlying market will absorb issues without difficulty if the correct expectations as to returns are generated. Of course, one of the most cited imperfections of this market is that its behaviour is so erratic and volatile, as in 1973–4, that the flow of equity capital virtually ceases. In such instances the market is merely responding to external factors, and within a relatively short space of time it provided very large sums of capital without the inducement of high profits or the abandonment of official controls on dividends. Allowing for such temporary interruptions (in what was after all a very severe recession) British companies of good credit standing have found no great difficulty in raising new equity capital, or indeed, in getting working capital from their bankers.

Less extreme than the suggestion of prescribed ratios is that institutional investors should abandon their traditional posture of 'arm's length' investment and assume an active 'policing' role. Rather than sell holdings on the market when an investment appears to be deteriorating, institutional investors should take a more direct and continuous interest in the way in which individual companies employ the funds provided to them. Presumably this would involve direct action on the part of major shareholders, and possibly major creditors, to remedy falling profits or mounting losses. It is doubtful, however, if the major institutional investors would wish or could identify the causes of likely failure; they are not equipped to take an active concern in the commercial performance of the many companies in which they have an interest. With considerable outlays such inadequacies could be remedied, but more serious is the objection that such intervention would probably do more to hinder industrial change than it would by way of improving industrial efficiency. An attempt to improve the effectiveness of institutions in managing their allocated savings might well diminish the efficiency with which they channel savings among alternative uses in industry and trade. It would certainly reduce the flexibility of their assets, and as a result dilute their primary responsibility to the holders of their liabilities. Accepting the highly specialized nature of the main institutional investors, and that they have a very developed capital market in which to operate, it might well be that the existing market mechanism is the best long-run method of allocating funds to alternative industrial and commercial uses.[30]

The pattern by which companies are financed in various countries arises from past economic development, the nature of the financial framework, the legal system and accounting practices. Therefore, to advocate the widespread adoption of foreign practices is at best naive, at worst merely foolish indulgence in transplanting institutional gadgetry. It is a very doubtful proposition that the supply of funds is the prime constraint on the investment performance of the U.K. It might well be for stagnant firms which anyway would have little claim on the savings of other sectors; it does not seem to be so for fast growing or creditworthy companies. Institutional manipulation cannot compensate for the prevailing low rate of return on capital employed in British industry. Taking the general picture of the changes in the sources of funds given in table 11.1 (p. 310), the impressive claim can be made that overall for the postwar years a high rate of capital accumulation has taken place while there has been a very considerable change in the flow of finance from internal to external sources. Periodically some strains have appeared but in general the financial system has shown a large degree of adaptation to the increased demands made upon it.

Notes

1 For an indication of trends in specific sources of funds see earlier chapters. Tables for industrial and commercial companies first appeared in the 1964 National Income Blue Book, which gave figures back to 1953, and capital items dating back to 1959. Prior to this figures were given for companies excluding insurance, banking and finance.

2 For a detailed description of the series see Rita Maurice (ed.), *National Accounts Statistics; Sources and Methods*, London, 1968, ch. VII.

3 Up to and including 1954 profit figures were 'an aggregation of the profits earned in varying accounting years which on average end about the beginning of December'. From 1955 accounting year figures were adjusted to a calendar year basis; Maurice, op. cit., p. 218.

4 J. L. Walker, 'Structure of Company Financing', *Economic Trends*, September 1975, p. 97. The changes are those associated with take-overs and amalgamations. In 1970 the series was rebased to cover companies with net assets over £2.0m., or gross income of £200,000 or more in 1968.

5 ibid., pp. 96–7. For some earlier accounts of the quoted company series see *Economic Trends*, February 1958, and April 1962.

6 'Company Finance; 1952–65', *Bank of England Quarterly Bulletin*, March 1967, p. 31.

7 J. L. Walker, 'Estimating Companies' Rate of Return on Capital Employed', *Economic Trends*, November 1974, pp. xxxv–xxxvii.

8 'Companies' Rate of Return on Capital Employed', *Trade and Industry*, 24 October 1975, pp. 244–7; 'Companies' Rate of Return on Capital Employed 1960 to 1976', *Trade and Industry*, 16 September 1977, pp. 519–22.

9 The Royal Commission on the Distribution of Income and Wealth in its second report, *Income from Companies and its Distribution*, Cmnd 6172, 1975, calculated that the average real return for the average standard rate of taxpayer for 1963–74 was a negative figure of −2.9%, compared with a figure of 7.4% for the period 1949–66; para. 173.

10 In 'Trends in Company Profitability', *Bank of England Quarterly Bulletin*, March 1976, and 'Industrial and Commercial Companies: Profitability and the Cost of Capital', *Bank of England Quarterly Bulletin*, June 1977, rates of return are given for 1960–76 after adjusting for inflation and taxation on profits and the value of the physical assets employed. The pre-tax real rate of return falls from 13.4% in 1960 to 4.6% in 1974 and to 3.5% in 1976; post-tax figures fall at a slower rate from 8.3% in 1960 to 4.3% in 1974 and to 2.4% in 1976 (without the stock relief provision this measure would be 0.3%). See also 'The Cost of Capital, Finance and Investment', *Bank of England Quarterly Bulletin*, June 1976.

11 For a discussion of the determinants of fixed investment see J. C. R. Dow, *The Management of the British Economy 1945–60*, Cambridge, 1964, pp. 286–92.

12 Due to the three-day week all industrial stocks fell sharply in the first quarter of 1974. Quarterly ratios of stocks to manufacturing production are given in *Economic Trends*.

13 J. M. Samuels, R. E. V. Groves and C. S. Goddard, *Company Finance in Europe*, London, 1975, pp. 238–50.

14 A. W. Clements, 'International Corporate Finance and Flexible Exchange Rates', *Journal of the Institute of Bankers*, October 1977, pp. 165–71.

15 G. D. Newbould, *Management and Merger Activity*, Liverpool, 1970, pp. 17–24; see also A. Singh, *Take-overs; Their Relevance to the Stock Market and the Theory of the Firm*, Cambridge, 1971, ch. 2.

16 In the analysis of large unlisted and quoted companies the debtors less creditors item is positive over 1964–9. During 1970–1 and 1973 it showed large negative figures suggesting that the quoted or 'big' companies sector took credit from other sectors; some caution needs to be exercised, however, in making firm conclusions, since the item creditors includes short-term loans received: Walker, 'Structure of Company Financing', op. cit., pp. 102–3. See also J. R. S. Revell, 'Trends in the Financing of Companies', *The Stock Exchange Journal*, December 1974, pp. 12–17.

17 Inter-company borrowing is not reported in these figures; see Chapter 9.

18 For a succinct description of gearing see *Income from Companies and its Distribution*, op. cit., pp. 72–3.

19 *Bank of England Quarterly Bulletin*, December 1973, p. 424.

20 Walker, 'Structure of Company Financing', op. cit., p. 101; Revell, op. cit., p. 12.

21 Company liquidity tends to increase in the fourth quarter of the year in readiness for the tax payments in the following quarter when there is an off-setting fall.

22 The figures are largely estimates on a residual basis having taken into account the holdings of all other sectors. Such an indirect method of assessment is very dependent on the accuracy and classification made by institutions and companies in other sectors.

23 'Department of Industry Survey of Company Liquidity', *Economic Trends*, November 1974, p. 7. The survey covered 236 large companies. For a later survey see J. C. D. Alexander, 'Department of Industry Survey of Company Liquidity; Compar-

ison with the Financial Accounts', *Economic Trends*, May 1977, pp. 87–99.

24 ibid., pp. 6–7.

25 In the second quarter of 1973 company holdings of CDs fell due to the provisions of the Finance Act 1973 which ended the tax free element in capital gains; they were rebuilt afterwards.

26 For a short period Import Deposits affected company liquidity positions. The deposits were payable in respect of imports of most manufactured goods over the period November 1968 to December 1970. The deposits were repayable after 180 days. The measure had little deterrent effect since additional borrowing costs could be passed on, and often the foreign supplier provided the necessary funds.

27 *Finance for Investment*, N.E.D.O., 1975, p. 57.

28 For a perceptive discussion on these issues see T. M. Rybczynski, 'Business Finance in the E.E.C., U.S.A. and Japan', *The Three Banks Review*, September 1974, pp. 58–72. For a detailed treatment see J. M. Samuels, R. E. V. Groves and C. S. Goddard, *Company Finance in Europe*, London, 1975.

29 *Bank of England Quarterly Bulletin*, December 1974, p. 201; 'Capital Requirements and Industrial Finance', *Midland Bank Review*, February 1976, pp. 14–15.

30 For details of these suggestions see 'Industrial Management and the Institutional Investor: Report of the Working Party', *Bank of England Quarterly Bulletin*, March 1973, 'Savings and Investment; Recent Developments in Financing Arrangements', *Bank of England Quarterly Bulletin*, September 1977.

Selected bibliography

Official Reports

Committee on Finance and Industry, *Minutes of Evidence*, London, 1931.
Committee on Finance and Industry, *Report*, Cmd 3897, 1931 (Macmillan Committee).
Committee of Inquiry on Small Firms, *Report*, Cmnd 4811, 1971 (Bolton Committee).
Committee on National Debt and Taxation, *Report*, Cmd 2800, 1927 (Colwyn Committee).
Committee on Turnover Taxation, *Report*, Cmnd 2300, 1964 (Richardson Committee).
Committee on the Working of the Monetary System, *Minutes of Evidence*, London, 1960.
Committee on the Working of the Monetary System, *Principal Memoranda of Evidence*, London, 1960.
Committee on the Working of the Monetary System, *Report*, Cmnd 827, 1959 (Radcliffe Committee).
The Financial and Economic Obligations of the Nationalised Industries, Cmnd 1337, 1961
Investment Incentives, Cmnd 2874, 1966.
Nationalised Industries: A Review of Economic and Financial Objectives, Cmnd 3437, 1967.
Reform of Corporation Tax, Cmnd 4955, 1972.
Report of the Commissioners of H.M. Inland Revenue, annual.
Report on the Proposed Merger of Barclays Bank, Lloyds Bank and Martins Bank, H.C. 319, 1968.
Royal Commission on the Distribution of Income and Wealth, Report no. 2, *Income from Companies and its Distribution*, Cmnd 6172, 1975.
Royal Commission on the Taxation of Profits and Income, *Final Report*, Cmnd 9474, 1955.
Select Committee on Nationalised Industries, 1967–8, *Ministerial Control of the Nationalised Industries*, H.C. 371, I–III.
Select Committee on Nationalised Industries, 1973–4, *Capital Investment Procedures*, H.C. 65.
Treasury Committee on Bank Amalgamation, *Report*, Cd 9052, 1918.

Books

ALDCROFT, D. H., *The Inter-war Economy: Britain 1919–39*, London, 1970.
ALDCROFT, D. H. and FEARON, P., *Economic Growth in 20th-Century Britain*, London, 1969.
ALLEN, C., *Small Firm Survey*, London, 1970 (I.C.F.C.).
ANDREWS, P. W. S. and BRUNNER, E., *The Life of Lord Nuffield*, London, 1955.
ASHWORTH, W., *Contracts and Finance*, London, 1953.

BALOGH, T., *Financial Organisation*, Cambridge, 1950.

BARRETT-WHALE, P., *Joint Stock Banking in Germany*, London, 1930.

BATES, J., *The Financing of Small Business*, 2nd ed., London, 1971.

CAIRNCROSS, A. K., *Home and Foreign Investment 1870–1913*, Cambridge, 1953.

CLARK, C., *National Income and Outlay*, London, 1937.

CLAY, H., *Lord Norman*, London, 1957.

CLAYTON, G. AND OSBORN, W. T., *Insurance Company Investment*, London, 1965.

COLE, G. D. H. (ed.), *Studies in Capital and Investment*, London, 1935.

COLEMAN, D. C., *Courtaulds: An Economic and Social History*, Oxford, 1969.

CRAEMER, D., DOBROVOLSKY, S. P. and BORENSTEIN, I., *Capital in Manufacturing and Mining*, Princeton, 1960.

Credit Management Databook, London, 1973.

DACEY, M., *The British Banking Mechanism*, London, 1958.

DAVIES, E., *National Enterprise: the Development of the Public Corporation*, London, 1946.

DAVIES, E. W. and YEOMANS, K. A., *Company Finance and the Capital Market*, Cambridge, 1974.

DOBROVOLSKY, S. P., *Corporate Income Retention 1915–43*, New York, 1951.

DOW., J. C. R., *The Management of the British Economy 1945–60*, Cambridge, 1964.

DUNNING, J. H. and THOMAS, L. J., *British Industry: An Economic Analysis*, London, 1961.

ECONOMISTS ADVISORY GROUP, *Financial Facilities for Small Firms*, Research Report no. 4, Committee of Inquiry on Small Firms, London, 1971.

FEINSTEIN, C. H., *Domestic Capital Formation in the United Kingdom 1920–1938*, Cambridge, 1965.

Finance for Investment, N.E.D.O., 1975.

FINNIE, D., *Capital Underwriting*, London, 1934.

FOSTER, C. D., *Politics, Finance and the Role of Economics*, London, 1971.

GILLETT BROTHERS, *The Bill on London*, London, 1952.

GOODHART, C. A. E., *The Business of Banking 1891–1914*, London, 1972.

GRANT, A. T. K., *A Study of the Capital Market in Britain from 1919–1936*, London, 1967.

HART, P. E., *Studies in Profit, Business Savings and Investment in the United Kingdom 1920–1962*, London, 1965.

HENDERSON, R. F., *The New Issue Market and the Finance of Industry*, Cambridge, 1951.

HOWSON, S., *Domestic Monetary Management 1919–38*, Cambridge, 1975.

HUTSON, T. G. and BUTTERWORTH, J., *Management of Trade Credit*, London, 1968.

JACOBY, W. H. and SAULNIER, R. J., *Business Finance and Banking*, New York, 1947.

KENAN, P. B., *British Monetary Policy and the Balance of Payments 1951–57*, Cambridge (Mass.), 1960.

KIRKALDY, A. W., (ed.), *British Finance 1914–21*, London, 1921.

KUZNETZ, S., *Capital in the American Economy: Its Formation and Financing*, Princeton, 1961.

LAVINGTON, F., *The English Capital Market*, London, 1921.

LEAKE, P. D., *Depreciation and Wasting Assets*, 5th ed., London, 1948.

LUTZ, F. A., *Corporate Cash Balances 1914–43*, New York, 1945.

MACRAE, N. A. D., *The London Capital Market*, London, 1957.

MAURICE, R. (ed.), *National Accounts Statistics: Sources and Methods*, London, 1968.

MAXCY, G. E. and SILBERTSON, A., *The Motor Industry*, London, 1959.

MERRETT, A. J., HOWE, M. and NEWBOULD, G. D., *Equity Issues and the London Capital Market*, London, 1967.

MORGAN, E. V., *Studies in British Financial Policy 1914–1925*, London, 1952.

NEVIN, E., *The Mechanism of Cheap Money*, Cardiff, 1955.

NEWBOULD, G. D., *Management and Merger Activity*, Liverpool, 1970.

NISHIMURA, S., *The Decline of Inland Bills of Exchange in the London Money Market 1855–1913*, Cambridge, 1971.

O.E.C.D., *Capital Markets Study*, vol. 3, Paris, 1967.

OSBORN, R. C., *Financing Small and Medium Sized Businesses*, London, 1972 (I.C.F.C.).

PAISH, F. W., *Business Finance*, 2nd ed., London, 1961.

PAISH, F. W., *Studies in an Inflationary Economy*, London, 1962.

PRYKE, R. W. S., *Public Enterprise in Practice*, London, 1971.

RADICE, E. A., *Savings in Great Britain 1922–35*, Oxford, 1939.

REVELL, J. R. S., *The Wealth of the Nation*, Cambridge, 1967.

ROBSON, W. A. (ed.), *Public Enterprise*, London, 1937.

ROBSON, W. A., *Nationalised Industry and Public Ownership*, London, 1962.

SAMUELS, J. M., GROVES, R. E. V. and GODDARD, C. S., *Company Finance in Europe*, London, 1975.

SAYERS, R. S., *Modern Banking*, 2nd ed., Oxford, 1947.

SAYERS, R. S., *Financial Policy 1939–45*, London, 1956.

SAYERS, R. S., *The Bank of England 1891–1944*, vols 1–3, Cambridge, 1977.

SINGH, A., *Take-overs: Their Relevance to the Stock Market and the Theory of the Firm*, Cambridge, 1971.

SYKES, J., *The Amalgamation Movement in English Banking*, London, 1926.

TAGGART, P., *Profits and Balance Sheet Adjustments*, London, 1934.

TEW, B. and HENDERSON, R. E. (eds), *Studies in Company Finance*, Cambridge, 1959.

THOMAS, W. A., *The Provincial Stock Exchanges*, London, 1973.

TRUPTIL, R. J., *British Banks and the London Money Market*, London, 1936.

WEBB, H. G., *The Economics of the Nationalised Industries*, London, 1973.

WHITTINGTON, G., *The Prediction of Profitability: and Other Studies of Company Behaviour*, London, 1971.

WILSON, T. and ANDREWS, P. W. S., *Oxford Studies in the Price Mechanism*, Oxford, 1951.

WORSWICK, G. D. N. and TIPPING, D. G., *Profits in the British Economy 1909–1938*, Oxford, 1967.

Articles

AITKEN, J., 'Official Regulation of Overseas Investment 1914–1931', *Economic History Review*, 1970.

ALEXANDER, J. D., 'Department of Industry Survey of Company Liquidity: Comparison with the Financial Accounts', *Economic Trends*, 1977.

ALLEN, A. M., 'Bank Advances', *The Banker*, 1936.

ASHTON, R. S., 'Investment Policy in Private Enterprise', *Lloyds Bank Review*, 1962.

BARNA, T., 'Valuation of Stocks and the National Income', *Economica*, 1942.

BATES, J., 'The Macmillan Gap in Britain and Canada', *The Bankers' Magazine*, 1962.

BIRD, R. M., 'Depreciation Allowances and Counter Cyclical Policy in the U.K. 1946–60', *Canadian Tax Journal*, 1963.

BLACK, J., 'Investment Allowances, Initial Allowances and Cheap Loans as Means of Encouraging Investment', *Review of Economic Studies*, 1959.

BRECHLING, F. P. and LIPSEY, R. G., 'Trade Credit and Monetary Policy', *Economic Journal*, 1963.

CARRUTHERS, A. S., 'The Trend of Net Profits of Commercial and Industrial Enterprises, 1928–37', *Journal of the Royal Statistical Society*, 1932.

CLAY, H., 'The Financing of Industrial Enterprise', *Manchester Statistical Society*, 1932.

CLEMENTS, A. W., 'International Corporate Finance and Flexible Exchange Rates', *Journal of the Institute of Bankers*, October 1977.

COATES, J. B., 'Trade Credit and Monetary Policy: A Study of the Accounts of 50 Companies', *Oxford Economic Papers*, 1967.

'Commercial Bills', *Bank of England Quarterly Bulletin*, 1961.

'Company Finance: 1952–65', *Bank of England Quarterly Bulletin*, 1967.

CORNER, D. C. and WILLIAMS, A., 'The Sensitivity of Business to Initial and Investment Allowances', *Economica*, 1965.

CRAWFORD, M., 'The 1965 Reforms in the British Tax System', *Moorgate and Wall Street*, 1965.

'Department of Industry Survey of Company Liquidity', *Economic Trends*, 1974.

EDGE, S. K., 'Shareholders' Reaction to Rights Issues', *Manchester School*, 1965.

EDGE, S. K., 'Sources of Funds from Rights Issues and their Cost', *Journal of Economic Studies*, 1966.

FOXWELL, H. F., 'The Financing of Industry and Trade', *Economic Journal*, 1917.

FRANKS, OLIVER, SIR, 'Bank Advances as an Object of Policy', *Lloyds Bank Review*, 1961.

FROST, R., 'The Macmillan Gap 1931–1953', *Oxford Economic Papers*, 1954.

GHANDI, J. K. S., 'Some Aspects of the Provincial New Issue Market', *Bulletin of the Oxford University Institute of Economics and Statistics*, 1964.

HARRIS, S. A., 'A Re-Analysis of the 1928 New Issue Boom', *Economic Journal*, 1933.

HARTFORD, T., 'Pricing a Flotation', *Journal of Business Finance*, 1969.

HICHENS, A., 'The Cost of Equipment Leasing', *Investment Analyst*, 1966.

HICKS, U. K., 'The Taxation of Excess Profits in War Time', *Transactions of the Manchester Statistical Society*, 1940.

HOLBORN, P. R. M. and EDWARDS, E. C. N., 'The U.K. Venture Capital Market', *The Banker*, 1971.

HOPE, R., 'Profits in British Industry from 1925–35', *Oxford Economic Papers*, 1949.

KIRKMAN, P. R. A. and USHER, J., 'Recent Developments in Preference Share Finance', *Journal of Business Finance*, 1971.

LAW, R., 'The Resurgence of the Commercial Bill', *The Bankers' Magazine*, 1965.

LEAKE, P. D., 'Shilling Deferred Shares', *Accountant*, 1928.

LEHR, M. E. and NEWBOULD, G. D., 'New Issues-Activity and Performance 1964 to 1967', *Investment Analyst*, 1967.

LEVITT, M. S., 'Monetary Theory and Trade Credit, An Historical Approach', *Yorkshire Bulletin*, 1964.

LITTLE, I. M. D., 'Higgledy Piggledy Growth', *Bulletin of the Oxford University Institute of Economics and Statistics*, 1962.

LUBOFF, A., 'Some Aspects of Post-War Company Finance: An Analysis of Tabulations of Company Accounts Published in *The Economist*', *Accounting Research*, 1956.

MCRAE, H., 'London's Shifting Money Markets', *The Banker*, 1970.

MACROSTY, H. W., 'Inflation and Deflation in the U.S. and the U.K., 1919–1923', *Journal of the Royal Statistical Society*, 1927.

MANLEY, P. S., 'The New Issue Revival', *Moorgate and Wall Street*, Spring 1976.

METZLER, A., 'Mercantile Credit, Monetary Policy, and Size of Firms', *Review of Economics and Statistics*, 1960.

MURPHY, G. W. and PRUSSMAN, D. F., 'Equity Placings on the New Issue Market', *Manchester School*, 1967.

MUSGRAVE, R. A. and MUSGRAVE, P. B., 'Fiscal Policy' in R. E. Caves (ed.), *Britain's Economic Prospects*, Washington, 1968.

PAISH, F. W., 'The London New Issue Market', *Economica*, 1951.

PARKINSON, H., 'British Industrial Profits, A Survey of Three Decades', *The Economist*, 1938.

PIERCY, LORD, 'The Macmillan Gap and the Shortage of Risk Capital', *Journal of the Royal Statistical Society*, 1955.

PREST, A. R., 'Corporation Tax', *District Bank Review*, 1965.

REVELL, J. R. S., 'Trends in the Financing of Companies', *The Stock Exchange Journal*, 1974.

ROSE, H. B., 'Monetary Policy and the Capital Market 1955–56', *Economic Journal*, 1957.

ROSE, H. B., 'Domestic Trade Credit and Economic Policy', Committee on the Working of the Monetary System, *Memoranda of Evidence*, vol. 3 (Radcliffe Committee, 1959).

RUBNER, A., 'The Irrelevancy of the British Differential Profits Tax', *Economic Journal*, 1964.

RYBCZYNSKI, T. M., 'Business Finance in the E.E.C., U.S.A. and Japan'. *The Three Banks Review*, 1974.

'Savings and Investment: Recent Developments in Financing Arrangements', *Bank of England Quarterly Bulletin*, September 1977.

SAYERS, R. S., 'Monetary Thought and Monetary Policy in England', *Economic Journal*, 1960.

SAYERS, R. S., 'The Timing of Tax Payments by Companies', *The Three Banks Review*, 1967.

SKERRATT, L. C. L., 'Convertible Loan Stocks 1958–1968: An Empirical Investigation', *Journal of Business Finance*, 1971.

SPARROW, J., 'Convertible Loan Stocks', *Journal of Business Finance*, 1969.

STAMP, J. C., 'Industrial Profits in the Past Twenty Years – a New Index Number', *Journal of the Royal Statistical Society*, 1932.

TEW, B., 'Edith', *The Three Banks Review*, 1955.

TEW, B., 'I.C.F.C. Revisited', *Economica*, 1955.

'The Cost of Capital, Finance and Investment', *Bank of England Quarterly Bulletin*, 1976.

THOMAS, ROY, 'The Change in Corporation Tax and the Incentive to Invest', *Journal of Business Finance*, 1973.

'Trends in Company Profitability', *Bank of England Quarterly Bulletin*, 1976.

VANN, J. C., 'Credit Insurance Expansion', *The Bankers' Magazine*, 1972.

WALKER, D., 'Some Economic Aspects of the Taxation of Companies', *Manchester School*, 1954.

WALKER, D., 'Depreciation Problems and Taxation', in J. L. Meij (ed.), *Depreciation and Replacement Policy*, Amsterdam, 1961.

WALKER, J. L., 'Estimating Companies' Rate of Return on Capital Employed', *Economic Trends*, 1974.

WALKER, J. L., 'Structure of Company Financing', *Economic Trends*, 1975.

WILLIAMS, A., 'Great Britain' in *Foreign Tax Policies and Economic Growth*, A Conference Report of the National Bureau of Economic Research and the Brookings Institution, Columbia, 1966.

Index